STOP

This is the back of the book! Start from the other side.

***NATIVE MANGA* readers read manga from *right to left*.**

1
2
1
3
2
3
5
4
4
6
5
8
7
6

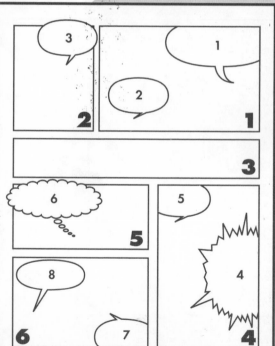

*If you run into our **Native Manga** logo on any of our books... you'll know that this manga is published in it's true original native Japanese right to left reading format, as it was intended. Turn to the other side of the book and start reading from right to left, top to bottom.*

Follow the diagram to see how its done.
Surf's Up!

NATIVE MANGA
READ RIGHT TO LEFT

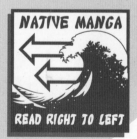

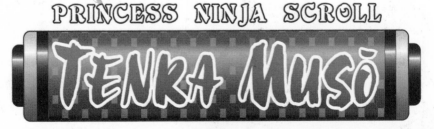

Evil Nobunaga possess the scroll of the Heavens and will stop at nothing to find the scroll of the Earth, because when the two scrolls meet they form the Tenka-Musō a near infinite source of power!

Just one small problem...
The scroll of the Earth
is located inside
13 year old
Hattori Hanzou!

Vol. 1 ISBN# 1-56970-955-6 $12.95
Vol. 2 ISBN# 1-56970-954-8 $12.95

An epic fictional adventure inspired by the true life stories of Hattori Hanzou

PRINCESS NINJA SCROLL

TENKA MUSŌ

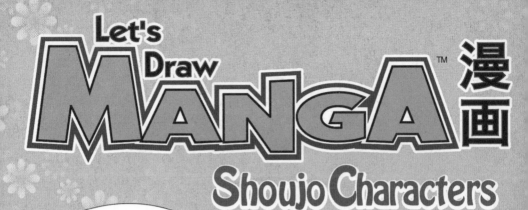

Shoujo Characters

Draw shoujo manga the way you like it!

"HEE HEE"

TEE HEE

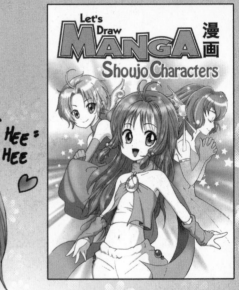

ISBN# 1-56970-966-1 SRP $19.95

Both beginner and intermediate artists can now learn to draw "shoujo" characters in the highly recognizable styles established by celebrated Japanese manga artists. With detailed coverage of classic characteristics and basic features, including signature costumes, hairstyles and accessories, this book is a dream come true for the aspiring "shoujo" manga artist.

Distributed Exclusively by:
Watson-Guptill Publications
770 Broadway
New York, NY 10003
www.watsonguptill.com

www.dmpbooks.com

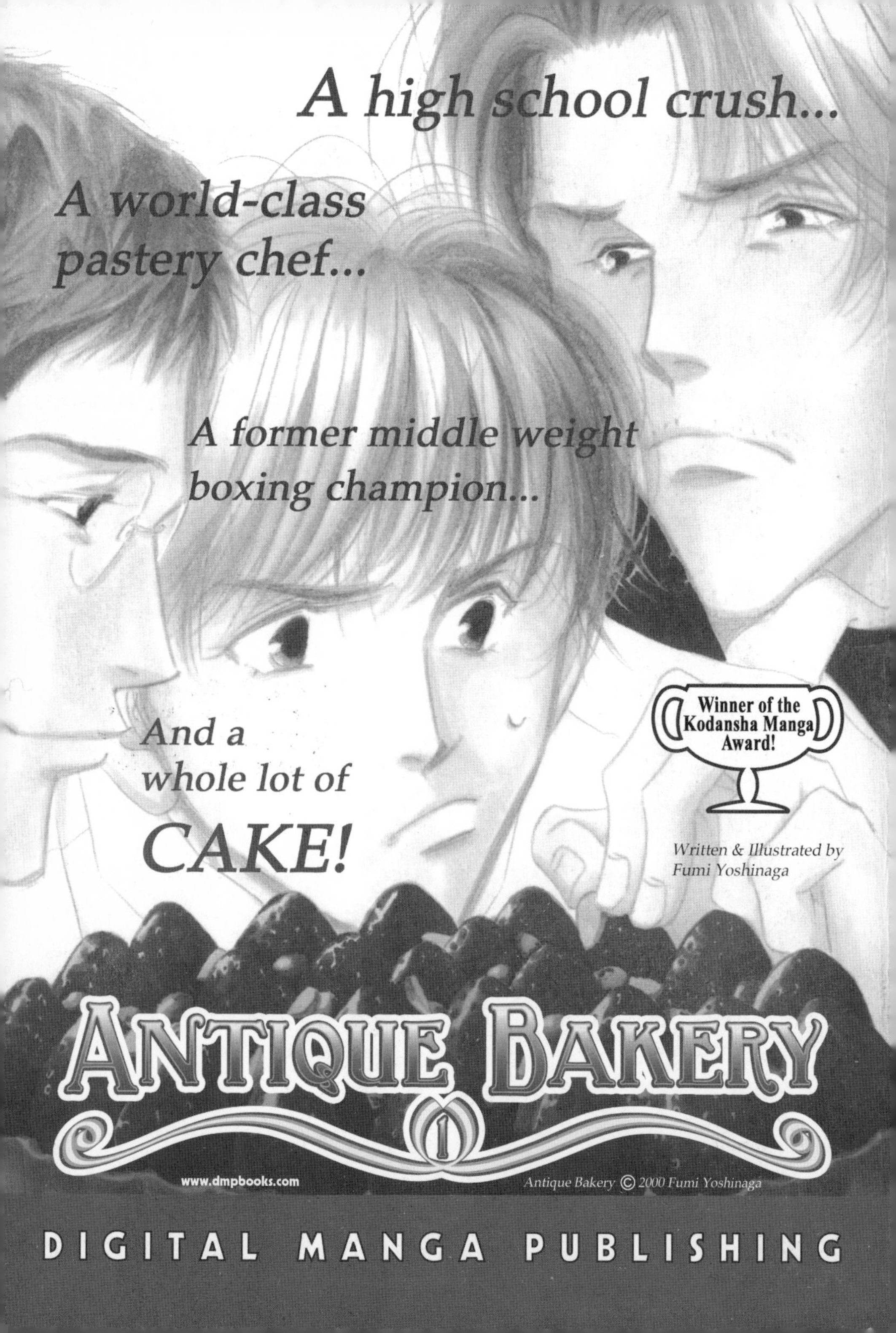
A high school crush...
A world-class pastery chef...
A former middle weight boxing champion...
And a whole lot of CAKE!
Winner of the Kodansha Manga Award!
Written & Illustrated by Fumi Yoshinaga
ANTIQUE BAKERY
1
www.dmpbooks.com
Antique Bakery © 2000 Fumi Yoshinaga
DIGITAL MANGA PUBLISHING

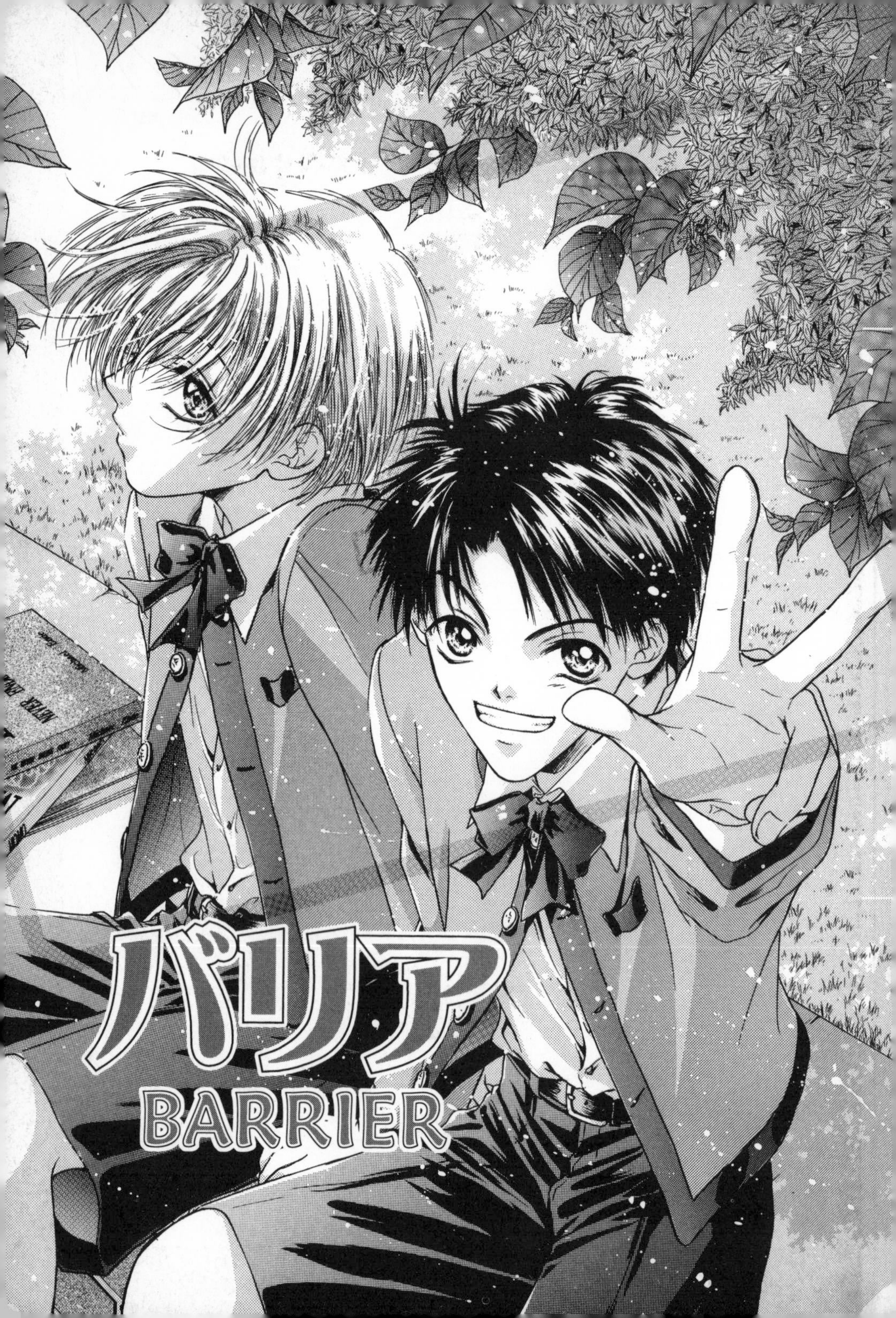
バリア
BARRIER

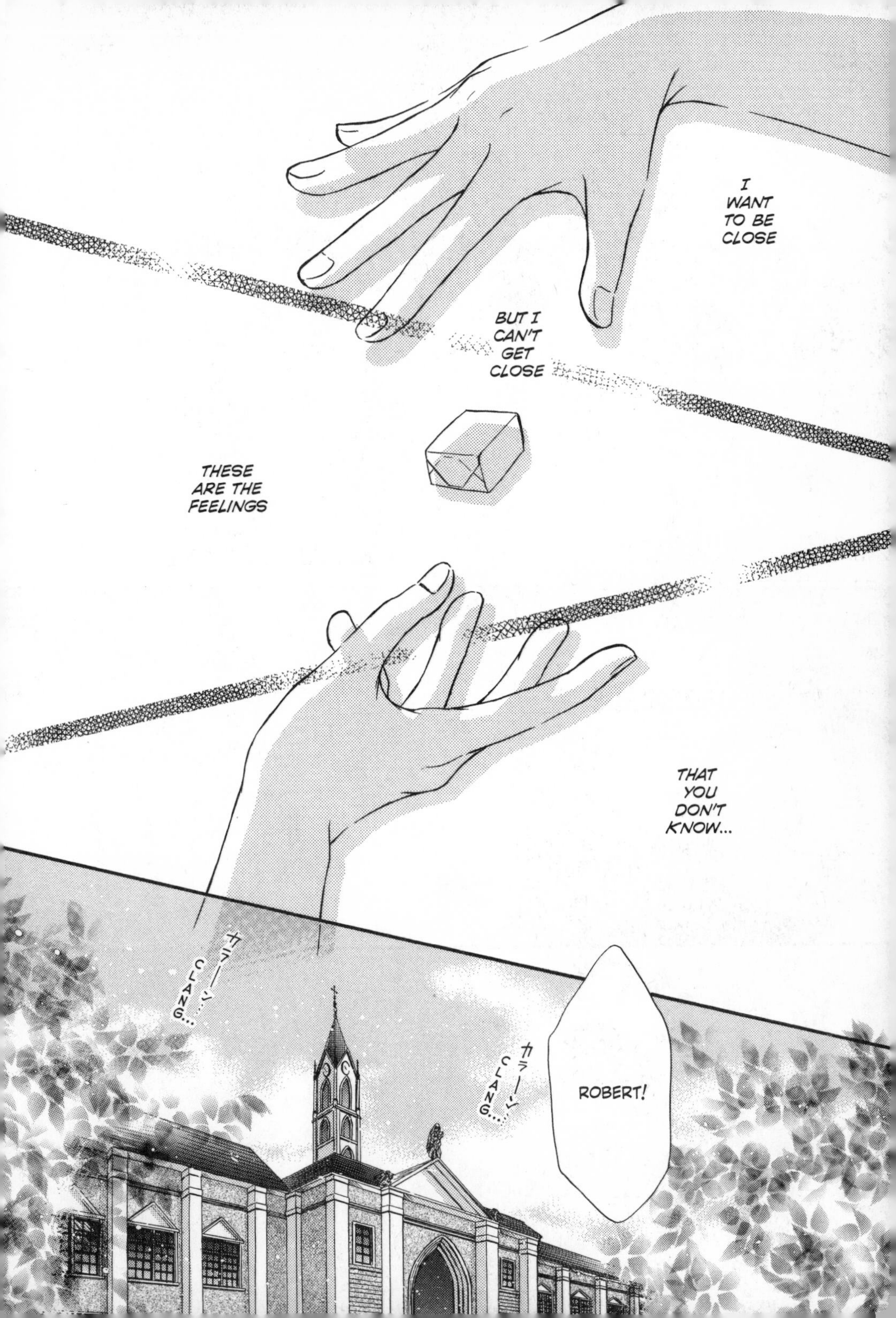
I WANT TO BE CLOSE
BUT I CAN'T GET CLOSE
THESE ARE THE FEELINGS
THAT YOU DON'T KNOW...
ROBERT!
カラーン CLANG...
カラーン CLANG...

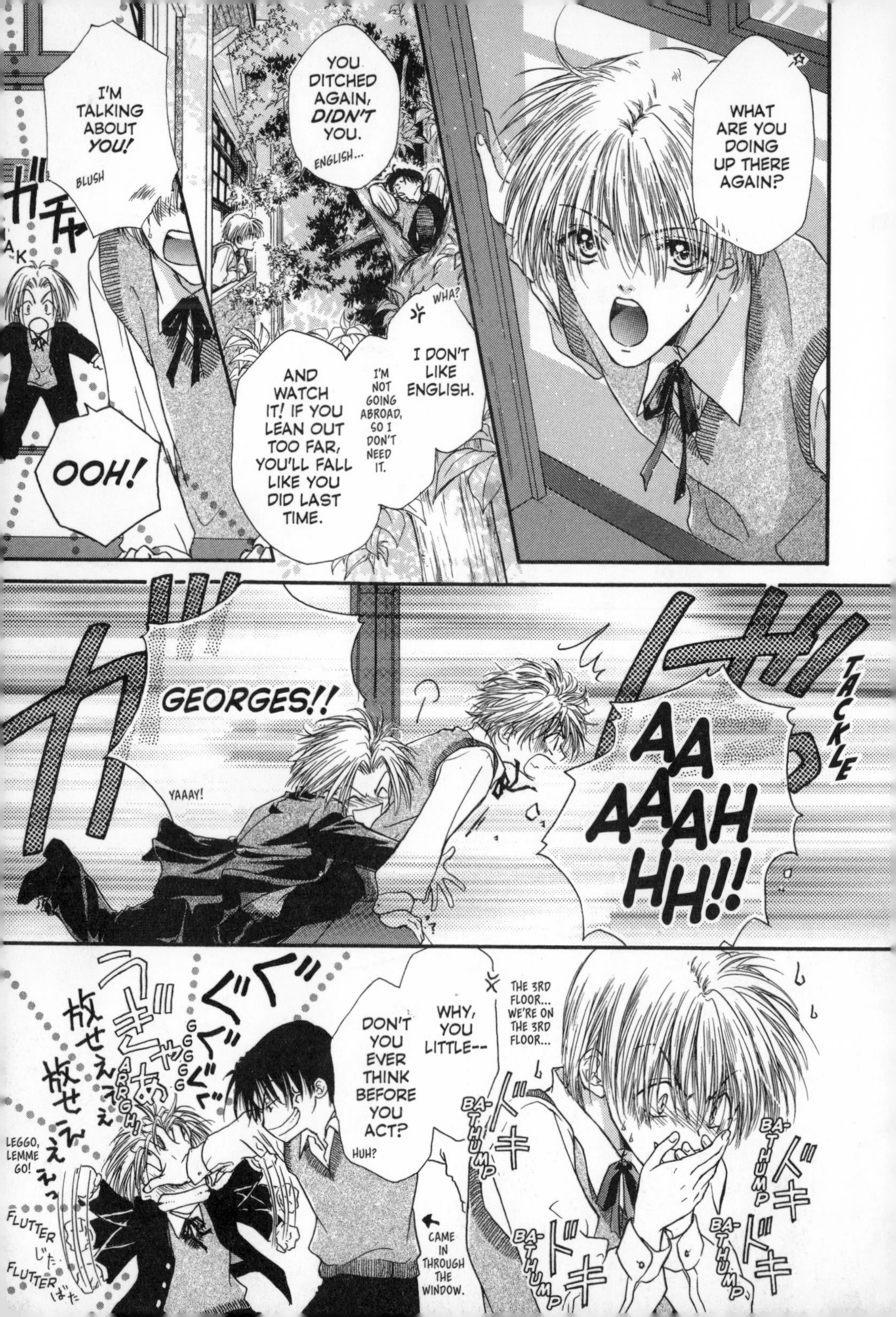

WHAT ARE YOU DOING UP THERE AGAIN?
YOU DITCHED AGAIN, DIDN'T YOU.
ENGLISH...
WHA?
I DON'T LIKE ENGLISH.
I'M NOT GOING ABROAD, SO I DON'T NEED IT.
AND WATCH IT! IF YOU LEAN OUT TOO FAR, YOU'LL FALL LIKE YOU DID LAST TIME.
I'M TALKING ABOUT YOU!
BLUSH
ガチャ
OOH!
TACKLE
AAAAAHHH!!
GEORGES!!
YAAAY!
THE 3RD FLOOR... WE'RE ON THE 3RD FLOOR...
BA-THUMP
ドキ
BA-THUMP
ドキ
BA-THUMP
ドキ
BA-THUMP
ドキ
WHY, YOU LITTLE--
DON'T YOU EVER THINK BEFORE YOU ACT?
HUH?
CAME IN THROUGH THE WINDOW.
ぐぐぐぐ
GGGG
うぎゃあ
ARRGH!
放せぇぇ
放せぇぇっ
LEGGO, LEMME GO!
FLUTTER じた
FLUTTER ばた

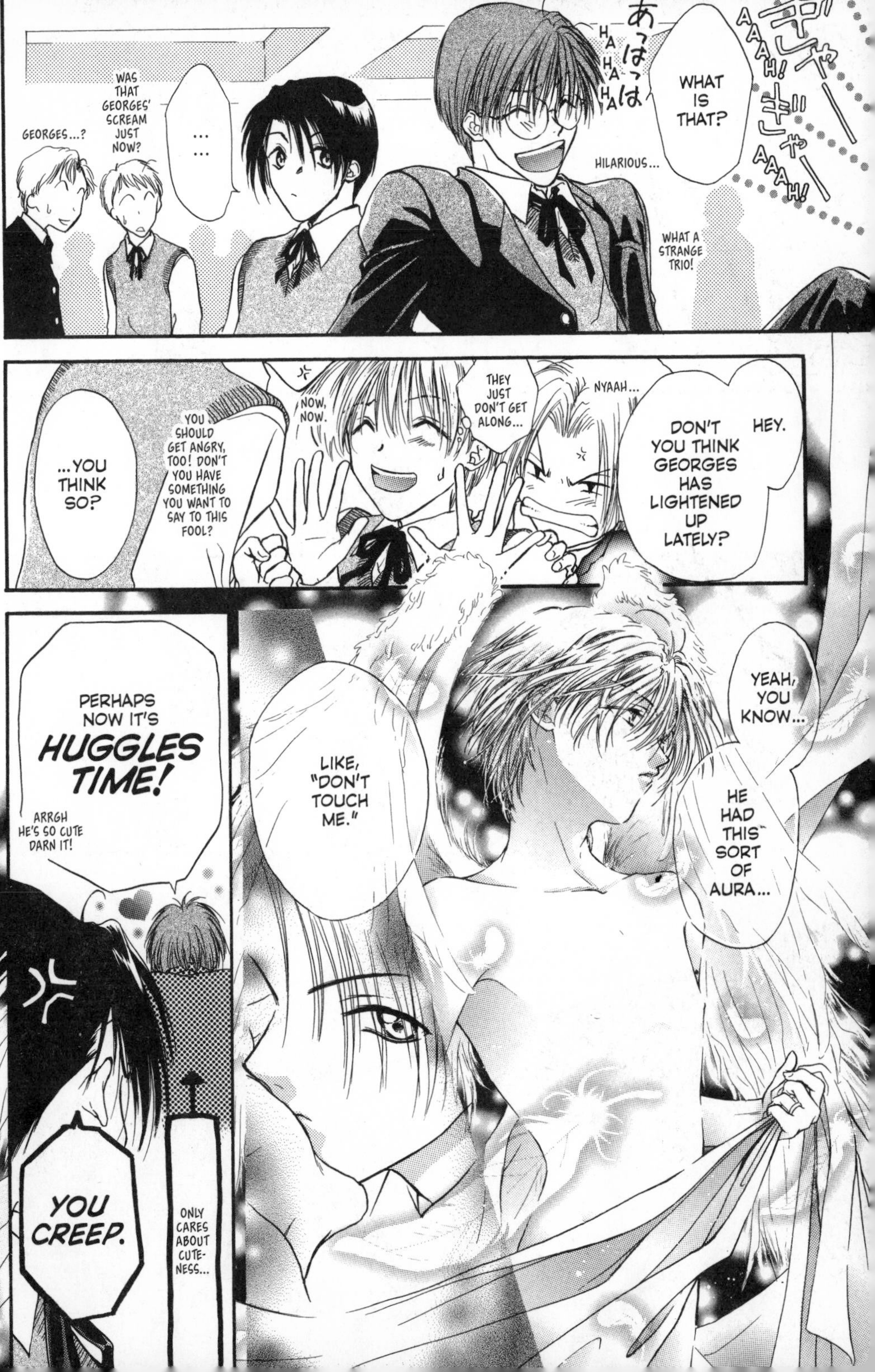
ぎゃーぎゃー
AAAAH! AAAAH!
WHAT IS THAT?
あっはっは
HA HA HA HA
HILARIOUS...
WHAT A STRANGE TRIO!
WAS THAT GEORGES' SCREAM JUST NOW?
... ...
GEORGES...?
HEY.
DON'T YOU THINK GEORGES HAS LIGHTENED UP LATELY?
NYAAH...
THEY JUST DON'T GET ALONG...
NOW, NOW.
YOU SHOULD GET ANGRY, TOO! DON'T YOU HAVE SOMETHING YOU WANT TO SAY TO THIS FOOL?
...YOU THINK SO?
YEAH, YOU KNOW...
HE HAD THIS SORT OF AURA...
LIKE, "DON'T TOUCH ME."
PERHAPS NOW IT'S HUGGLES TIME!
ARRGH HE'S SO CUTE DARN IT!
ONLY CARES ABOUT CUTE-NESS...
YOU CREEP.

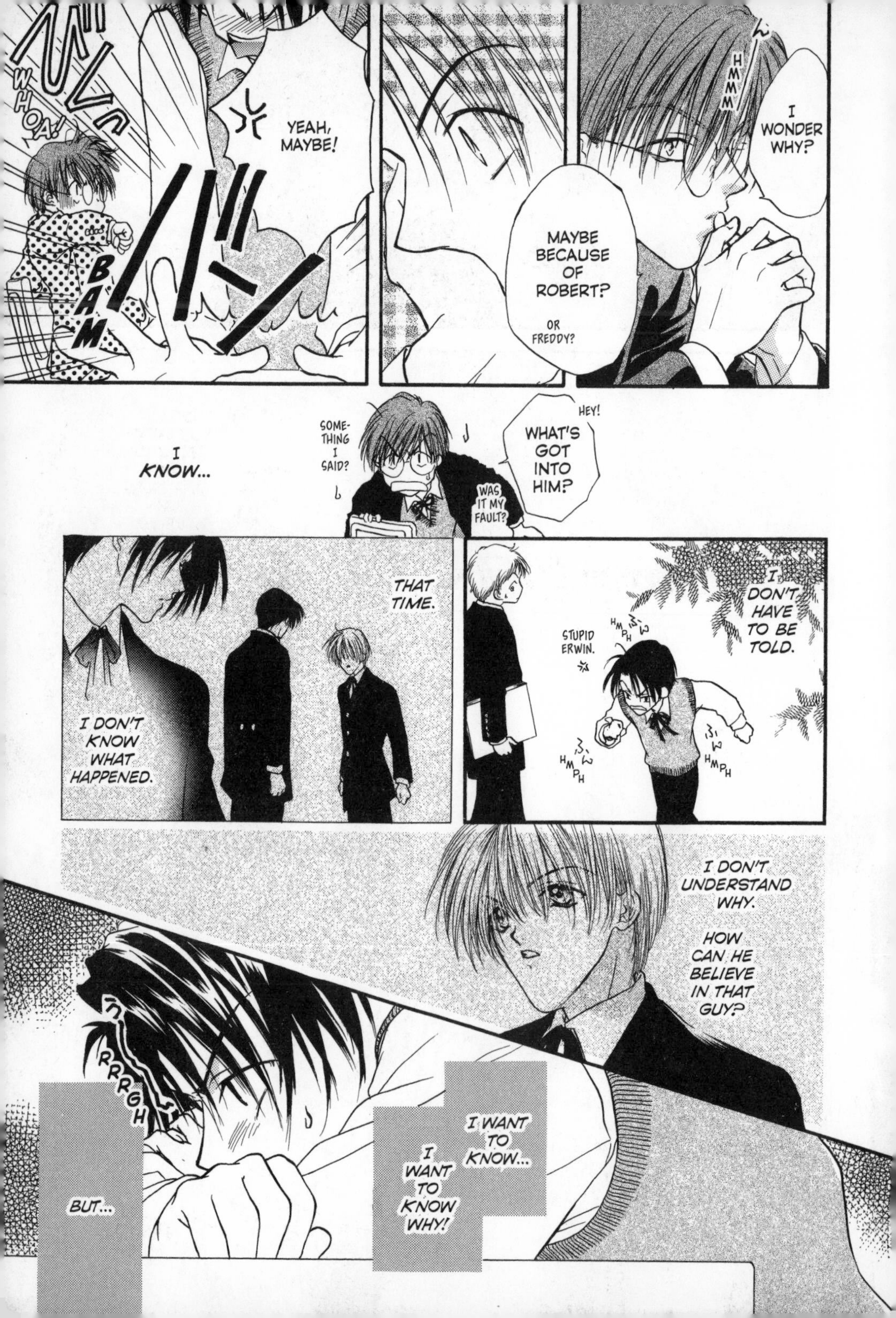
HMMM
I WONDER WHY?
MAYBE BECAUSE OF ROBERT?
OR FREDDY?
YEAH, MAYBE!
BAM
WHOA!
HEY!
WHAT'S GOT INTO HIM?
WAS IT MY FAULT?
SOMETHING I SAID?
I KNOW...
I DON'T HAVE TO BE TOLD.
HMPH
STUPID ERWIN.
HMPH
HMPH
THAT TIME.
I DON'T KNOW WHAT HAPPENED.
I DON'T UNDERSTAND WHY.
HOW CAN HE BELIEVE IN THAT GUY?
RRRGH
I WANT TO KNOW...
I WANT TO KNOW WHY!
BUT...

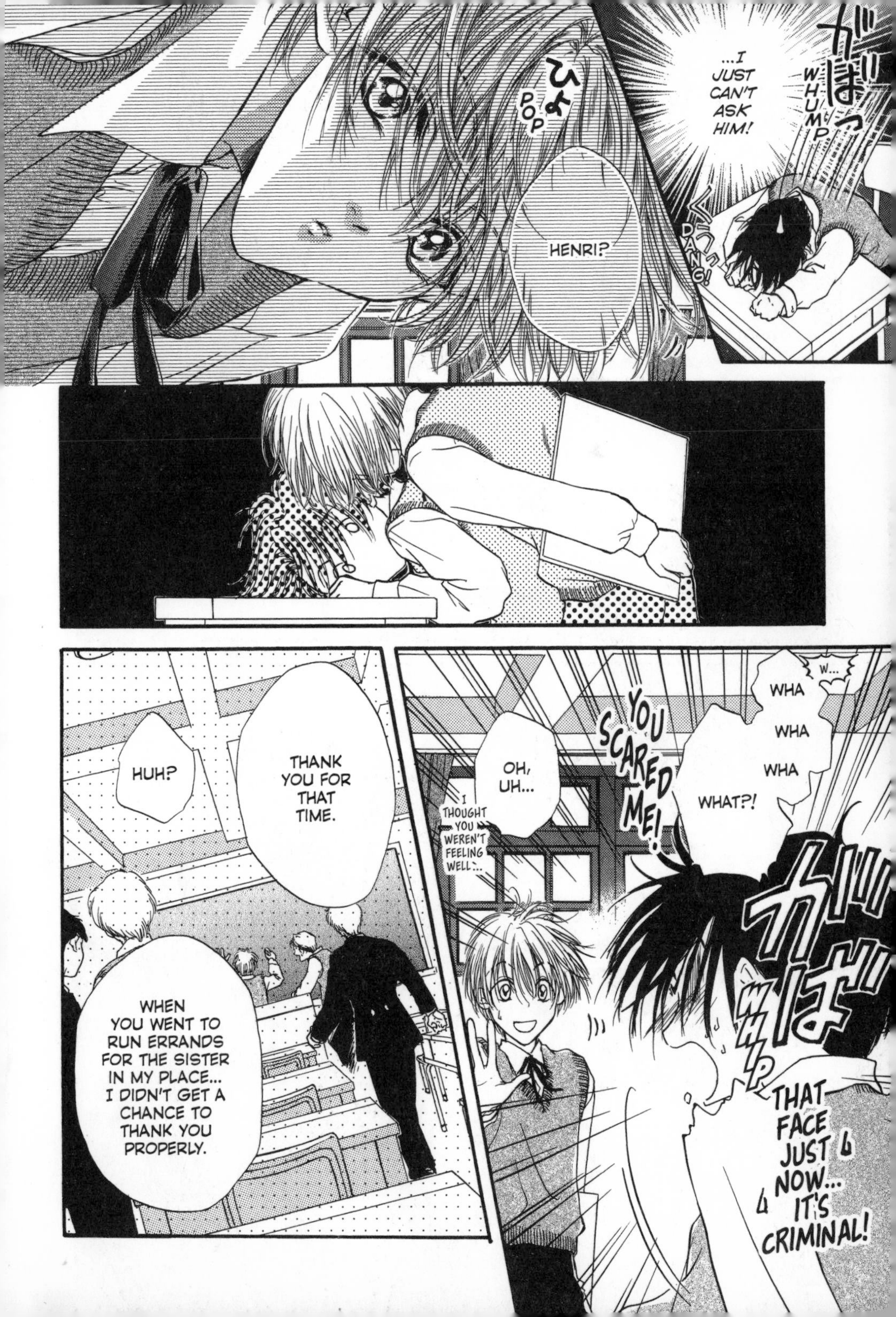
WHUMP
...I JUST CAN'T ASK HIM!
DANG!
ひょ POP
HENRI?
W...
WHA
WHA
WHA
WHAT?!
YOU SCARED ME!
OH, UH...
I THOUGHT YOU WEREN'T FEELING WELL...
WHIP
THAT FACE JUST NOW... IT'S CRIMINAL!
THANK YOU FOR THAT TIME.
HUH?
WHEN YOU WENT TO RUN ERRANDS FOR THE SISTER IN MY PLACE... I DIDN'T GET A CHANCE TO THANK YOU PROPERLY.

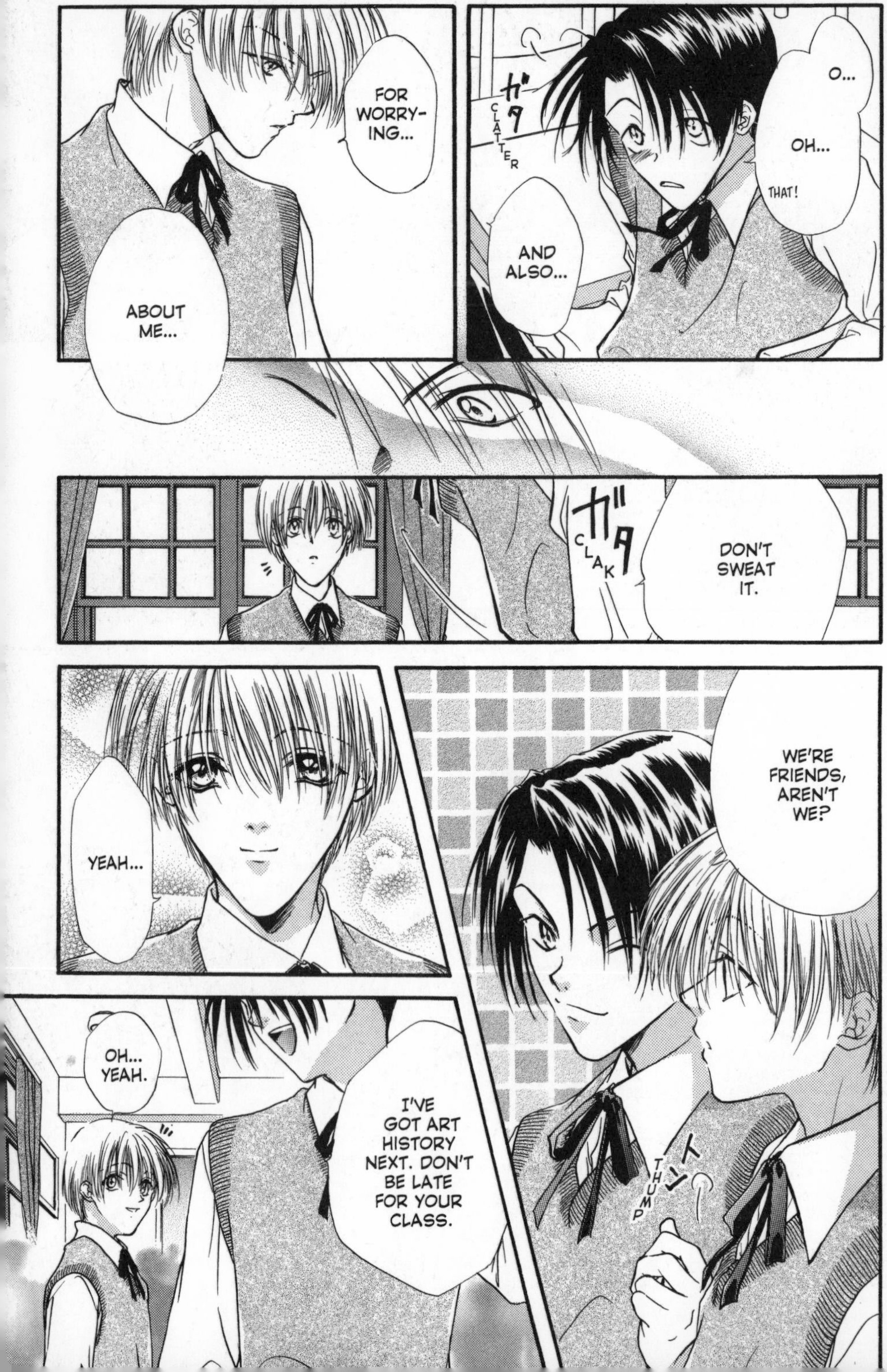
O...
OH...
THAT!
ガタ
CLATTER
AND ALSO...
FOR WORRYING...
ABOUT ME...
ガタ
CLAK
DON'T SWEAT IT.
WE'RE FRIENDS, AREN'T WE?
トン
THUMP
YEAH...
I'VE GOT ART HISTORY NEXT. DON'T BE LATE FOR YOUR CLASS.
OH... YEAH.

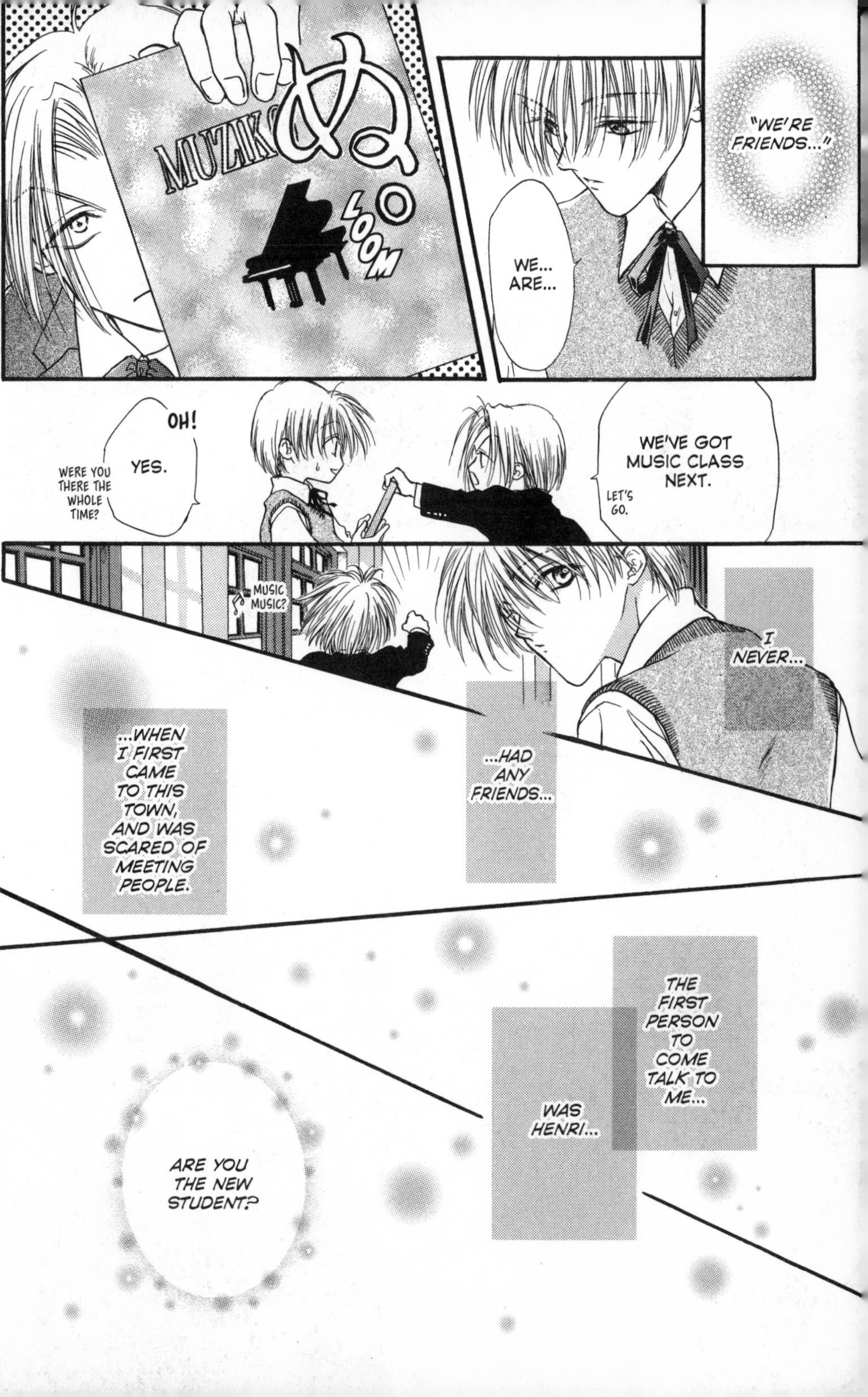
"WE'RE FRIENDS..."
WE... ARE...
MUZIK
LOOM
WE'VE GOT MUSIC CLASS NEXT.
LET'S GO.
OH!
YES.
WERE YOU THERE THE WHOLE TIME?
I NEVER...
...HAD ANY FRIENDS...
MUSIC MUSIC?
...WHEN I FIRST CAME TO THIS TOWN, AND WAS SCARED OF MEETING PEOPLE.
THE FIRST PERSON TO COME TALK TO ME...
WAS HENRI...
ARE YOU THE NEW STUDENT?

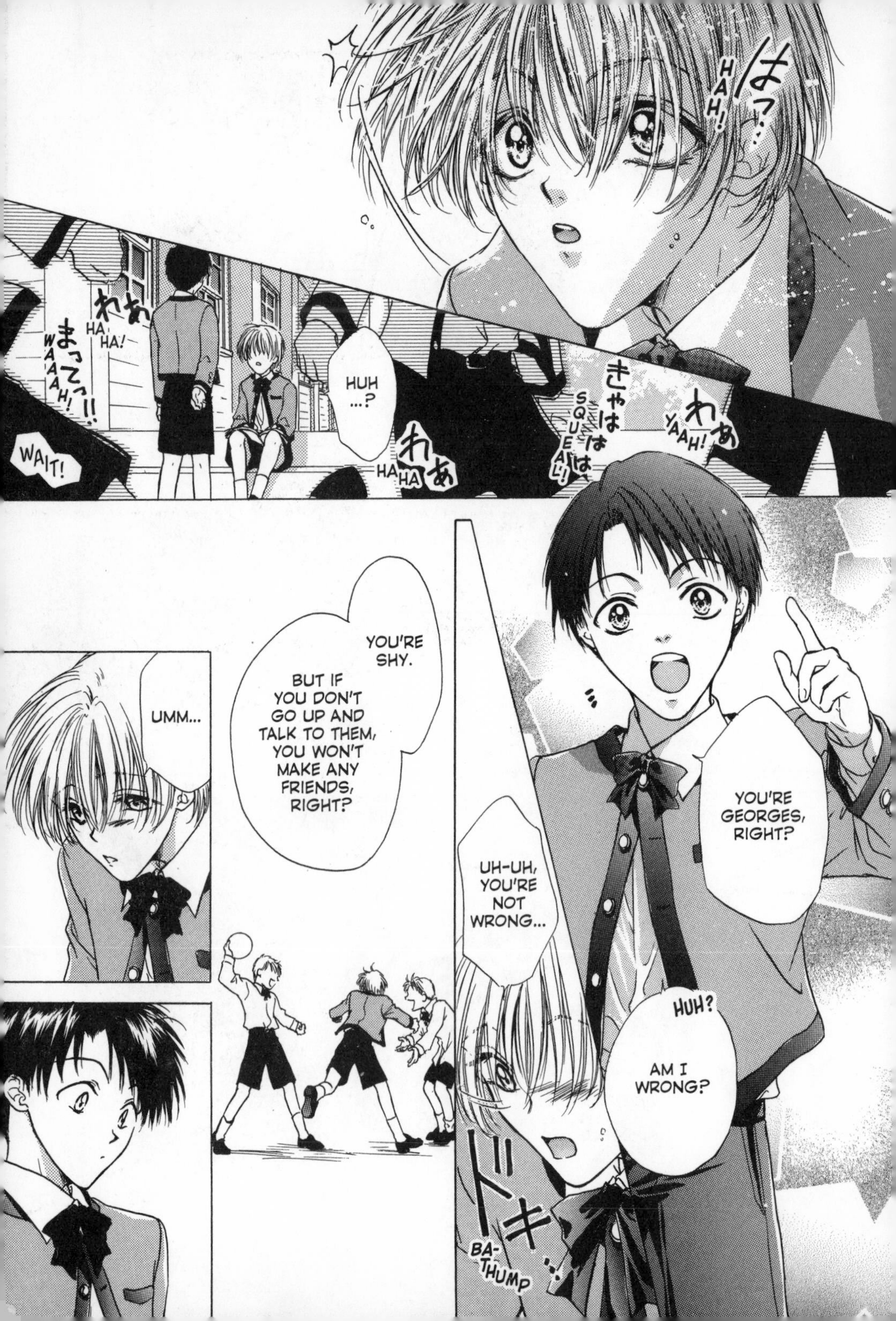

はっ…
HAH!
わあ
YAAAH!
きゃははは
SQUEAL!
わあ
HA HA
HUH ...?
わあ
HA HA!
まってっ!!
WAAAAH!
WAIT!
YOU'RE GEORGES, RIGHT?
UH-UH, YOU'RE NOT WRONG...
HUH?
AM I WRONG?
ドキ
BA-THUMP
YOU'RE SHY.
BUT IF YOU DON'T GO UP AND TALK TO THEM, YOU WON'T MAKE ANY FRIENDS, RIGHT?
UMM...

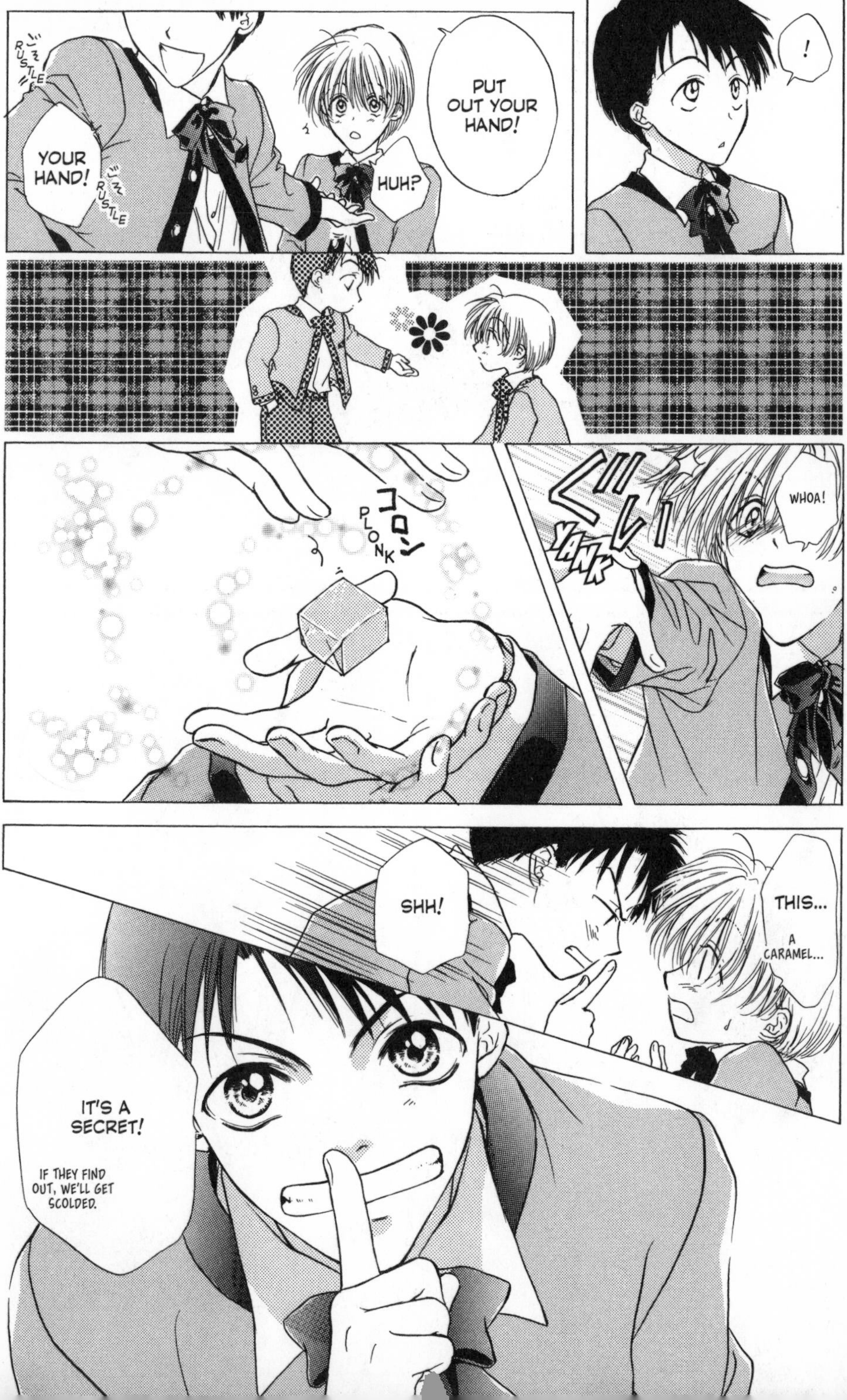
!
PUT OUT YOUR HAND!
RUSTLE
HUH?
YOUR HAND!
RUSTLE
WHOA!
YANK
PLONK
THIS...
A CARAMEL...
SHH!
IT'S A SECRET!
IF THEY FIND OUT, WE'LL GET SCOLDED.

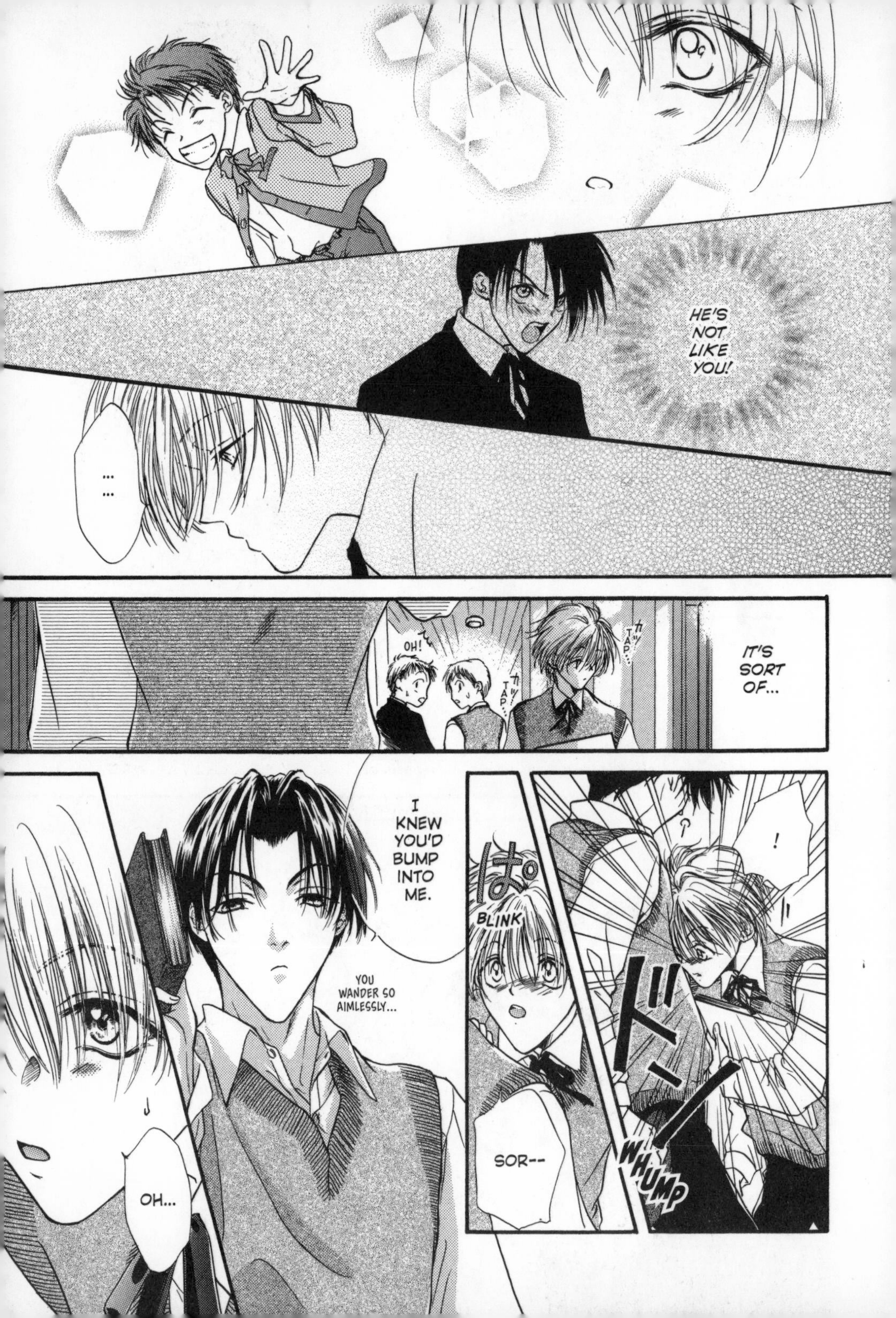
HE'S NOT LIKE YOU!
... ...
IT'S SORT OF...
TAP... TAP...
OH!
!
はっ
BLINK
SOR--
ドン
WHUMP
I KNEW YOU'D BUMP INTO ME.
YOU WANDER SO AIMLESSLY...
OH...

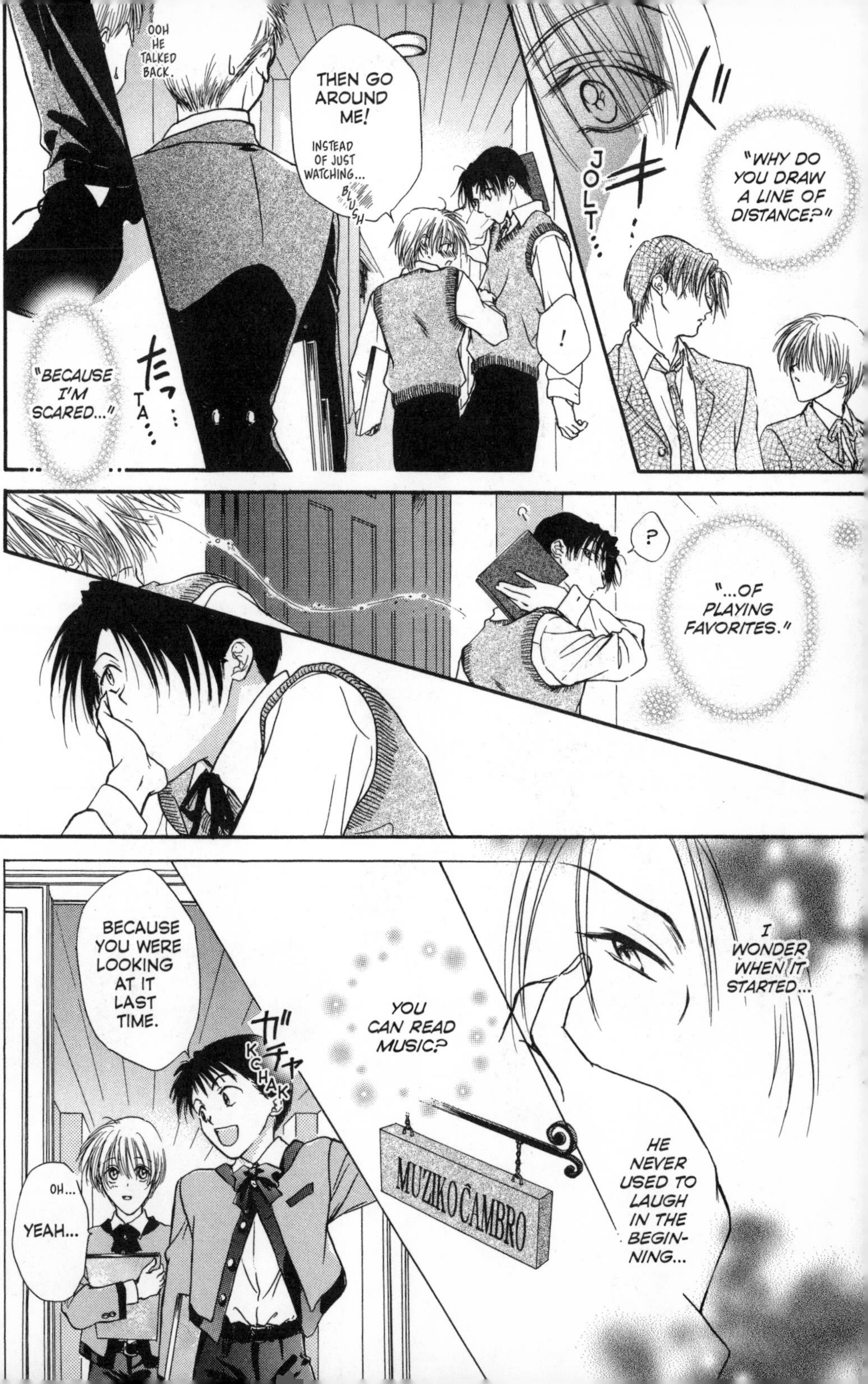
"WHY DO YOU DRAW A LINE OF DISTANCE?"
JOLT...
THEN GO AROUND ME!
INSTEAD OF JUST WATCHING...
BLUSH
!
OOH HE TALKED BACK.
"BECAUSE I'M SCARED..."
TA...
"...OF PLAYING FAVORITES."
?
I WONDER WHEN IT STARTED...
HE NEVER USED TO LAUGH IN THE BEGIN-NING...
MUZIKO CAMBRO
YOU CAN READ MUSIC?
KCHAK
BECAUSE YOU WERE LOOKING AT IT LAST TIME.
OH...
YEAH...

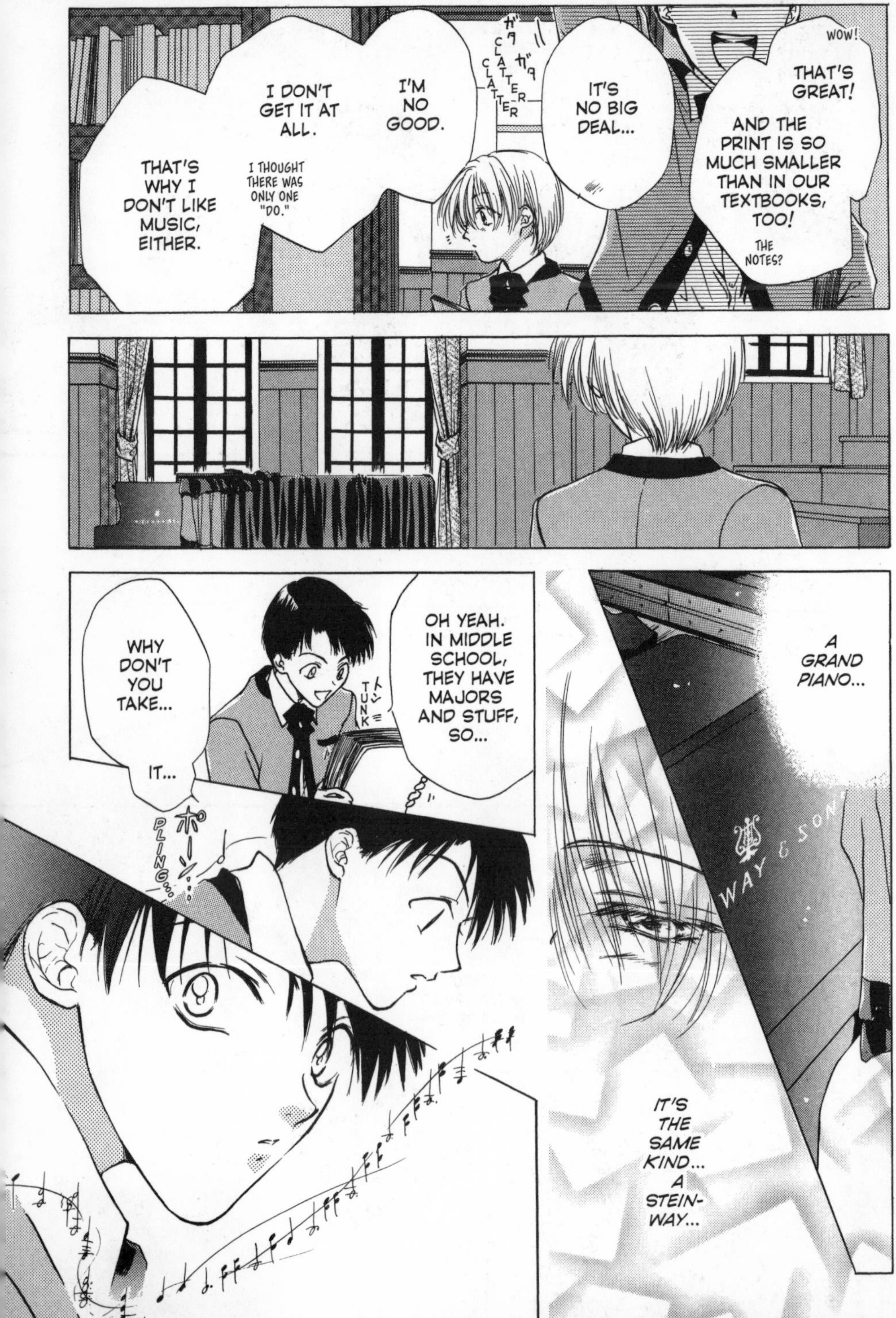
WOW!
THAT'S GREAT!
AND THE PRINT IS SO MUCH SMALLER THAN IN OUR TEXTBOOKS, TOO!
THE NOTES?
IT'S NO BIG DEAL...
ガタ CLATTER ガタ CLATTER
I'M NO GOOD.
I DON'T GET IT AT ALL.
I THOUGHT THERE WAS ONLY ONE "DO."
THAT'S WHY I DON'T LIKE MUSIC, EITHER.
A GRAND PIANO...
WAY & SONS
IT'S THE SAME KIND... A STEIN-WAY...
OH YEAH. IN MIDDLE SCHOOL, THEY HAVE MAJORS AND STUFF, SO...
TUNK
WHY DON'T YOU TAKE...
IT...
PLING...

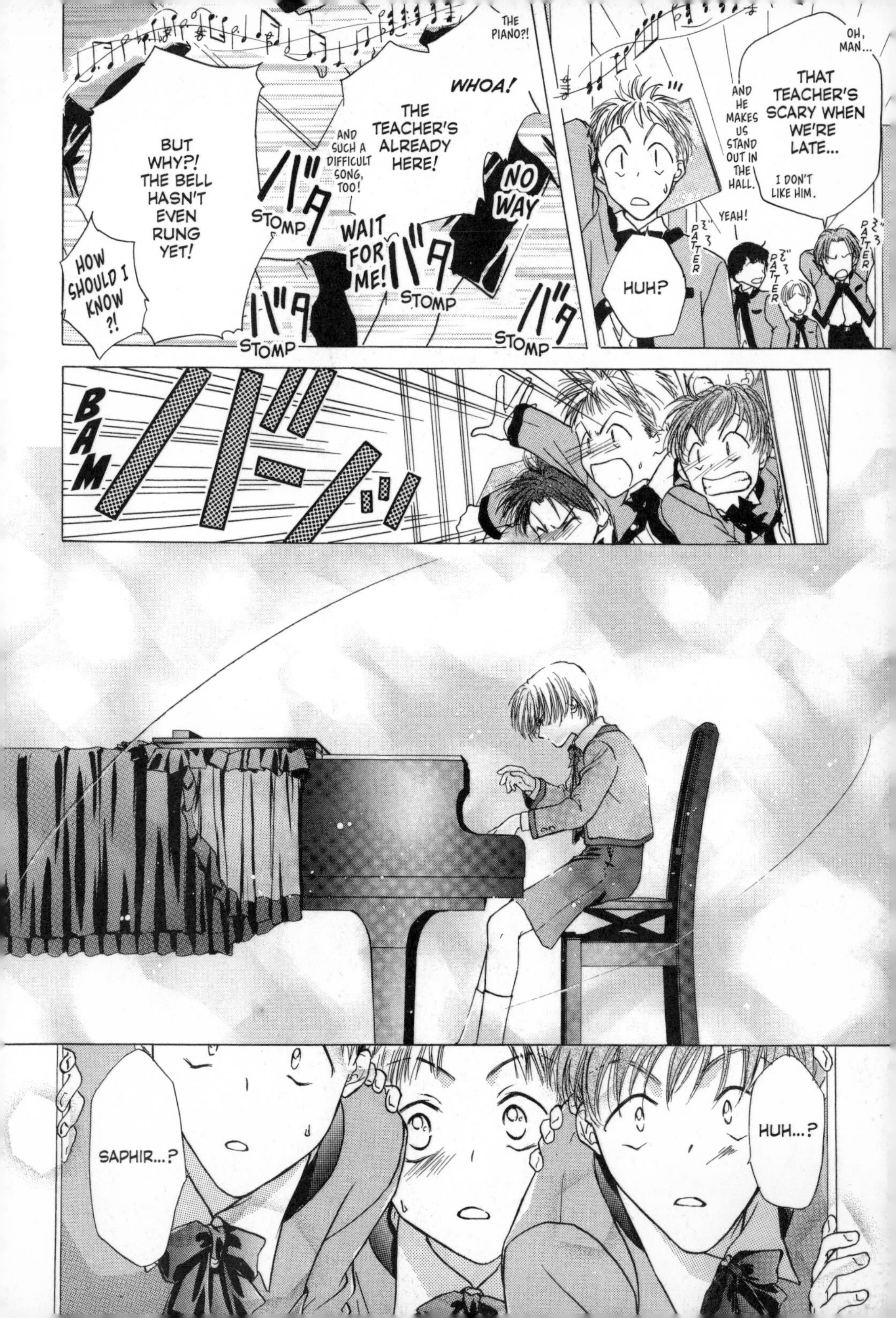
OH, MAN...
THAT TEACHER'S SCARY WHEN WE'RE LATE...
I DON'T LIKE HIM.
AND HE MAKES US STAND OUT IN THE HALL.
YEAH!
PATTER
PATTER
PATTER
HUH?
THE PIANO?!
WHOA!
THE TEACHER'S ALREADY HERE!
AND SUCH A DIFFICULT SONG, TOO!
NO WAY
BUT WHY?! THE BELL HASN'T EVEN RUNG YET!
HOW SHOULD I KNOW ?!
バタ STOMP
WAIT FOR ME!
バタ STOMP
バタ STOMP
バタ STOMP
BAM
HUH...?
SAPHIR...?

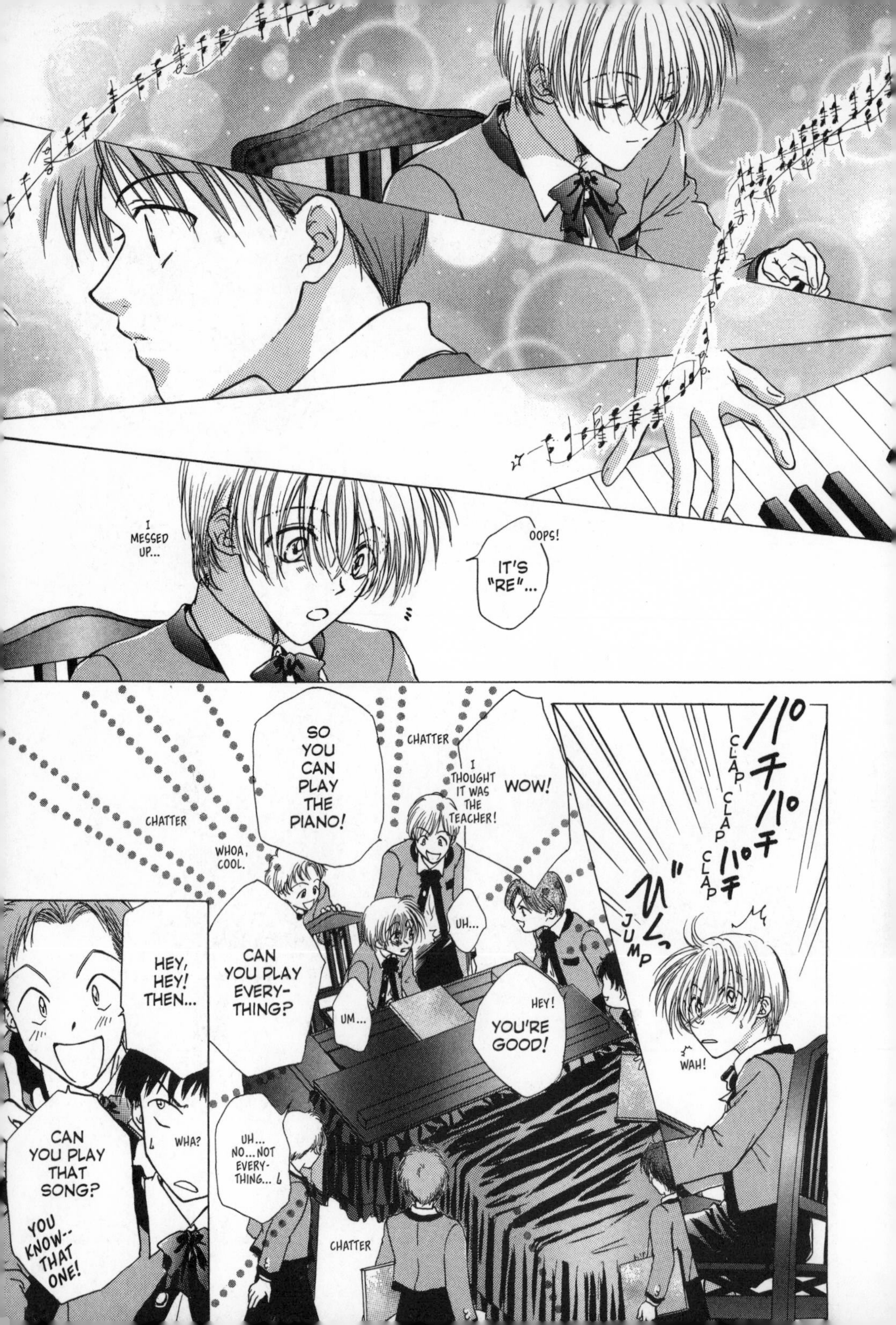
OOPS!
IT'S "RE"...
I MESSED UP...
パチパチパチ
CLAP CLAP CLAP
びくっ
JUMP
WAH!
WOW!
I THOUGHT IT WAS THE TEACHER!
CHATTER
SO YOU CAN PLAY THE PIANO!
WHOA, COOL.
CHATTER
UH...
HEY! YOU'RE GOOD!
CAN YOU PLAY EVERYTHING?
UM...
UH... NO... NOT EVERYTHING...
CHATTER
HEY, HEY! THEN...
WHA?
CAN YOU PLAY THAT SONG?
YOU KNOW-- THAT ONE!

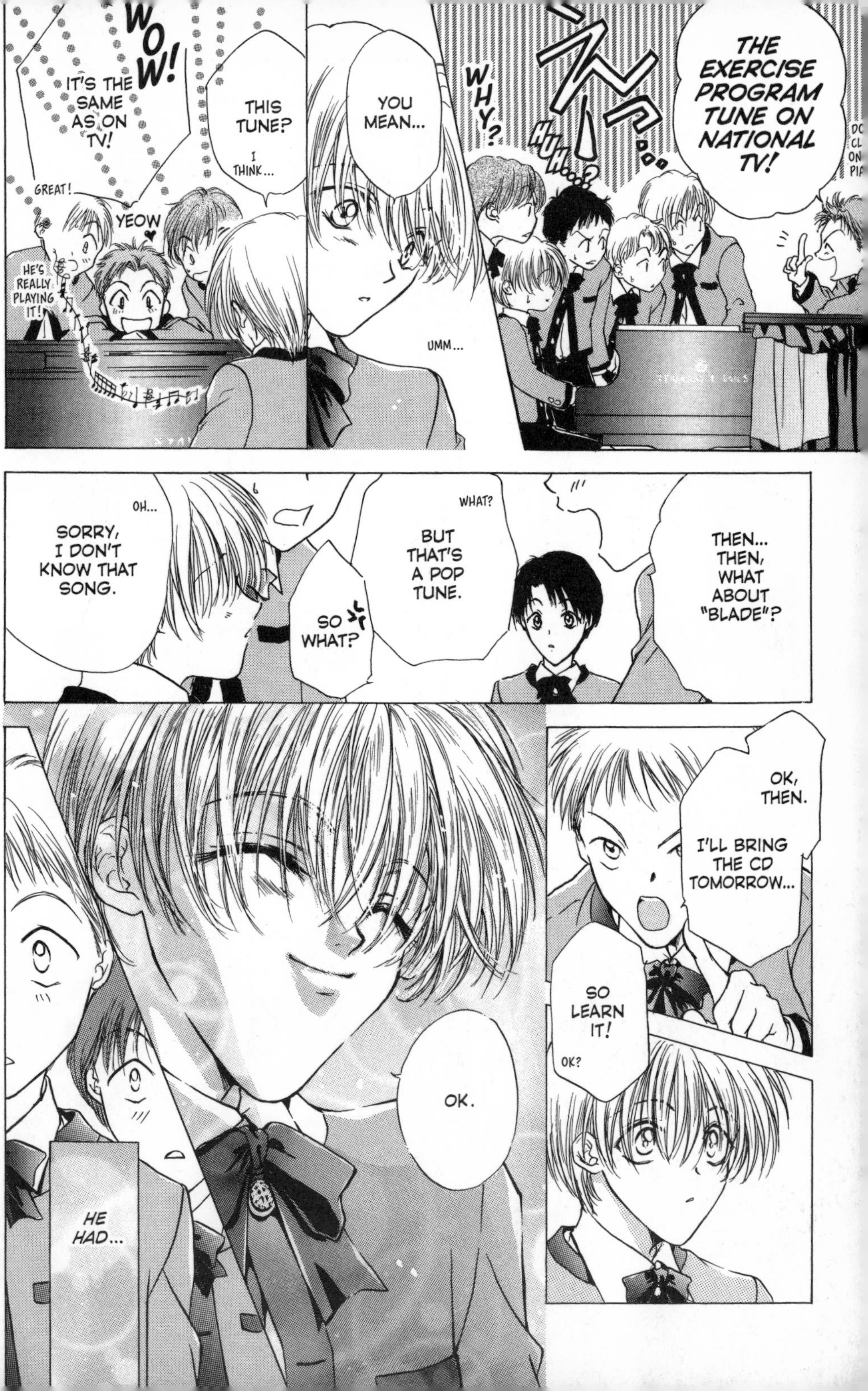
THE EXERCISE PROGRAM TUNE ON NATIONAL TV!
WHY?
HUH...?
YOU MEAN...
UMM...
THIS TUNE?
I THINK...
WOW!
IT'S THE SAME AS ON TV!
GREAT!
YEOW
HE'S REALLY PLAYING IT!
THEN... THEN, WHAT ABOUT "BLADE"?
WHAT?
BUT THAT'S A POP TUNE.
SO WHAT?
OH...
SORRY, I DON'T KNOW THAT SONG.
OK, THEN.
I'LL BRING THE CD TOMORROW...
SO LEARN IT!
OK?
OK.
HE HAD...

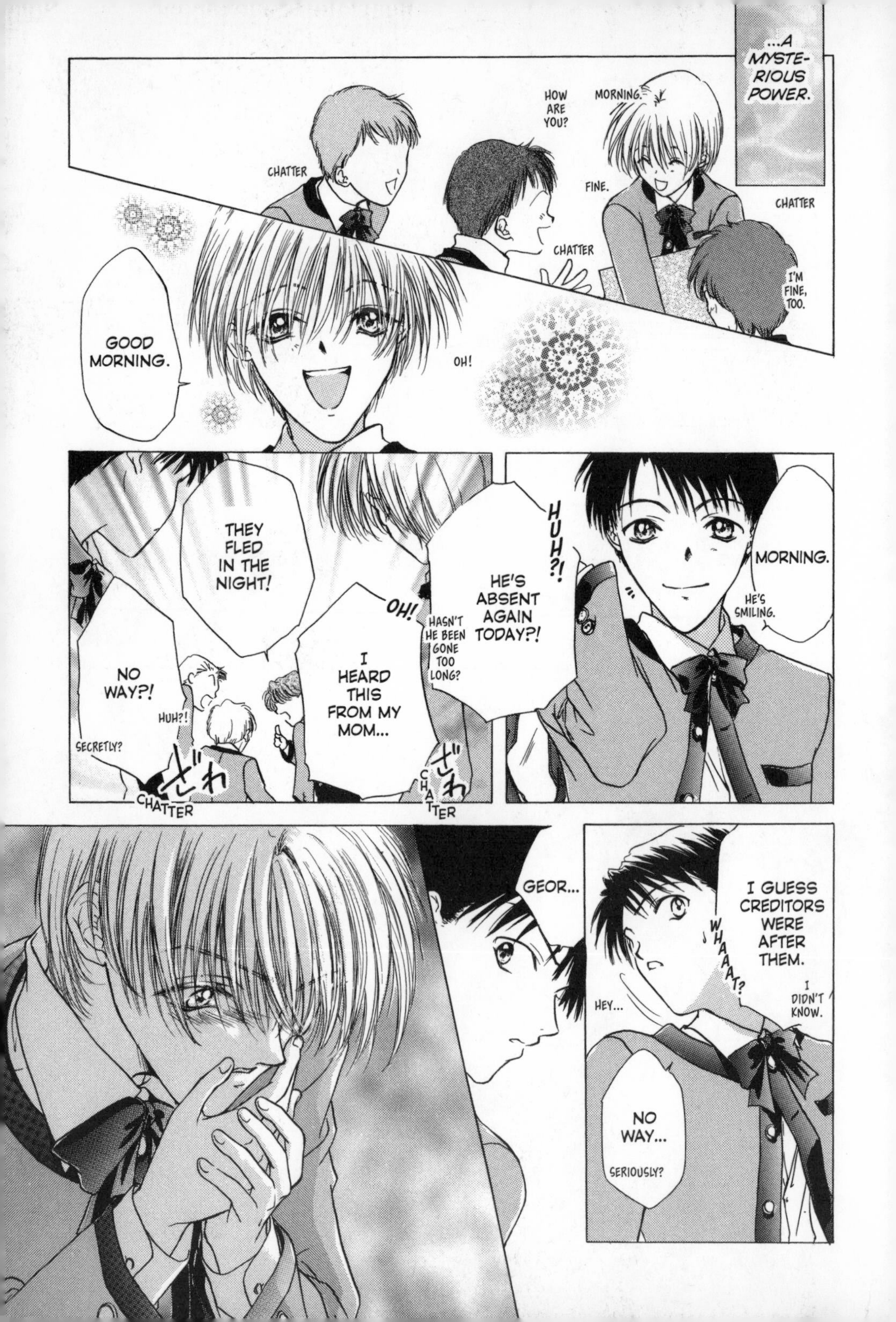
...A MYSTERIOUS POWER.
MORNING.
HOW ARE YOU?
FINE.
CHATTER
I'M FINE, TOO.
CHATTER
CHATTER
OH!
GOOD MORNING.
HUH?!
MORNING.
HE'S SMILING.
HE'S ABSENT AGAIN TODAY?!
HASN'T HE BEEN GONE TOO LONG?
OH!
ざわ
CHATTER
THEY FLED IN THE NIGHT!
I HEARD THIS FROM MY MOM...
NO WAY?!
HUH?!
SECRETLY?
ざわ
CHATTER
I GUESS CREDITORS WERE AFTER THEM.
WHAAAT?
I DIDN'T KNOW.
HEY...
NO WAY...
SERIOUSLY?
GEOR...

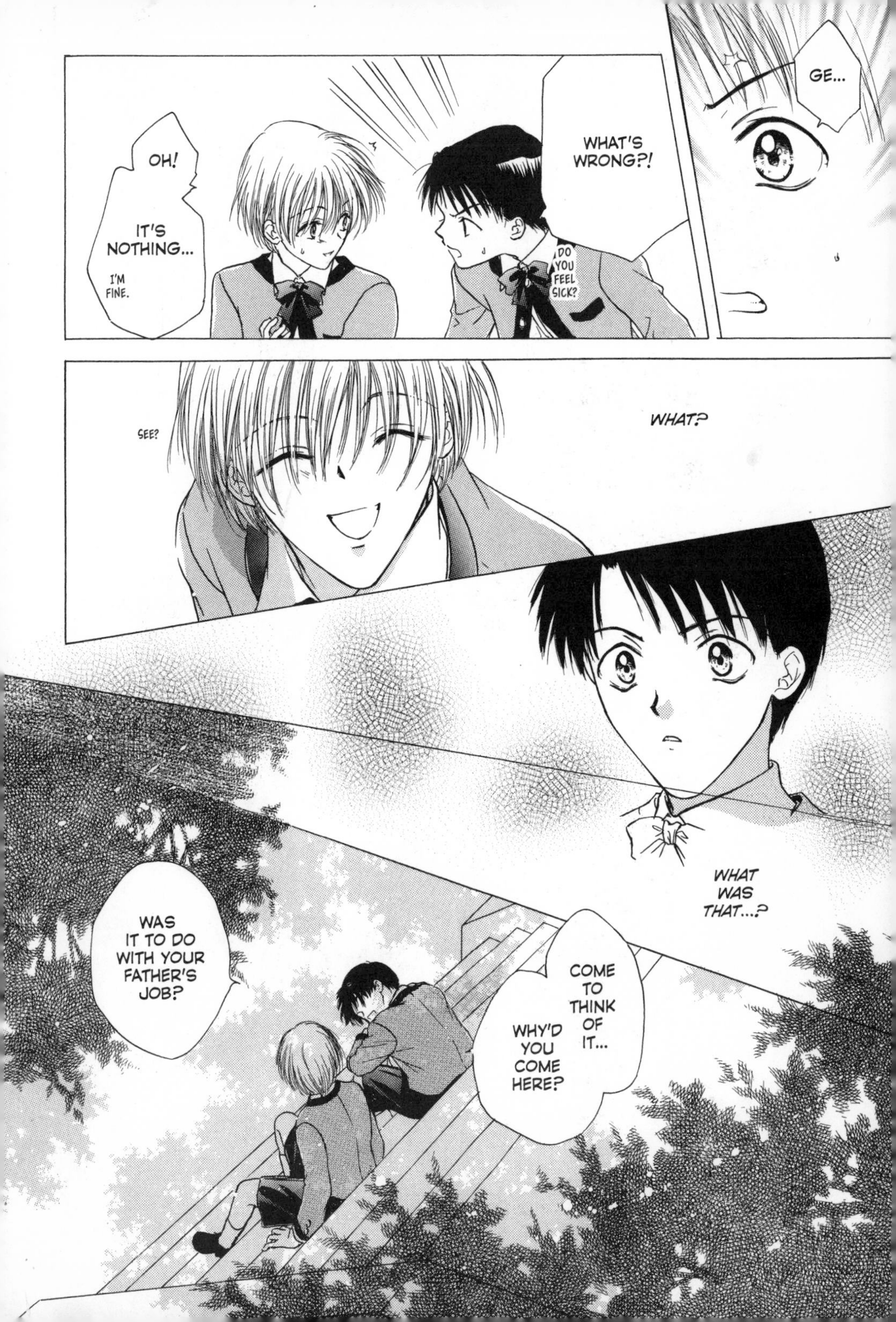
GE...
WHAT'S WRONG?!
DO YOU FEEL SICK?
OH!
IT'S NOTHING...
I'M FINE.
SEE?
WHAT?
WHAT WAS THAT...?
COME TO THINK OF IT...
WHY'D YOU COME HERE?
WAS IT TO DO WITH YOUR FATHER'S JOB?

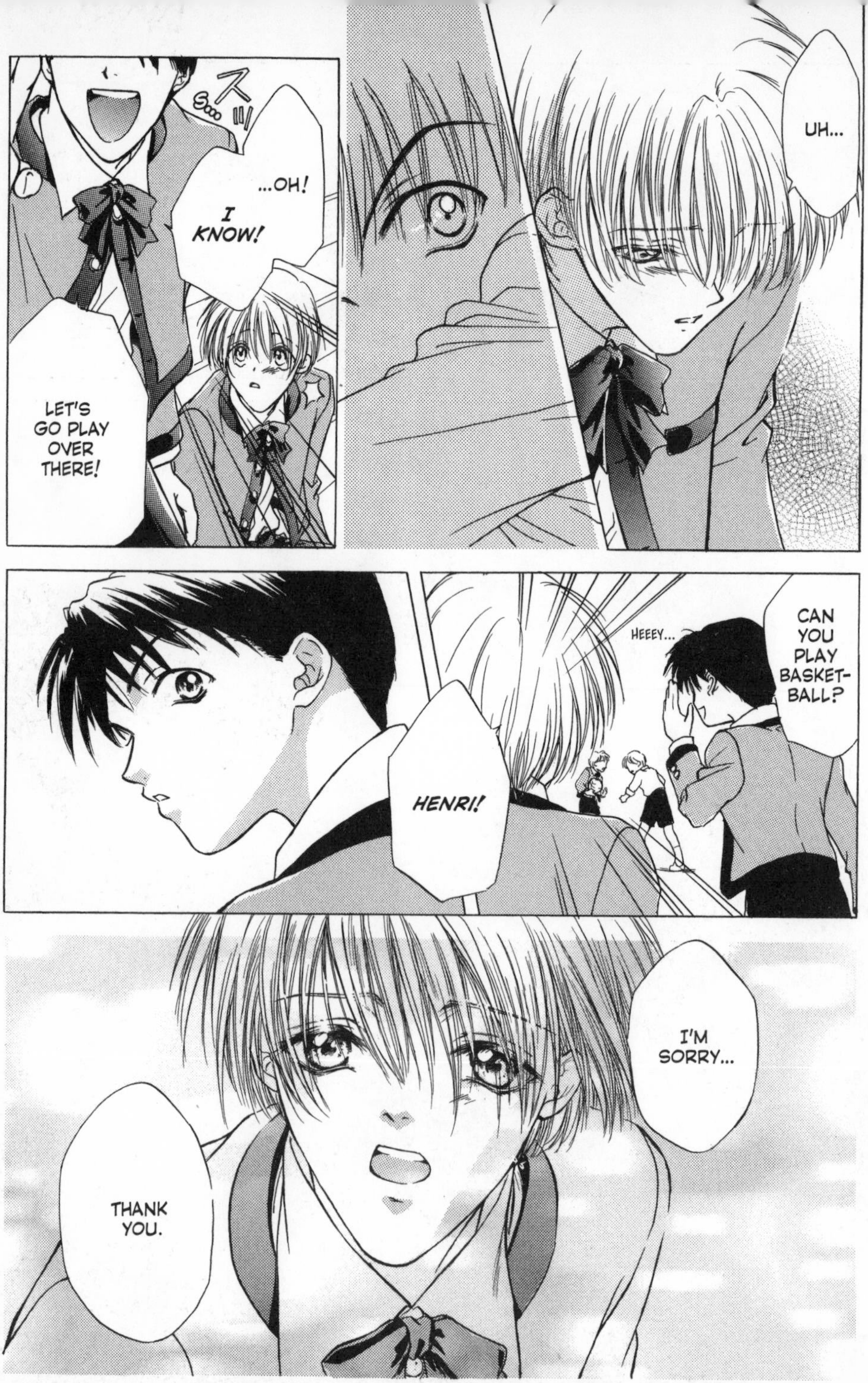
UH...
...OH!
I KNOW!
S...
LET'S GO PLAY OVER THERE!
HEEEY...
CAN YOU PLAY BASKET-BALL?
HENRI!
I'M SORRY...
THANK YOU.

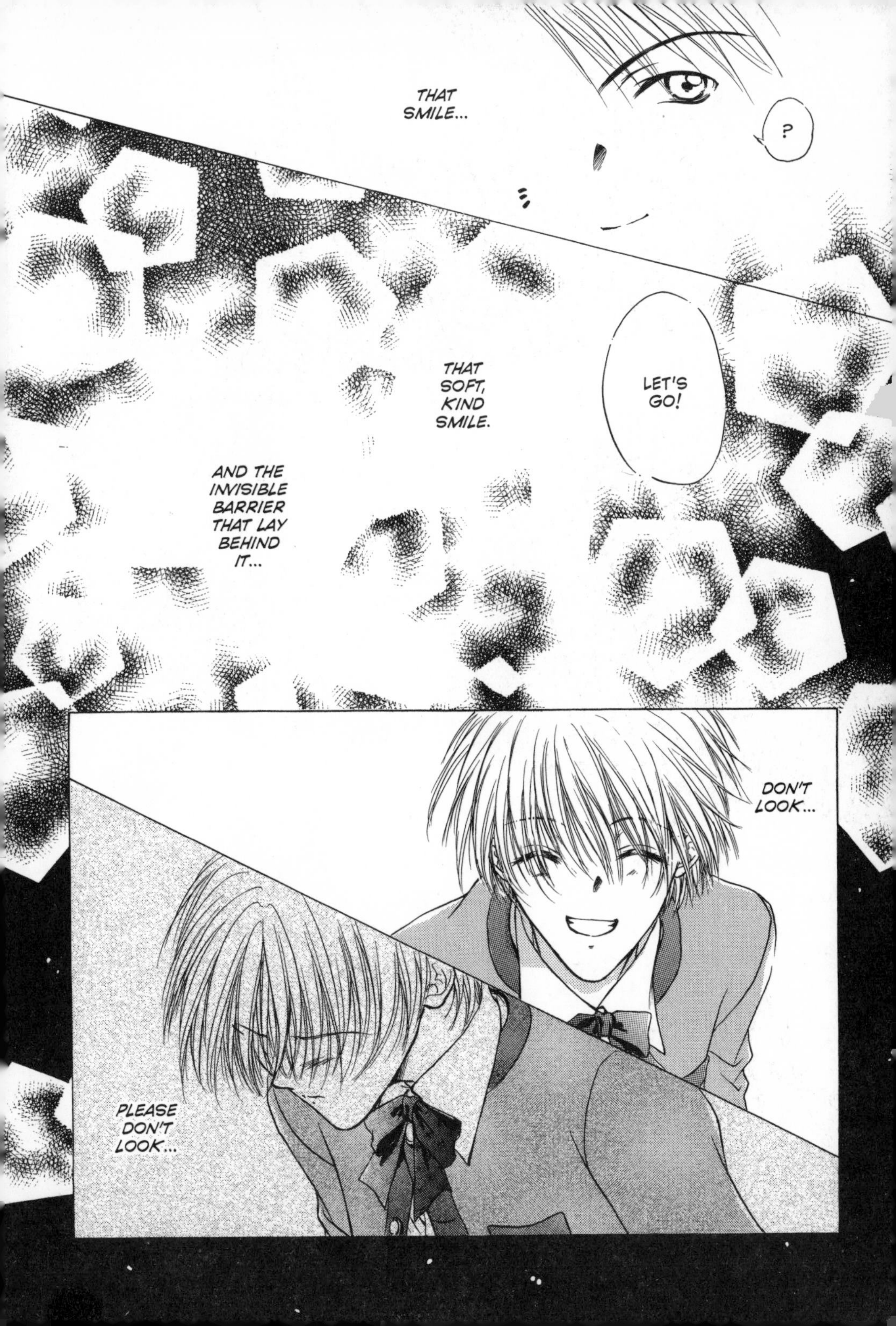
THAT SMILE...
?
LET'S GO!
THAT SOFT, KIND SMILE.
AND THE INVISIBLE BARRIER THAT LAY BEHIND IT...
DON'T LOOK...
PLEASE DON'T LOOK...

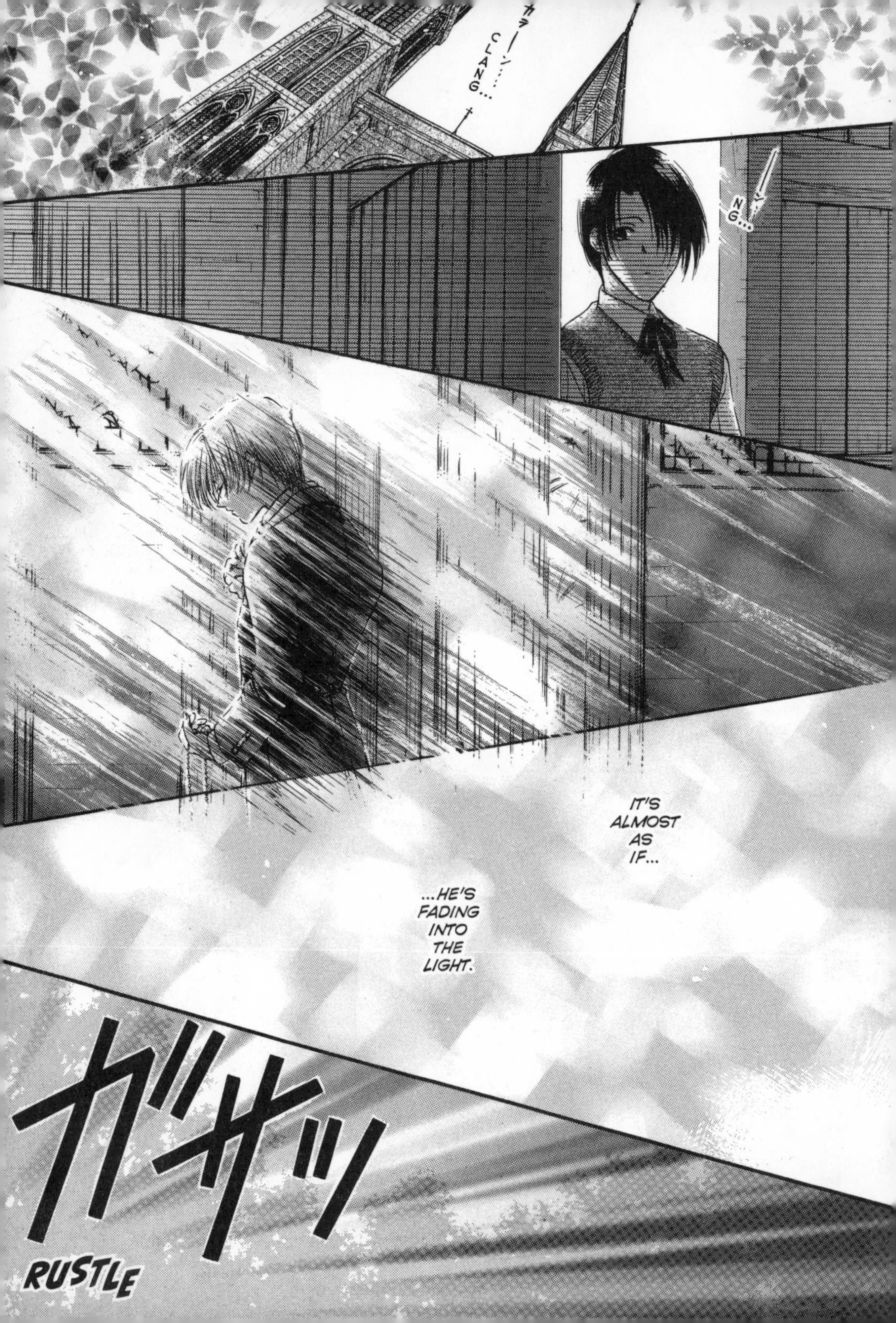
カラーン……
CLANG...
NG...
IT'S ALMOST AS IF...
...HE'S FADING INTO THE LIGHT.
ガザッ
RUSTLE

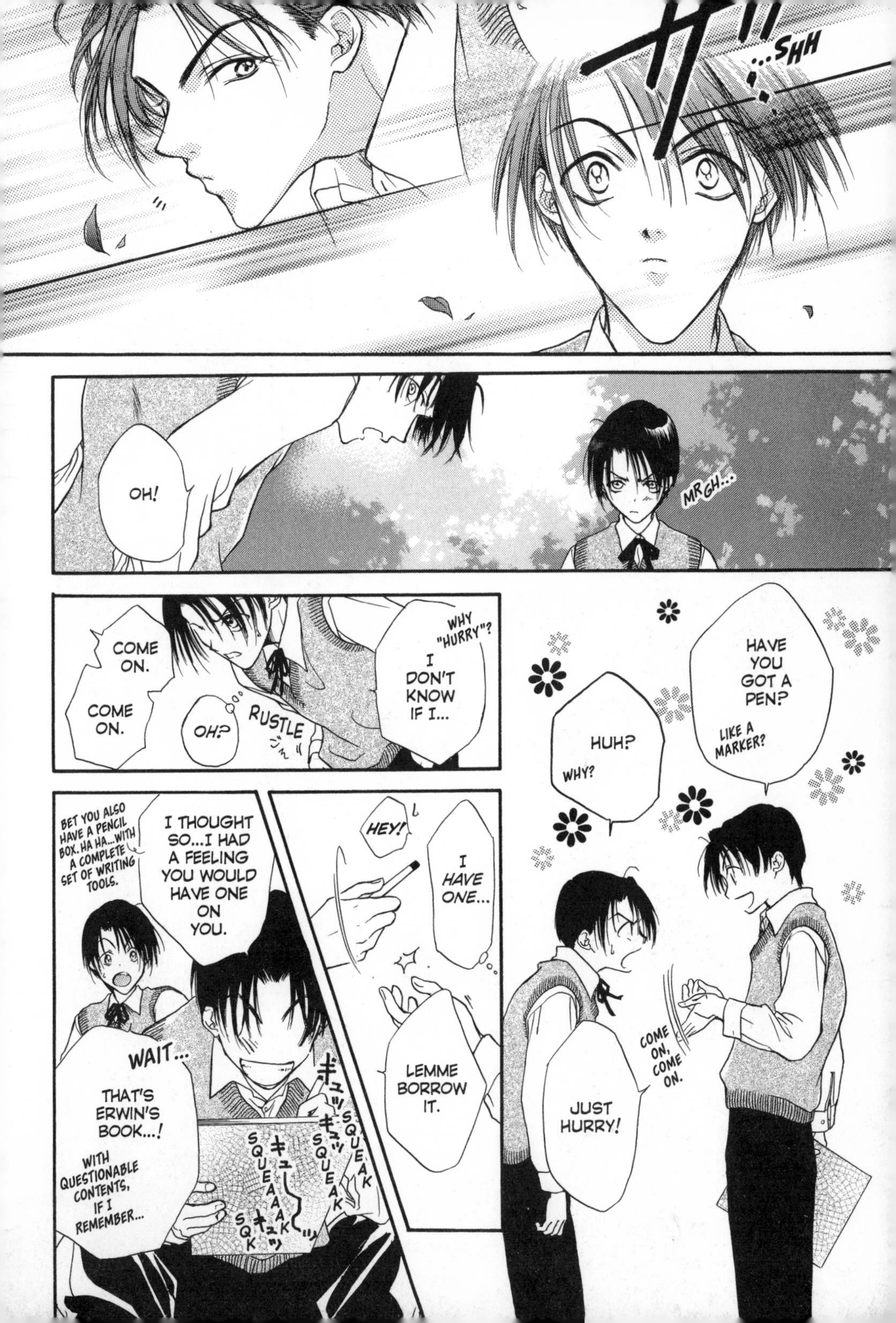
...SHH
MRGH...
OH!
HAVE YOU GOT A PEN?
LIKE A MARKER?
HUH?
WHY?
COME ON, COME ON.
JUST HURRY!
WHY "HURRY"?
I DON'T KNOW IF I...
OH?
RUSTLE
COME ON.
COME ON.
HEY!
I HAVE ONE...
LEMME BORROW IT.
I THOUGHT SO...I HAD A FEELING YOU WOULD HAVE ONE ON YOU.
BET YOU ALSO HAVE A PENCIL BOX. HA HA...WITH A COMPLETE SET OF WRITING TOOLS.
WAIT...
THAT'S ERWIN'S BOOK...!
WITH QUESTIONABLE CONTENTS, IF I REMEMBER...
SQUEAK
SQUEAK
SQUEAAAAK
SQK

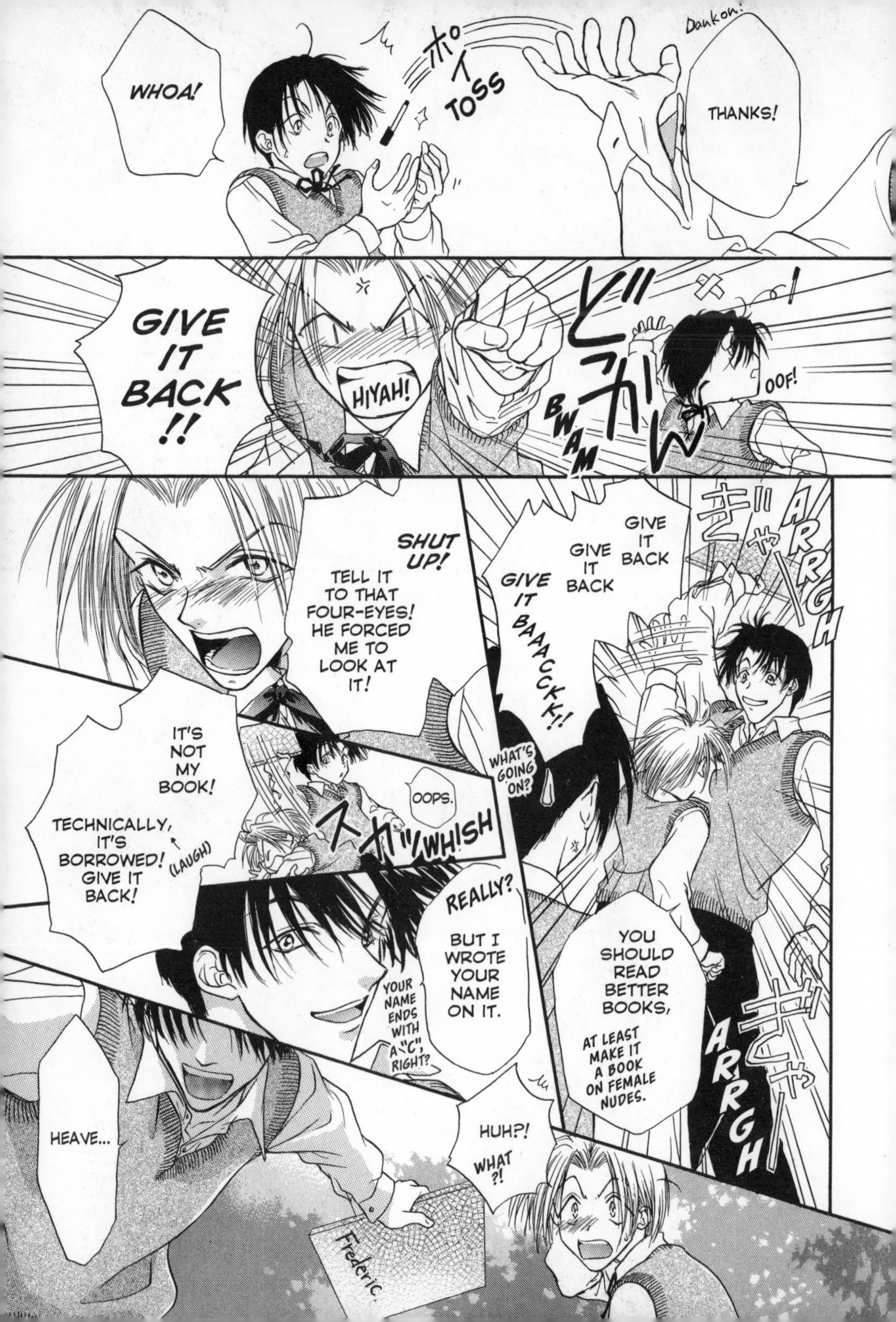

Dankon!
THANKS!
TOSS
WHOA!
OOF!
BWAM
HIYAH!
GIVE IT BACK!!
ARRGH
GIVE IT BACK
GIVE IT BACK
GIVE IT BAAACKK!!
WHAT'S GOING ON?
YOU SHOULD READ BETTER BOOKS,
AT LEAST MAKE IT A BOOK ON FEMALE NUDES.
ARRGH
SHUT UP!
TELL IT TO THAT FOUR-EYES! HE FORCED ME TO LOOK AT IT!
IT'S NOT MY BOOK!
OOPS.
WHISH
TECHNICALLY, IT'S BORROWED! GIVE IT BACK!
(LAUGH)
REALLY?
BUT I WROTE YOUR NAME ON IT.
YOUR NAME ENDS WITH A "C", RIGHT?
HUH?!
WHAT?!
HEAVE...
Frederic

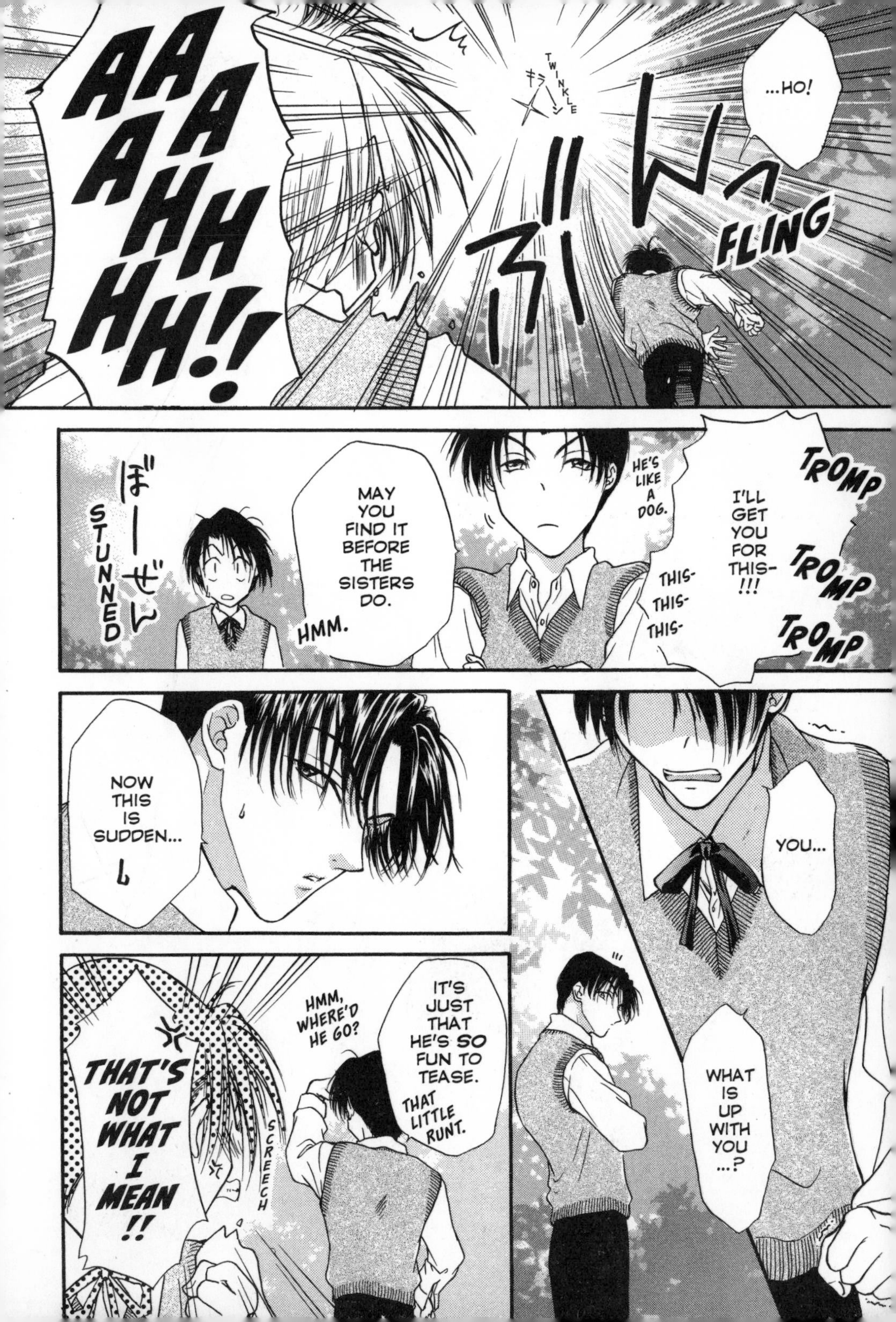
...HO!
FLING
TWINKLE
AAAAAHHHHHH!!
TROMP
TROMP
TROMP
I'LL GET YOU FOR THIS-!!!
THIS- THIS- THIS-
HE'S LIKE A DOG.
MAY YOU FIND IT BEFORE THE SISTERS DO.
HMM.
STUNNED
YOU...
WHAT IS UP WITH YOU ...?
NOW THIS IS SUDDEN...
IT'S JUST THAT HE'S SO FUN TO TEASE.
THAT LITTLE RUNT.
HMM, WHERE'D HE GO?
SCREECH
THAT'S NOT WHAT I MEAN!!

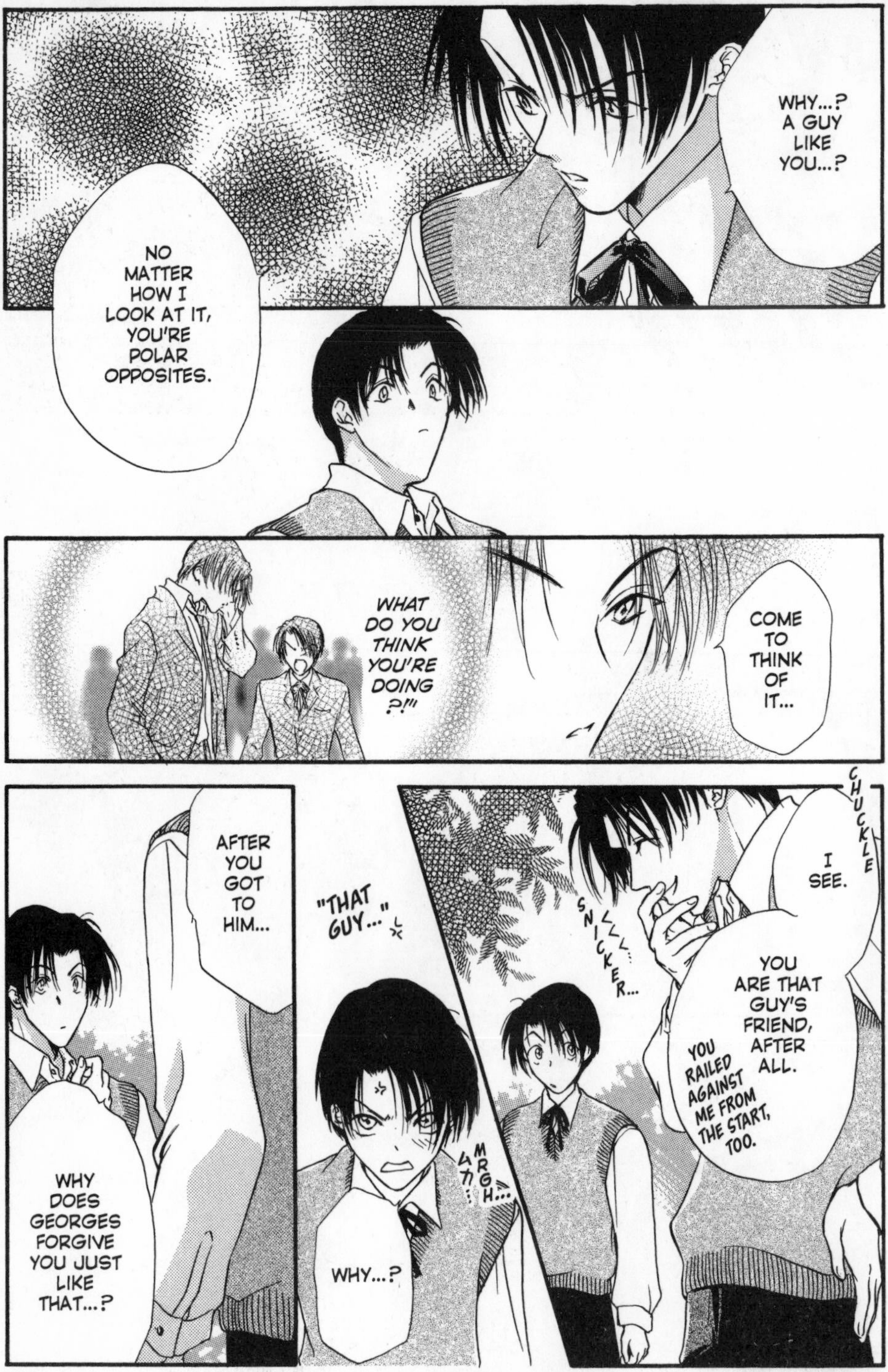
WHY...? A GUY LIKE YOU...?
NO MATTER HOW I LOOK AT IT, YOU'RE POLAR OPPOSITES.
COME TO THINK OF IT...
WHAT DO YOU THINK YOU'RE DOING?!"
CHUCKLE
I SEE.
SNICKER...
YOU ARE THAT GUY'S FRIEND, AFTER ALL.
YOU RAILED AGAINST ME FROM THE START, TOO.
MRGH...
"THAT GUY..."
WHY...?
AFTER YOU GOT TO HIM...
WHY DOES GEORGES FORGIVE YOU JUST LIKE THAT...?

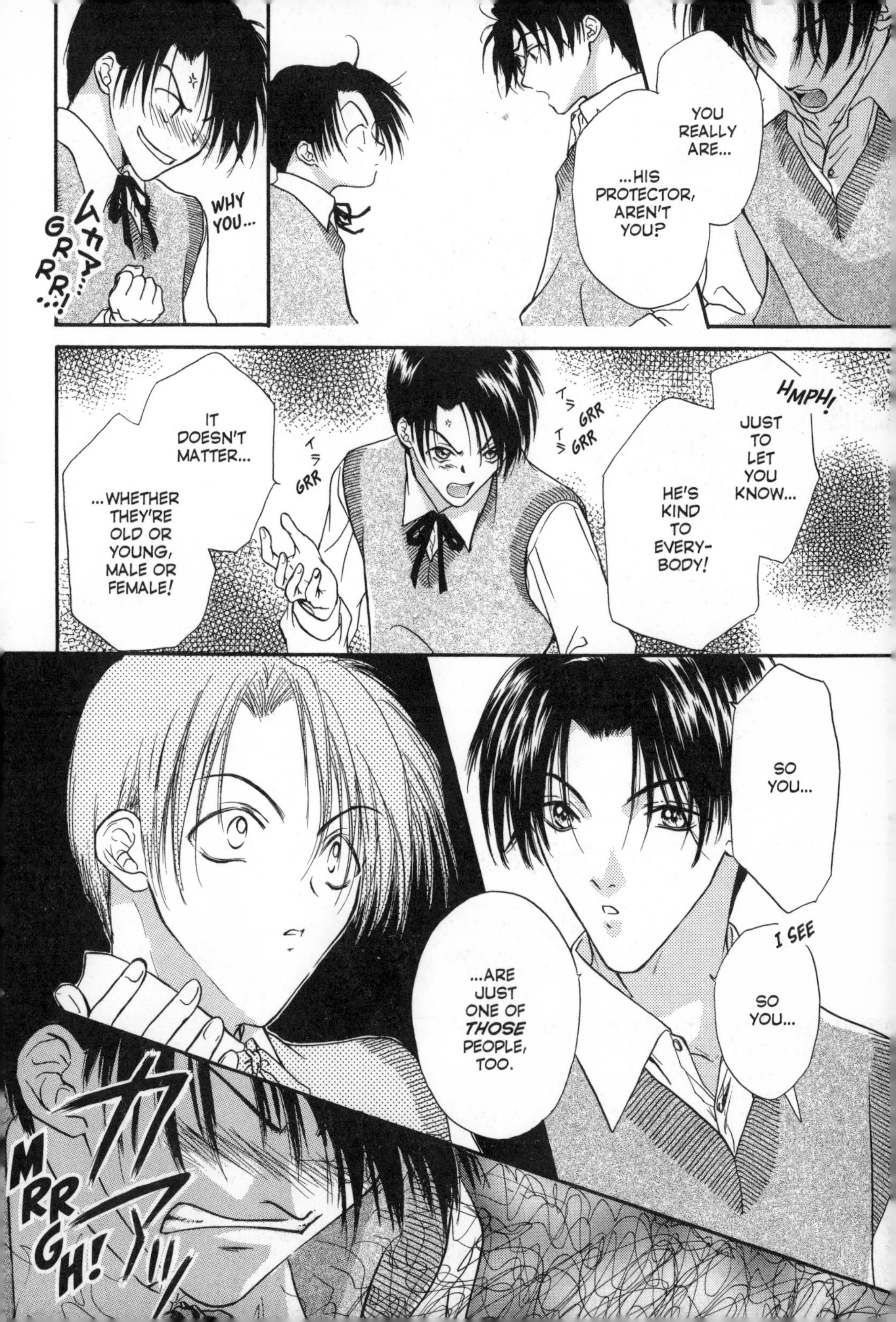
YOU REALLY ARE...
...HIS PROTECTOR, AREN'T YOU?
WHY YOU...
GRRRR..!!
HMPH!
JUST TO LET YOU KNOW...
HE'S KIND TO EVERY-BODY!
GRR GRR
GRR
IT DOESN'T MATTER...
...WHETHER THEY'RE OLD OR YOUNG, MALE OR FEMALE!
SO YOU...
I SEE
SO YOU...
...ARE JUST ONE OF *THOSE* PEOPLE, TOO.
MRRGH!

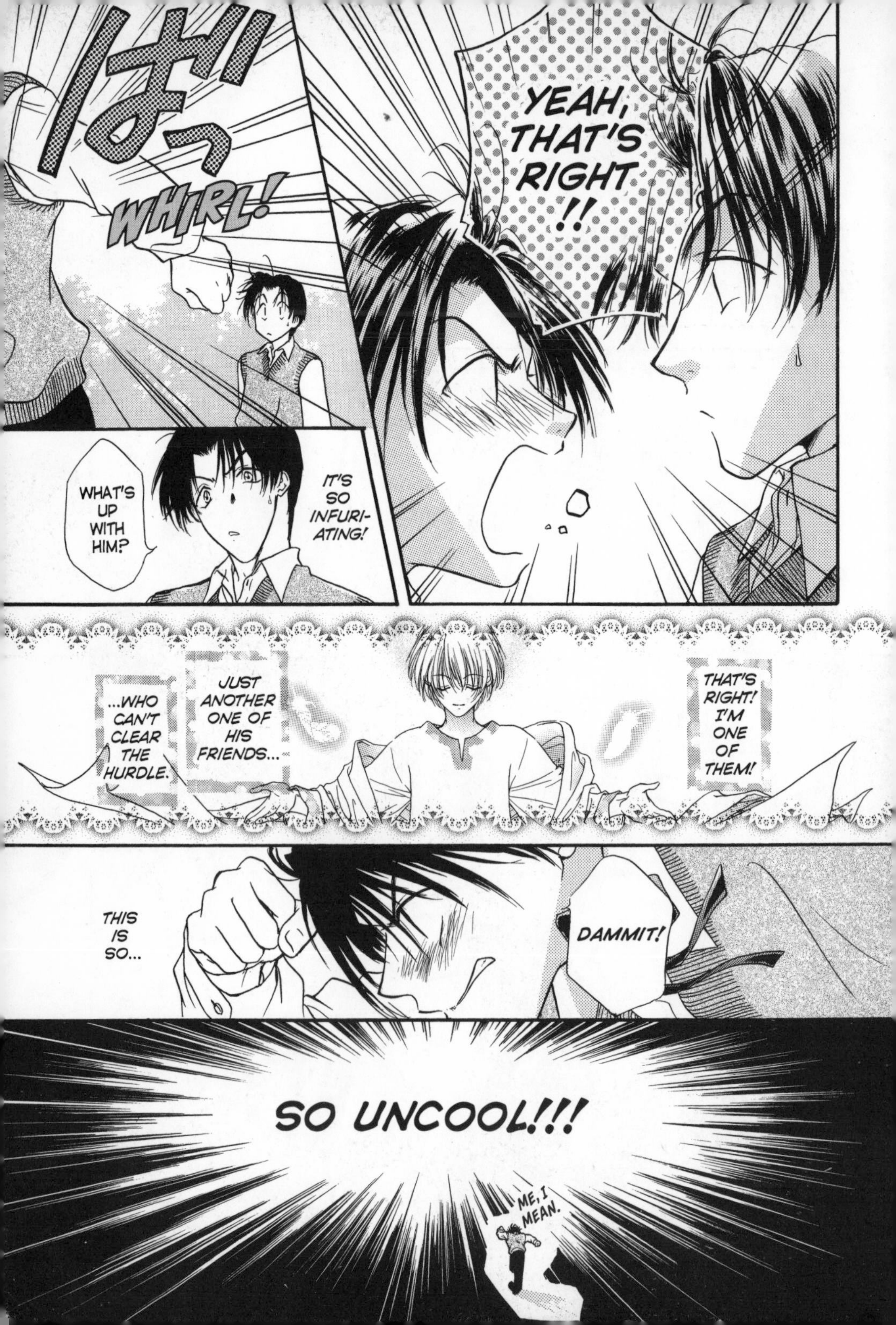
YEAH, THAT'S RIGHT !!
はっ
WHIRL!
IT'S SO INFURIATING!
WHAT'S UP WITH HIM?
THAT'S RIGHT! I'M ONE OF THEM!
JUST ANOTHER ONE OF HIS FRIENDS...
...WHO CAN'T CLEAR THE HURDLE.
DAMMIT!
THIS IS SO...
SO UNCOOL!!!
ME, I MEAN.

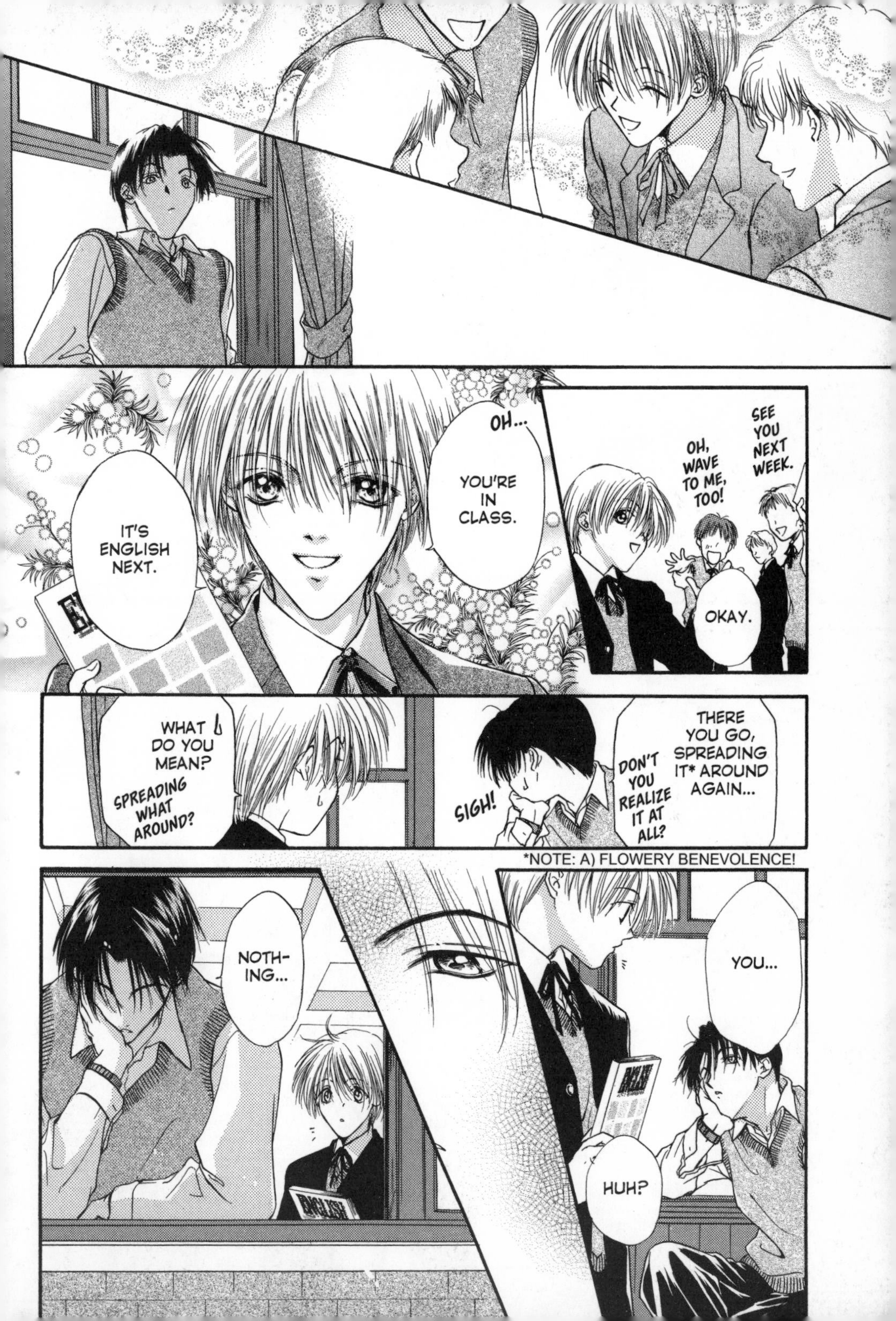
SEE YOU NEXT WEEK.
OH, WAVE TO ME, TOO!
OKAY.
OH...
YOU'RE IN CLASS.
IT'S ENGLISH NEXT.
THERE YOU GO, SPREADING IT* AROUND AGAIN...
DON'T YOU REALIZE IT AT ALL?
SIGH!
WHAT DO YOU MEAN?
SPREADING WHAT AROUND?
*NOTE: A) FLOWERY BENEVOLENCE!
YOU...
HUH?
NOTH-ING...

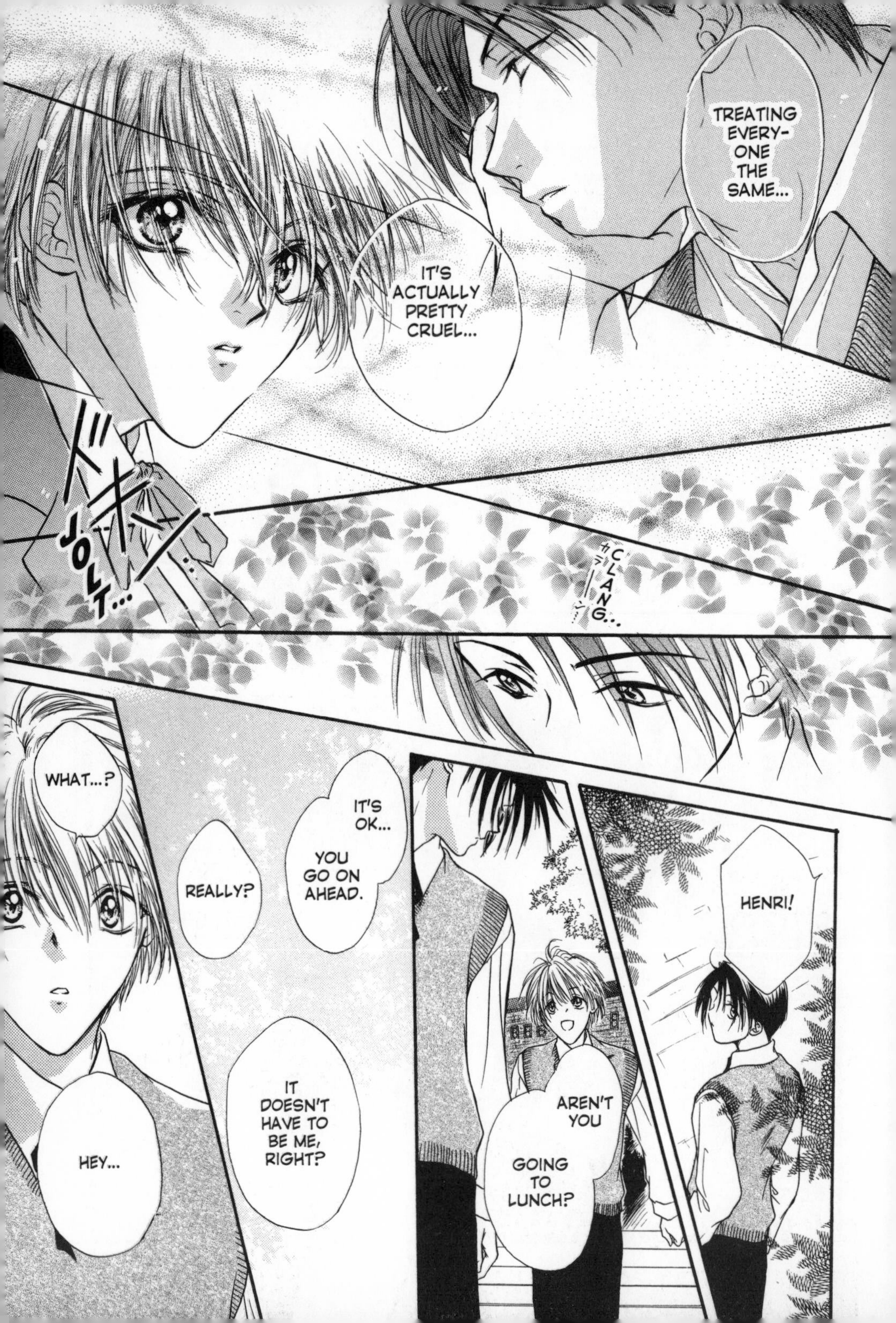
TREATING EVERY-ONE THE SAME...
IT'S ACTUALLY PRETTY CRUEL...
ドキン
JOLT...
CLANG...
HENRI!
AREN'T YOU GOING TO LUNCH?
IT'S OK... YOU GO ON AHEAD.
REALLY?
WHAT...?
IT DOESN'T HAVE TO BE ME, RIGHT?
HEY...

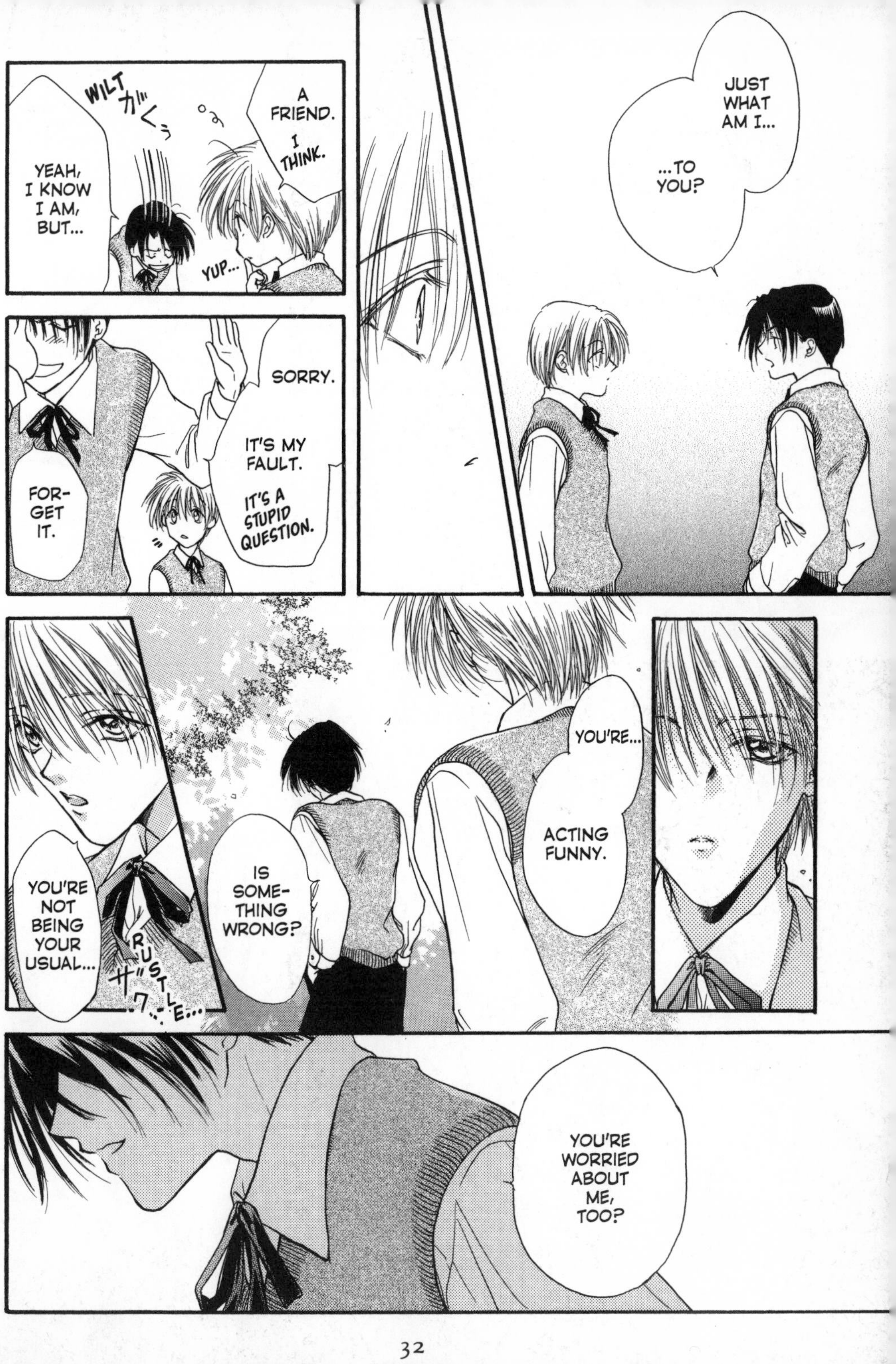
JUST WHAT AM I...
...TO YOU?
A FRIEND.
I THINK.
WILT ガくぅ
YUP...
YEAH, I KNOW I AM, BUT...
SORRY.
IT'S MY FAULT.
IT'S A STUPID QUESTION.
FOR-GET IT.
YOU'RE...
ACTING FUNNY.
IS SOME-THING WRONG?
YOU'RE NOT BEING YOUR USUAL...
RUSTLE...
YOU'RE WORRIED ABOUT ME, TOO?

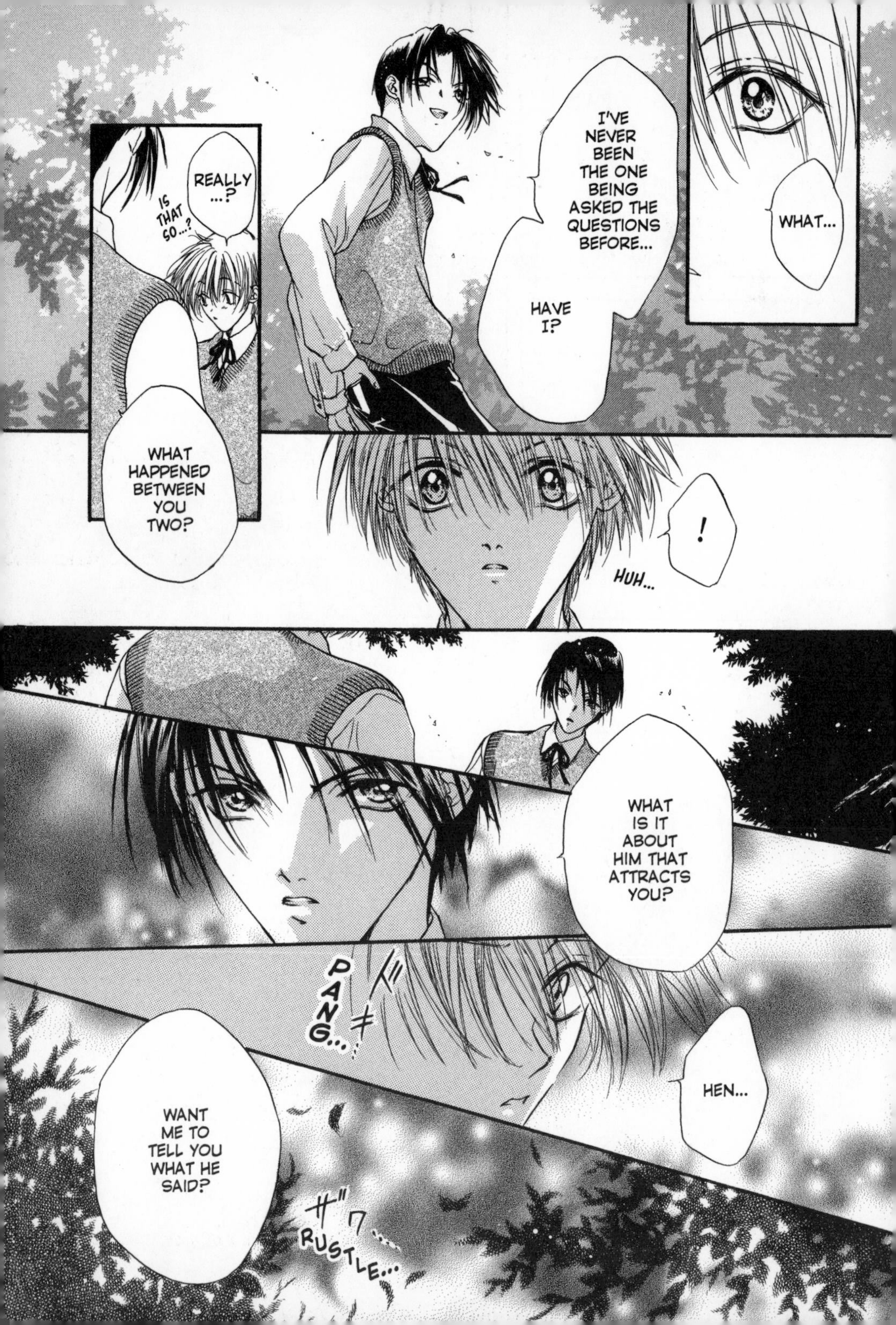
WHAT...
I'VE NEVER BEEN THE ONE BEING ASKED THE QUESTIONS BEFORE...
HAVE I?
REALLY ...?
IS THAT SO...?
WHAT HAPPENED BETWEEN YOU TWO?
!
HUH...
WHAT IS IT ABOUT HIM THAT ATTRACTS YOU?
HEN...
ズキ
PANG...
WANT ME TO TELL YOU WHAT HE SAID?
ザワ...
RUSTLE...

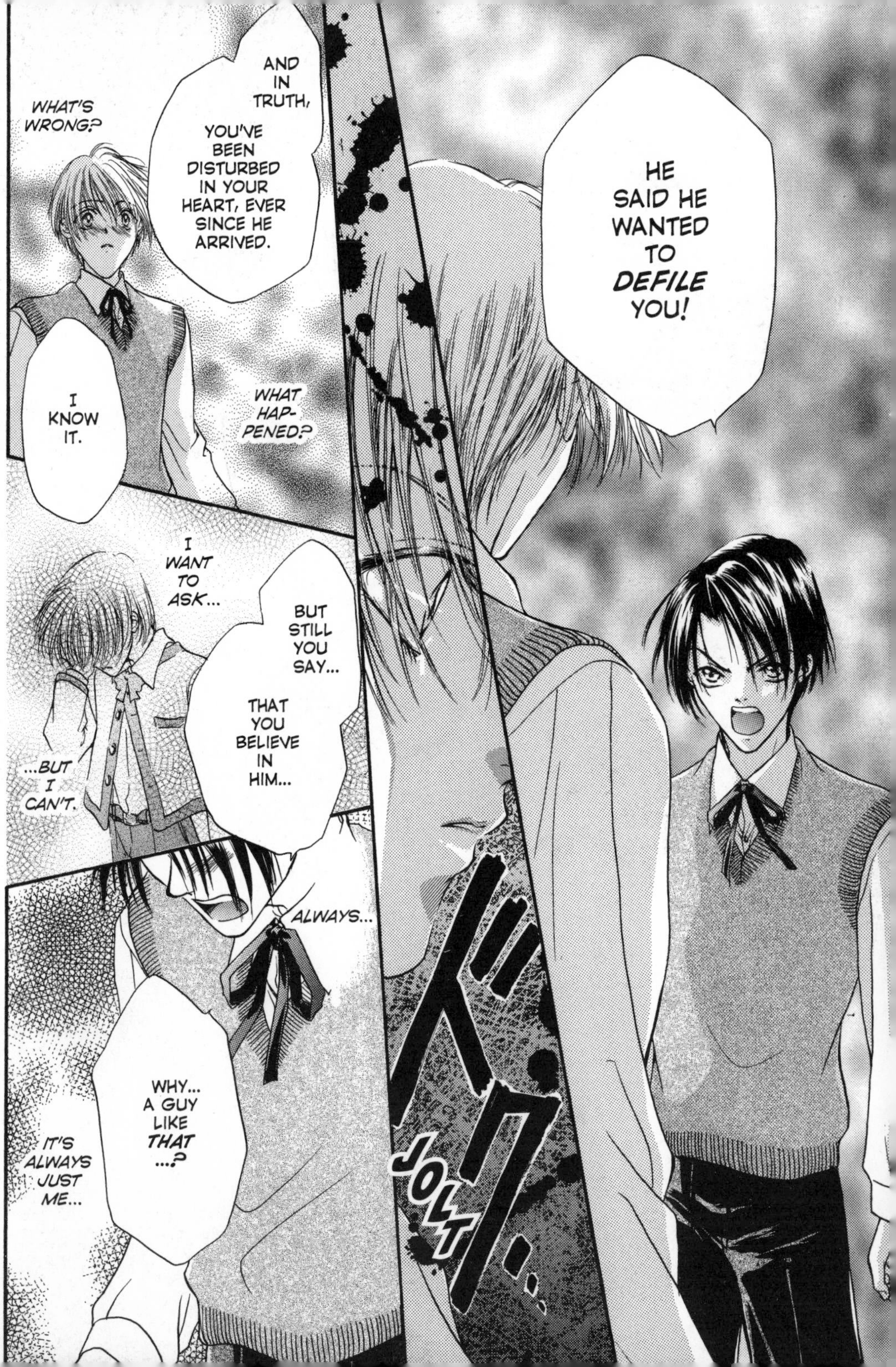
HE SAID HE WANTED TO *DEFILE* YOU!
JOLT...
AND IN TRUTH, YOU'VE BEEN DISTURBED IN YOUR HEART, EVER SINCE HE ARRIVED.
WHAT'S WRONG?
WHAT HAP-PENED?
I KNOW IT.
BUT STILL YOU SAY... THAT YOU BELIEVE IN HIM...
I WANT TO ASK...
...BUT I CAN'T.
ALWAYS...
WHY... A GUY LIKE *THAT* ...?
IT'S ALWAYS JUST ME...

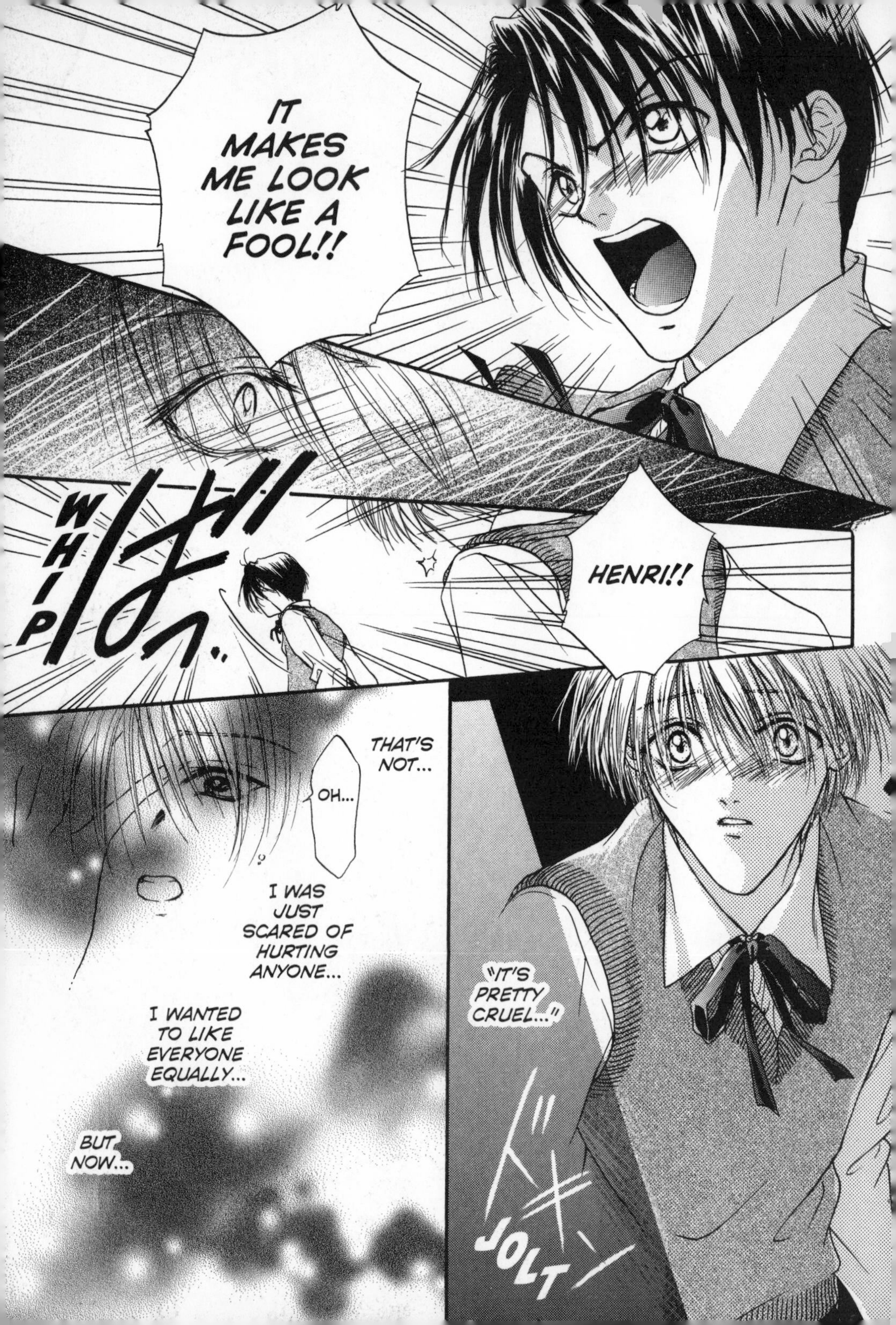
IT MAKES ME LOOK LIKE A FOOL!!
HENRI!!
WHIP
"IT'S PRETTY CRUEL..."
JOLT
THAT'S NOT...
OH...
I WAS JUST SCARED OF HURTING ANYONE...
I WANTED TO LIKE EVERYONE EQUALLY...
BUT NOW...

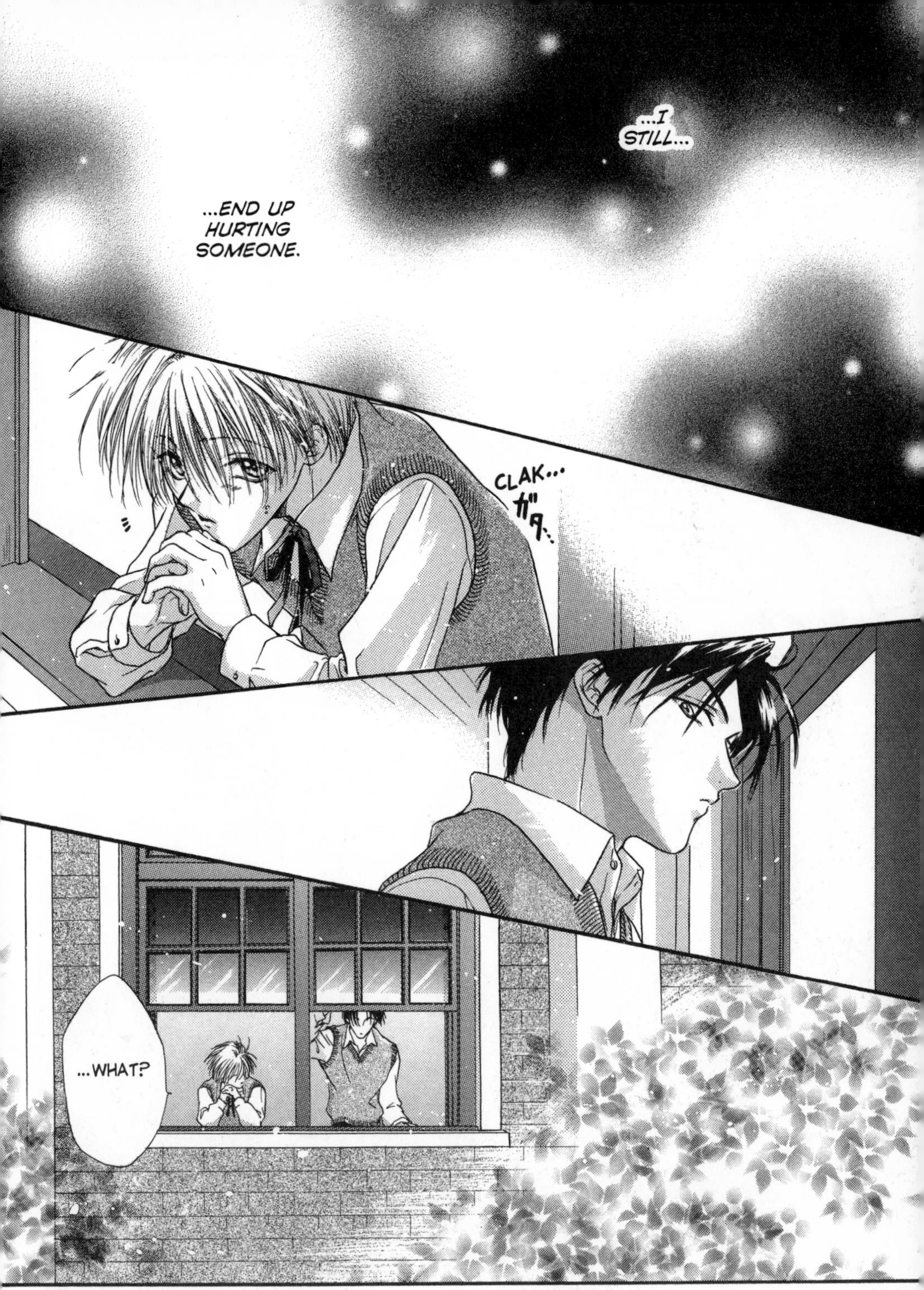
...I STILL...
...END UP HURTING SOMEONE.
CLAK...
ガタ...
...WHAT?

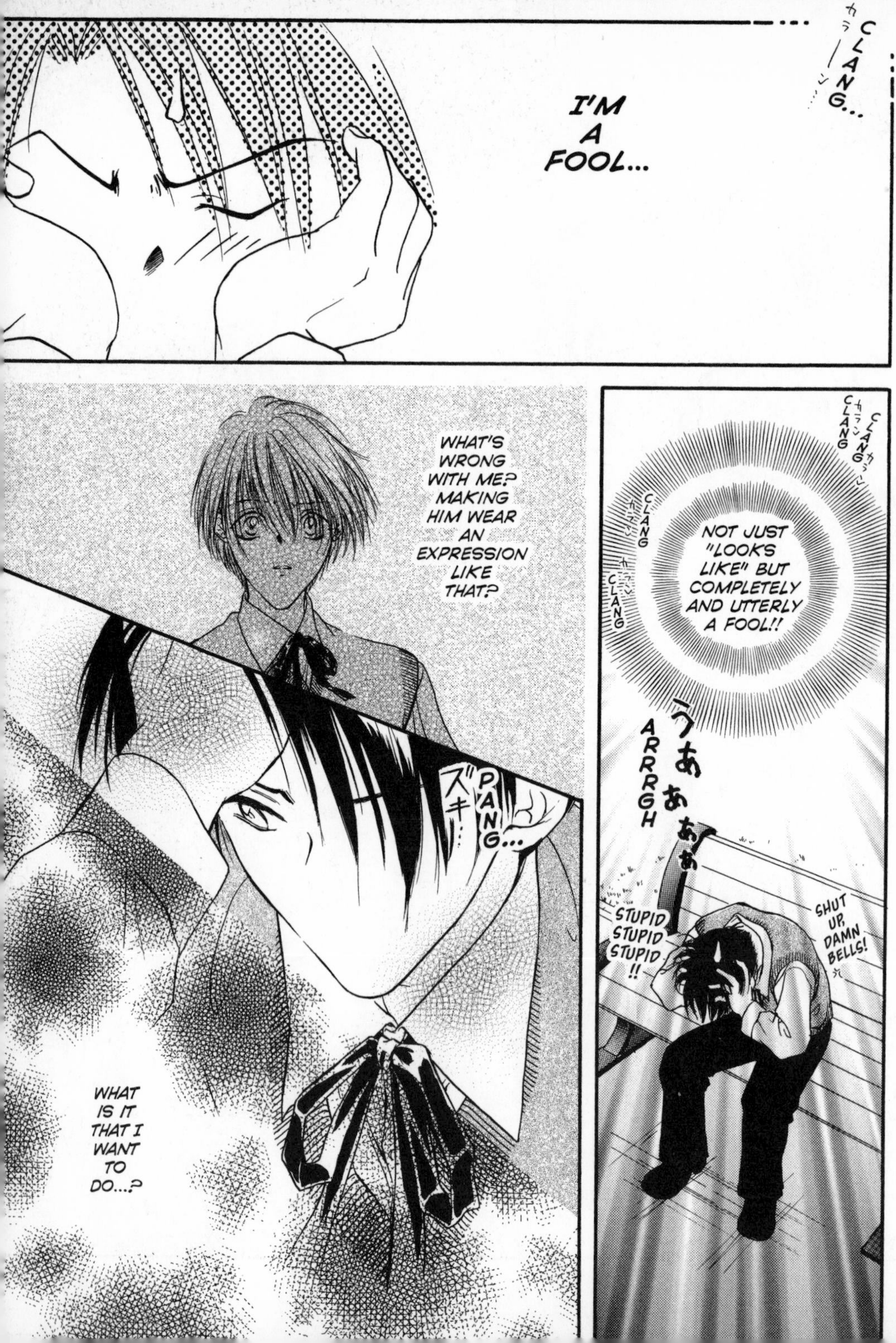
カラーン…
CLANG…
I'M A FOOL…
カラン カラン
CLANG CLANG
NOT JUST "LOOKS LIKE" BUT COMPLETELY AND UTTERLY A FOOL!!
カラン カラン
CLANG CLANG
うあぁぁぁ
ARRRGH
SHUT UP, DAMN BELLS!
STUPID STUPID STUPID!!
WHAT'S WRONG WITH ME? MAKING HIM WEAR AN EXPRESSION LIKE THAT?
ズキ…
PANG…
WHAT IS IT THAT I WANT TO DO…?

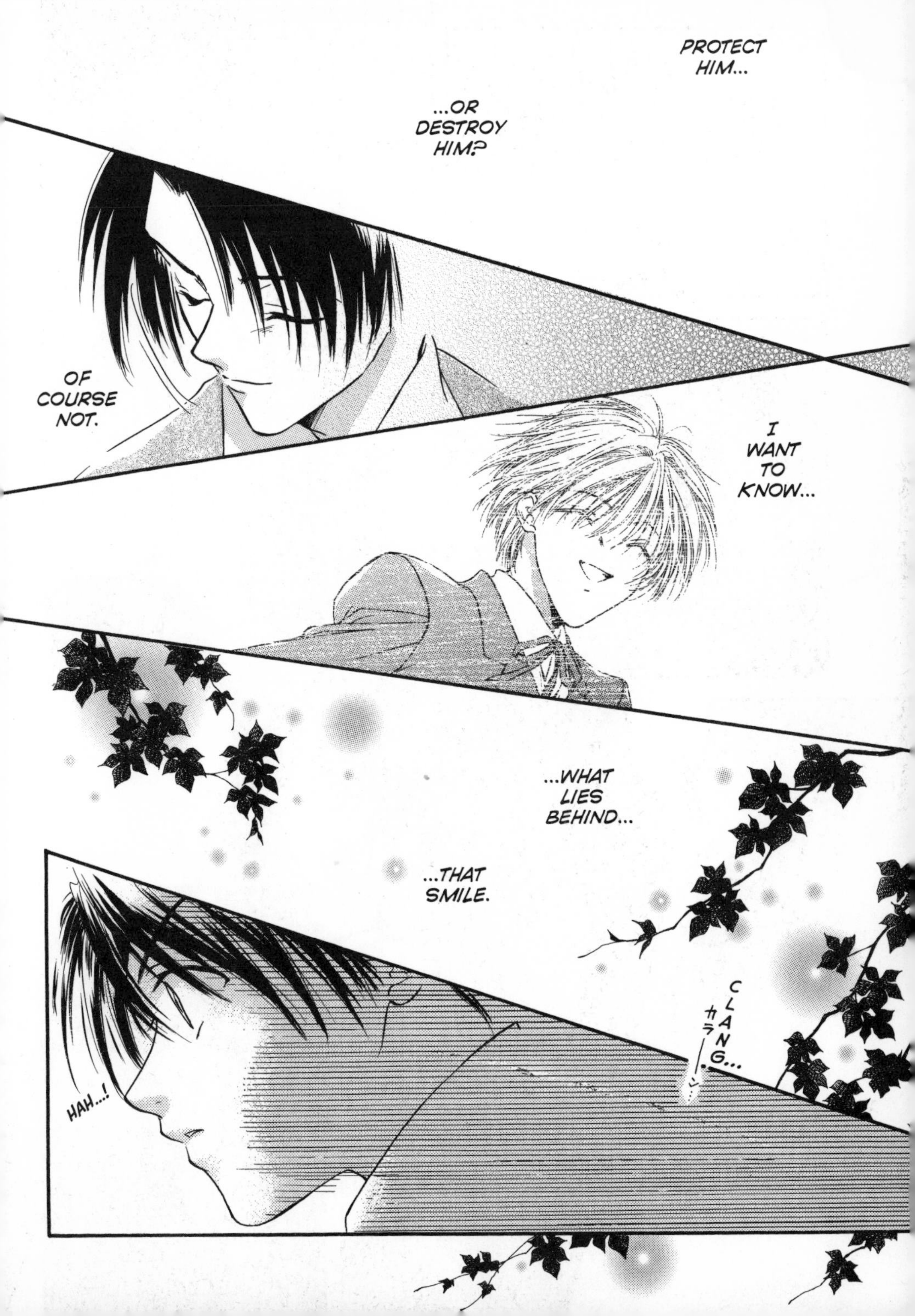
PROTECT HIM...
...OR DESTROY HIM?
OF COURSE NOT.
I WANT TO KNOW...
...WHAT LIES BEHIND...
...THAT SMILE.
CLANG...
カラーン
HAH..!

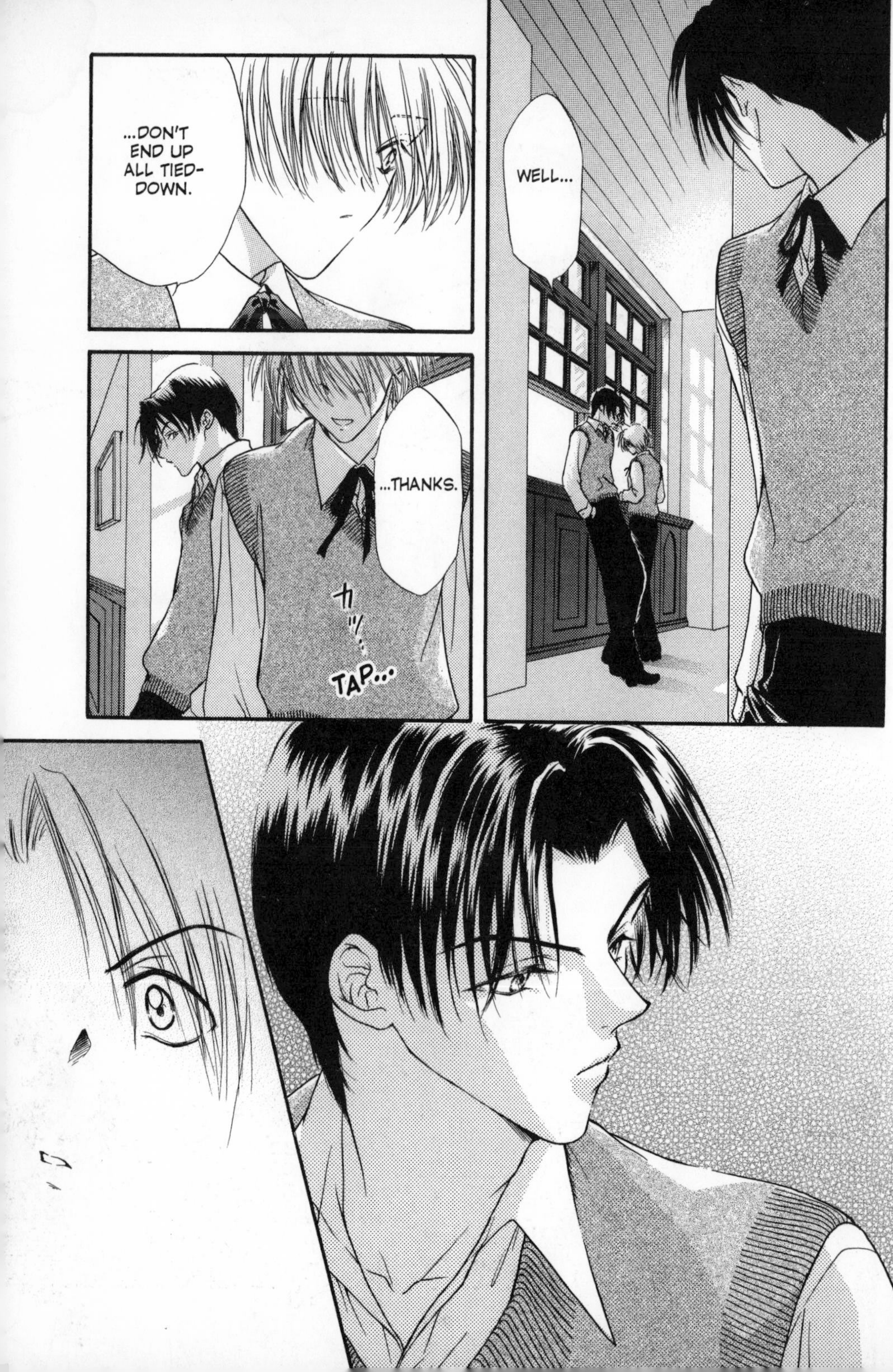
WELL...
...DON'T END UP ALL TIED-DOWN.
...THANKS.
カッ...
TAP...

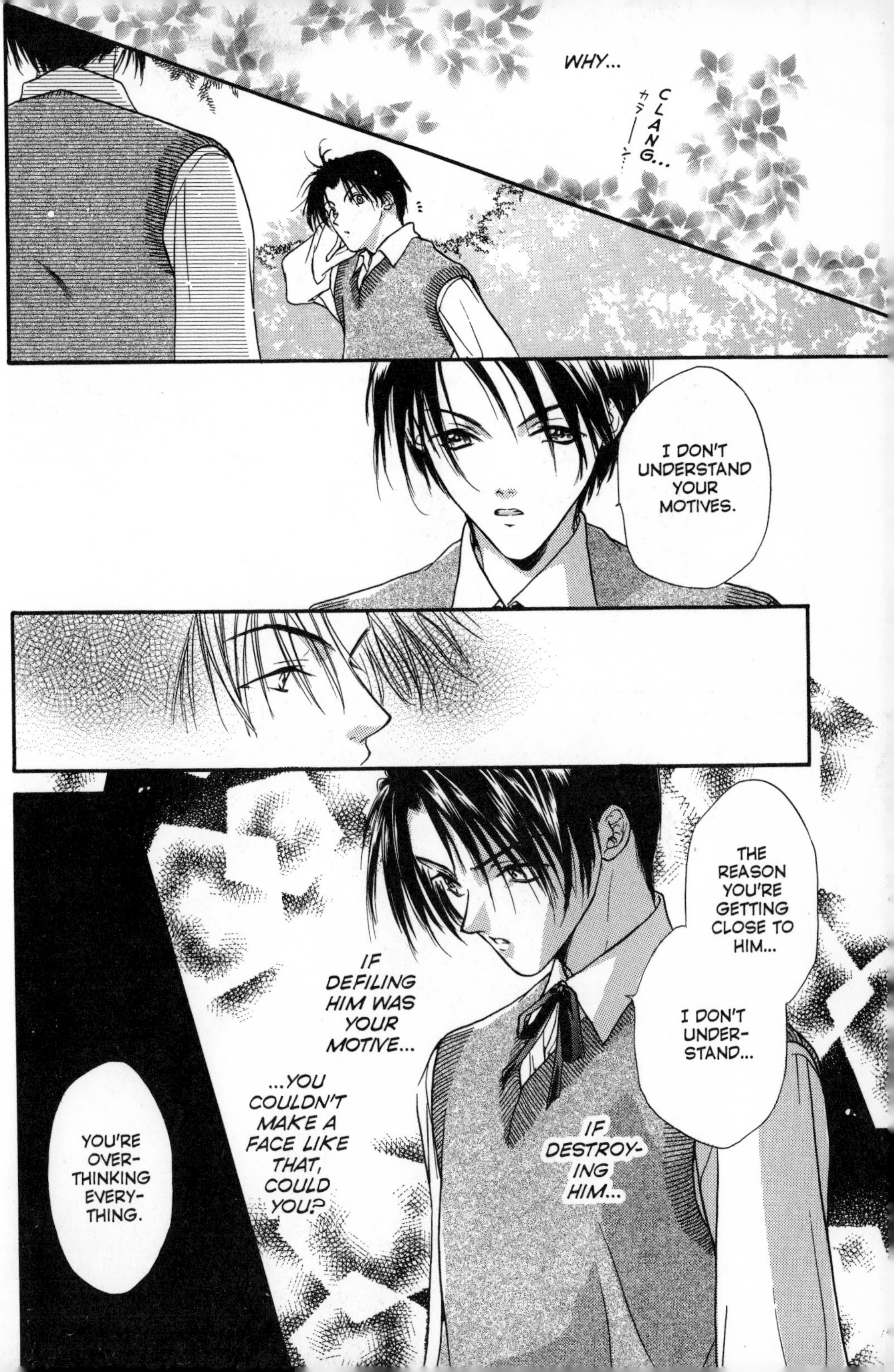
WHY...
CLANG...
I DON'T UNDERSTAND YOUR MOTIVES.
THE REASON YOU'RE GETTING CLOSE TO HIM...
I DON'T UNDER-STAND...
IF DESTROY-ING HIM...
IF DEFILING HIM WAS YOUR MOTIVE...
...YOU COULDN'T MAKE A FACE LIKE THAT, COULD YOU?
YOU'RE OVER-THINKING EVERY-THING.

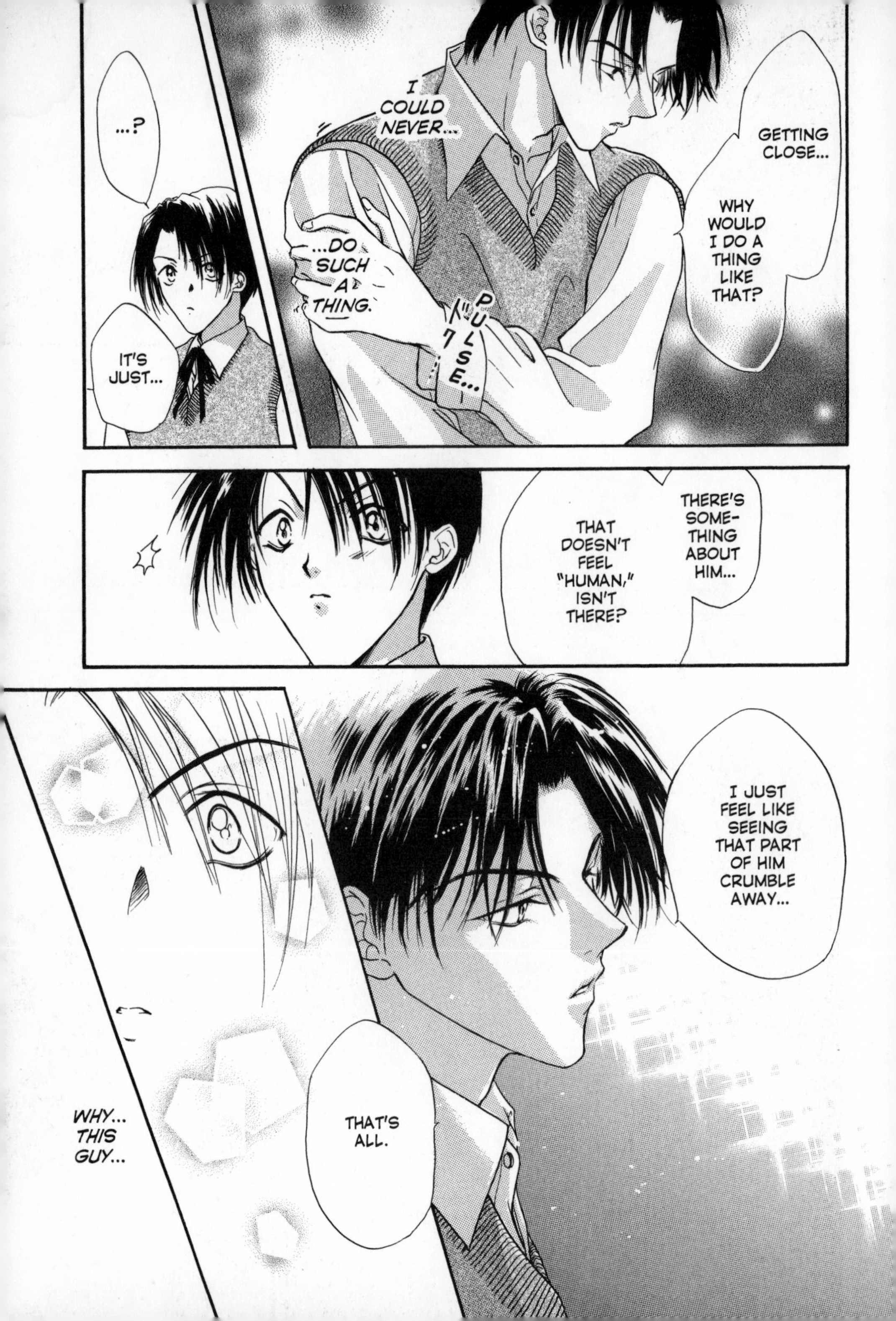
GETTING CLOSE...
WHY WOULD I DO A THING LIKE THAT?
I COULD NEVER...
...DO SUCH A THING.
PULSE...
...?
IT'S JUST...
THERE'S SOME-THING ABOUT HIM...
THAT DOESN'T FEEL "HUMAN," ISN'T THERE?
I JUST FEEL LIKE SEEING THAT PART OF HIM CRUMBLE AWAY...
THAT'S ALL.
WHY... THIS GUY...

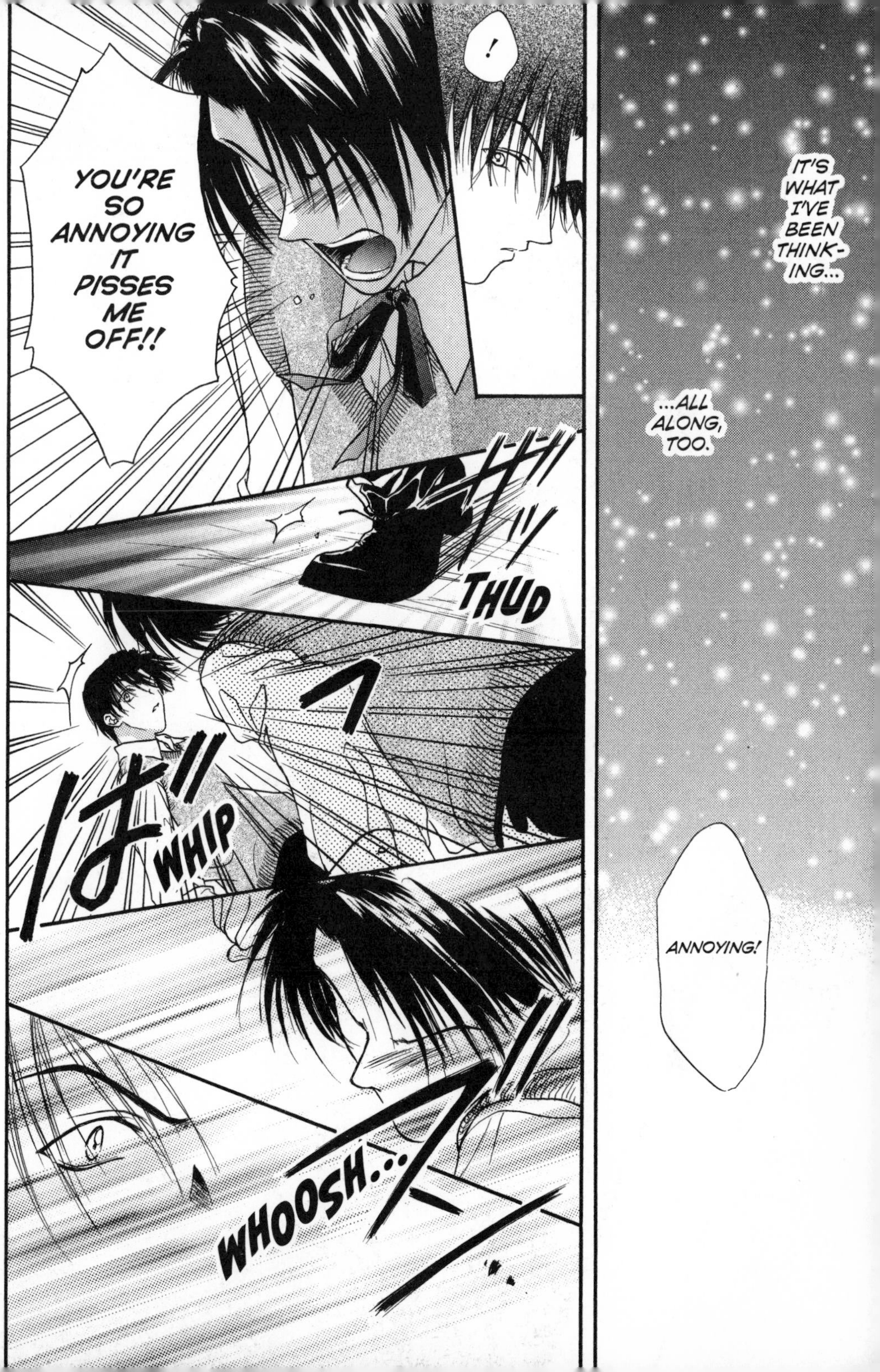
IT'S WHAT I'VE BEEN THINKING...
...ALL ALONG, TOO.
ANNOYING!
!
YOU'RE SO ANNOYING IT PISSES ME OFF!!
THUD
WHIP
WHOOSH...

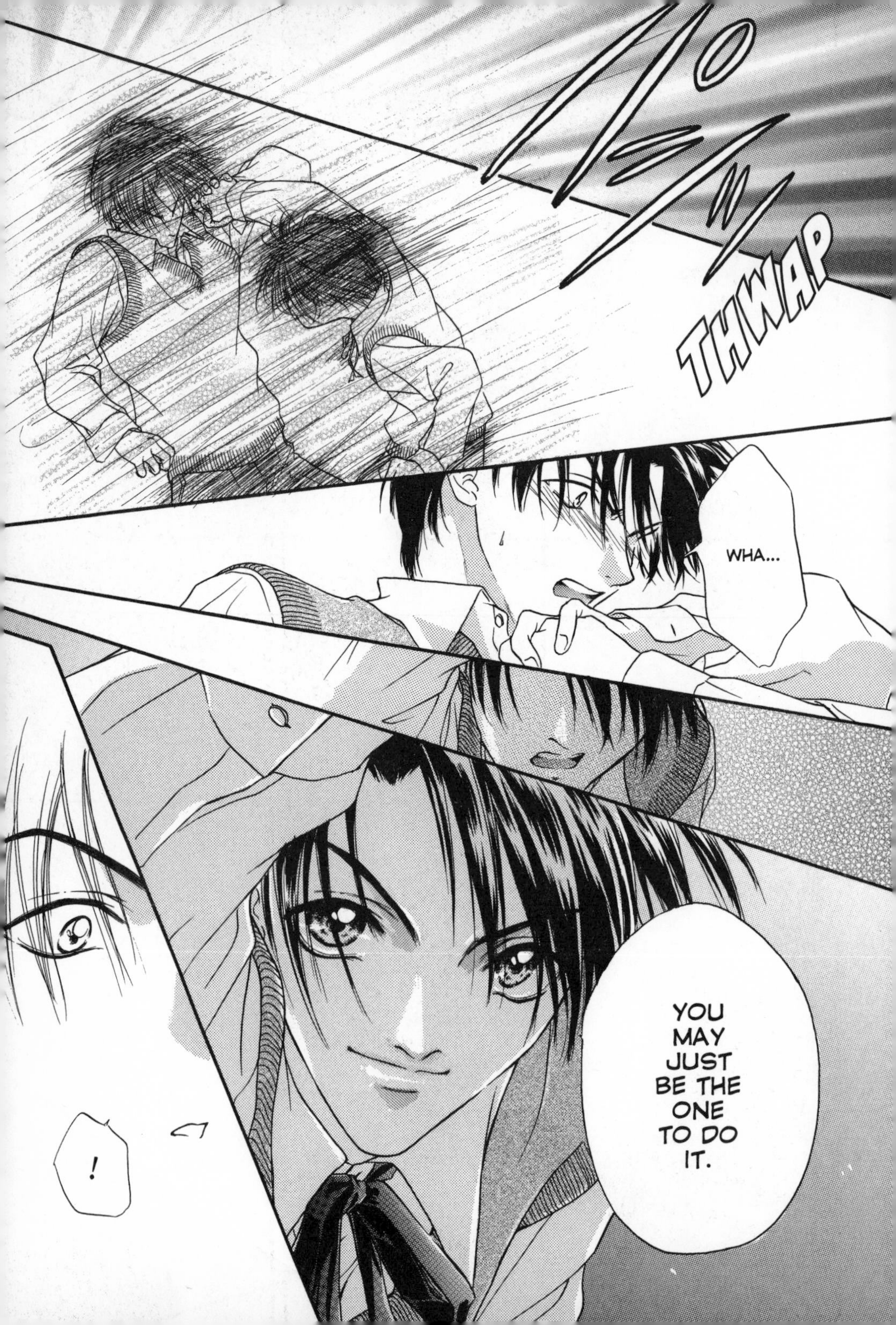
THWAP
WHA...
YOU MAY JUST BE THE ONE TO DO IT.
!

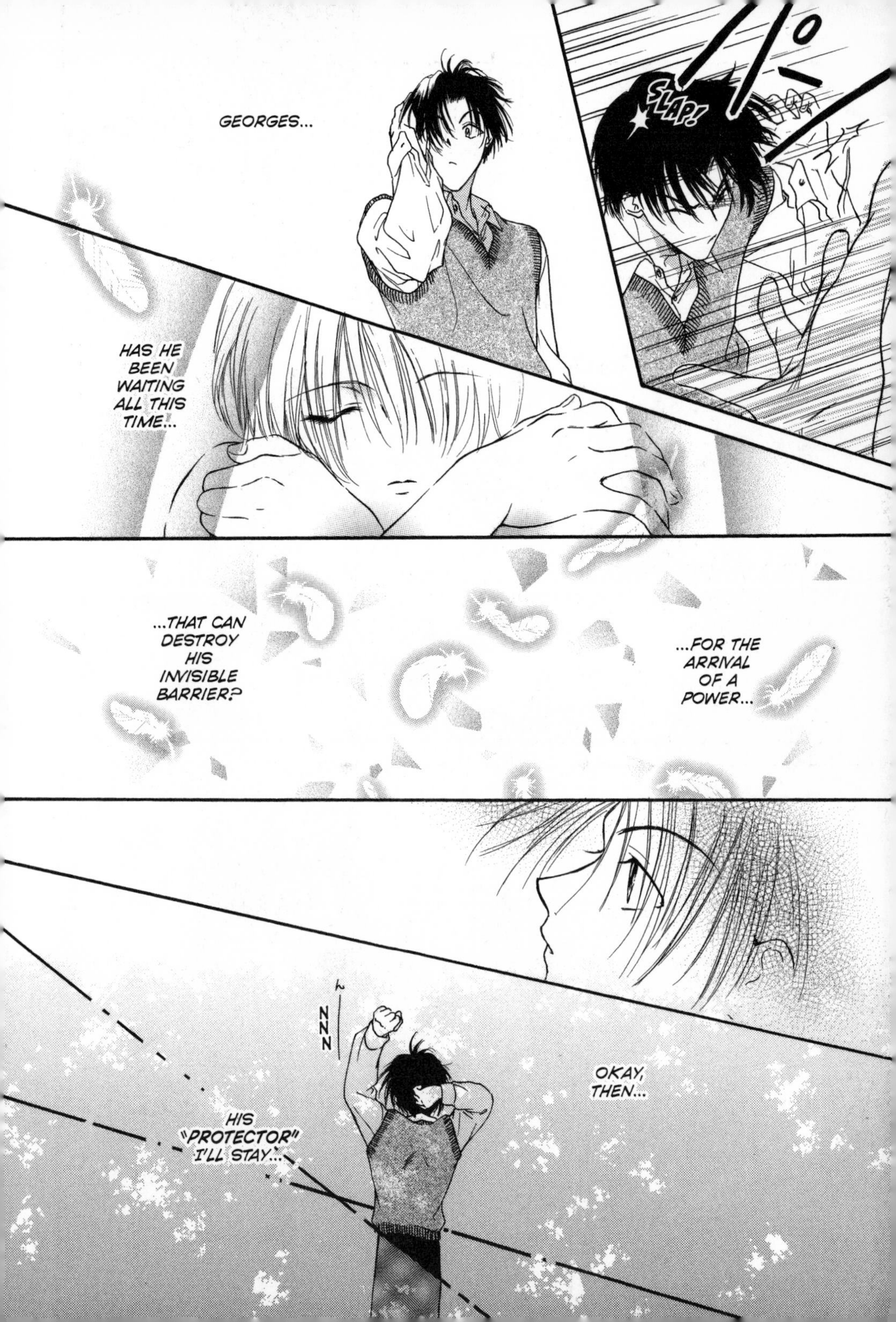
パ
SLAP!
GEORGES...
HAS HE BEEN WAITING ALL THIS TIME...
...FOR THE ARRIVAL OF A POWER...
...THAT CAN DESTROY HIS INVISIBLE BARRIER?
NNN
OKAY, THEN...
HIS "PROTECTOR" I'LL STAY...

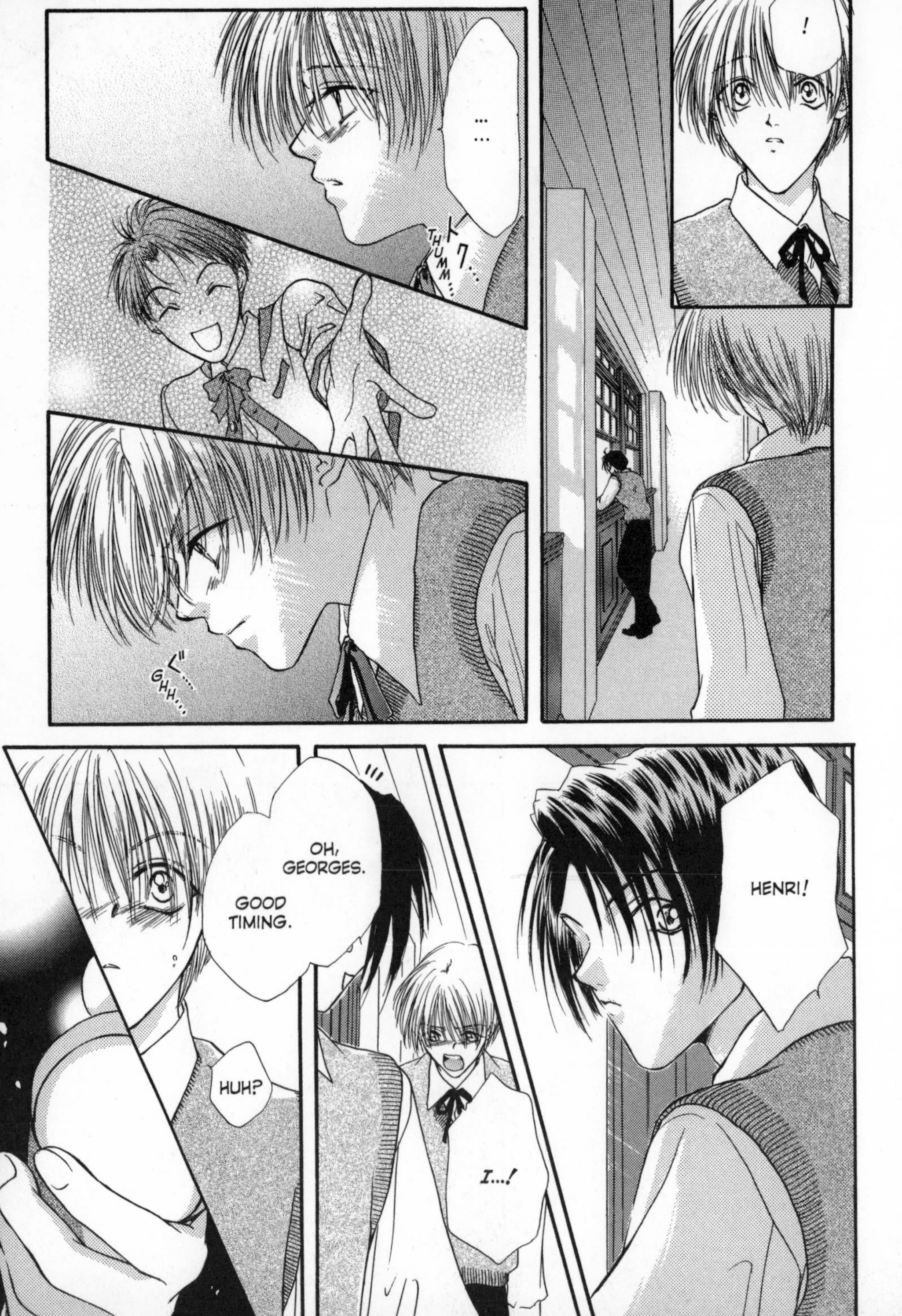

!
...
...
THUMM...
GHH...
HENRI!
I...!
OH, GEORGES.
GOOD TIMING.
HUH?

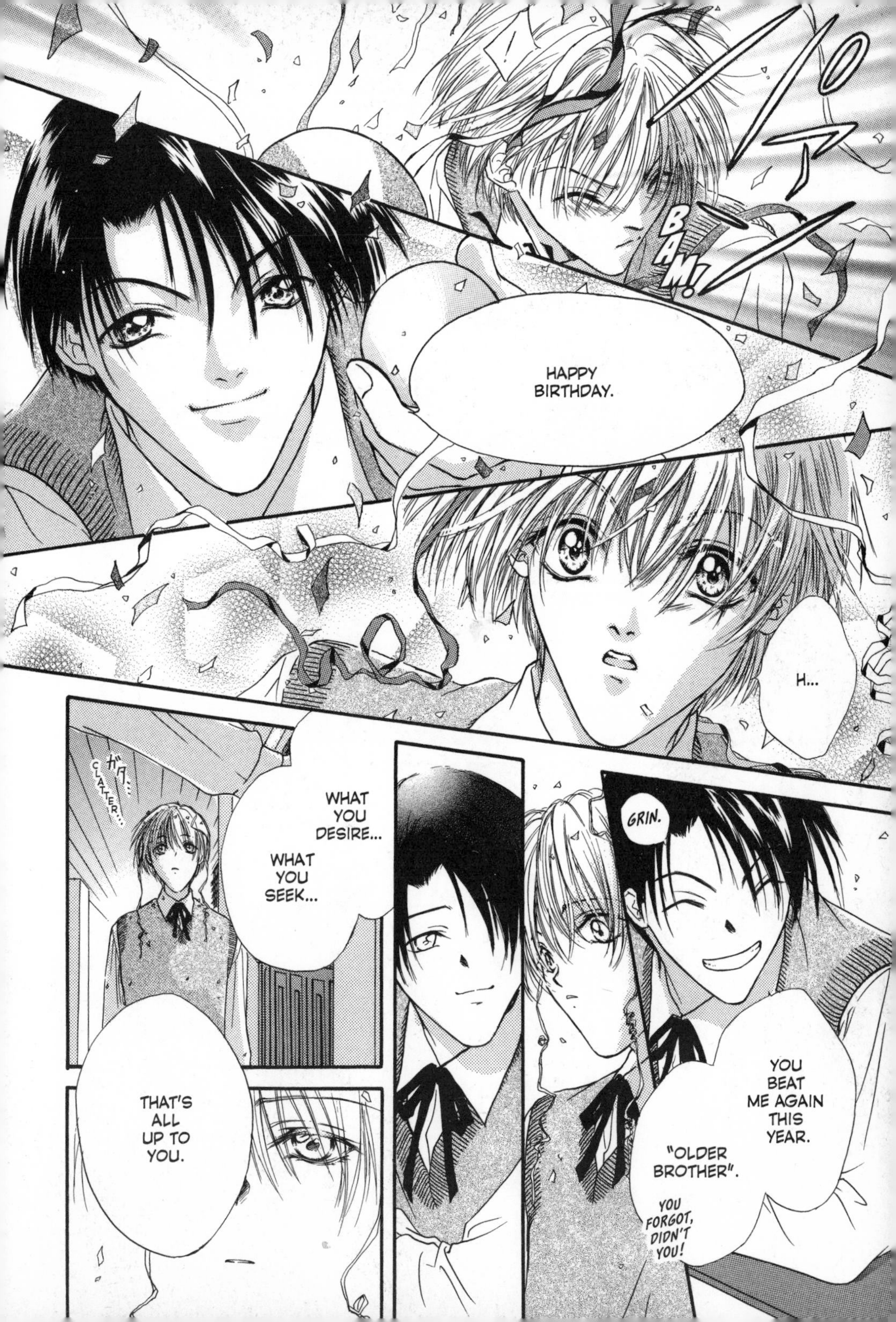
BAM!
HAPPY BIRTHDAY.
H...
GRIN.
YOU BEAT ME AGAIN THIS YEAR.
"OLDER BROTHER".
YOU FORGOT, DIDN'T YOU!
CLATTER...
WHAT YOU DESIRE...
WHAT YOU SEEK...
THAT'S ALL UP TO YOU.

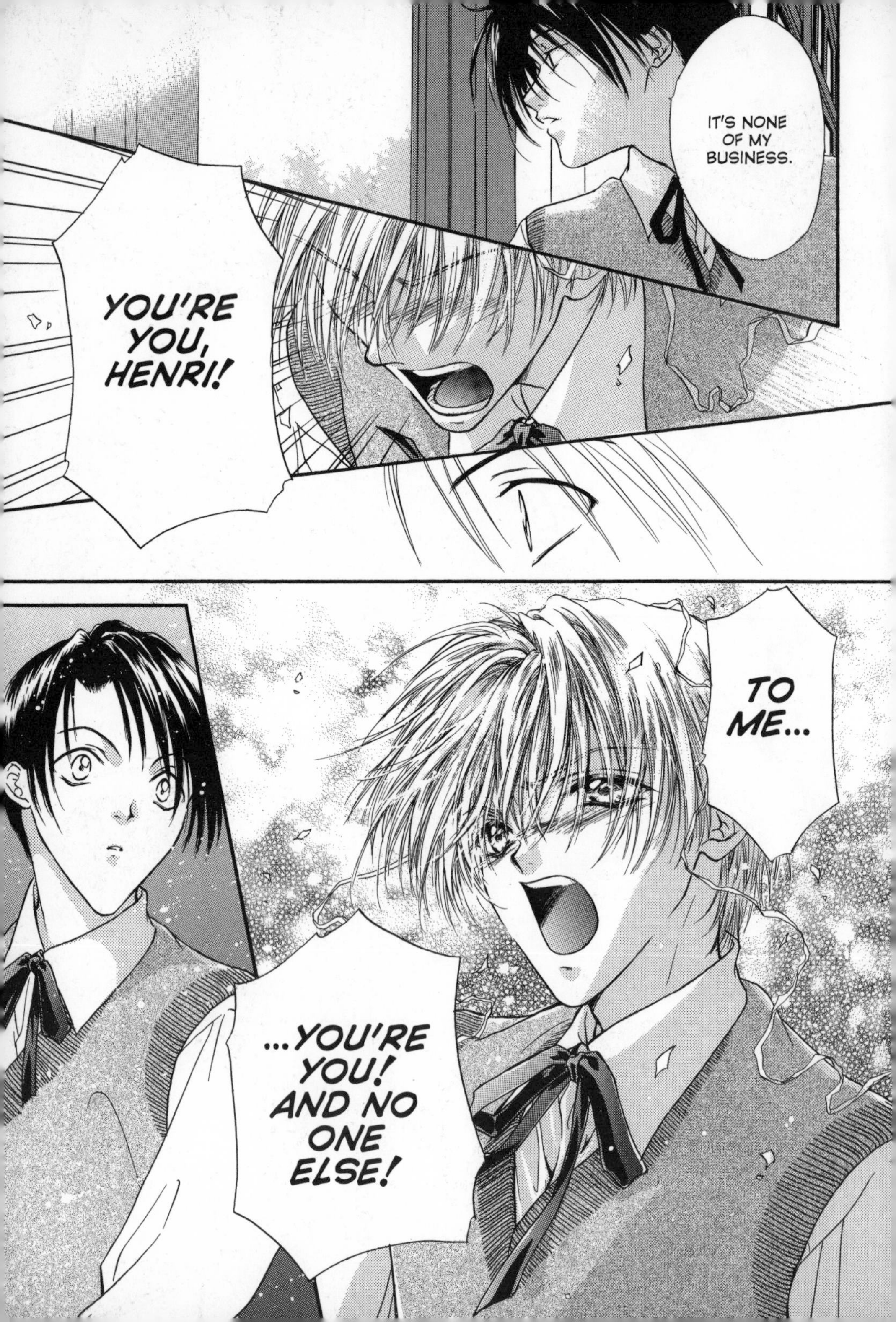
IT'S NONE OF MY BUSINESS.
YOU'RE YOU, HENRI!
TO ME...
...YOU'RE YOU! AND NO ONE ELSE!

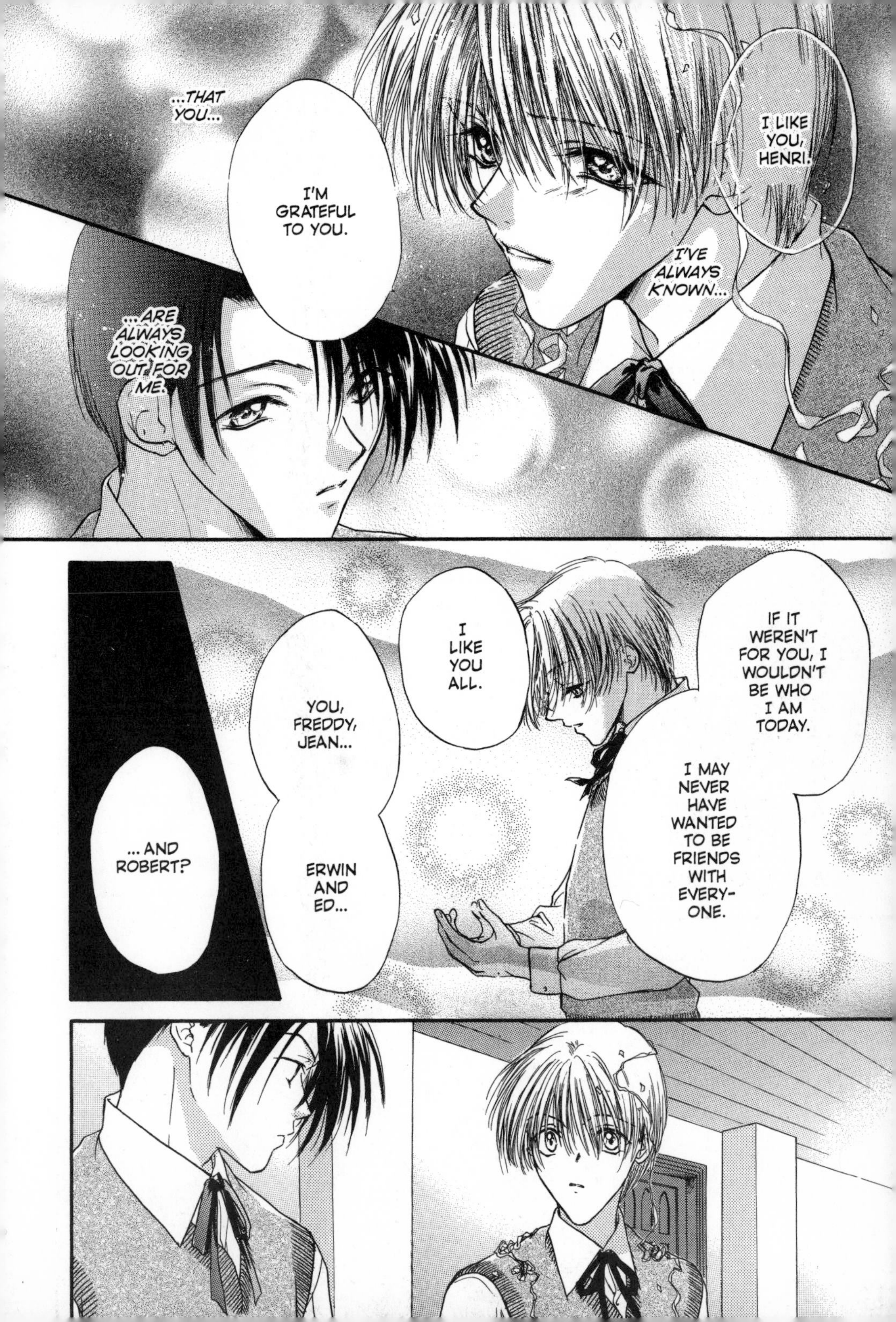

I LIKE YOU, HENRI.
I'VE ALWAYS KNOWN...
...THAT YOU...
...ARE ALWAYS LOOKING OUT FOR ME.
I'M GRATEFUL TO YOU.
IF IT WEREN'T FOR YOU, I WOULDN'T BE WHO I AM TODAY.
I MAY NEVER HAVE WANTED TO BE FRIENDS WITH EVERY-ONE.
I LIKE YOU ALL.
YOU, FREDDY, JEAN...
ERWIN AND ED...
... AND ROBERT?

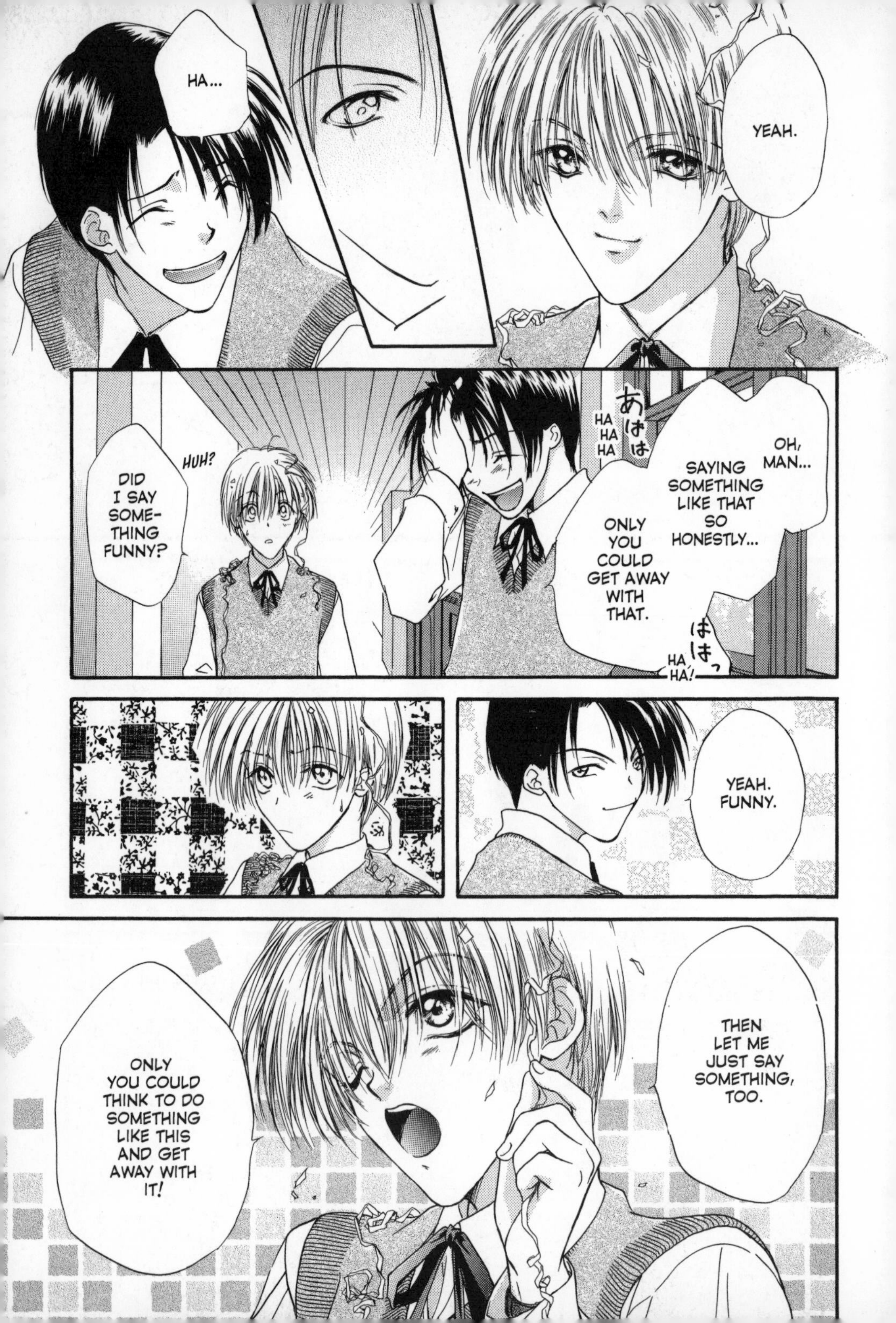
YEAH.
HA...
OH, MAN...
SAYING SOMETHING LIKE THAT SO HONESTLY...
ONLY YOU COULD GET AWAY WITH THAT.
あはは HA HA HA
ははっ HA HA!
HUH?
DID I SAY SOMETHING FUNNY?
YEAH. FUNNY.
THEN LET ME JUST SAY SOMETHING, TOO.
ONLY YOU COULD THINK TO DO SOMETHING LIKE THIS AND GET AWAY WITH IT!

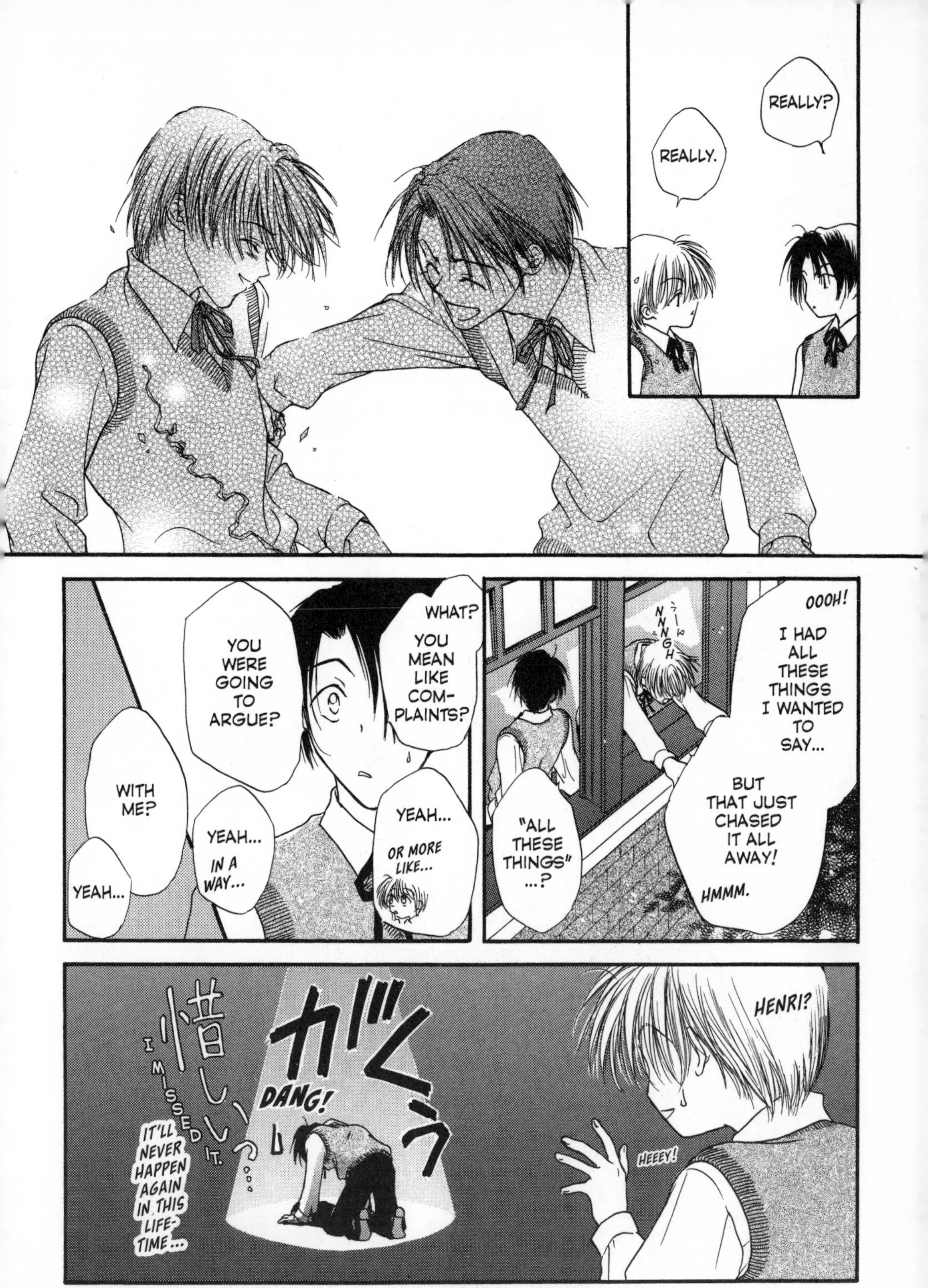
REALLY?
REALLY.
OOOH!
I HAD ALL THESE THINGS I WANTED TO SAY...
BUT THAT JUST CHASED IT ALL AWAY!
HMMM.
NNNGH
"ALL THESE THINGS"...?
WHAT?
YOU MEAN LIKE COM-PLAINTS?
YOU WERE GOING TO ARGUE?
YEAH...
OR MORE LIKE...
WITH ME?
YEAH... IN A WAY...
YEAH...
HENRI?
HEEEY!
がくう
DANG!
惜しい...
I MISSED IT.
IT'LL NEVER HAPPEN AGAIN IN THIS LIFE-TIME...

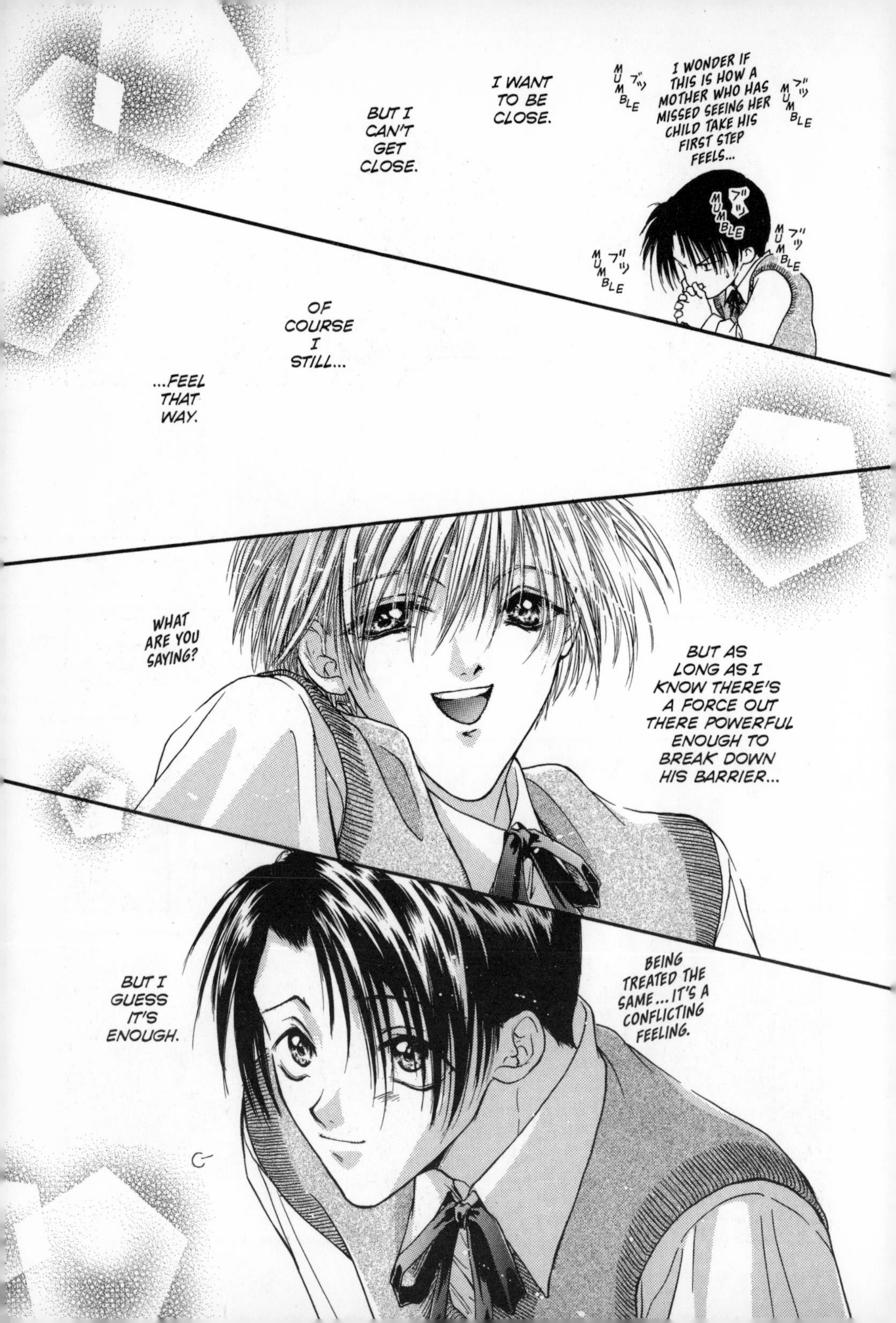
MUMBLE ブツ
I WONDER IF THIS IS HOW A MOTHER WHO HAS MISSED SEEING HER CHILD TAKE HIS FIRST STEP FEELS...
MUMBLE ブツ
I WANT TO BE CLOSE.
MUMBLE ブツ
BUT I CAN'T GET CLOSE.
MUMBLE ブツ
MUMBLE ブツ
MUMBLE ブツ
OF COURSE I STILL...
...FEEL THAT WAY.
BUT AS LONG AS I KNOW THERE'S A FORCE OUT THERE POWERFUL ENOUGH TO BREAK DOWN HIS BARRIER...
WHAT ARE YOU SAYING?
BEING TREATED THE SAME... IT'S A CONFLICTING FEELING.
BUT I GUESS IT'S ENOUGH.

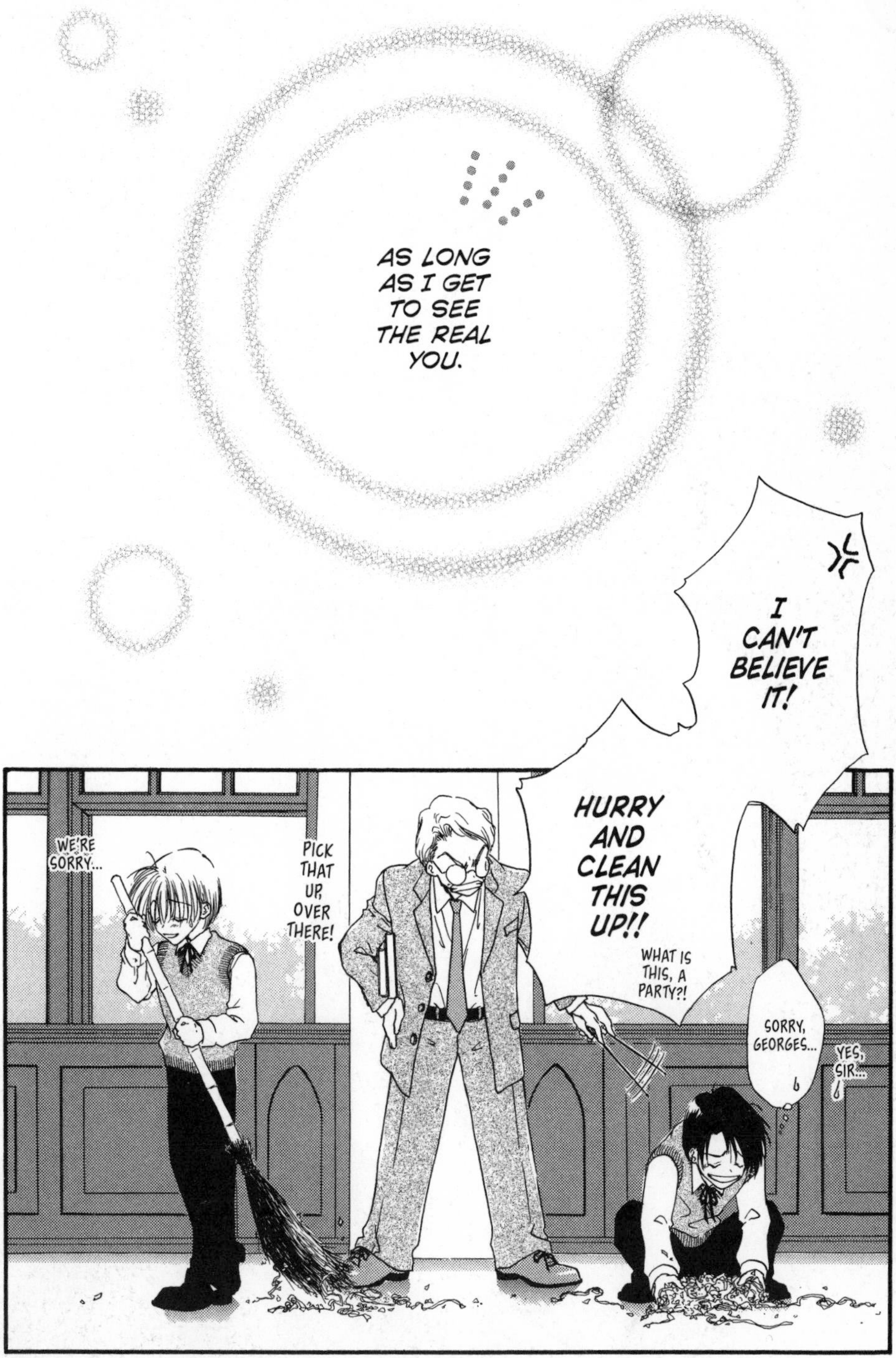
AS LONG AS I GET TO SEE THE REAL YOU.
I CAN'T BELIEVE IT!
HURRY AND CLEAN THIS UP!!
YES, SIR...
SORRY, GEORGES...
WHAT IS THIS, A PARTY?!
PICK THAT UP, OVER THERE!
WE'RE SORRY...

Barrier ◆END

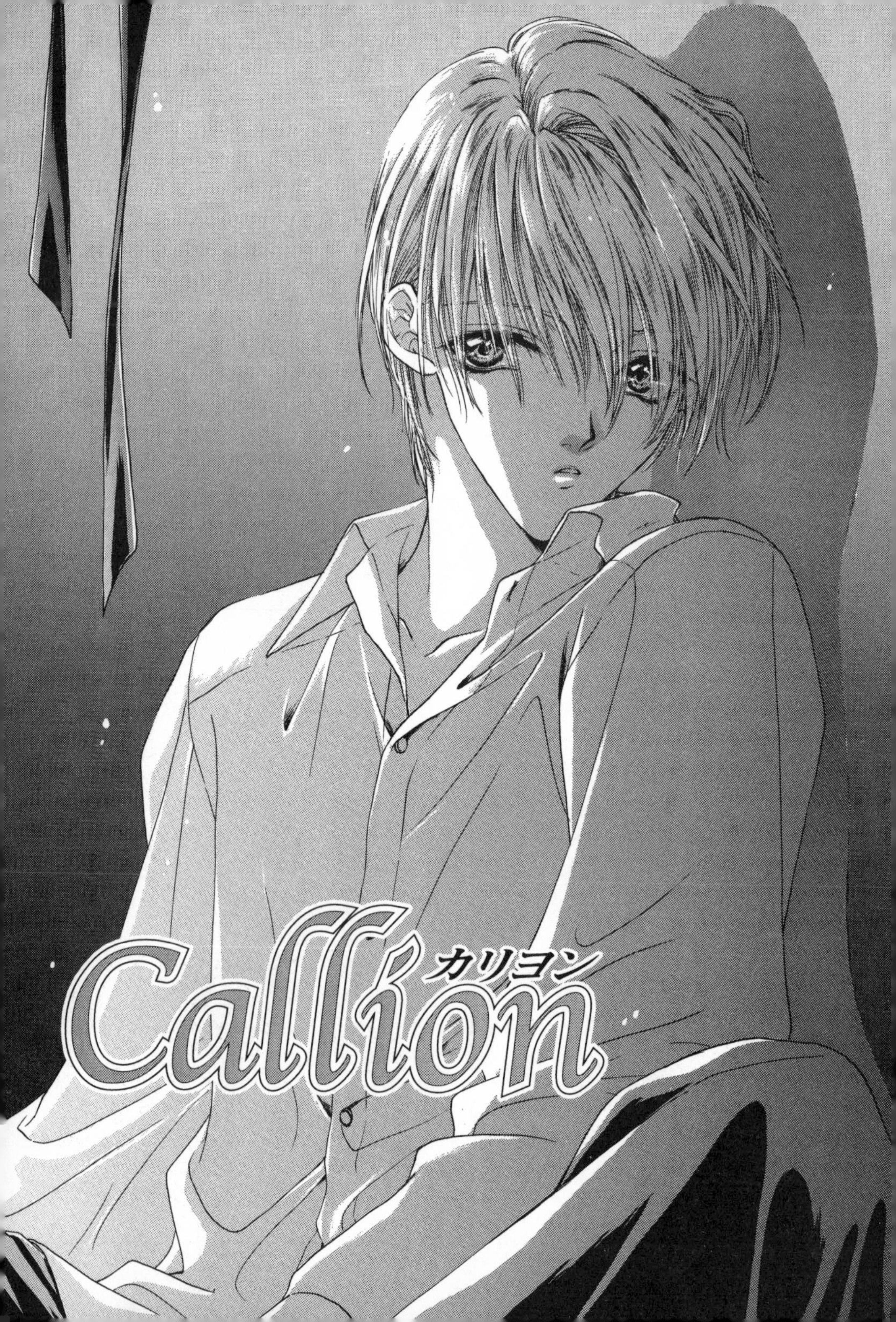
Callion
カリヨン

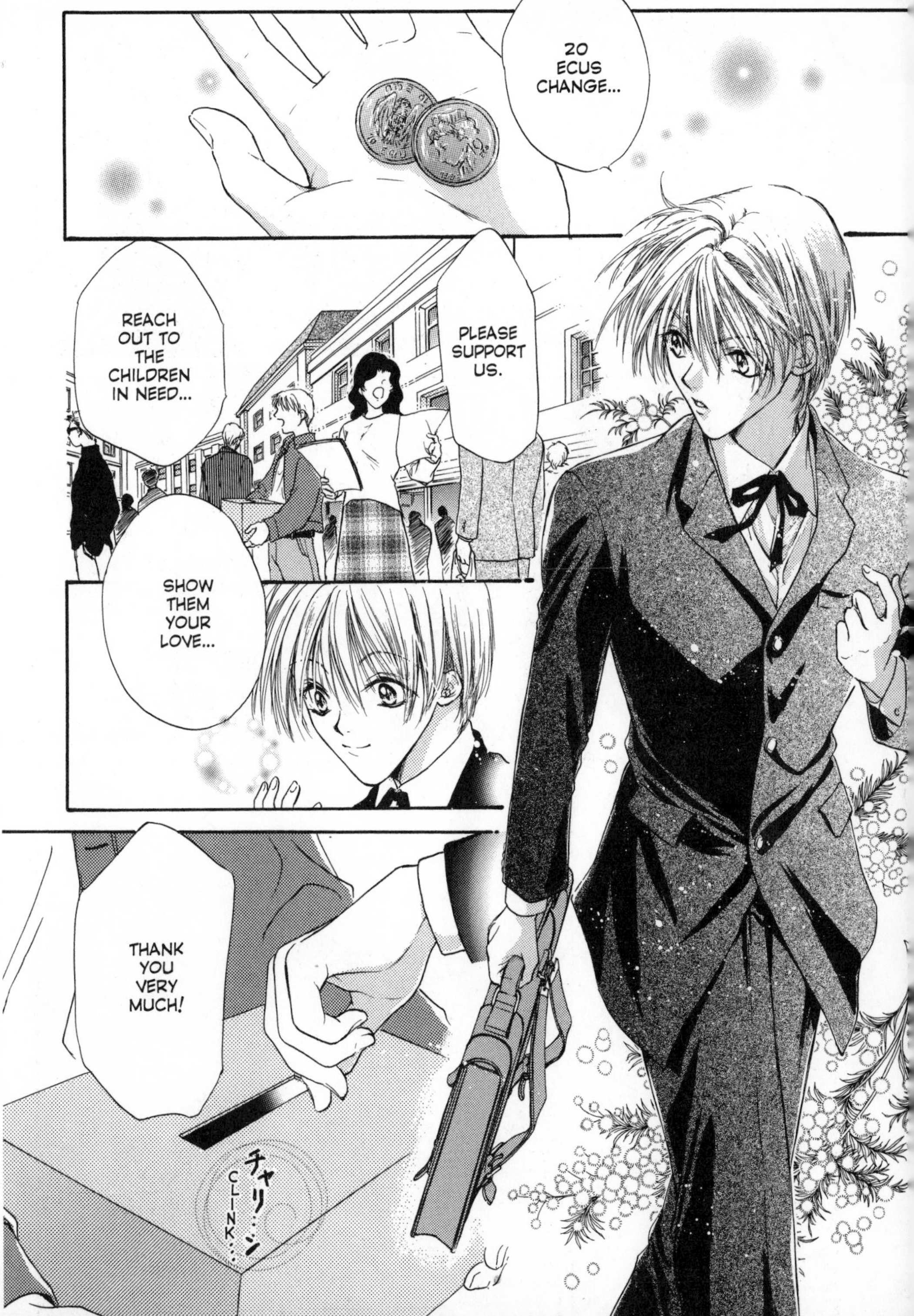
20 ECUS CHANGE...
PLEASE SUPPORT US.
REACH OUT TO THE CHILDREN IN NEED...
SHOW THEM YOUR LOVE...
THANK YOU VERY MUCH!
チャリ…ン
CLINK...

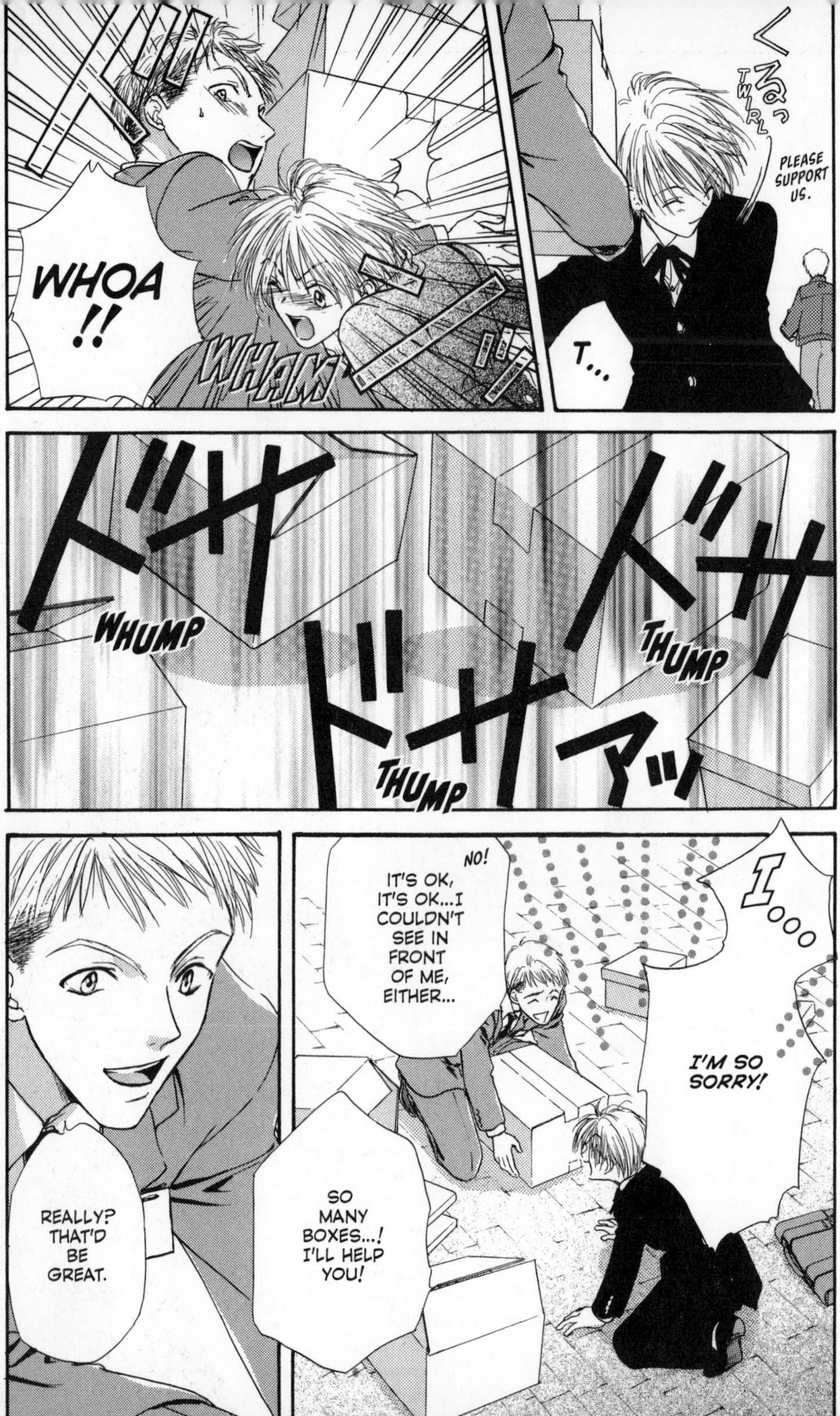
くるっ
TWIRL
PLEASE SUPPORT US.
T...
WHOA!!
WHAM
ドサ
THUMP
ドサァッ
THUMP
ドサ
WHUMP
IOOO
I'M SO SORRY!
NO!
IT'S OK, IT'S OK...I COULDN'T SEE IN FRONT OF ME, EITHER...
SO MANY BOXES...! I'LL HELP YOU!
REALLY? THAT'D BE GREAT.

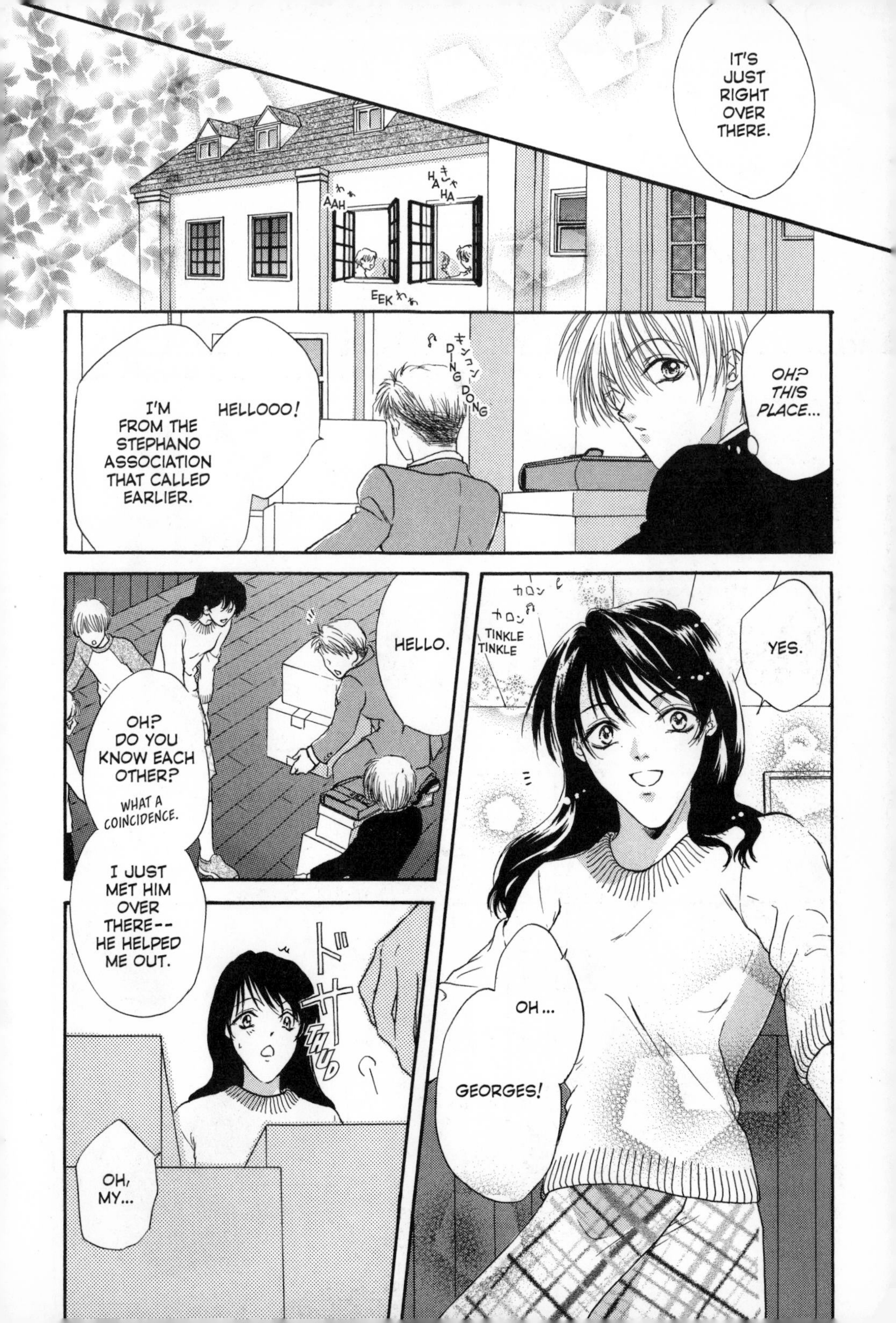
IT'S JUST RIGHT OVER THERE.
HA HA
AAH
EEK
OH? THIS PLACE...
DING DONG
HELLOOO!
I'M FROM THE STEPHANO ASSOCIATION THAT CALLED EARLIER.
YES.
TINKLE TINKLE
OH...
GEORGES!
HELLO.
OH? DO YOU KNOW EACH OTHER?
WHAT A COINCIDENCE.
I JUST MET HIM OVER THERE-- HE HELPED ME OUT.
THUD
OH, MY...

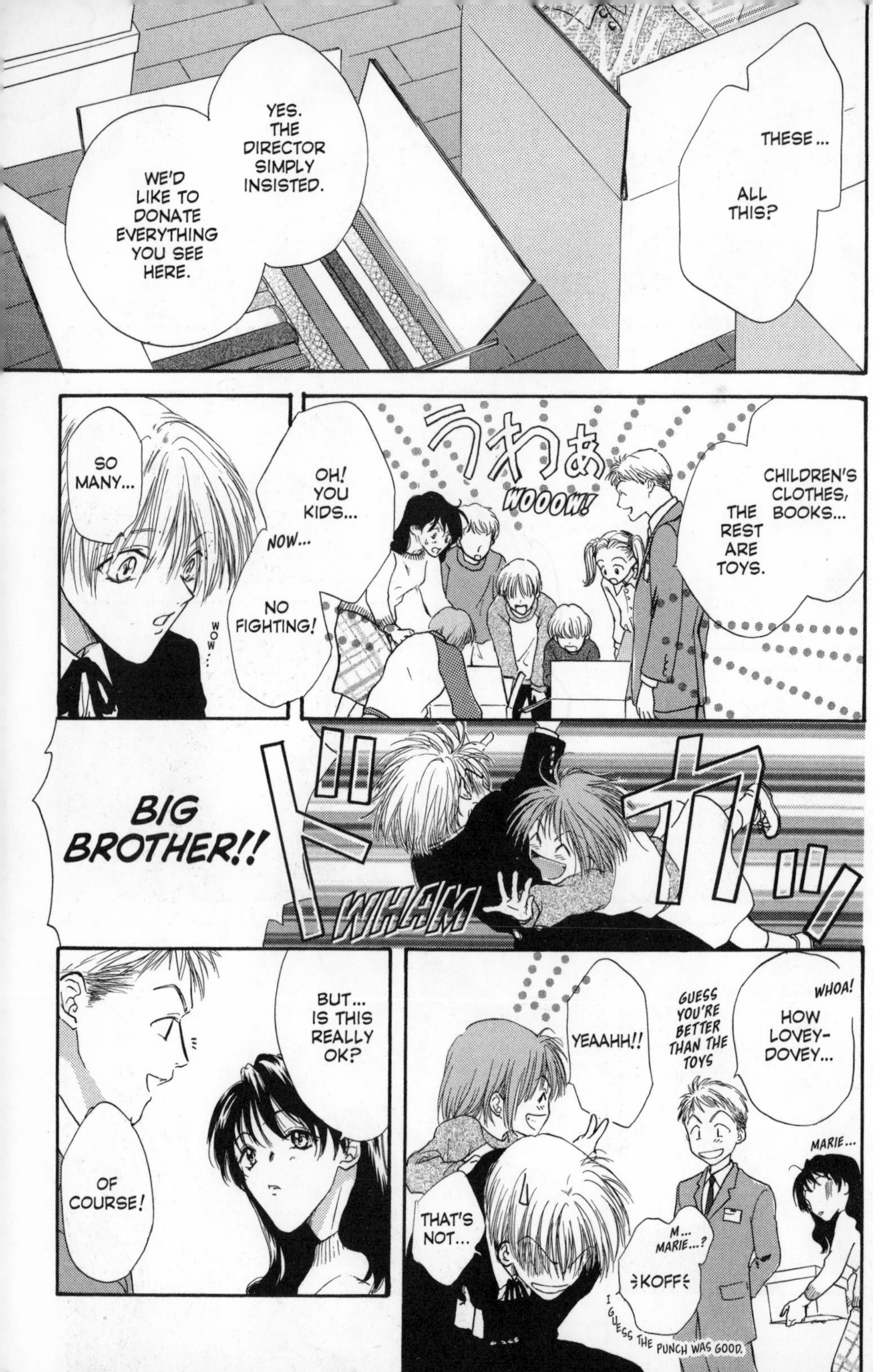
THESE... ALL THIS?
YES. THE DIRECTOR SIMPLY INSISTED.
WE'D LIKE TO DONATE EVERYTHING YOU SEE HERE.
CHILDREN'S CLOTHES, BOOKS... THE REST ARE TOYS.
うわぁ
WOOOW!
OH! YOU KIDS... NOW... NO FIGHTING!
SO MANY...
WOW...
ドカッ
WHAM
BIG BROTHER!!
WHOA! HOW LOVEY-DOVEY...
GUESS YOU'RE BETTER THAN THE TOYS
YEAAHH!!
MARIE...
M... MARIE...?
KOFF
I GUESS THE PUNCH WAS GOOD.
THAT'S NOT...
BUT... IS THIS REALLY OK?
OF COURSE!

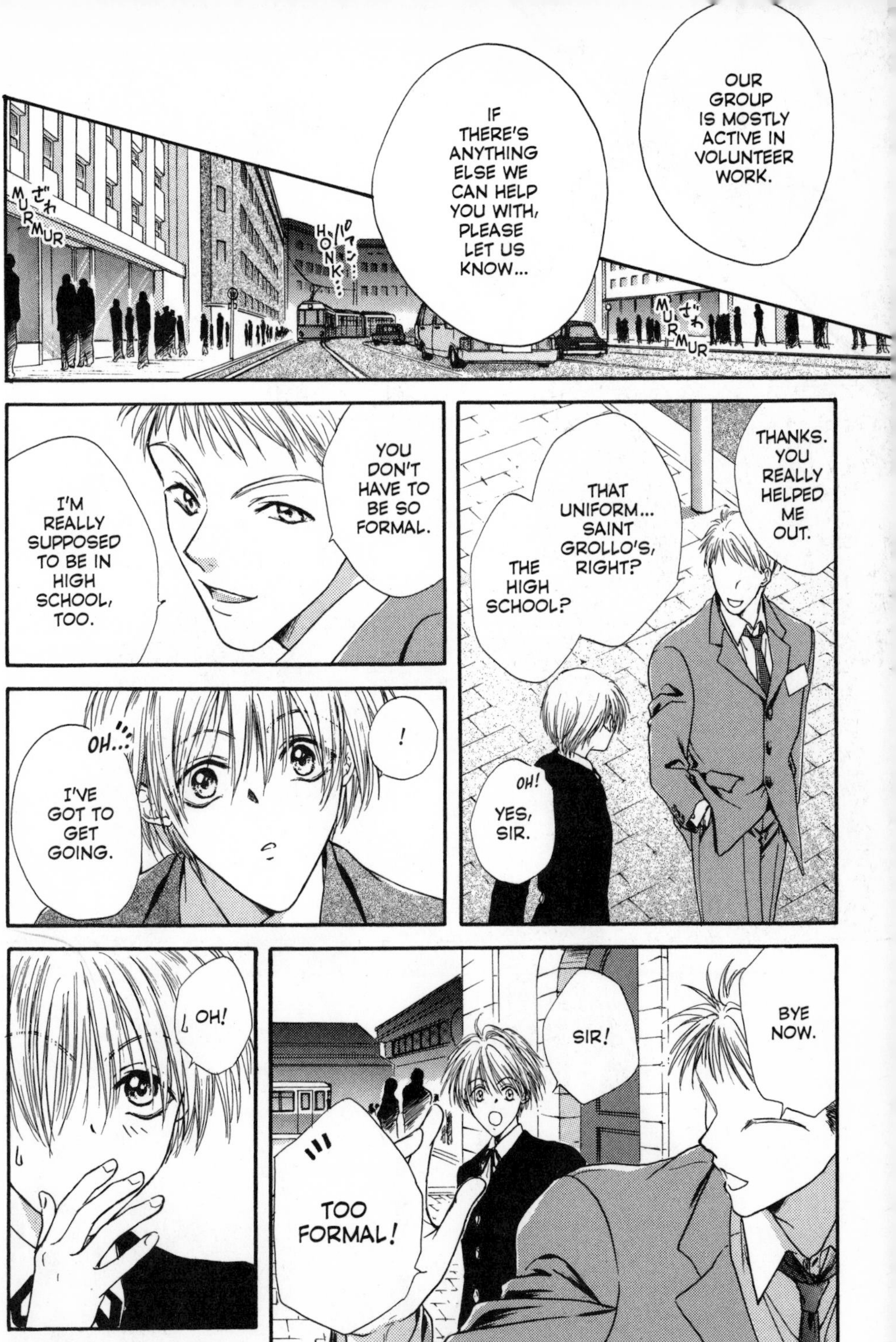
OUR GROUP IS MOSTLY ACTIVE IN VOLUNTEER WORK.
IF THERE'S ANYTHING ELSE WE CAN HELP YOU WITH, PLEASE LET US KNOW...
ざわ MURMUR
HONK... パァン…
ざわ MURMUR
THANKS. YOU REALLY HELPED ME OUT.
THAT UNIFORM... SAINT GROLLO'S, RIGHT?
THE HIGH SCHOOL?
OH!
YES, SIR.
YOU DON'T HAVE TO BE SO FORMAL.
I'M REALLY SUPPOSED TO BE IN HIGH SCHOOL, TOO.
!
OH...
I'VE GOT TO GET GOING.
BYE NOW.
SIR!
TOO FORMAL!
OH!

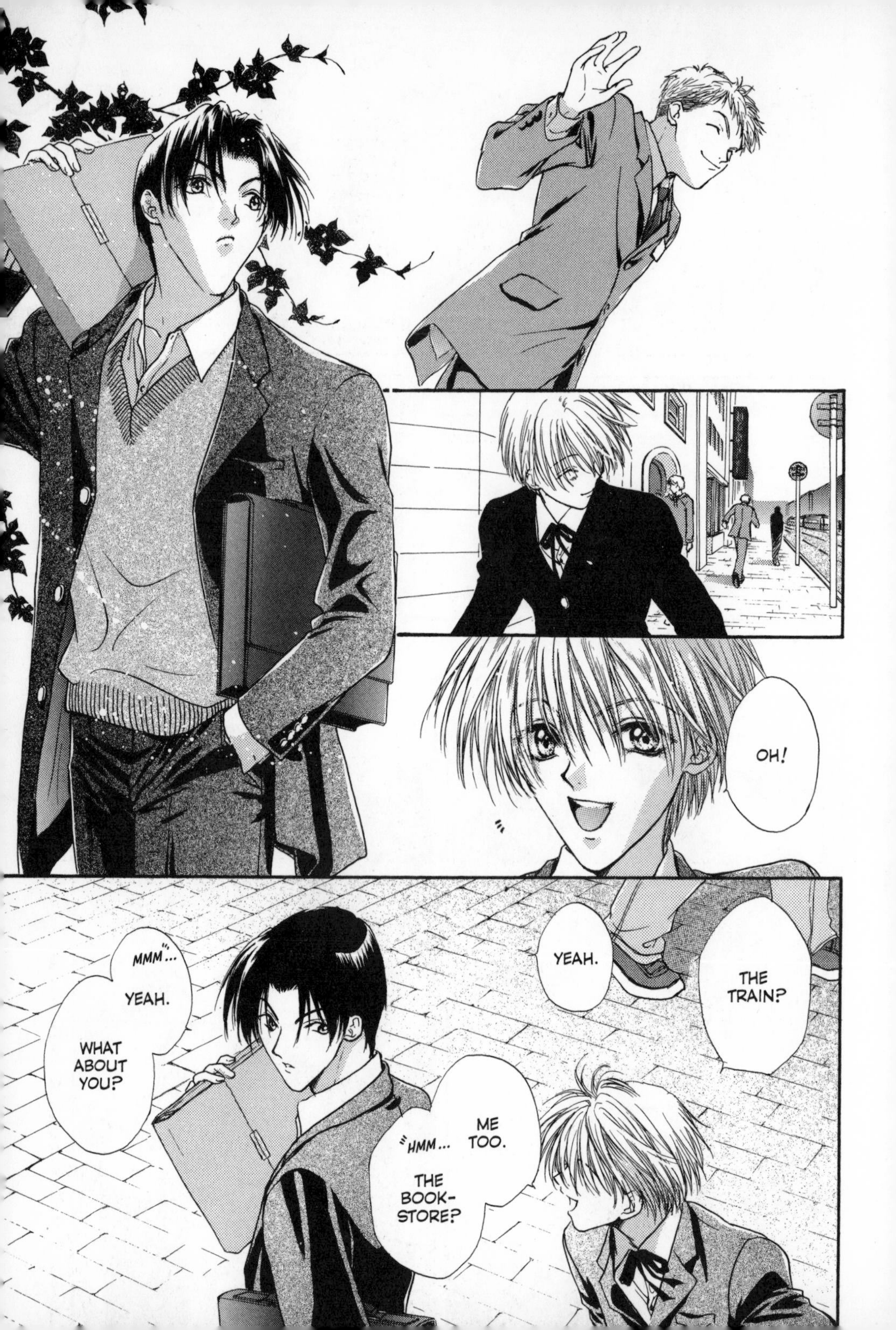
OH!
THE TRAIN?
YEAH.
MMM... YEAH. WHAT ABOUT YOU?
HMM... ME TOO. THE BOOK-STORE?

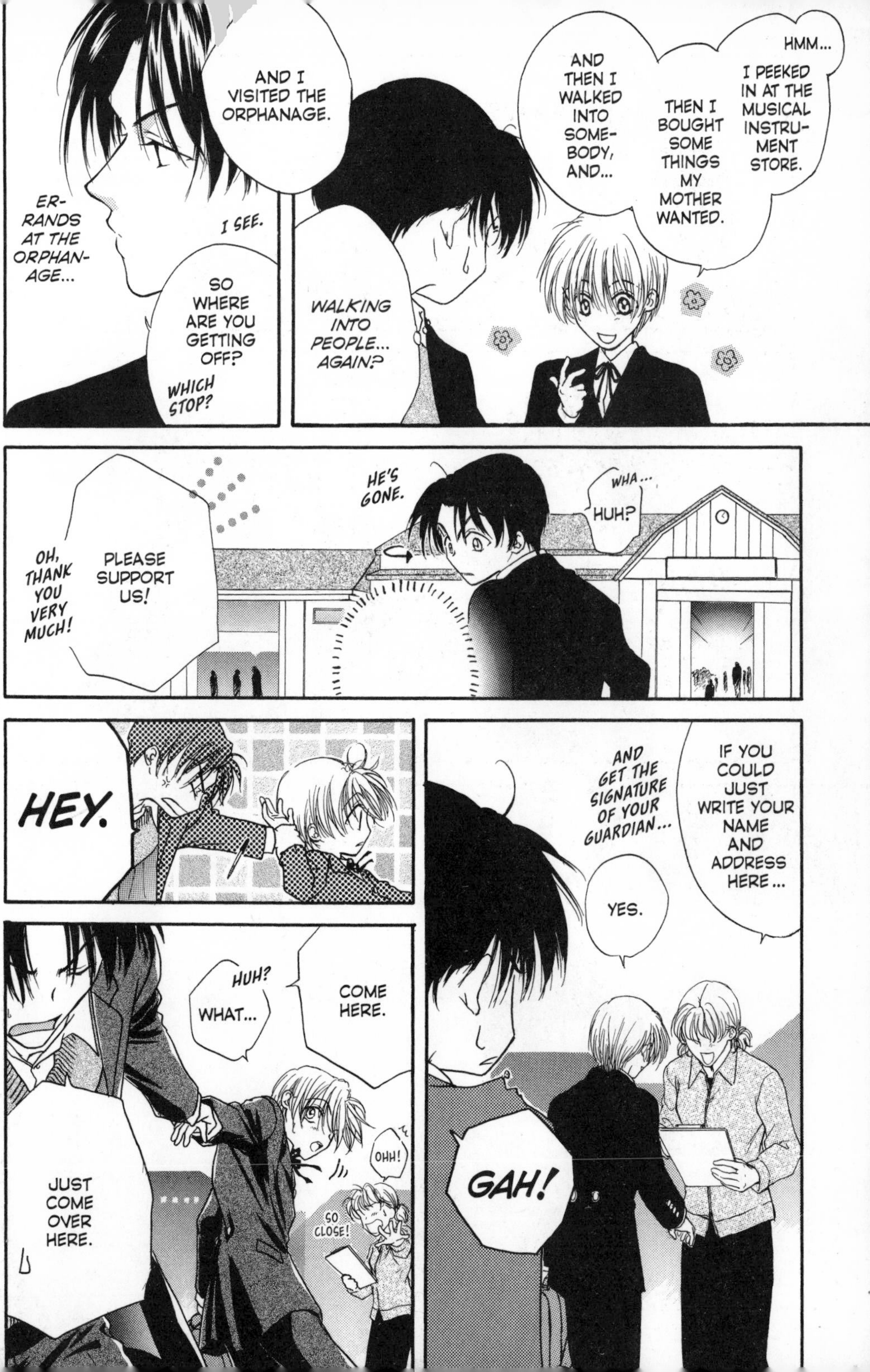
HMM...
I PEEKED IN AT THE MUSICAL INSTRU-MENT STORE.
THEN I BOUGHT SOME THINGS MY MOTHER WANTED.
AND THEN I WALKED INTO SOME-BODY, AND...
WALKING INTO PEOPLE... AGAIN?
AND I VISITED THE ORPHANAGE.
I SEE.
ER-RANDS AT THE ORPHAN-AGE...
SO WHERE ARE YOU GETTING OFF?
WHICH STOP?
WHA...
HUH?
HE'S GONE.
PLEASE SUPPORT US!
OH, THANK YOU VERY MUCH!
IF YOU COULD JUST WRITE YOUR NAME AND ADDRESS HERE...
AND GET THE SIGNATURE OF YOUR GUARDIAN...
YES.
GAH!
HEY.
COME HERE.
HUH?
WHAT...
OHH!
SO CLOSE!
JUST COME OVER HERE.

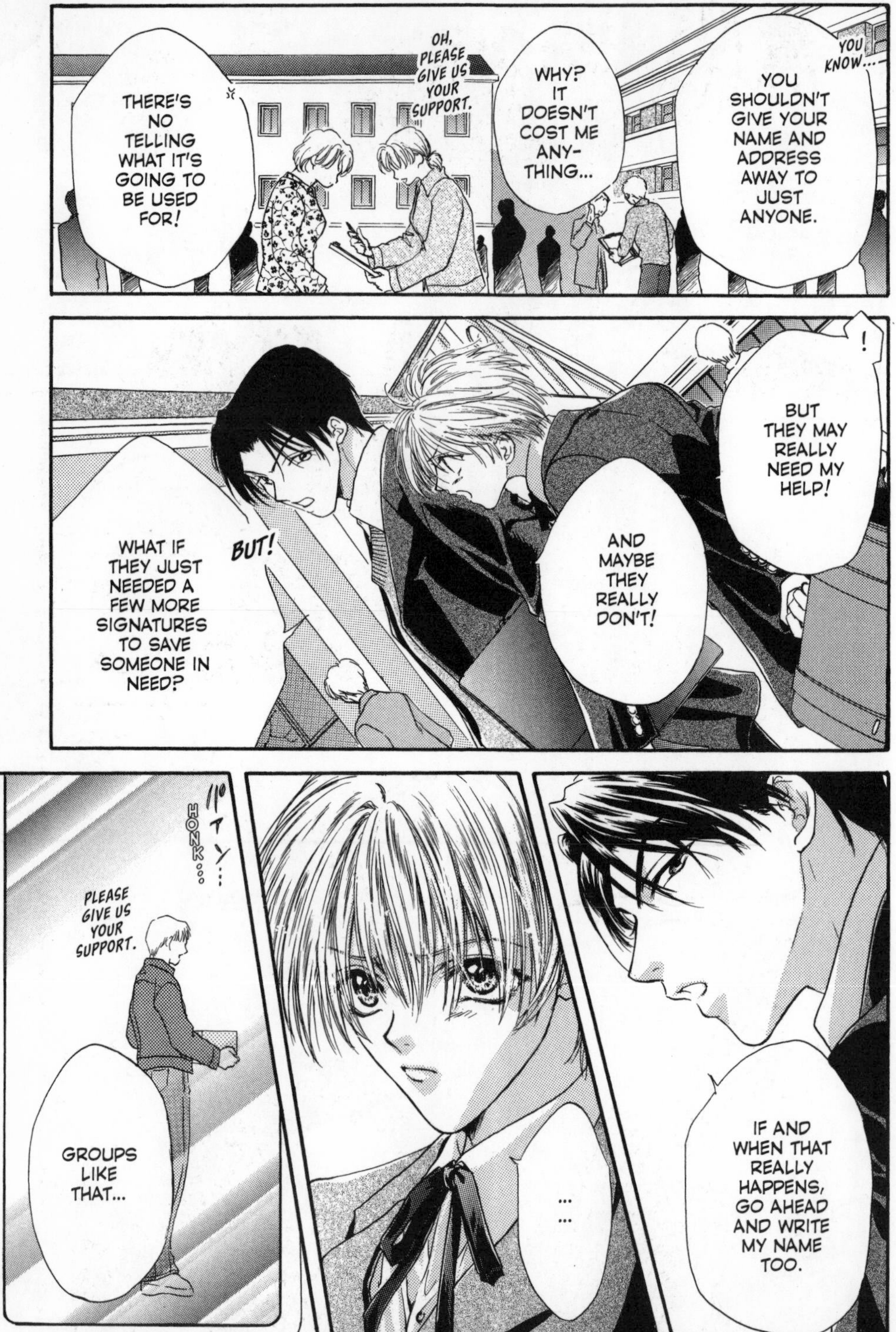
YOU KNOW...
YOU SHOULDN'T GIVE YOUR NAME AND ADDRESS AWAY TO JUST ANYONE.
WHY? IT DOESN'T COST ME ANY-THING...
OH, PLEASE GIVE US YOUR SUPPORT.
THERE'S NO TELLING WHAT IT'S GOING TO BE USED FOR!
!
BUT THEY MAY REALLY NEED MY HELP!
AND MAYBE THEY REALLY DON'T!
BUT!
WHAT IF THEY JUST NEEDED A FEW MORE SIGNATURES TO SAVE SOMEONE IN NEED?
IF AND WHEN THAT REALLY HAPPENS, GO AHEAD AND WRITE MY NAME TOO.
... ...
HONK...
PLEASE GIVE US YOUR SUPPORT.
GROUPS LIKE THAT...

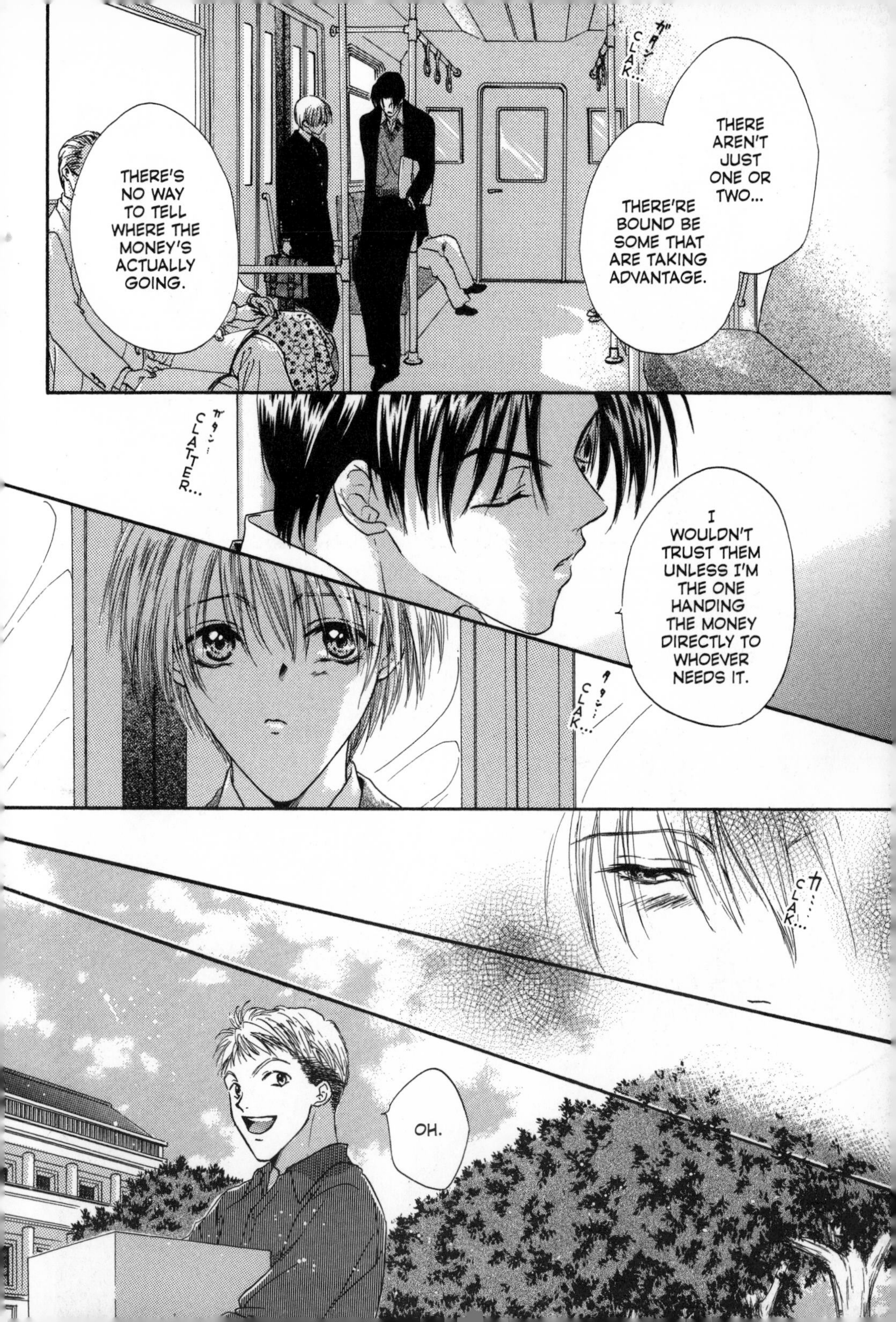
ガタン CLAK...
THERE AREN'T JUST ONE OR TWO...
THERE'RE BOUND BE SOME THAT ARE TAKING ADVANTAGE.
THERE'S NO WAY TO TELL WHERE THE MONEY'S ACTUALLY GOING.
I WOULDN'T TRUST THEM UNLESS I'M THE ONE HANDING THE MONEY DIRECTLY TO WHOEVER NEEDS IT.
カタン… CLAK...
ガタン… CLATTER...
カ… CLAK...
OH.

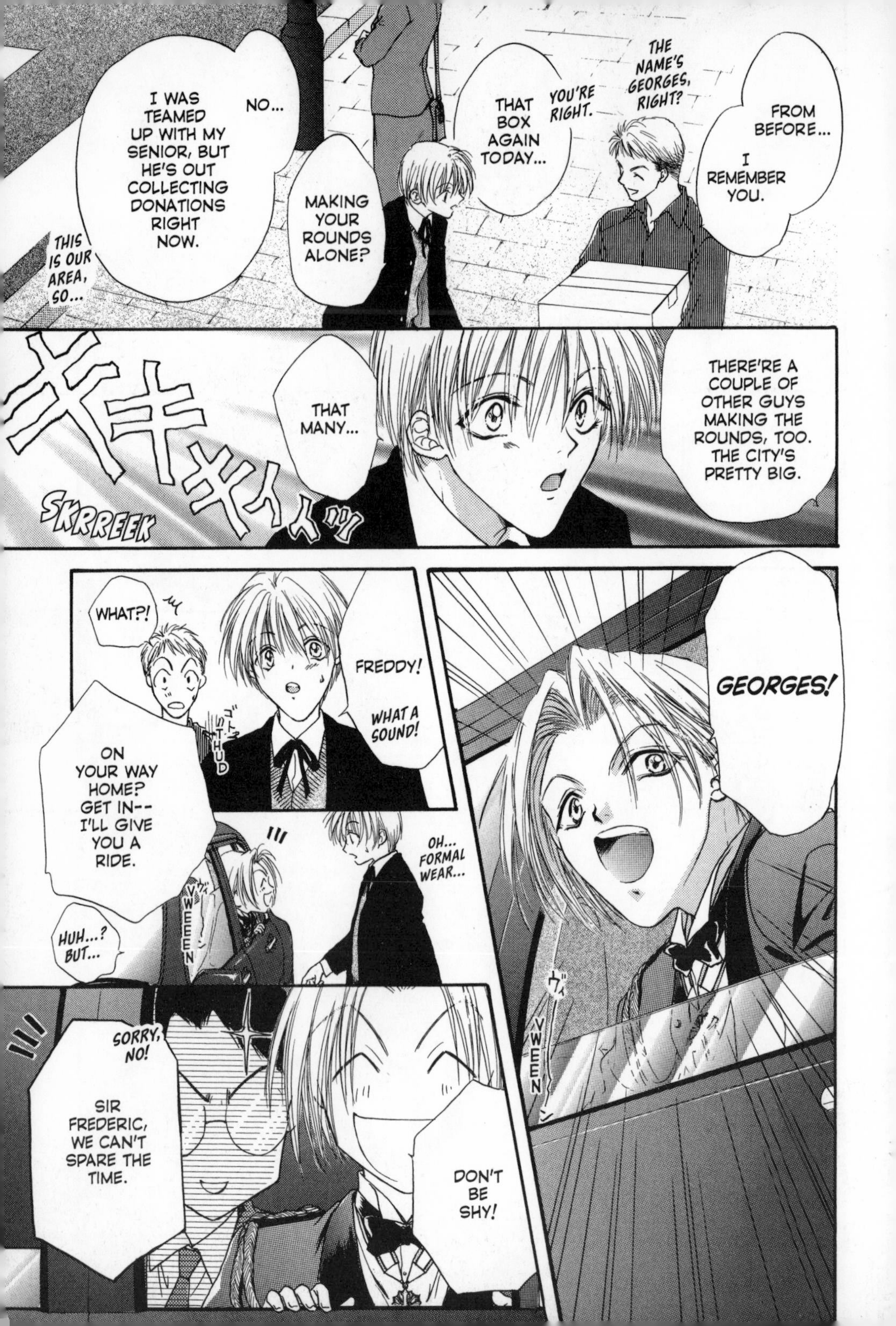
FROM BEFORE...
I REMEMBER YOU.
THE NAME'S GEORGES, RIGHT?
YOU'RE RIGHT.
THAT BOX AGAIN TODAY...
MAKING YOUR ROUNDS ALONE?
NO...
I WAS TEAMED UP WITH MY SENIOR, BUT HE'S OUT COLLECTING DONATIONS RIGHT NOW.
THIS IS OUR AREA, SO...
THERE'RE A COUPLE OF OTHER GUYS MAKING THE ROUNDS, TOO. THE CITY'S PRETTY BIG.
THAT MANY...
キキキイィッ
SKRREEK
GEORGES!
ヴィ
VWEEN
FREDDY!
WHAT A SOUND!
WHAT?!
ゴトッ
THUD
OH... FORMAL WEAR...
ON YOUR WAY HOME? GET IN-- I'LL GIVE YOU A RIDE.
ヴィ
VWEEN
HUH...? BUT...
DON'T BE SHY!
SORRY, NO!
SIR FREDERIC, WE CAN'T SPARE THE TIME.

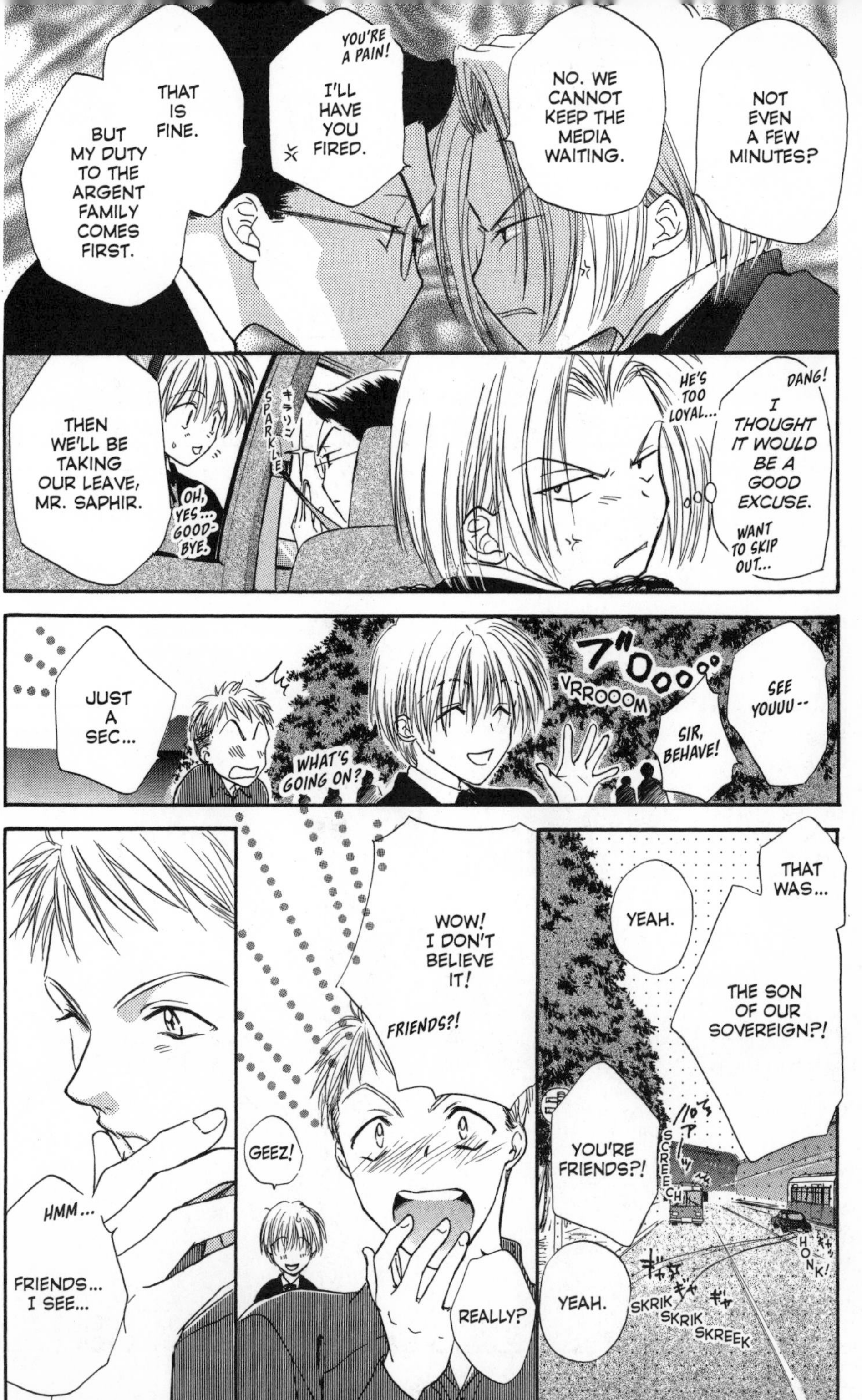
NOT EVEN A FEW MINUTES?
NO. WE CANNOT KEEP THE MEDIA WAITING.
YOU'RE A PAIN!
I'LL HAVE YOU FIRED.
THAT IS FINE.
BUT MY DUTY TO THE ARGENT FAMILY COMES FIRST.
DANG!
I THOUGHT IT WOULD BE A GOOD EXCUSE.
HE'S TOO LOYAL...
WANT TO SKIP OUT...
SPARKLE
THEN WE'LL BE TAKING OUR LEAVE, MR. SAPHIR.
OH, YES... GOOD-BYE.
SEE YOUUU--
VRROOOM
SIR, BEHAVE!
WHAT'S GOING ON?
JUST A SEC...
THAT WAS...
YEAH.
THE SON OF OUR SOVEREIGN?!
SCREECH
YOU'RE FRIENDS?!
HONK!
YEAH.
SKRIK SKRIK SKREEK
WOW! I DON'T BELIEVE IT!
FRIENDS?!
GEEZ!
REALLY?
HMM...
FRIENDS... I SEE...

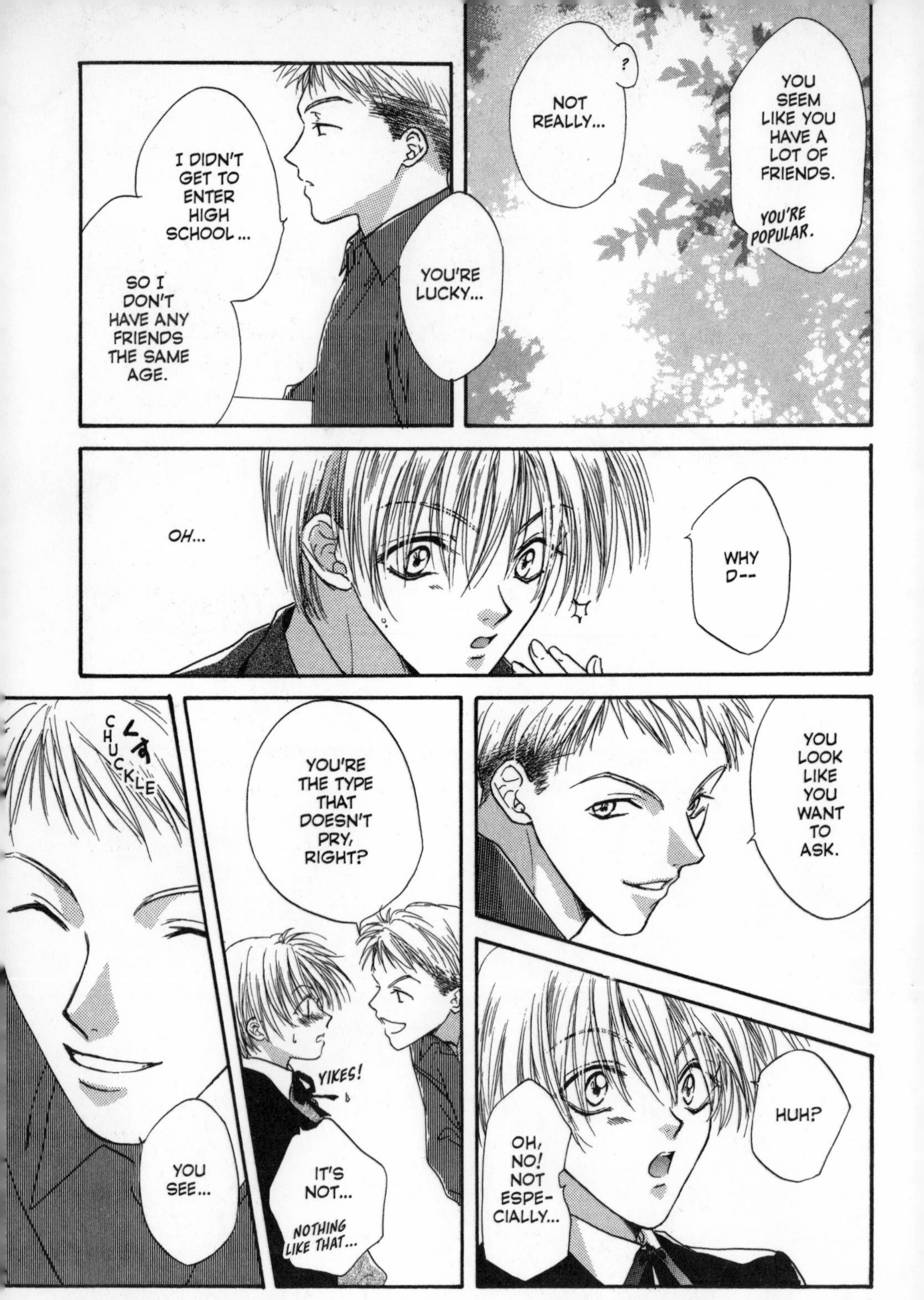

YOU SEEM LIKE YOU HAVE A LOT OF FRIENDS.
YOU'RE POPULAR.
?
NOT REALLY...
YOU'RE LUCKY...
I DIDN'T GET TO ENTER HIGH SCHOOL...
SO I DON'T HAVE ANY FRIENDS THE SAME AGE.
WHY D--
OH...
YOU LOOK LIKE YOU WANT TO ASK.
HUH?
OH, NO! NOT ESPE-CIALLY...
YOU'RE THE TYPE THAT DOESN'T PRY, RIGHT?
YIKES!
IT'S NOT...
NOTHING LIKE THAT...
くす
CHUCKLE
YOU SEE...

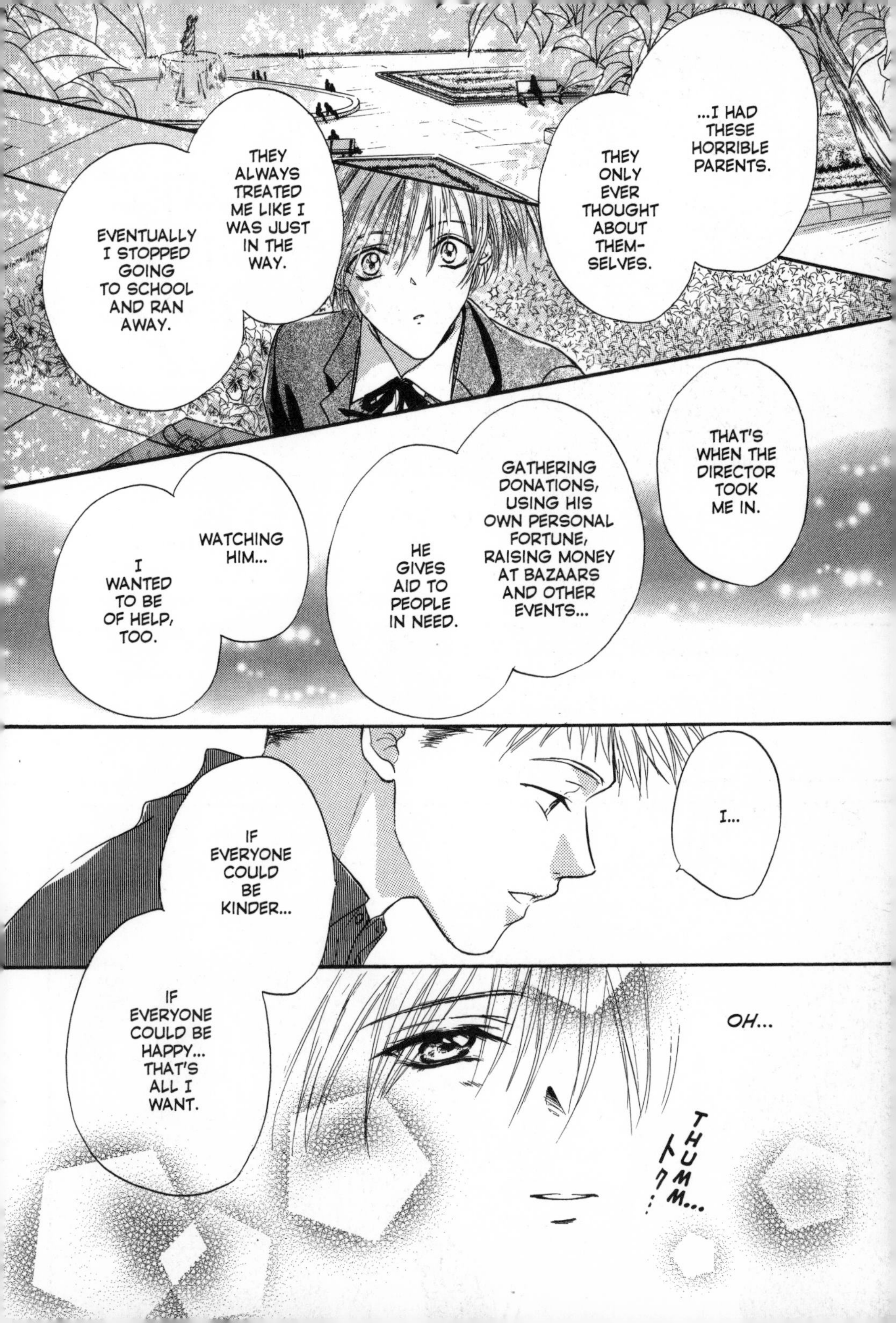
...I HAD THESE HORRIBLE PARENTS.
THEY ONLY EVER THOUGHT ABOUT THEM-SELVES.
THEY ALWAYS TREATED ME LIKE I WAS JUST IN THE WAY.
EVENTUALLY I STOPPED GOING TO SCHOOL AND RAN AWAY.
THAT'S WHEN THE DIRECTOR TOOK ME IN.
GATHERING DONATIONS, USING HIS OWN PERSONAL FORTUNE, RAISING MONEY AT BAZAARS AND OTHER EVENTS...
HE GIVES AID TO PEOPLE IN NEED.
WATCHING HIM...
I WANTED TO BE OF HELP, TOO.
I...
IF EVERYONE COULD BE KINDER...
OH...
THUMM...
トク…
IF EVERYONE COULD BE HAPPY... THAT'S ALL I WANT.

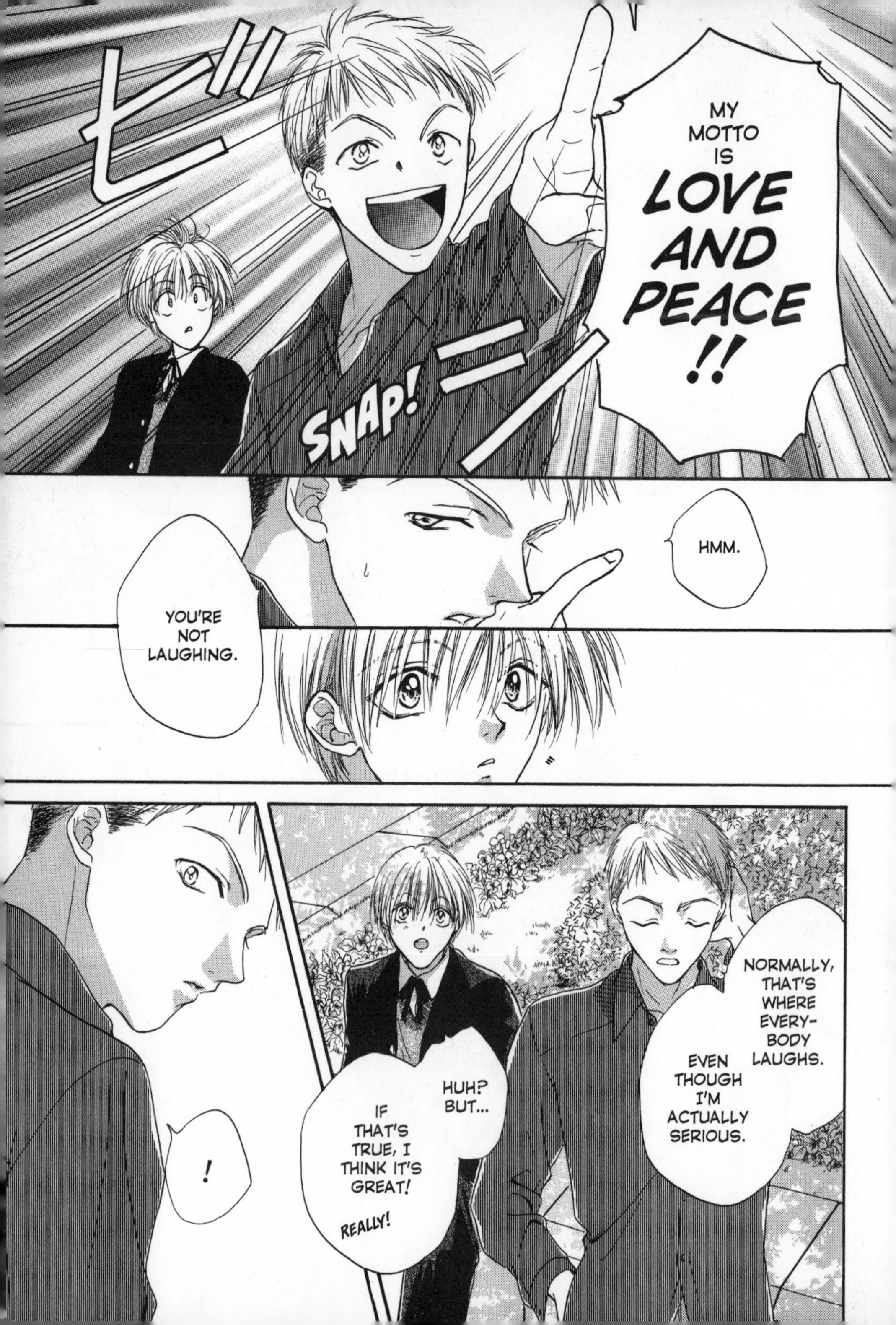
MY MOTTO IS LOVE AND PEACE!!
SNAP!
ビ
HMM.
YOU'RE NOT LAUGHING.
NORMALLY, THAT'S WHERE EVERY-BODY LAUGHS.
EVEN THOUGH I'M ACTUALLY SERIOUS.
HUH? BUT...
IF THAT'S TRUE, I THINK IT'S GREAT!
REALLY!
!

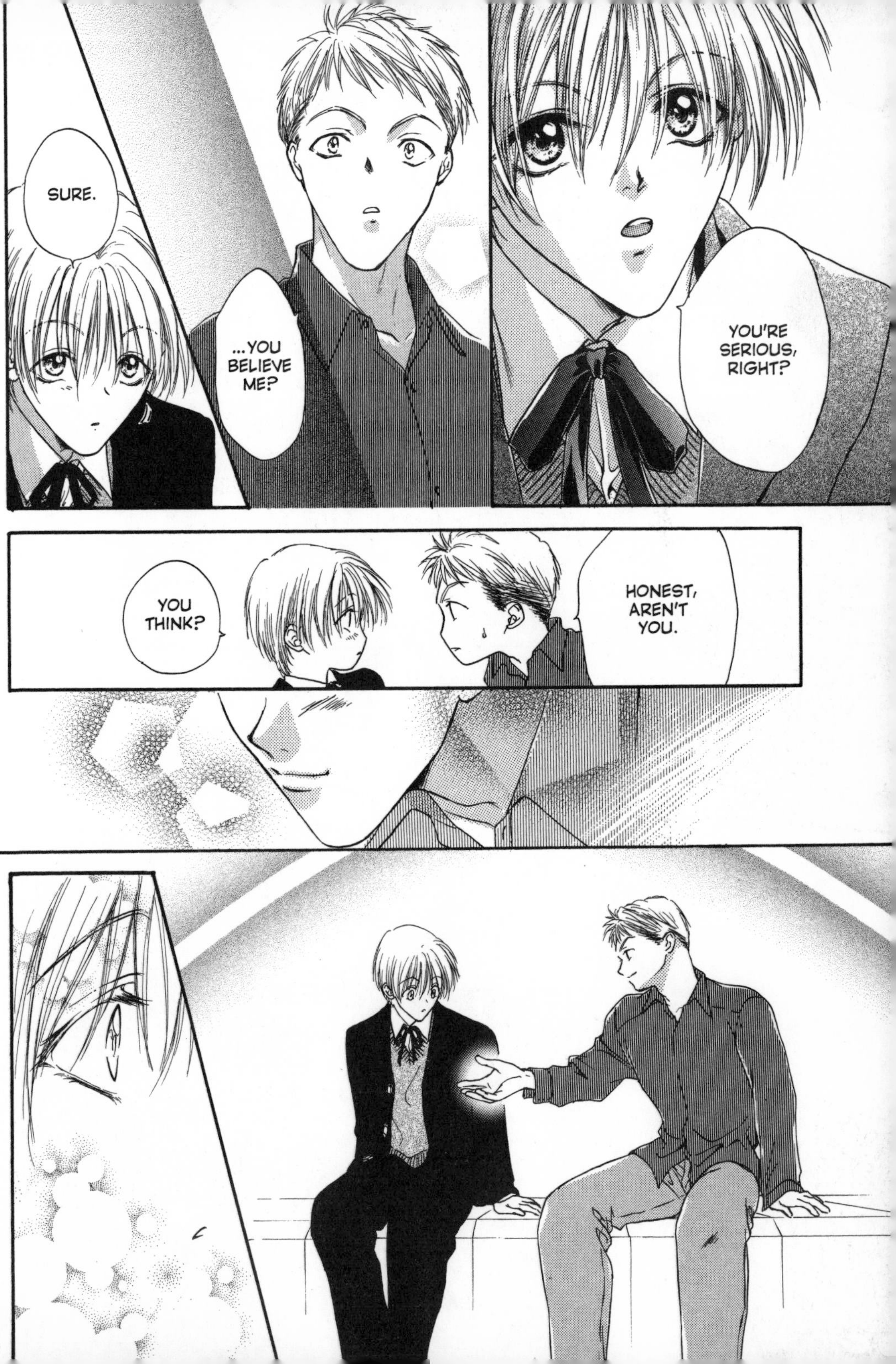
YOU'RE SERIOUS, RIGHT?
...YOU BELIEVE ME?
SURE.
HONEST, AREN'T YOU.
YOU THINK?

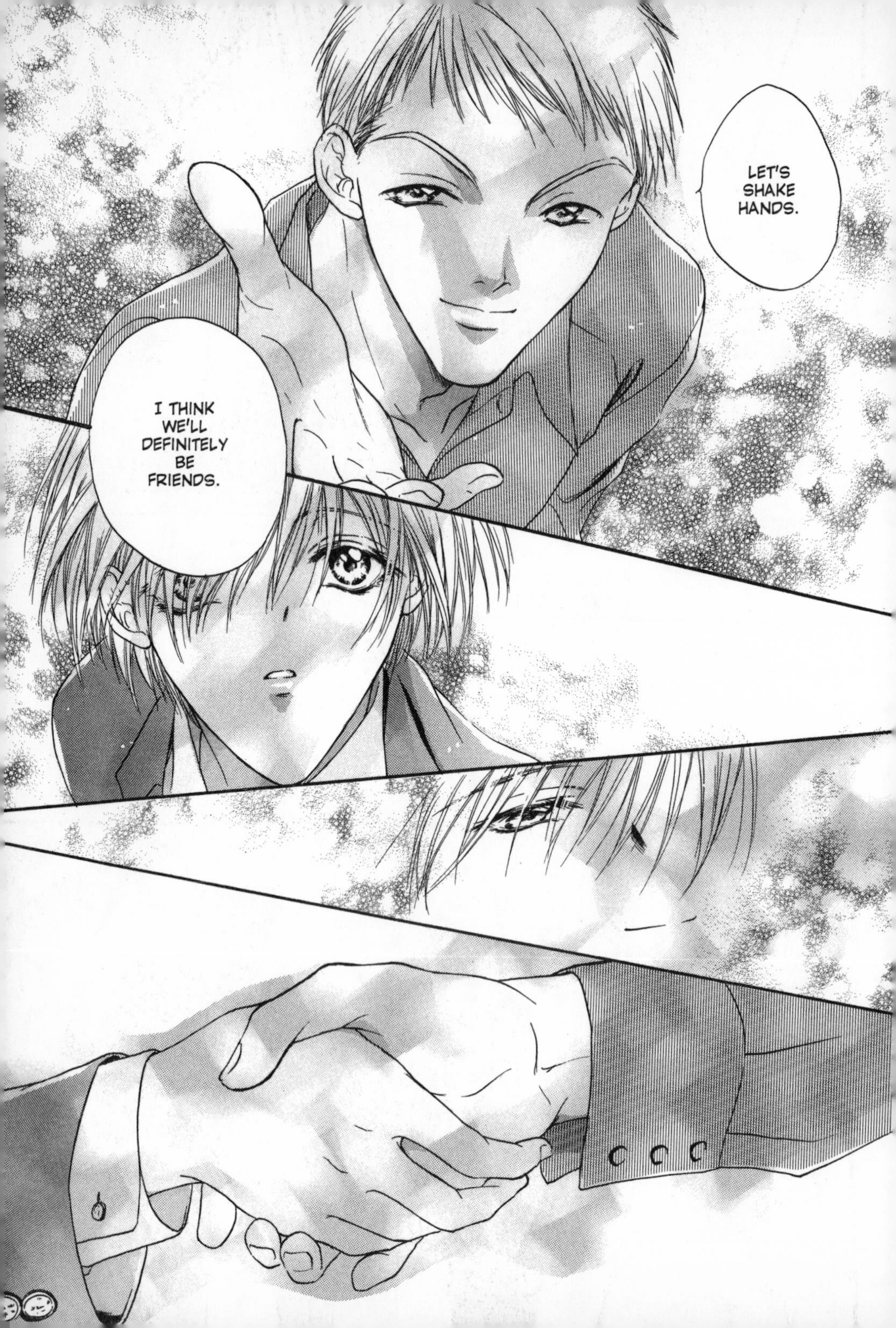
LET'S SHAKE HANDS.
I THINK WE'LL DEFINITELY BE FRIENDS.

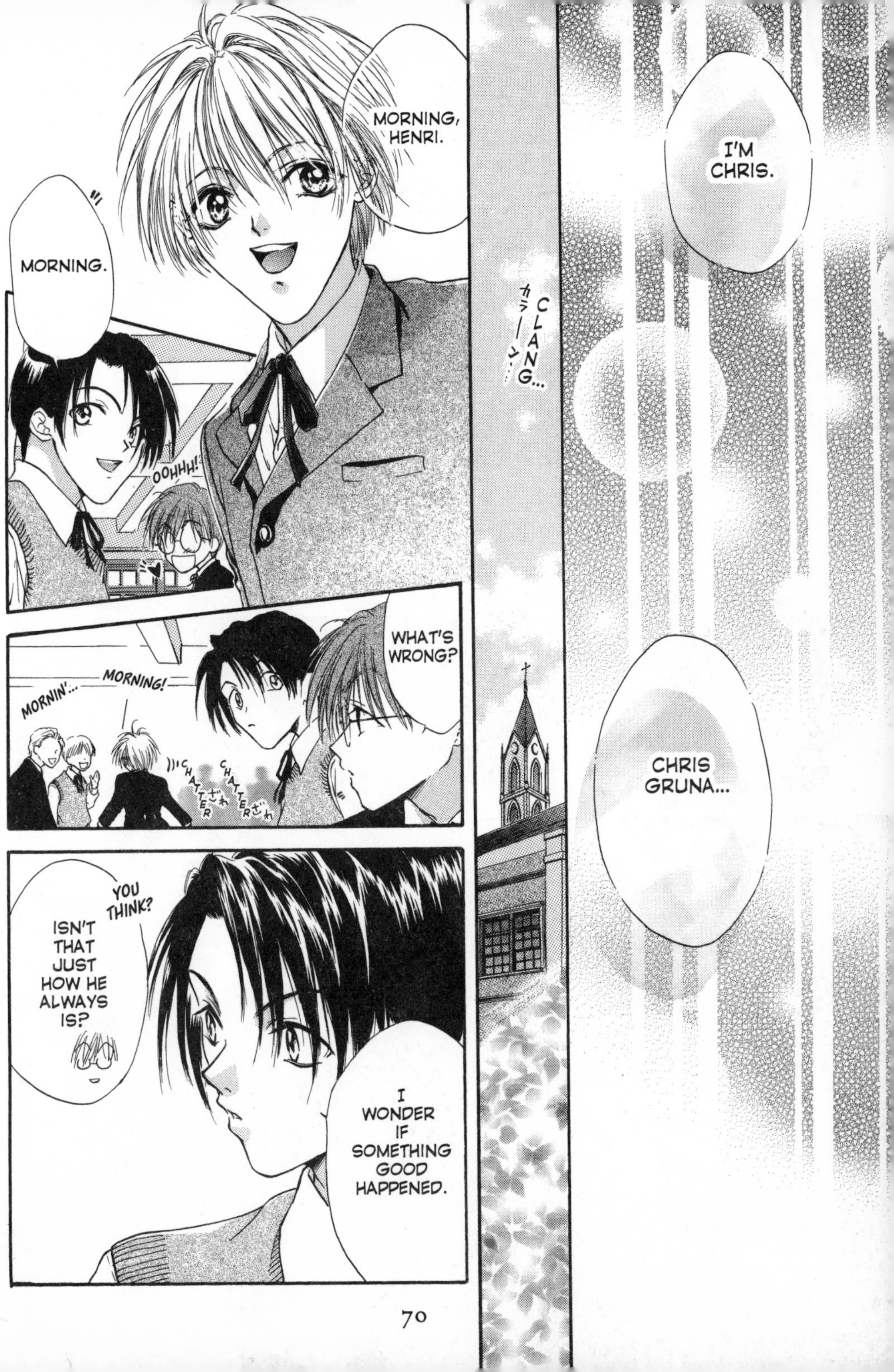
I'M CHRIS.
CHRIS GRUNA...
CLANG...
MORNING, HENRI.
MORNING.
OOHHH!
WHAT'S WRONG?
MORNING!
MORNIN'...
CHATTER
CHATTER
I WONDER IF SOMETHING GOOD HAPPENED.
YOU THINK?
ISN'T THAT JUST HOW HE ALWAYS IS?

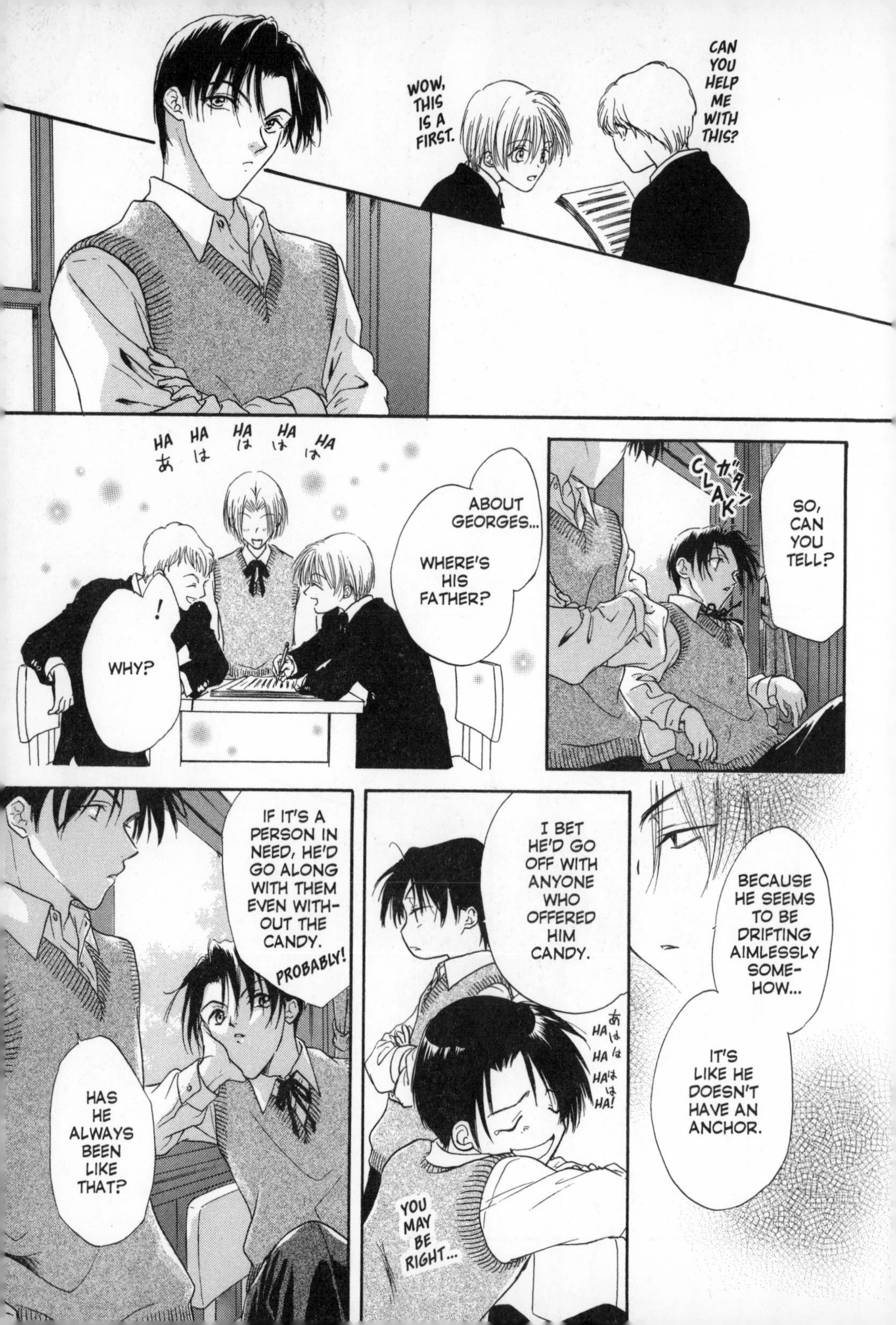
CAN YOU HELP ME WITH THIS?
WOW, THIS IS A FIRST.
CLAK ガタン
SO, CAN YOU TELL?
HA HA HA HA HA あははは
ABOUT GEORGES...
WHERE'S HIS FATHER?
!
WHY?
BECAUSE HE SEEMS TO BE DRIFTING AIMLESSLY SOME-HOW...
IT'S LIKE HE DOESN'T HAVE AN ANCHOR.
I BET HE'D GO OFF WITH ANYONE WHO OFFERED HIM CANDY.
HA HA HA HA HA! あははは
YOU MAY BE RIGHT...
IF IT'S A PERSON IN NEED, HE'D GO ALONG WITH THEM EVEN WITH-OUT THE CANDY.
PROBABLY!
HAS HE ALWAYS BEEN LIKE THAT?

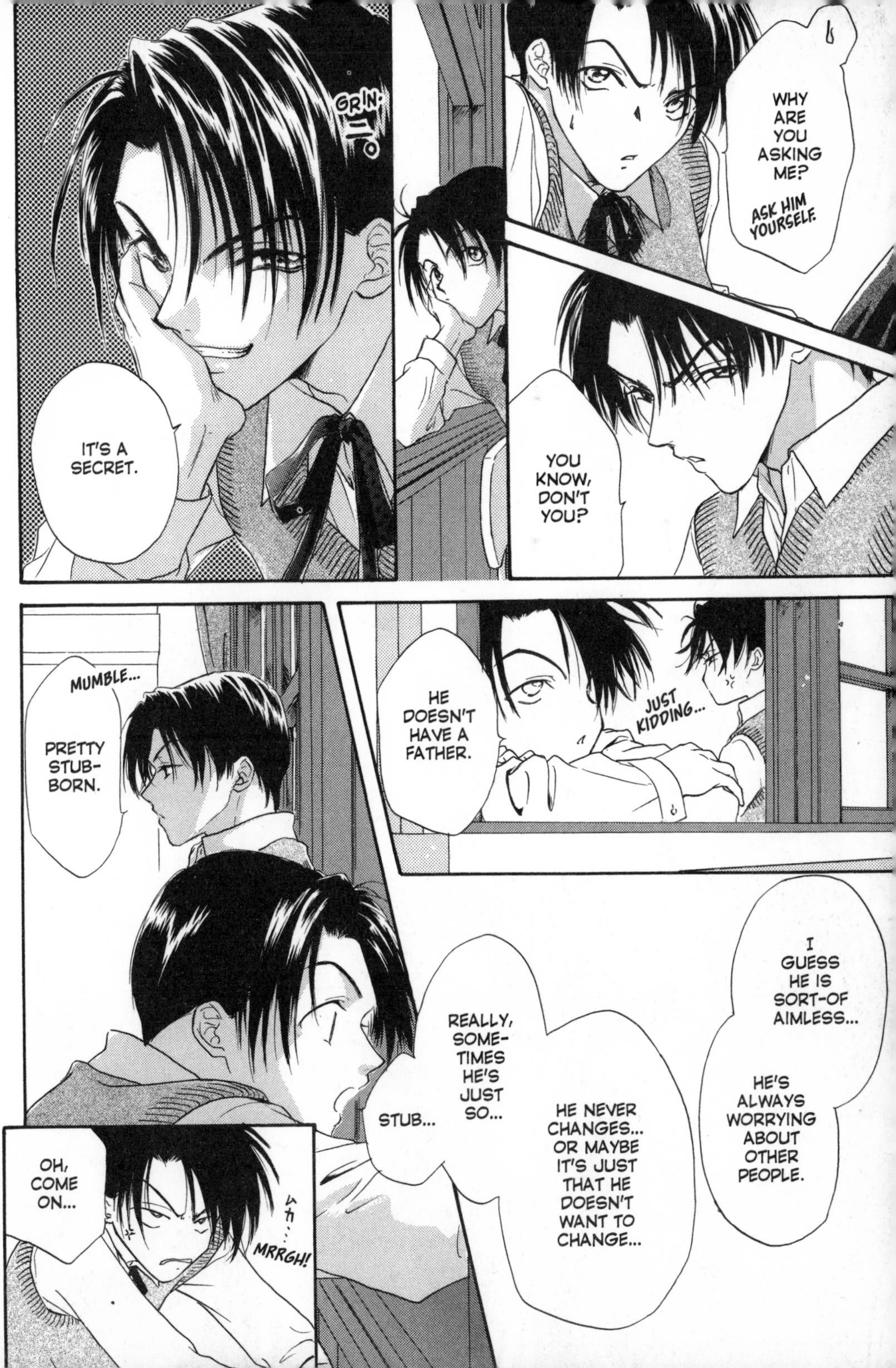
WHY ARE YOU ASKING ME?
ASK HIM YOURSELF.
YOU KNOW, DON'T YOU?
GRIN- ニコ
IT'S A SECRET.
JUST KIDDING...
HE DOESN'T HAVE A FATHER.
MUMBLE...
PRETTY STUB-BORN.
I GUESS HE IS SORT-OF AIMLESS...
HE'S ALWAYS WORRYING ABOUT OTHER PEOPLE.
HE NEVER CHANGES... OR MAYBE IT'S JUST THAT HE DOESN'T WANT TO CHANGE...
REALLY, SOMETIMES HE'S JUST SO...
STUB...
ムカ... MRRGH!
OH, COME ON...

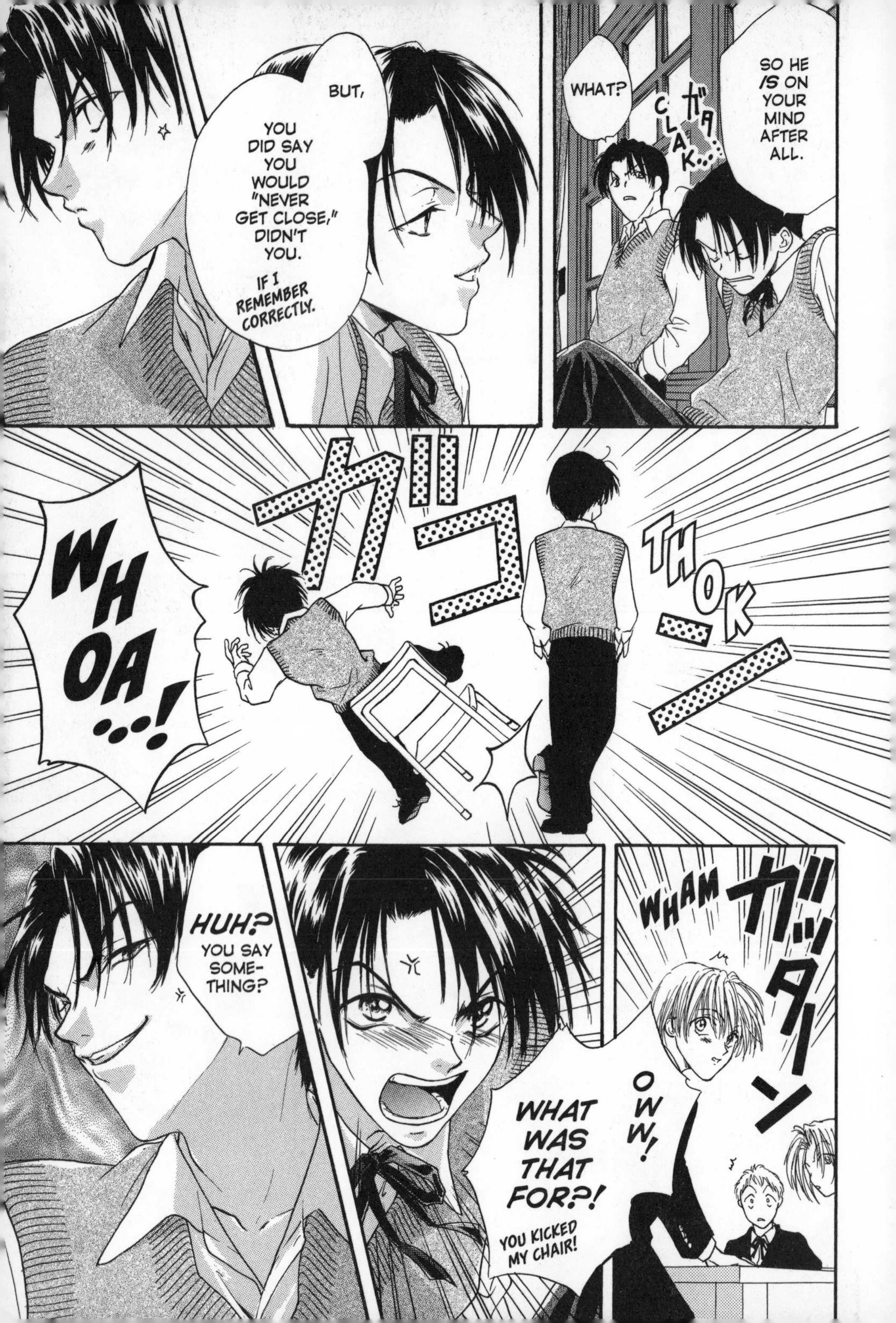
SO HE *IS* ON YOUR MIND AFTER ALL.
WHAT?
CLAK...
ガタ
BUT,
YOU DID SAY YOU WOULD "NEVER GET CLOSE," DIDN'T YOU.
IF I REMEMBER CORRECTLY.
THOK
ガゴ
WHOA...!
WHAM
ガッタン
OWW!
WHAT WAS THAT FOR?!
YOU KICKED MY CHAIR!
HUH? YOU SAY SOME-THING?

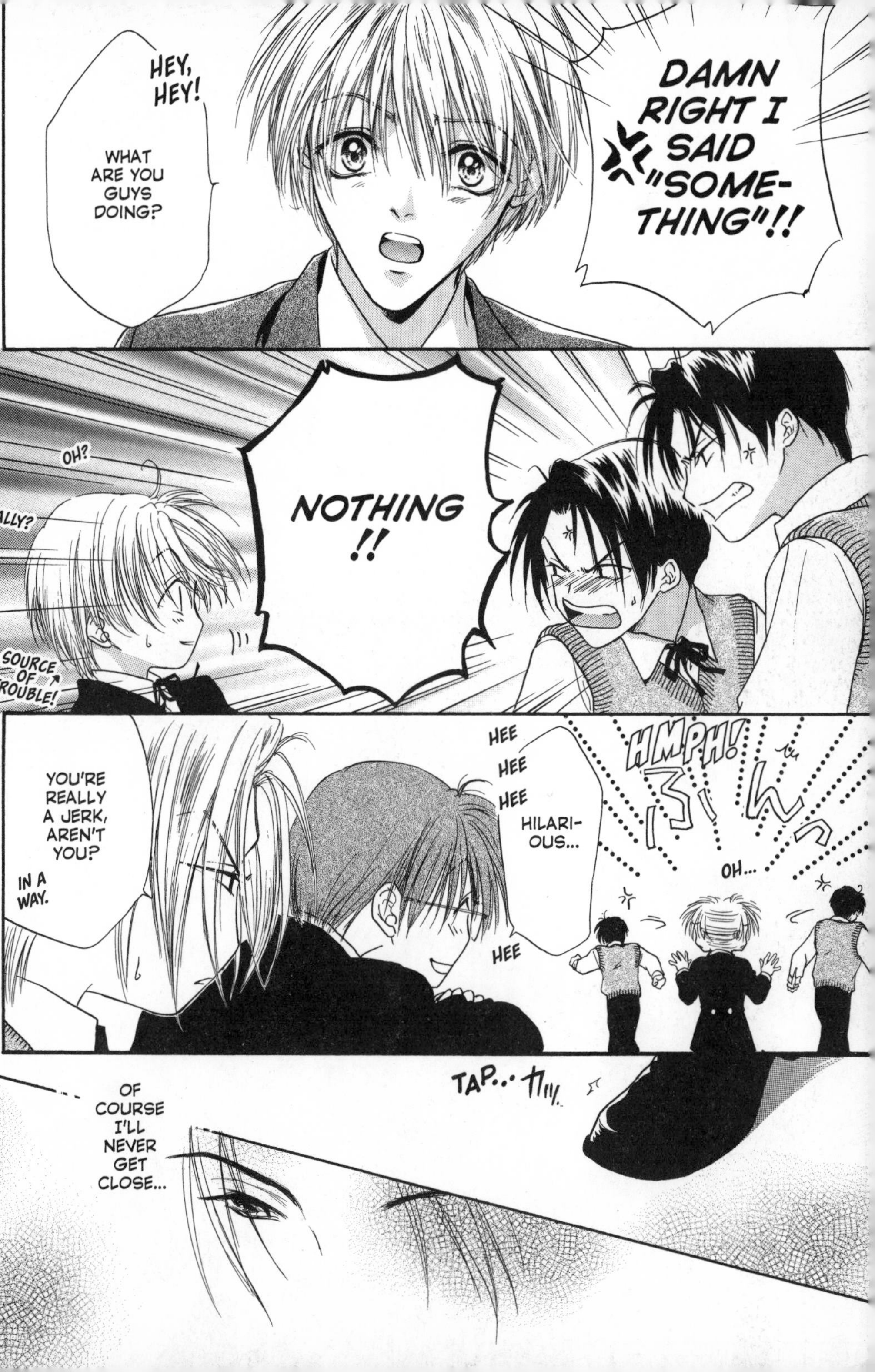
DAMN RIGHT I SAID "SOME-THING"!!
HEY, HEY!
WHAT ARE YOU GUYS DOING?
NOTHING!!
OH?
REALLY?
SOURCE OF TROUBLE!
HMPH!
ふん
OH...
HEE HEE HEE
HILARI-OUS...
HEE
YOU'RE REALLY A JERK, AREN'T YOU?
IN A WAY.
TAP...
OF COURSE I'LL NEVER GET CLOSE...

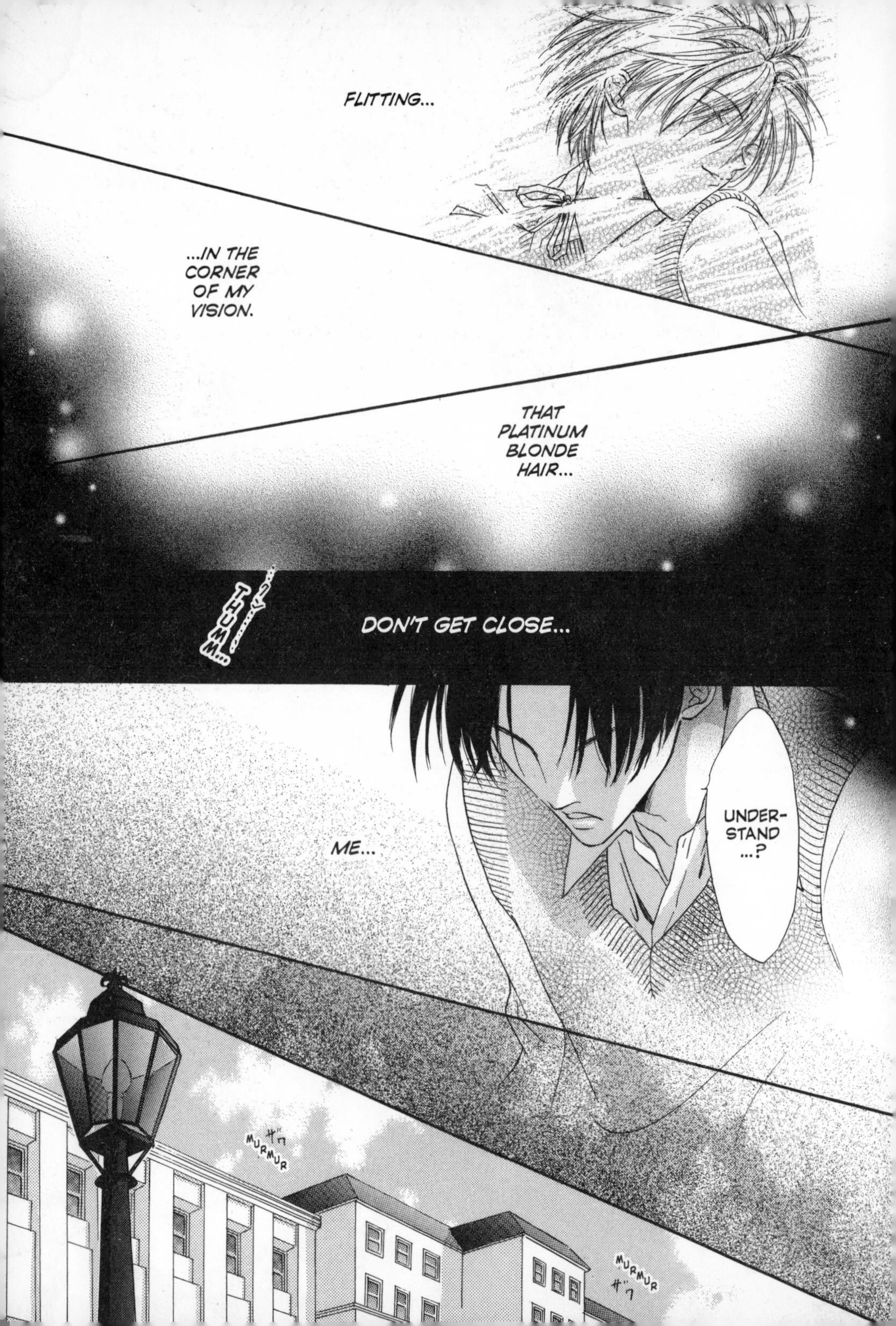
FLITTING...
...IN THE CORNER OF MY VISION.
THAT PLATINUM BLONDE HAIR...
DON'T GET CLOSE...
THUMM...
UNDER-STAND ...?
ME...
ザワ
MURMUR
MURMUR
ザワ

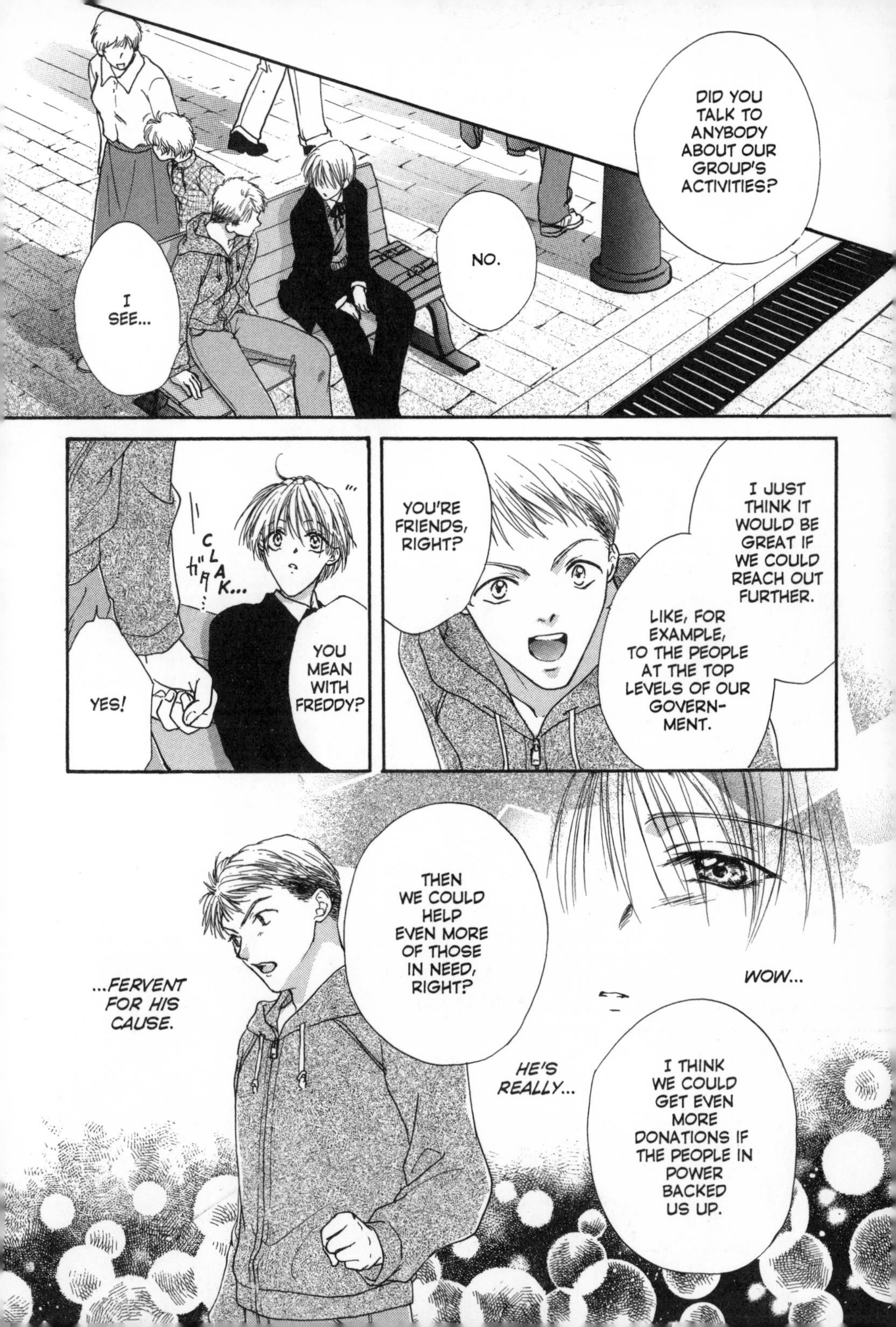
DID YOU TALK TO ANYBODY ABOUT OUR GROUP'S ACTIVITIES?
NO.
I SEE...
I JUST THINK IT WOULD BE GREAT IF WE COULD REACH OUT FURTHER.
LIKE, FOR EXAMPLE, TO THE PEOPLE AT THE TOP LEVELS OF OUR GOVERNMENT.
YOU'RE FRIENDS, RIGHT?
YOU MEAN WITH FREDDY?
CLAK...
YES!
THEN WE COULD HELP EVEN MORE OF THOSE IN NEED, RIGHT?
WOW...
I THINK WE COULD GET EVEN MORE DONATIONS IF THE PEOPLE IN POWER BACKED US UP.
HE'S REALLY...
...FERVENT FOR HIS CAUSE.

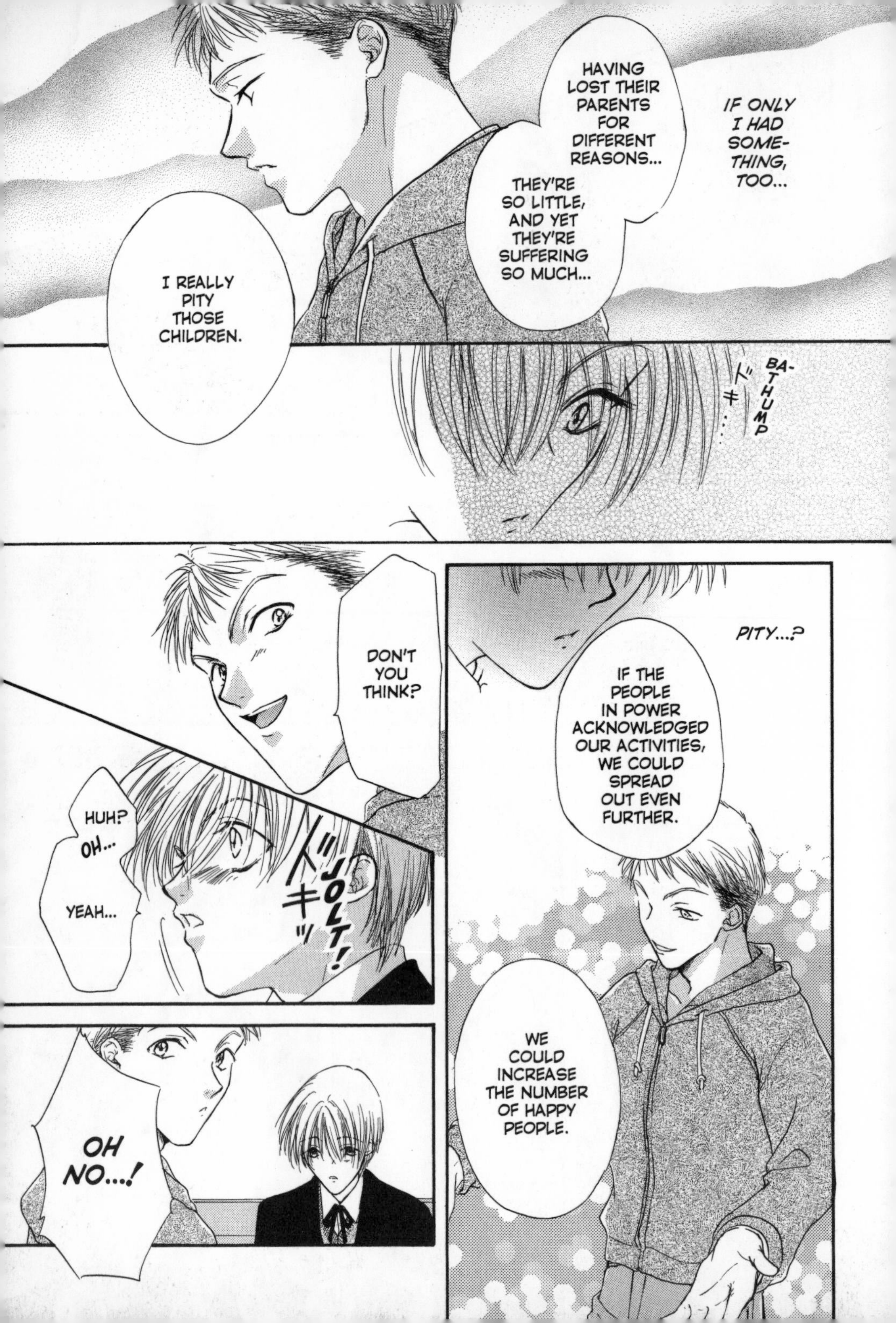
IF ONLY I HAD SOME-THING, TOO...
HAVING LOST THEIR PARENTS FOR DIFFERENT REASONS...
THEY'RE SO LITTLE, AND YET THEY'RE SUFFERING SO MUCH...
I REALLY PITY THOSE CHILDREN.
BA-THUMP
PITY...?
IF THE PEOPLE IN POWER ACKNOWLEDGED OUR ACTIVITIES, WE COULD SPREAD OUT EVEN FURTHER.
WE COULD INCREASE THE NUMBER OF HAPPY PEOPLE.
DON'T YOU THINK?
HUH? OH... YEAH...
JOLT!
OH NO...!

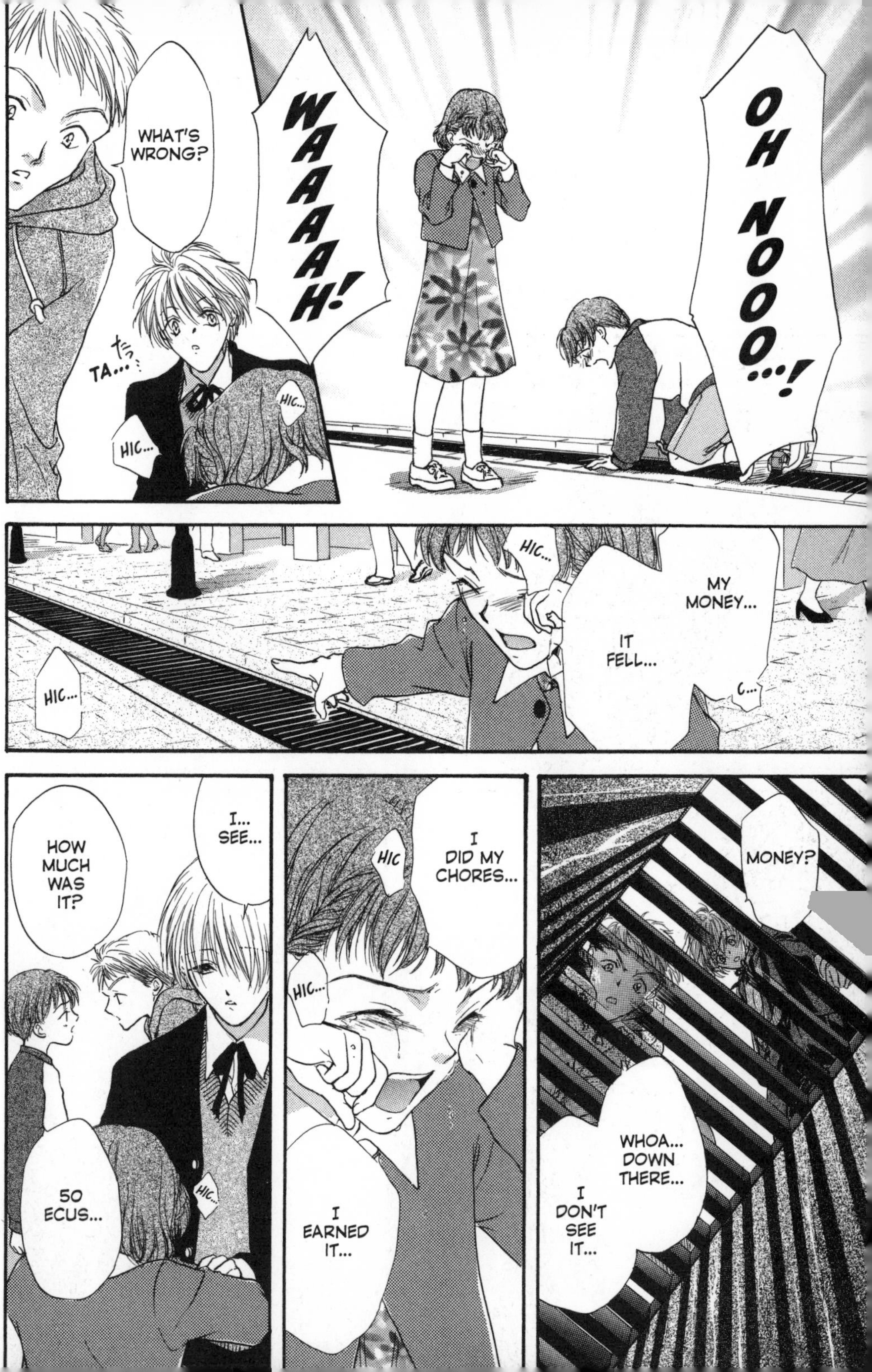
OH NOOOO...!
WAAAAAH!
WHAT'S WRONG?
TA...
HIC...
HIC...
HIC...
MY MONEY...
IT FELL...
C...
HIC...
MONEY?
WHOA... DOWN THERE...
I DON'T SEE IT...
HIC
I DID MY CHORES...
HIC...
I EARNED IT...
I... SEE...
HOW MUCH WAS IT?
HIC...
50 ECUS...

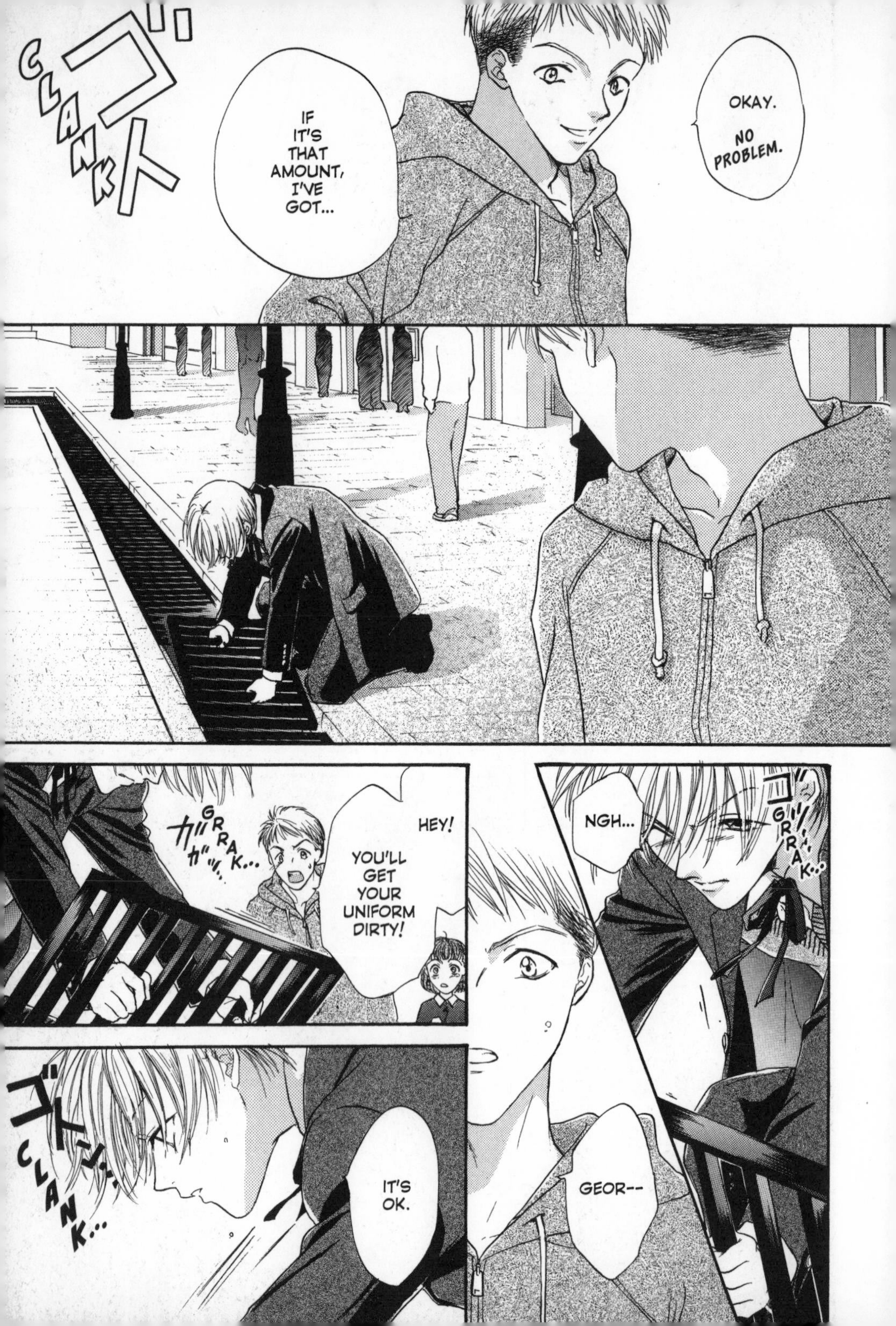

CLANK
OKAY.
NO PROBLEM.
IF IT'S THAT AMOUNT, I'VE GOT...
GRRAK...
NGH...
GEOR--
HEY!
YOU'LL GET YOUR UNIFORM DIRTY!
GRRAK...
CLANK...
IT'S OK.

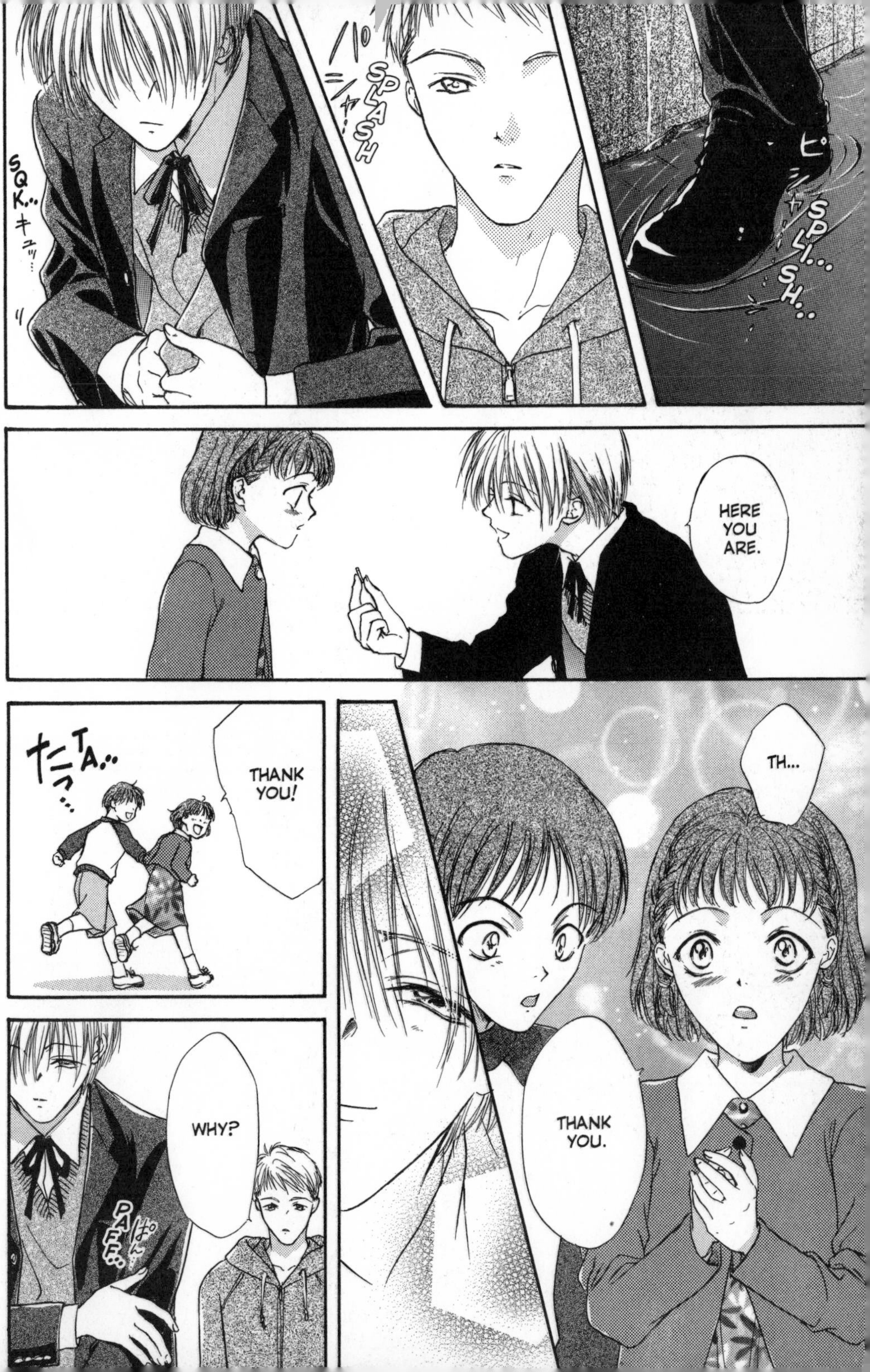
SPLI... SH...
SPLASH
SQK...
HERE YOU ARE.
TH...
THANK YOU.
THANK YOU!
TA...
WHY?
PAFF..

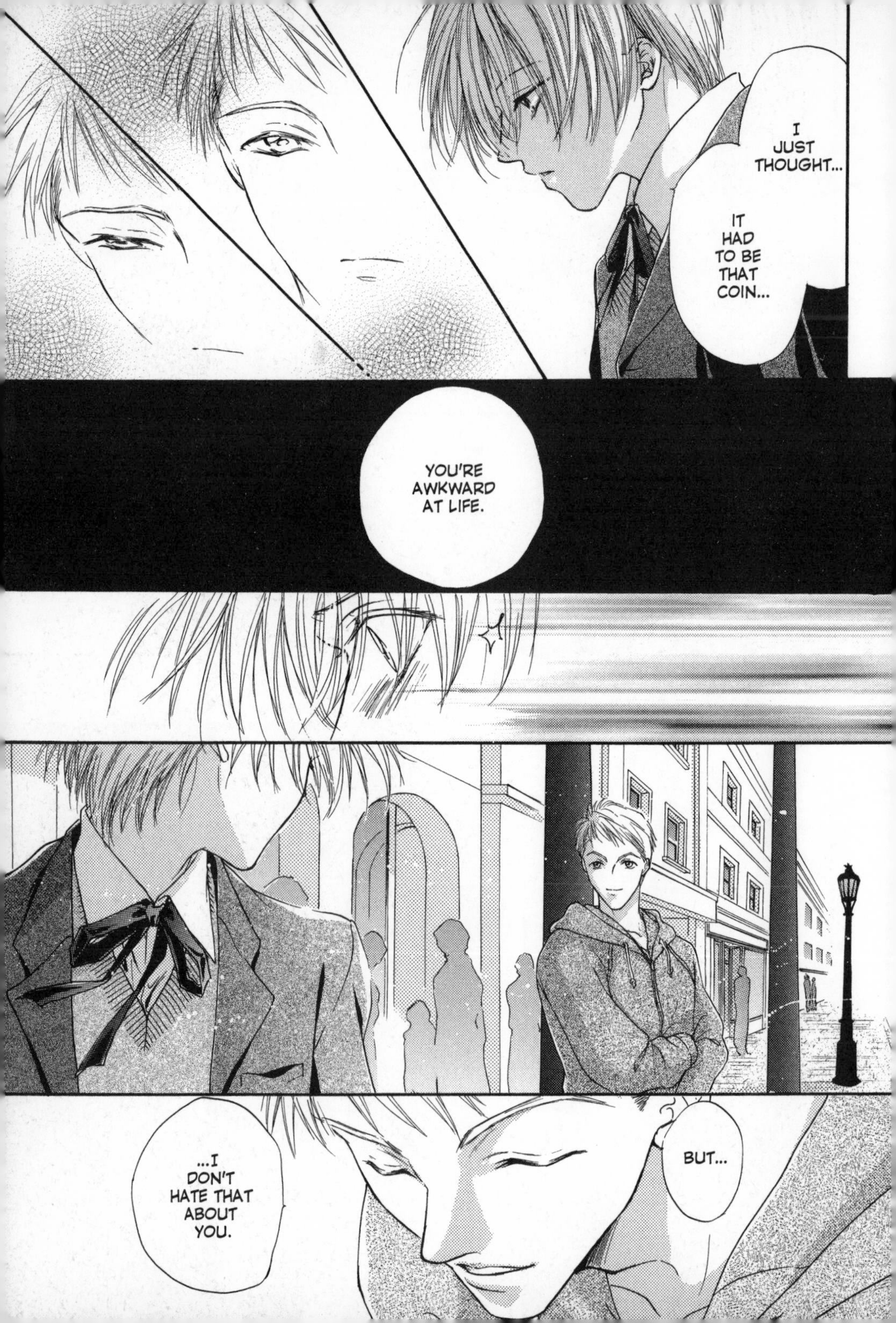
I JUST THOUGHT...
IT HAD TO BE THAT COIN...
YOU'RE AWKWARD AT LIFE.
BUT...
...I DON'T HATE THAT ABOUT YOU.

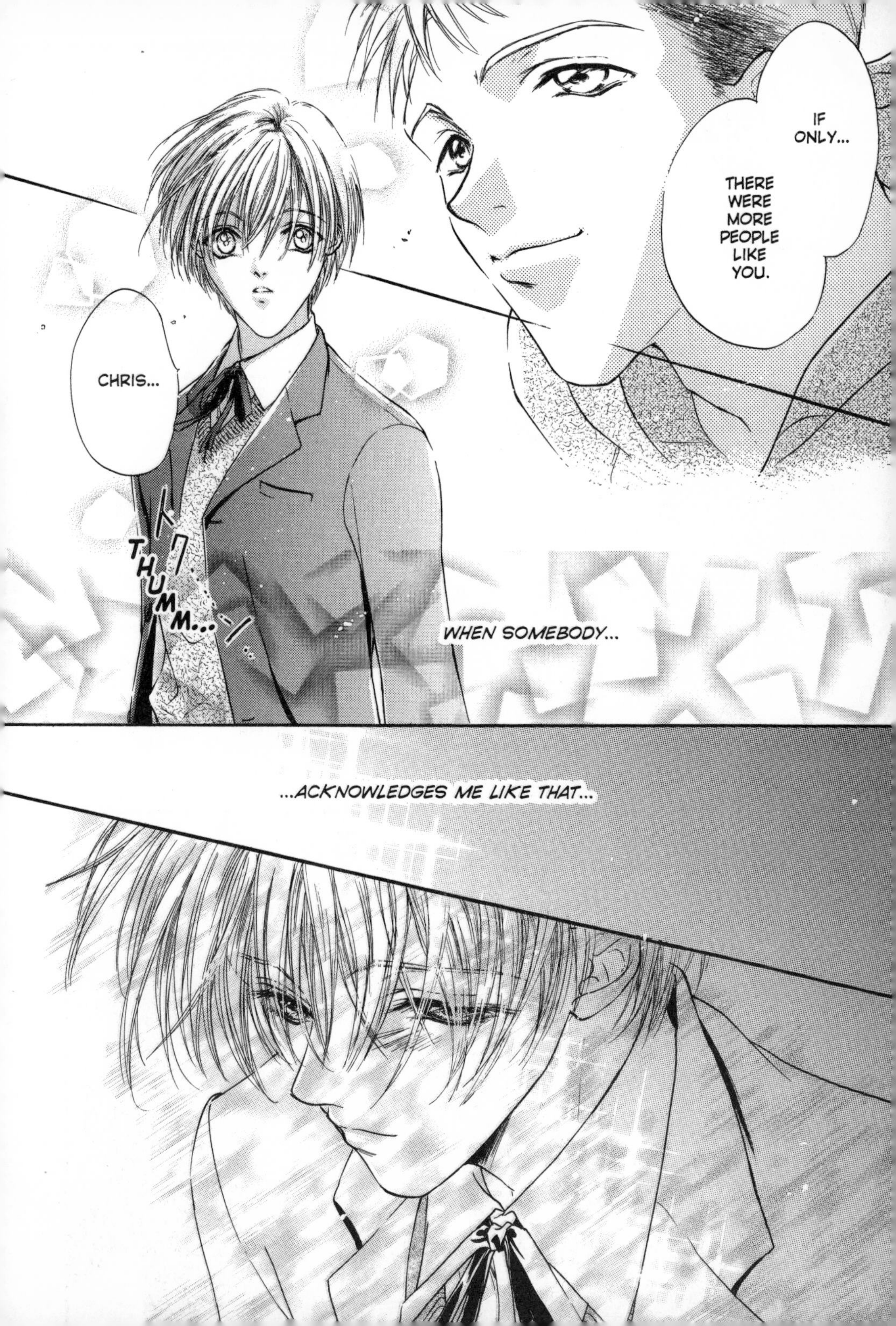
IF ONLY...
THERE WERE MORE PEOPLE LIKE YOU.
CHRIS...
THUMM...
WHEN SOMEBODY...
...ACKNOWLEDGES ME LIKE THAT...

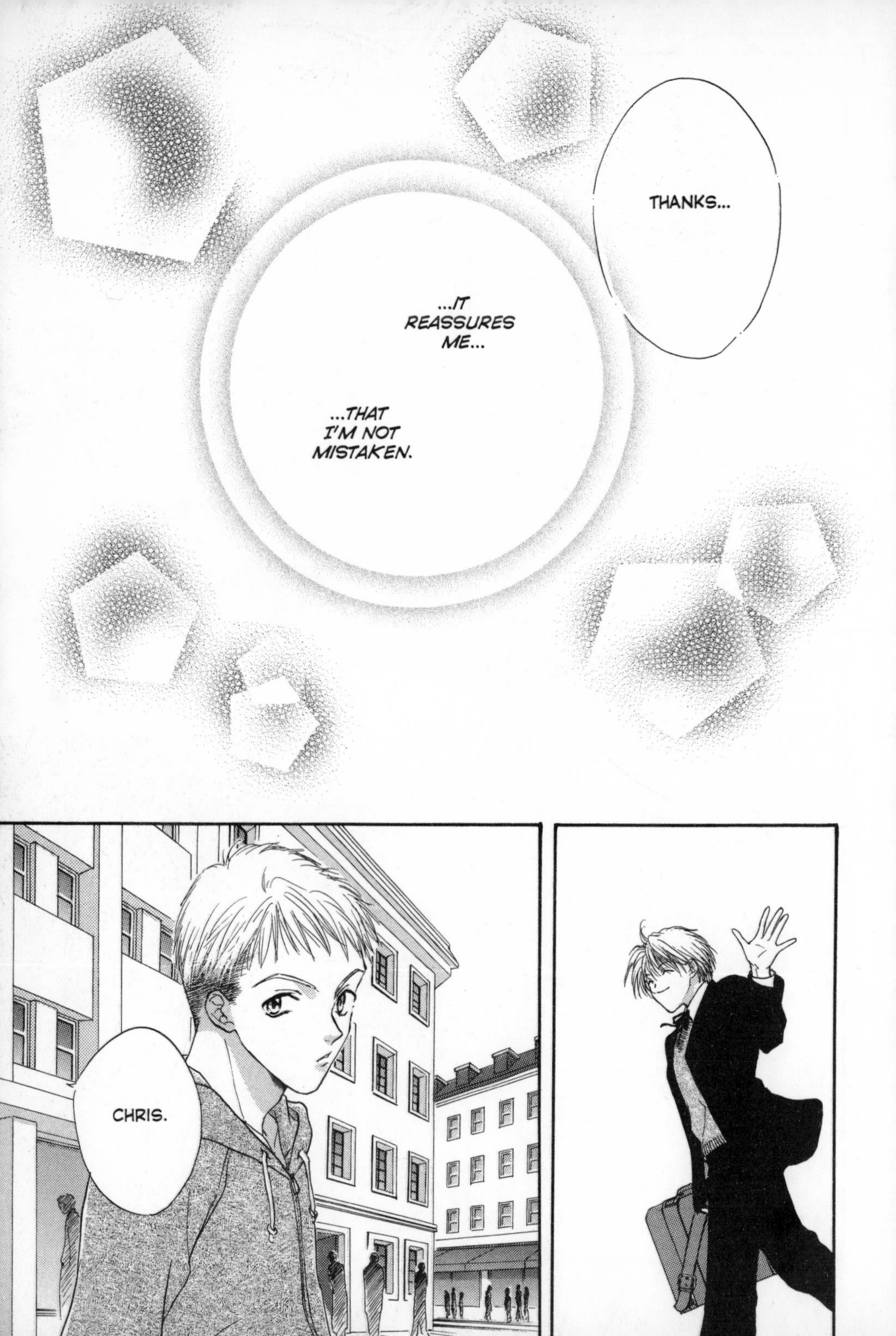
THANKS...
...IT REASSURES ME...
...THAT I'M NOT MISTAKEN.
CHRIS.

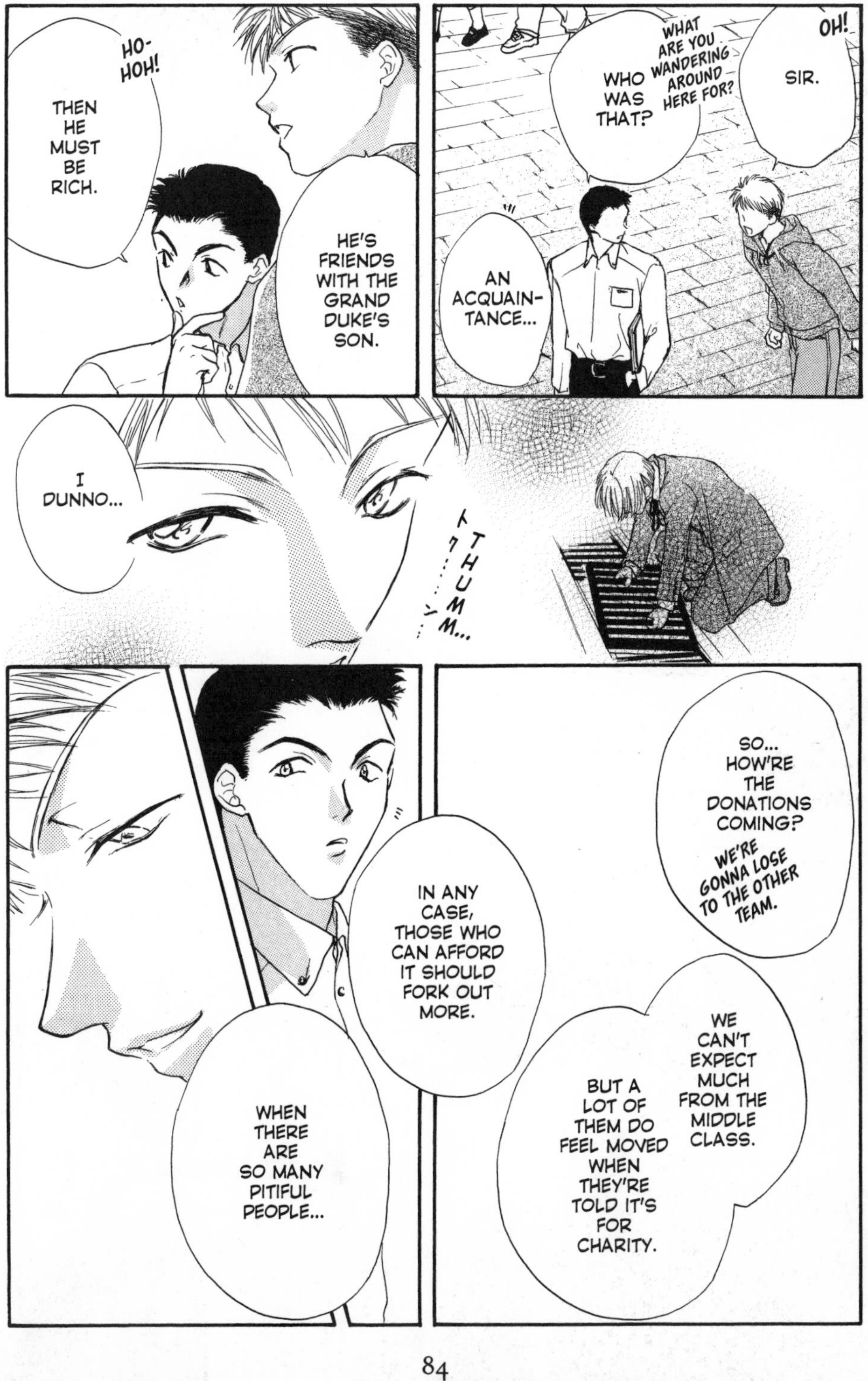
OH!
SIR.
WHAT ARE YOU WANDERING AROUND HERE FOR?
WHO WAS THAT?
AN ACQUAINTANCE...
HE'S FRIENDS WITH THE GRAND DUKE'S SON.
HO-HOH!
THEN HE MUST BE RICH.
THUMM THUMM...
I DUNNO...
SO... HOW'RE THE DONATIONS COMING?
WE'RE GONNA LOSE TO THE OTHER TEAM.
WE CAN'T EXPECT MUCH FROM THE MIDDLE CLASS.
BUT A LOT OF THEM DO FEEL MOVED WHEN THEY'RE TOLD IT'S FOR CHARITY.
IN ANY CASE, THOSE WHO CAN AFFORD IT SHOULD FORK OUT MORE.
WHEN THERE ARE SO MANY PITIFUL PEOPLE...

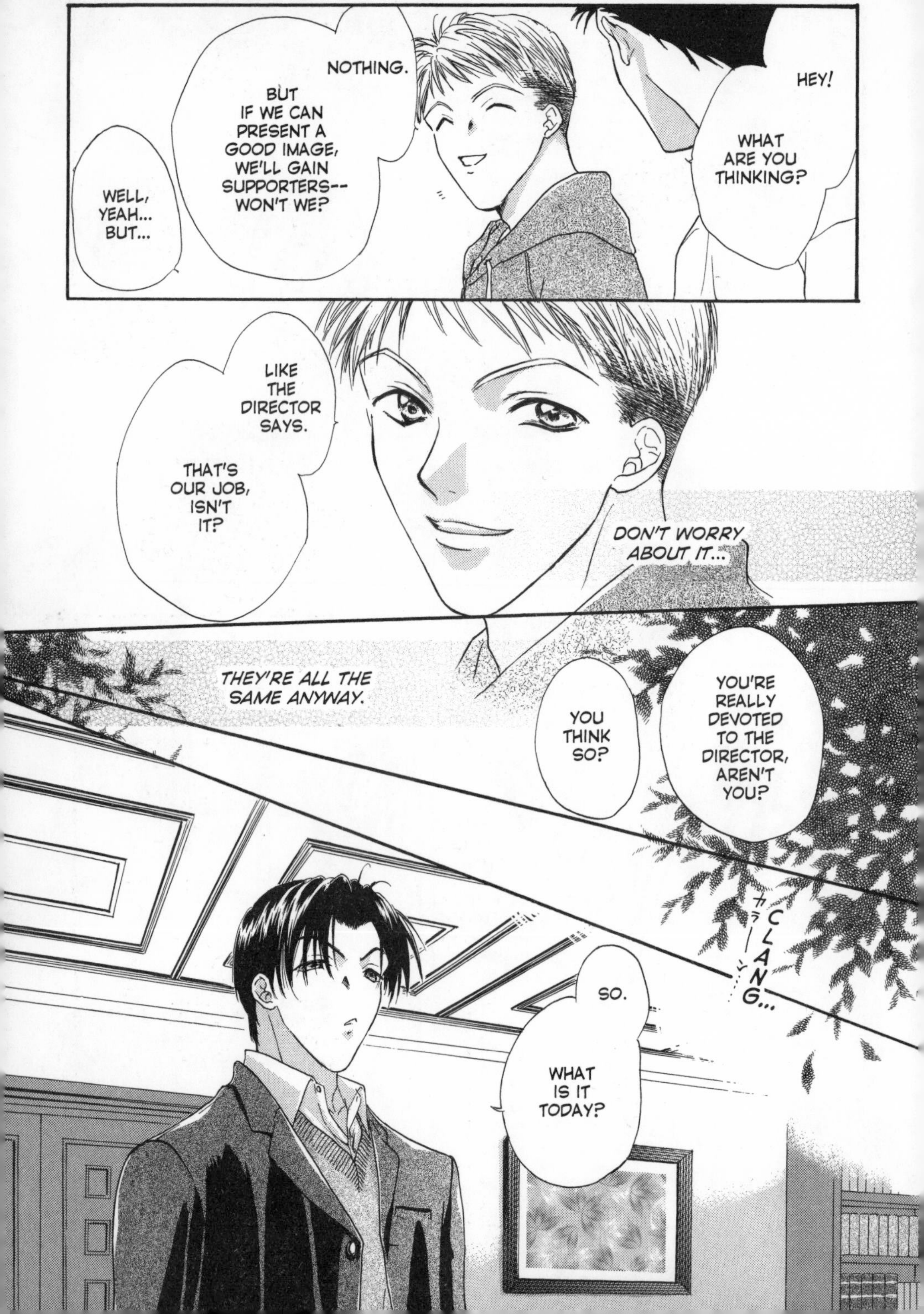
HEY!
WHAT ARE YOU THINKING?
NOTHING.
BUT IF WE CAN PRESENT A GOOD IMAGE, WE'LL GAIN SUPPORTERS-- WON'T WE?
WELL, YEAH... BUT...
LIKE THE DIRECTOR SAYS.
THAT'S OUR JOB, ISN'T IT?
YOU'RE REALLY DEVOTED TO THE DIRECTOR, AREN'T YOU?
YOU THINK SO?
DON'T WORRY ABOUT IT...
THEY'RE ALL THE SAME ANYWAY.
カラーン
CLANG...
SO.
WHAT IS IT TODAY?

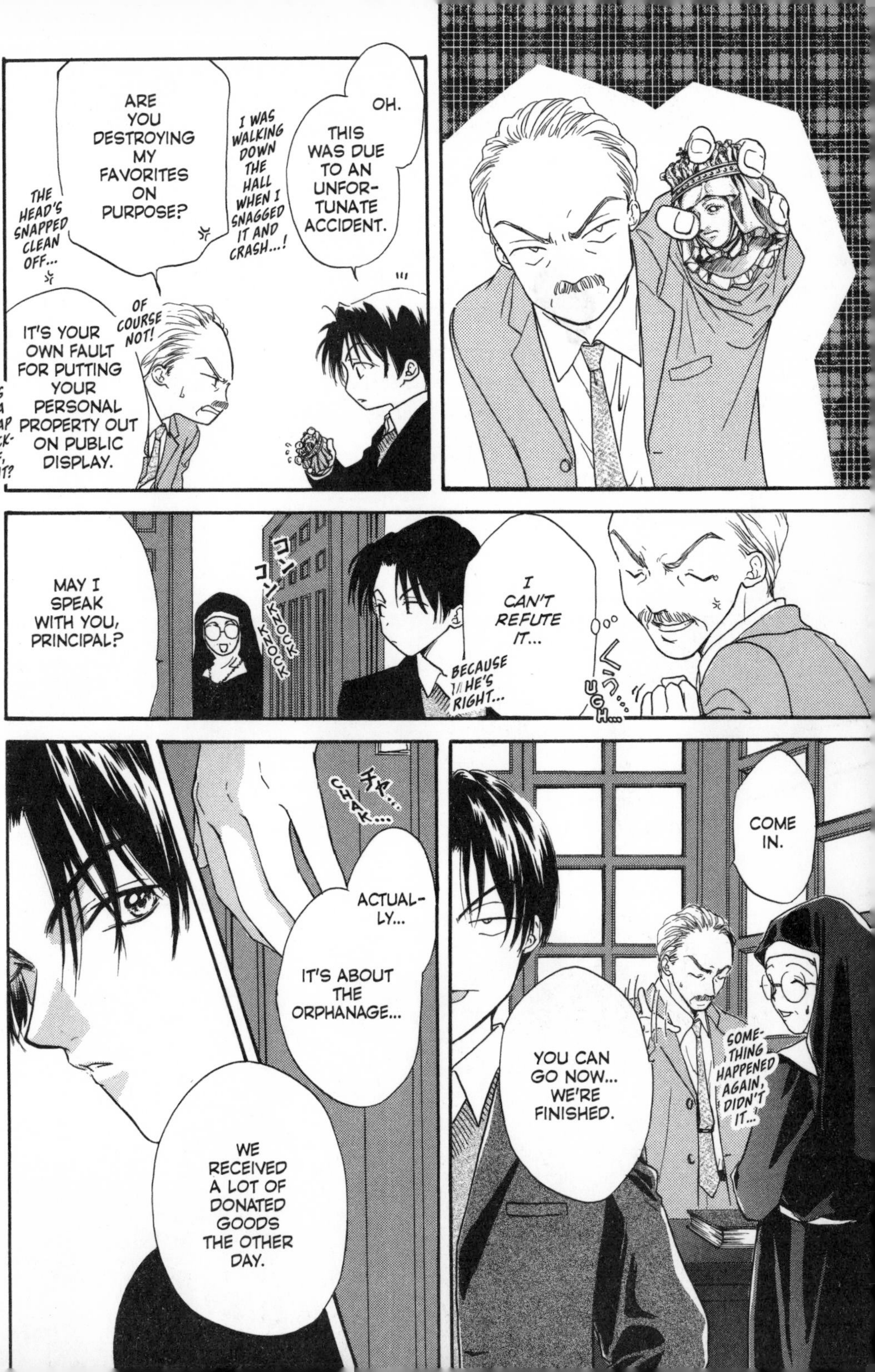
OH.
THIS WAS DUE TO AN UNFORTUNATE ACCIDENT.
I WAS WALKING DOWN THE HALL WHEN I SNAGGED IT AND CRASH...!
ARE YOU DESTROYING MY FAVORITES ON PURPOSE?
THE HEAD'S SNAPPED CLEAN OFF...
OF COURSE NOT!
IT'S YOUR OWN FAULT FOR PUTTING YOUR PERSONAL PROPERTY OUT ON PUBLIC DISPLAY.
THIS IS A CHEAP KNOCK-OFF, RIGHT?
UGH...
I CAN'T REFUTE IT...
BECAUSE HE'S RIGHT...
コン コン KNOCK KNOCK
MAY I SPEAK WITH YOU, PRINCIPAL?
COME IN.
SOMETHING HAPPENED AGAIN, DIDN'T IT...
YOU CAN GO NOW... WE'RE FINISHED.
チャ... CHAK...
ACTUALLY...
IT'S ABOUT THE ORPHANAGE...
WE RECEIVED A LOT OF DONATED GOODS THE OTHER DAY.

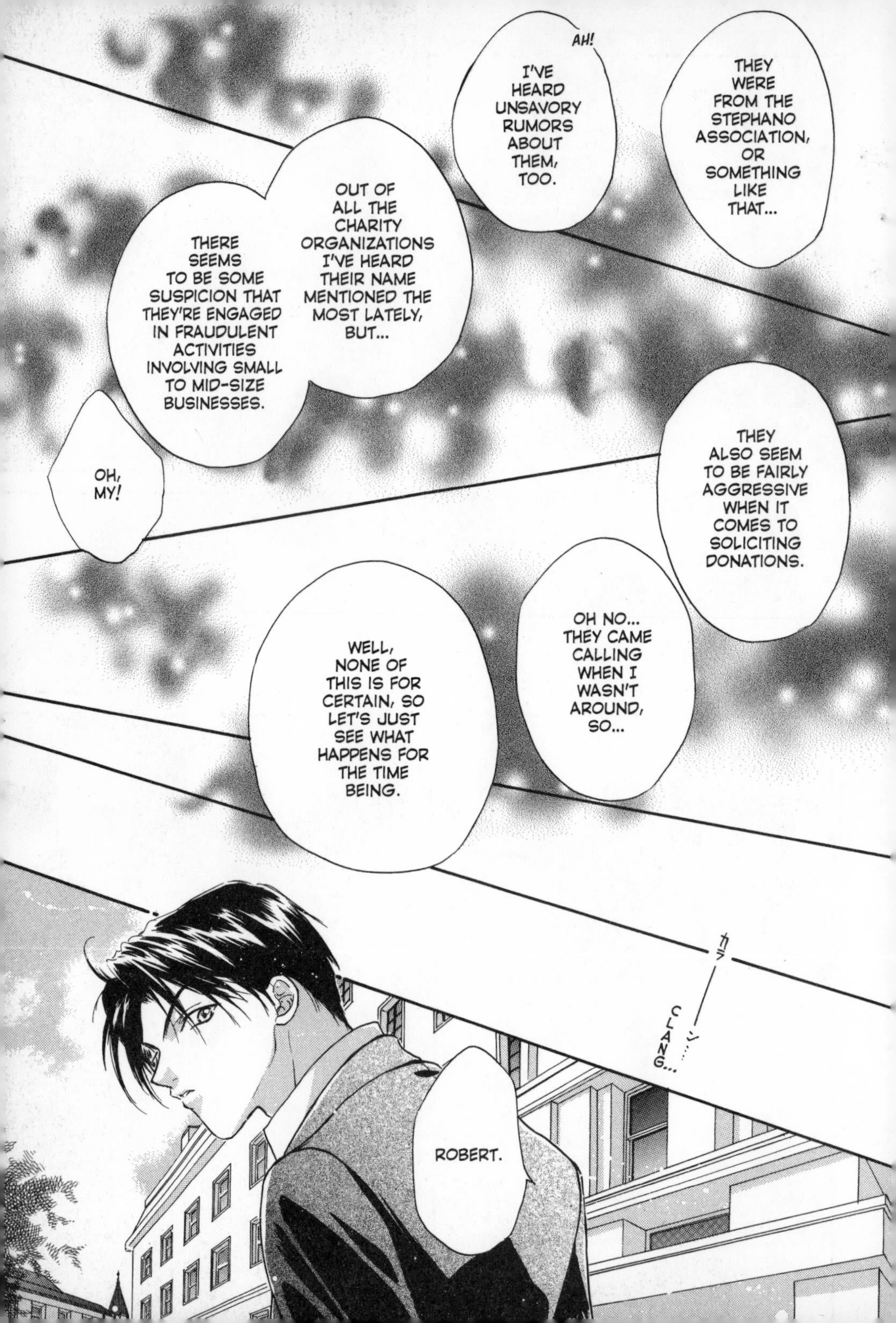
THEY WERE FROM THE STEPHANO ASSOCIATION, OR SOMETHING LIKE THAT...
AH! I'VE HEARD UNSAVORY RUMORS ABOUT THEM, TOO.
OUT OF ALL THE CHARITY ORGANIZATIONS I'VE HEARD THEIR NAME MENTIONED THE MOST LATELY, BUT...
THERE SEEMS TO BE SOME SUSPICION THAT THEY'RE ENGAGED IN FRAUDULENT ACTIVITIES INVOLVING SMALL TO MID-SIZE BUSINESSES.
OH, MY!
THEY ALSO SEEM TO BE FAIRLY AGGRESSIVE WHEN IT COMES TO SOLICITING DONATIONS.
OH NO... THEY CAME CALLING WHEN I WASN'T AROUND, SO...
WELL, NONE OF THIS IS FOR CERTAIN, SO LET'S JUST SEE WHAT HAPPENS FOR THE TIME BEING.
CLANG...
ROBERT.

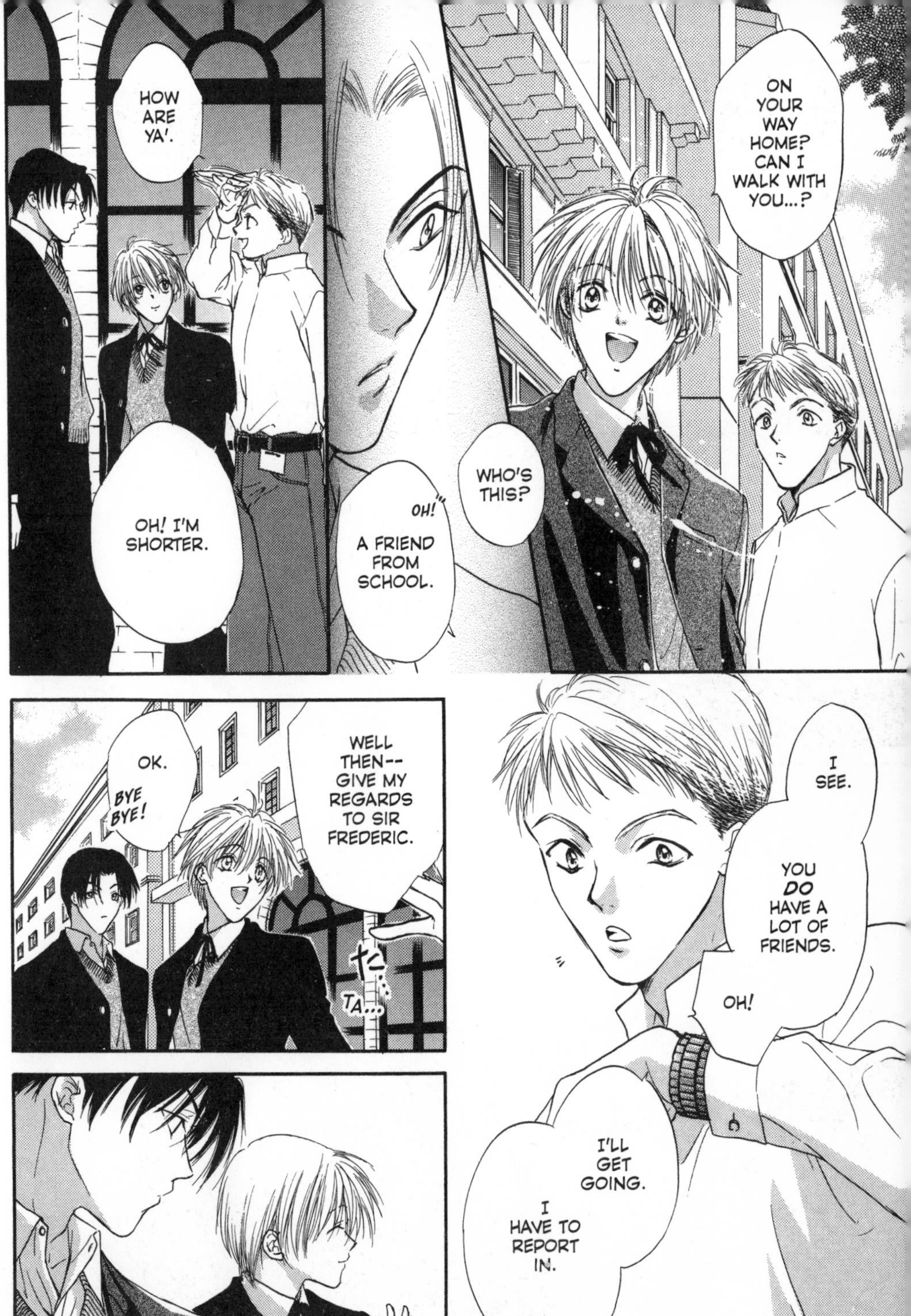
ON YOUR WAY HOME? CAN I WALK WITH YOU...?
WHO'S THIS?
OH!
A FRIEND FROM SCHOOL.
HOW ARE YA'.
OH! I'M SHORTER.
I SEE.
YOU *DO* HAVE A LOT OF FRIENDS.
OH!
I'LL GET GOING.
I HAVE TO REPORT IN.
WELL THEN-- GIVE MY REGARDS TO SIR FREDERIC.
OK.
BYE BYE!
た...
TA...

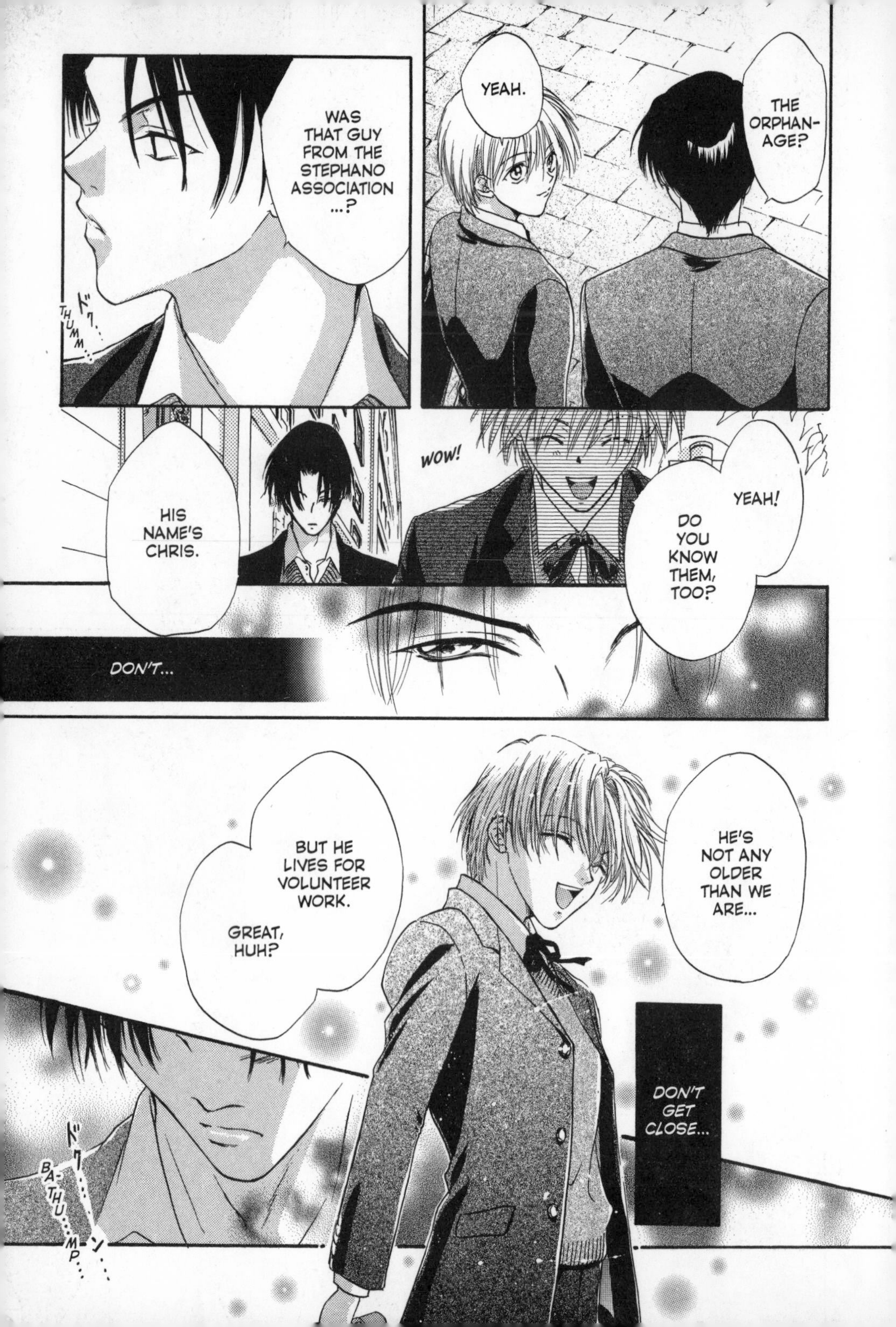
THE ORPHAN-AGE?
YEAH.
WAS THAT GUY FROM THE STEPHANO ASSOCIATION ...?
ドク…
THUMM...
YEAH! DO YOU KNOW THEM, TOO?
WOW!
HIS NAME'S CHRIS.
DON'T...
HE'S NOT ANY OLDER THAN WE ARE...
BUT HE LIVES FOR VOLUNTEER WORK.
GREAT, HUH?
DON'T GET CLOSE...
ドク…ン
BATHU...MP...

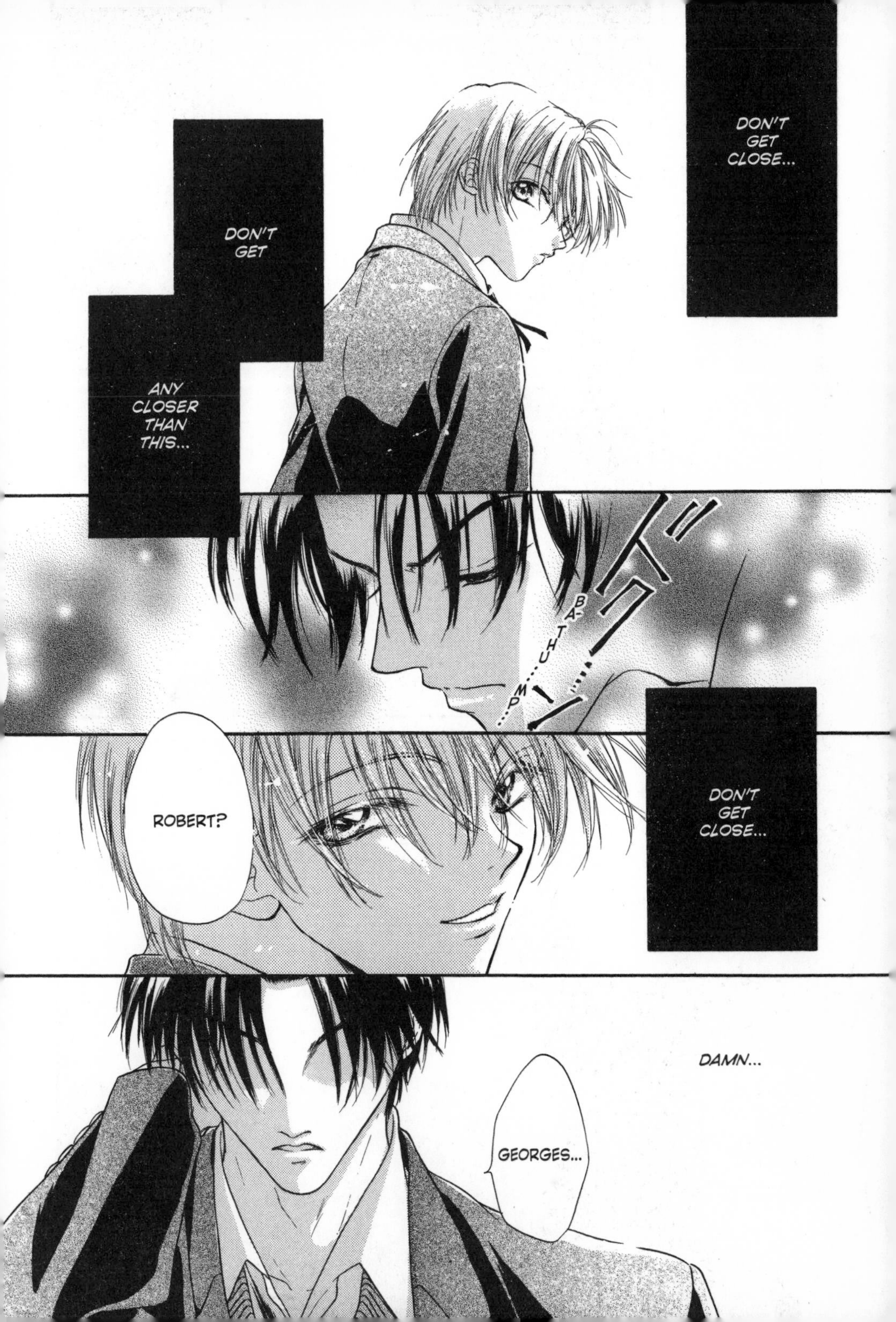
DON'T GET CLOSE...
DON'T GET
ANY CLOSER THAN THIS...
BA-THUMP...
DON'T GET CLOSE...
ROBERT?
DAMN...
GEORGES...

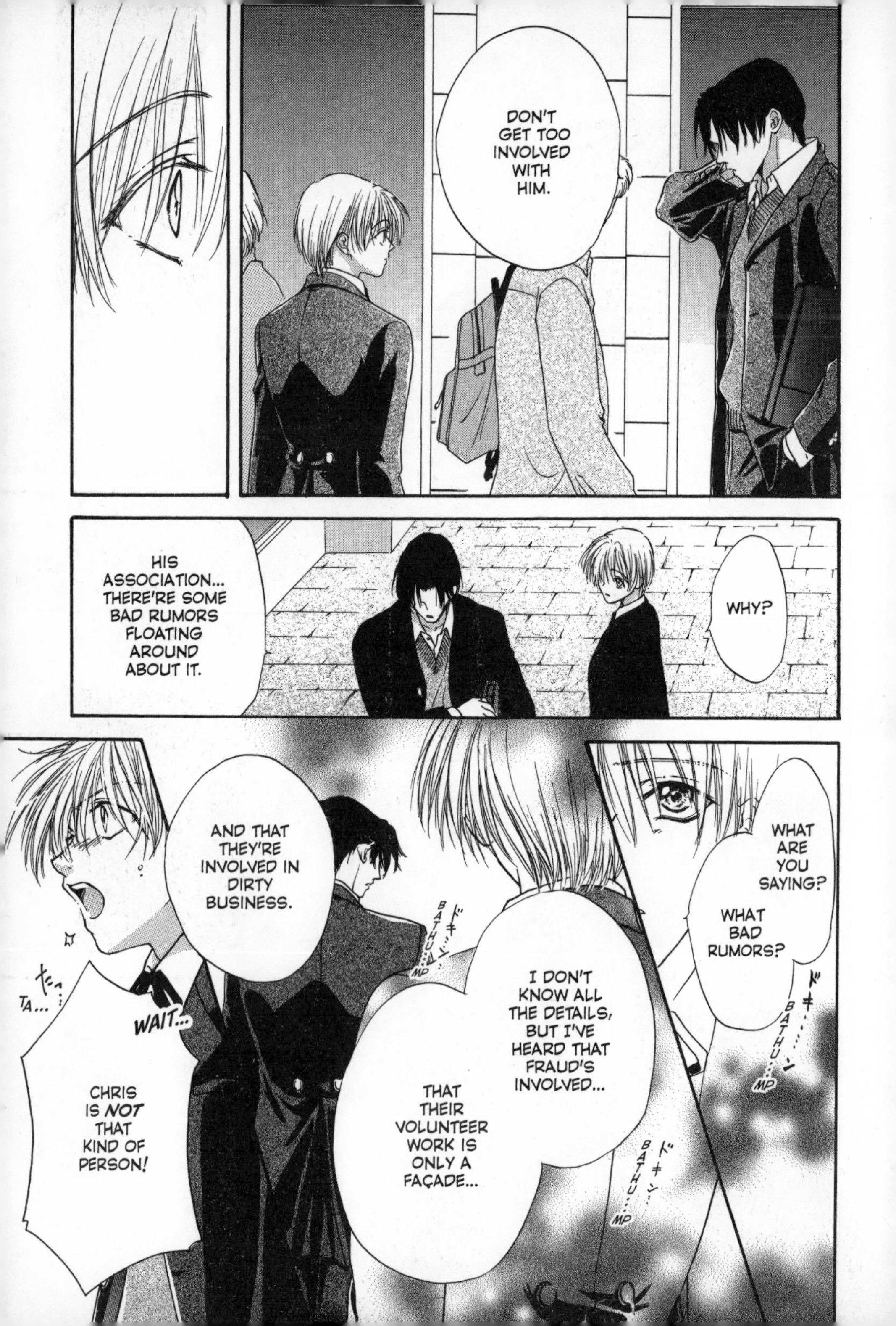
DON'T GET TOO INVOLVED WITH HIM.
WHY?
HIS ASSOCIATION... THERE'RE SOME BAD RUMORS FLOATING AROUND ABOUT IT.
WHAT ARE YOU SAYING?
WHAT BAD RUMORS?
ドキ… BATHU…MP
I DON'T KNOW ALL THE DETAILS, BUT I'VE HEARD THAT FRAUD'S INVOLVED...
THAT THEIR VOLUNTEER WORK IS ONLY A FAÇADE...
ドキン… BATHU…MP
AND THAT THEY'RE INVOLVED IN DIRTY BUSINESS.
ドキン BATHUMP
WAIT...
CHRIS IS NOT THAT KIND OF PERSON!
たっ… TA...

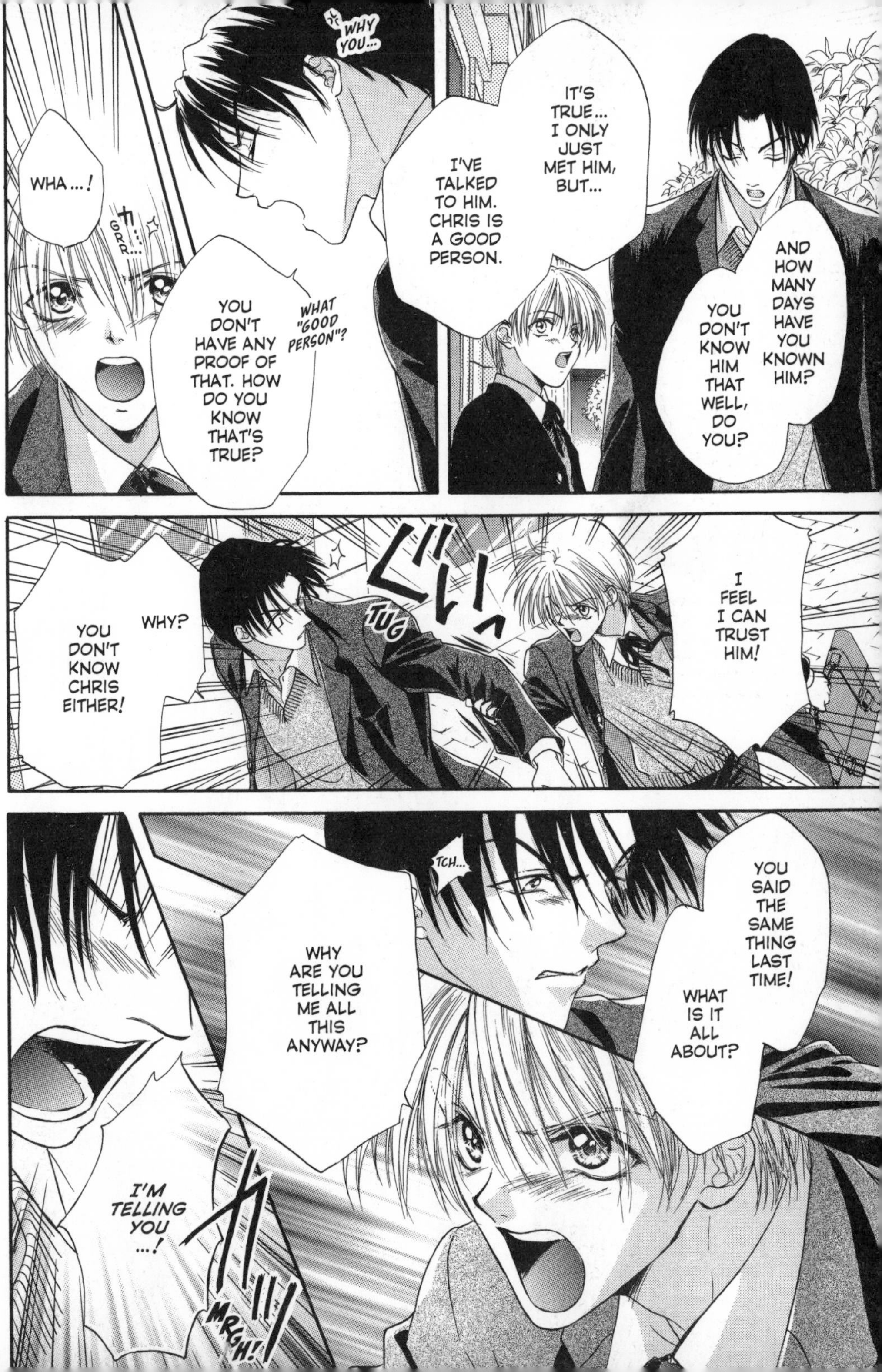
AND HOW MANY DAYS HAVE YOU KNOWN HIM?
YOU DON'T KNOW HIM THAT WELL, DO YOU?
IT'S TRUE... I ONLY JUST MET HIM, BUT...
I'VE TALKED TO HIM. CHRIS IS A GOOD PERSON.
WHY YOU...
WHAT "GOOD PERSON"?
YOU DON'T HAVE ANY PROOF OF THAT. HOW DO YOU KNOW THAT'S TRUE?
WHA...!
GRR...
I FEEL I CAN TRUST HIM!
TUG
WHY?
YOU DON'T KNOW CHRIS EITHER!
YOU SAID THE SAME THING LAST TIME!
WHAT IS IT ALL ABOUT?
TCH...
WHY ARE YOU TELLING ME ALL THIS ANYWAY?
I'M TELLING YOU ...!
MRGH!

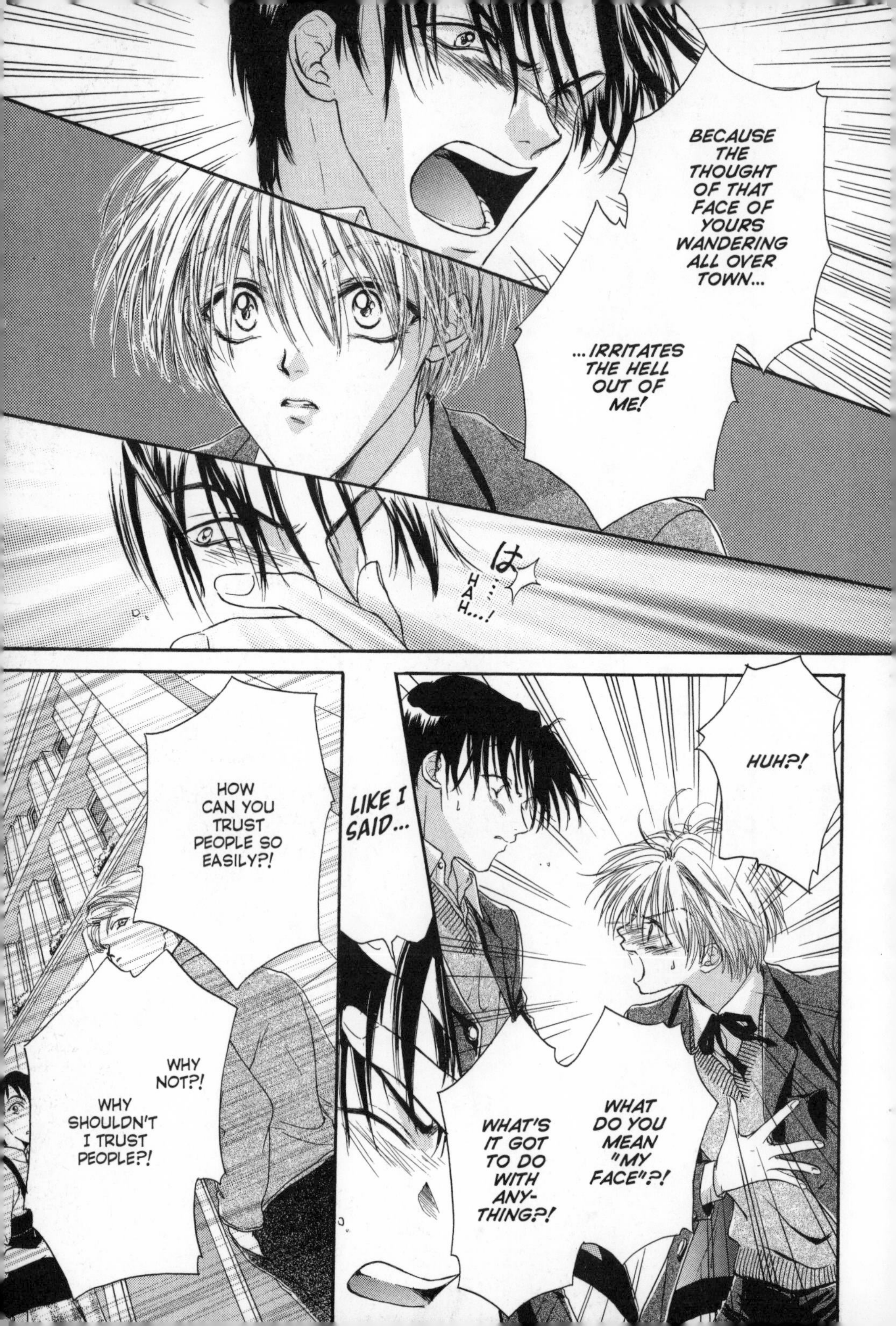
BECAUSE THE THOUGHT OF THAT FACE OF YOURS WANDERING ALL OVER TOWN...
...IRRITATES THE HELL OUT OF ME!
は
HAH...!
HUH?!
LIKE I SAID...
WHAT DO YOU MEAN "MY FACE"?!
WHAT'S IT GOT TO DO WITH ANY-THING?!
HOW CAN YOU TRUST PEOPLE SO EASILY?!
WHY NOT?!
WHY SHOULDN'T I TRUST PEOPLE?!

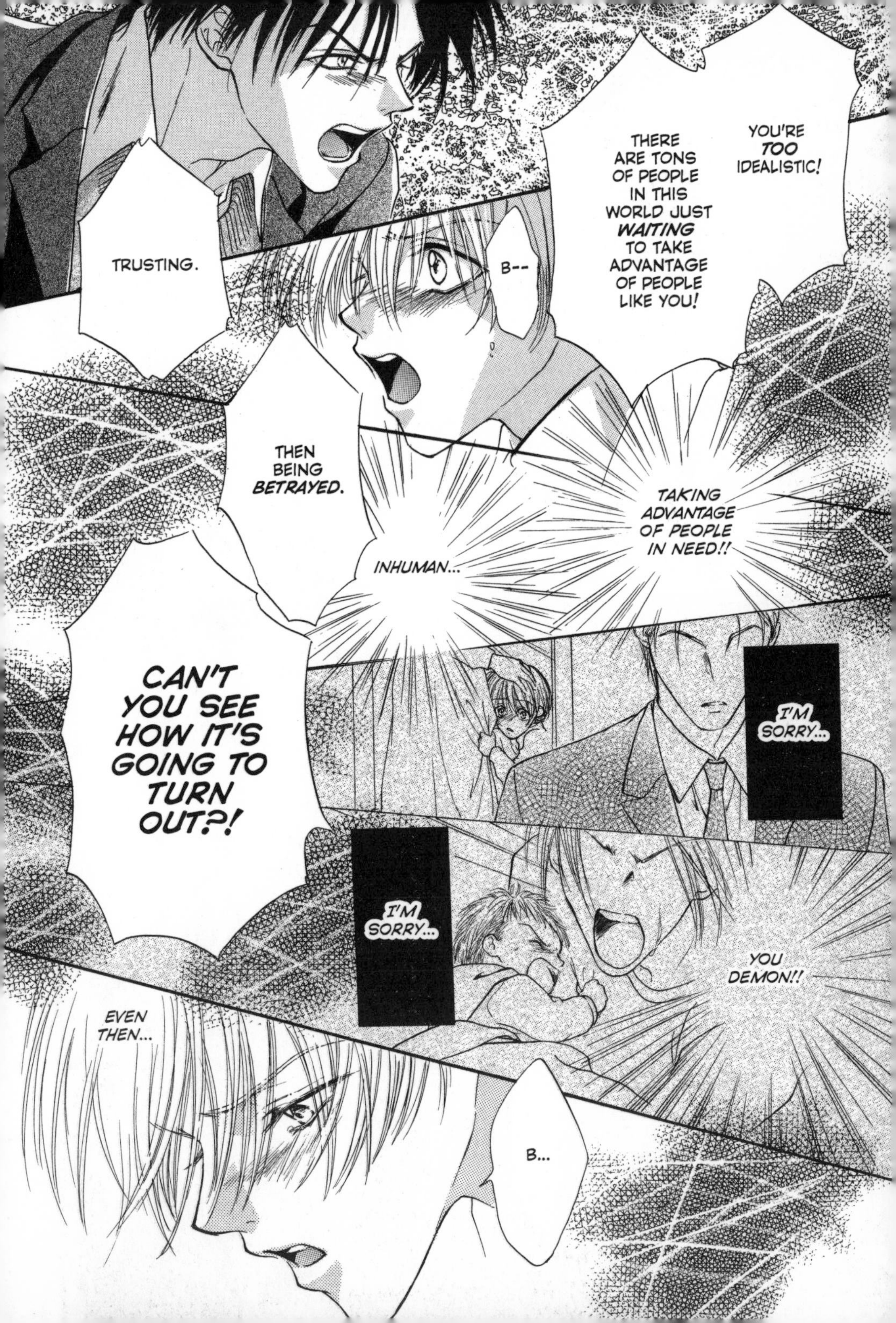

YOU'RE *TOO* IDEALISTIC!
THERE ARE TONS OF PEOPLE IN THIS WORLD JUST *WAITING* TO TAKE ADVANTAGE OF PEOPLE LIKE YOU!
B--
TRUSTING.
THEN BEING *BETRAYED*.
TAKING ADVANTAGE OF PEOPLE IN NEED!!
INHUMAN...
I'M SORRY...
CAN'T YOU SEE HOW IT'S GOING TO TURN OUT?!
YOU DEMON!!
I'M SORRY...
EVEN THEN...
B...

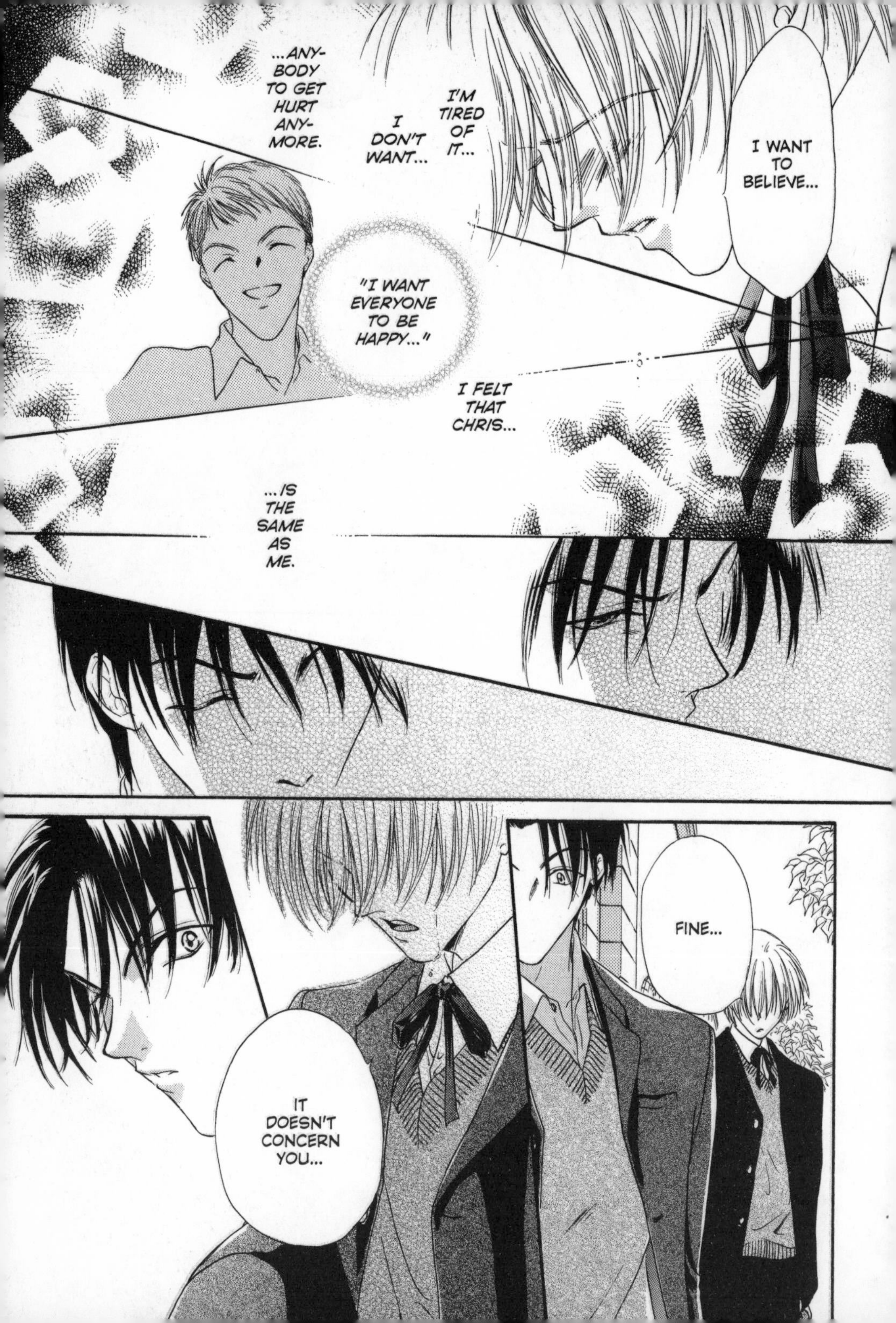
I WANT TO BELIEVE...
I'M TIRED OF IT...
I DON'T WANT...
...ANYBODY TO GET HURT ANYMORE.
"I WANT EVERYONE TO BE HAPPY..."
I FELT THAT CHRIS...
...IS THE SAME AS ME.
FINE...
IT DOESN'T CONCERN YOU...

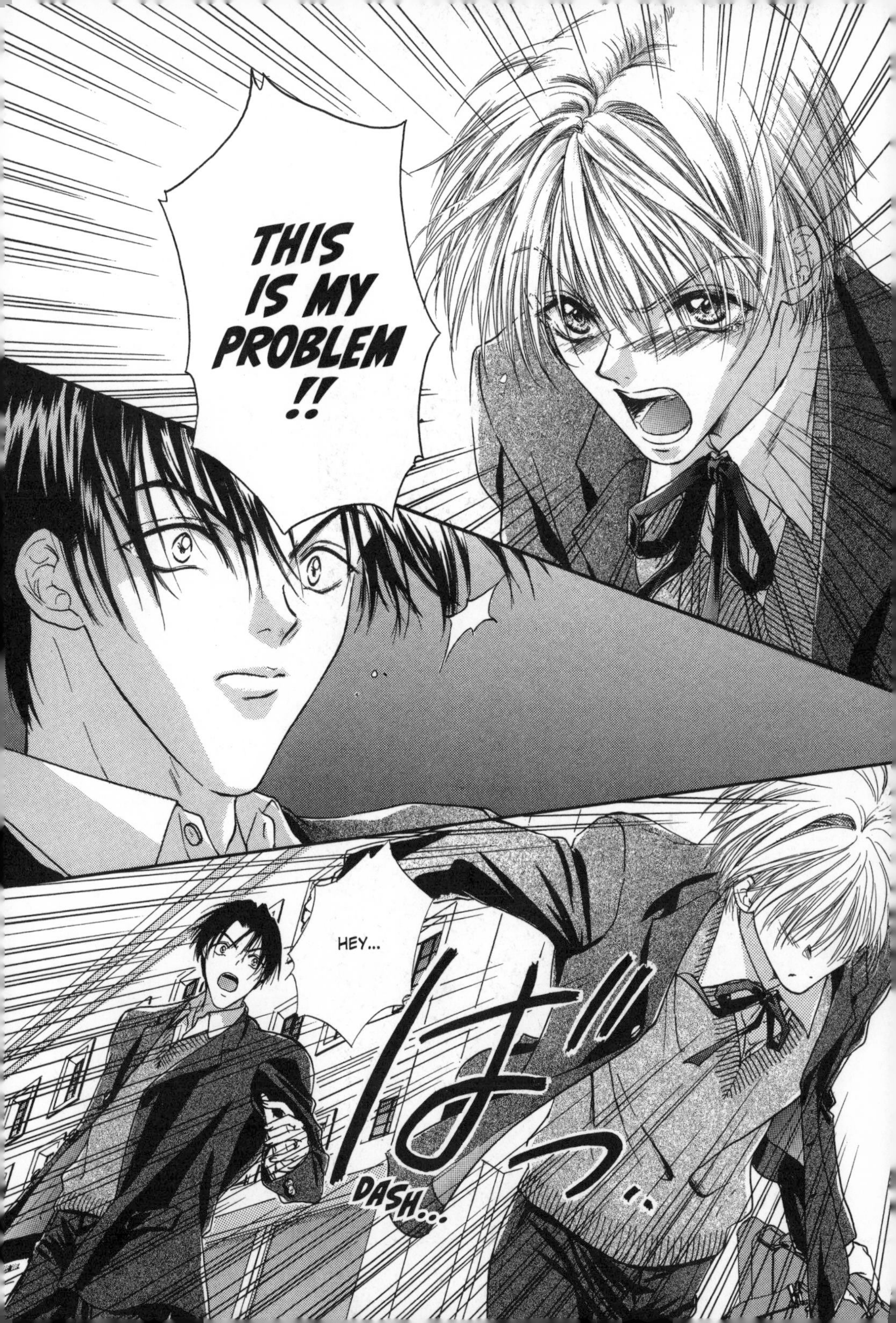
THIS IS MY PROBLEM !!
HEY...
はっ
DASH...

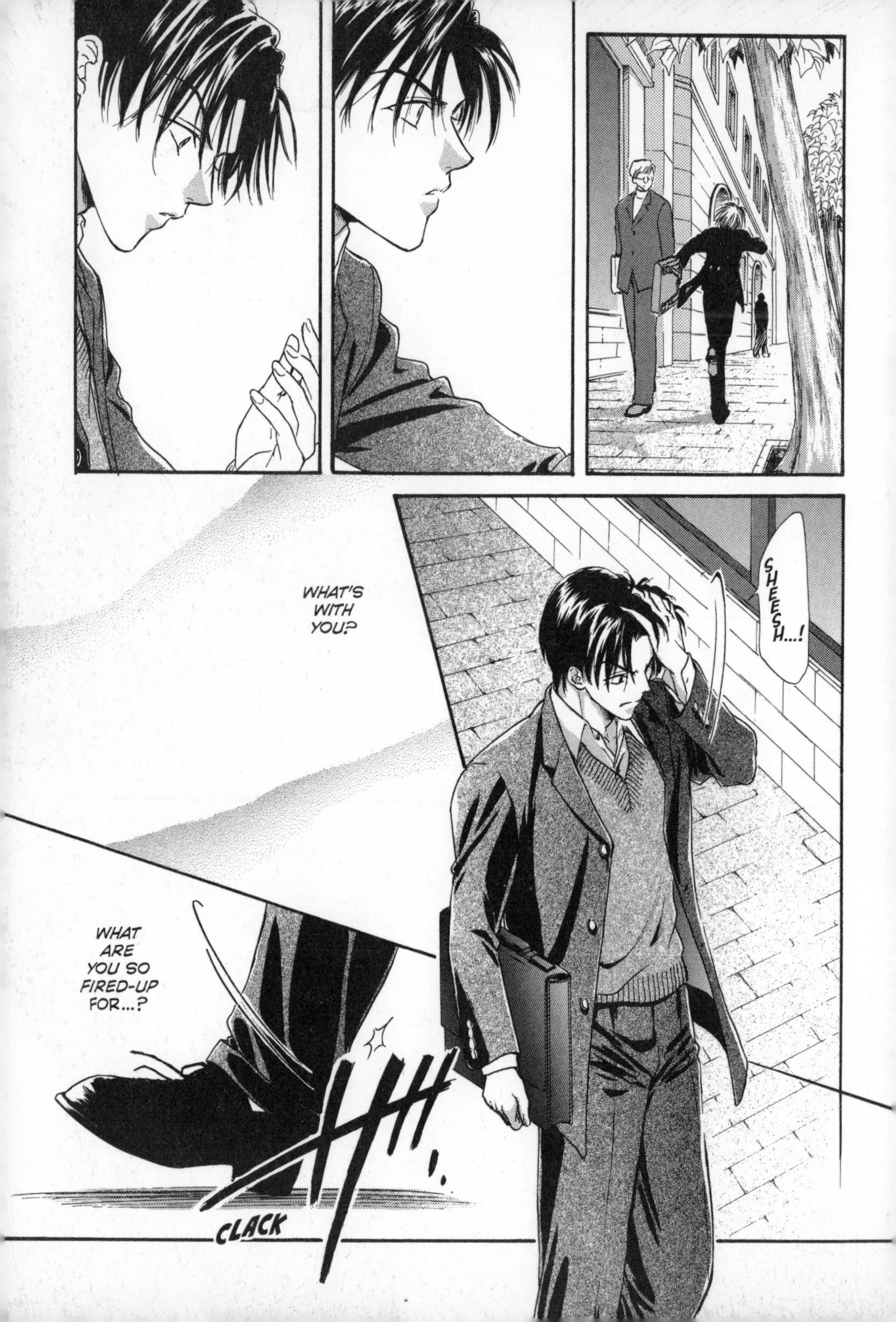
SHEESH...!
WHAT'S WITH YOU?
WHAT ARE YOU SO FIRED-UP FOR...?
CLACK

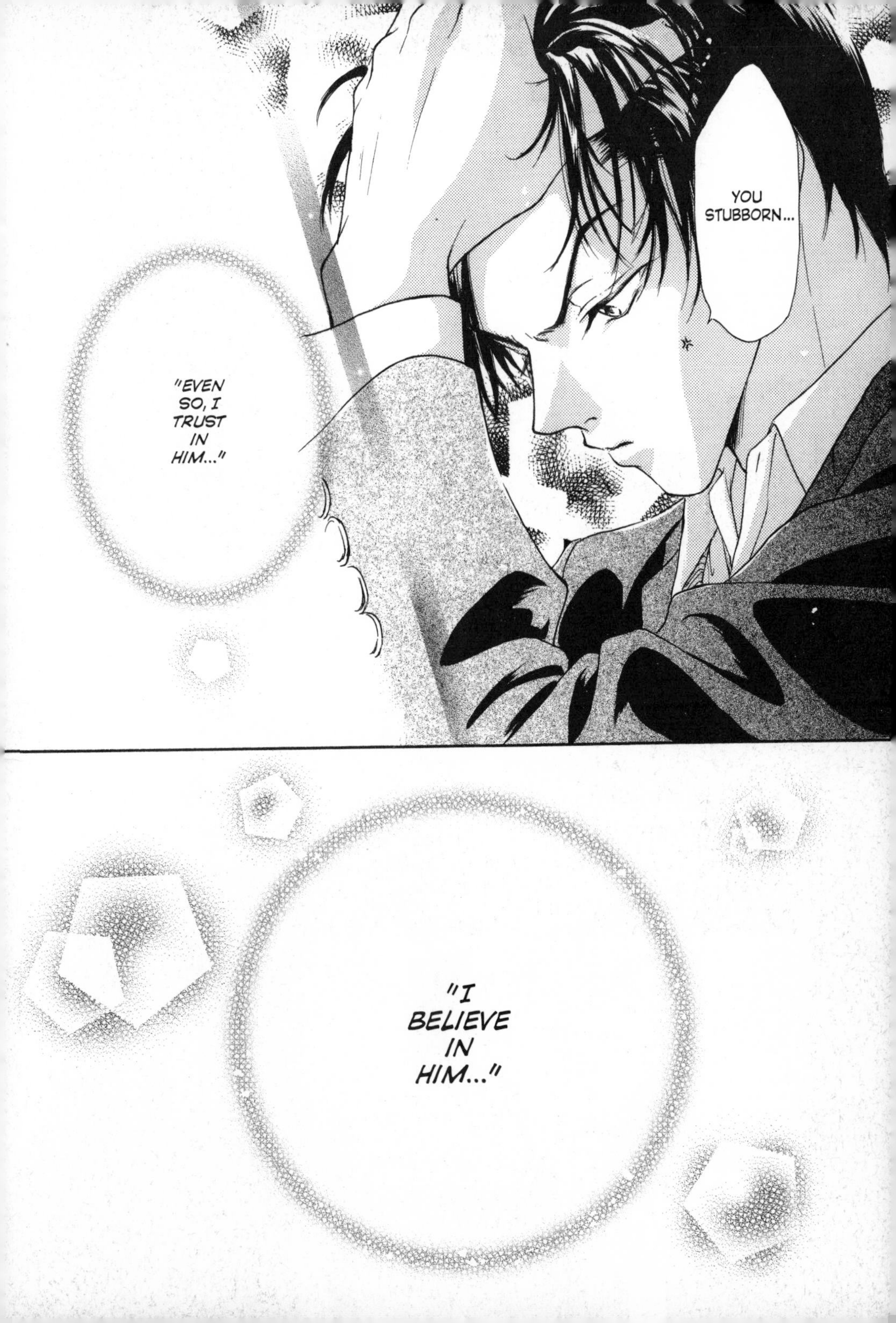
YOU STUBBORN...
"EVEN SO, I TRUST IN HIM..."
"I BELIEVE IN HIM..."

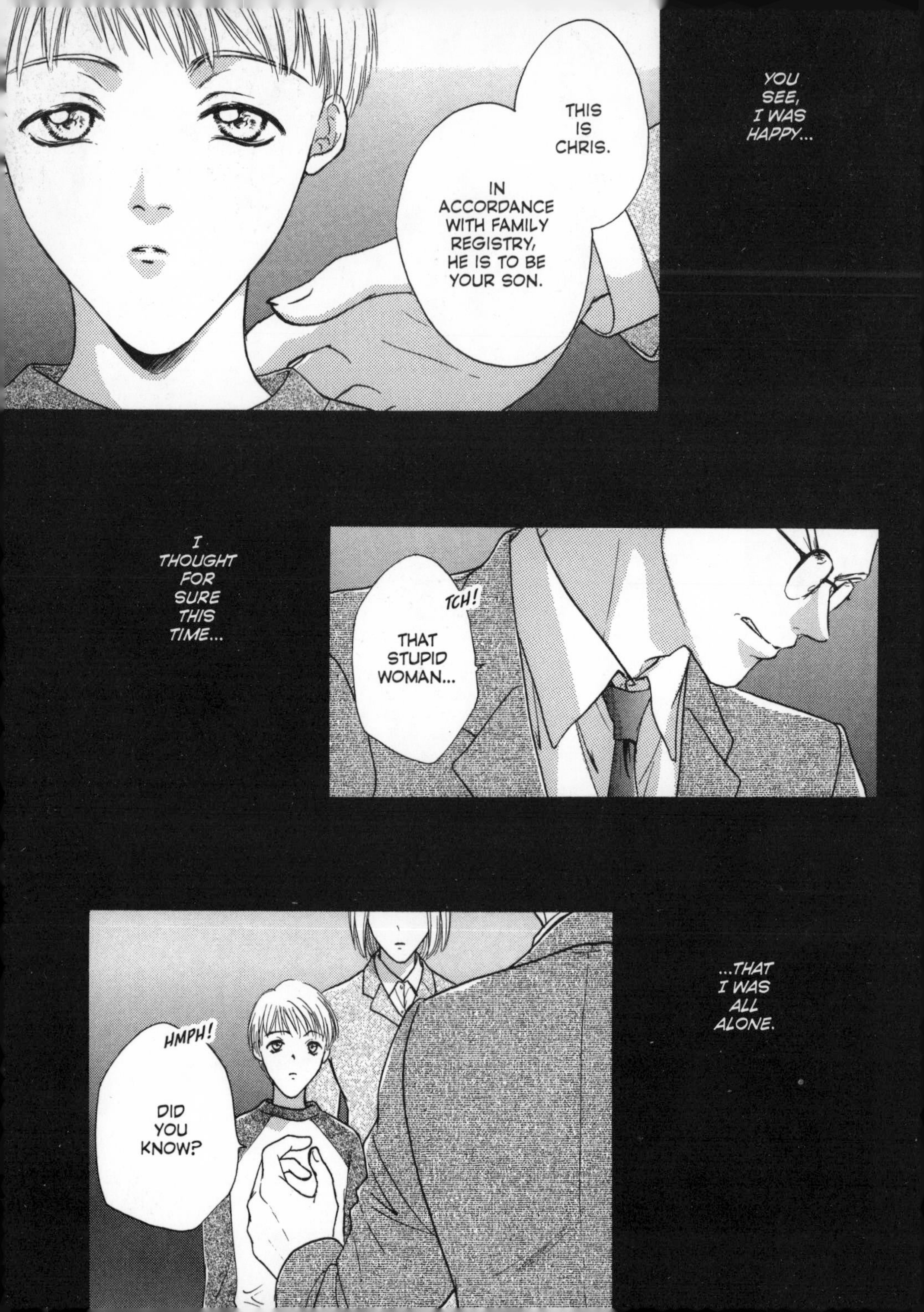
YOU SEE, I WAS HAPPY...
THIS IS CHRIS.
IN ACCORDANCE WITH FAMILY REGISTRY, HE IS TO BE YOUR SON.
TCH!
THAT STUPID WOMAN...
I THOUGHT FOR SURE THIS TIME...
...THAT I WAS ALL ALONE.
HMPH!
DID YOU KNOW?

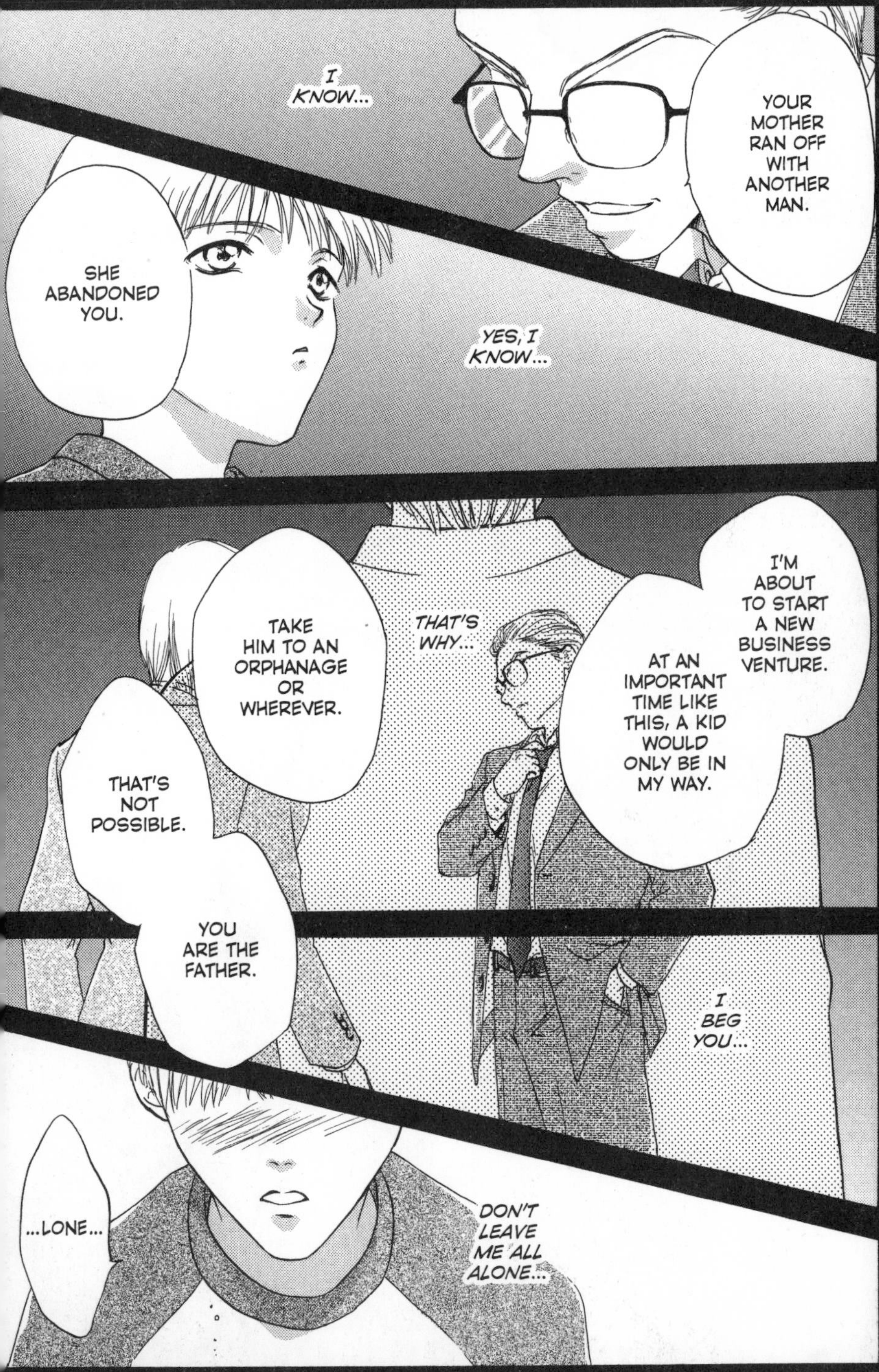
YOUR MOTHER RAN OFF WITH ANOTHER MAN.
I KNOW...
SHE ABANDONED YOU.
YES, I KNOW...
I'M ABOUT TO START A NEW BUSINESS VENTURE.
AT AN IMPORTANT TIME LIKE THIS, A KID WOULD ONLY BE IN MY WAY.
THAT'S WHY...
TAKE HIM TO AN ORPHANAGE OR WHEREVER.
THAT'S NOT POSSIBLE.
YOU ARE THE FATHER.
I BEG YOU...
DON'T LEAVE ME ALL ALONE...
...LONE...

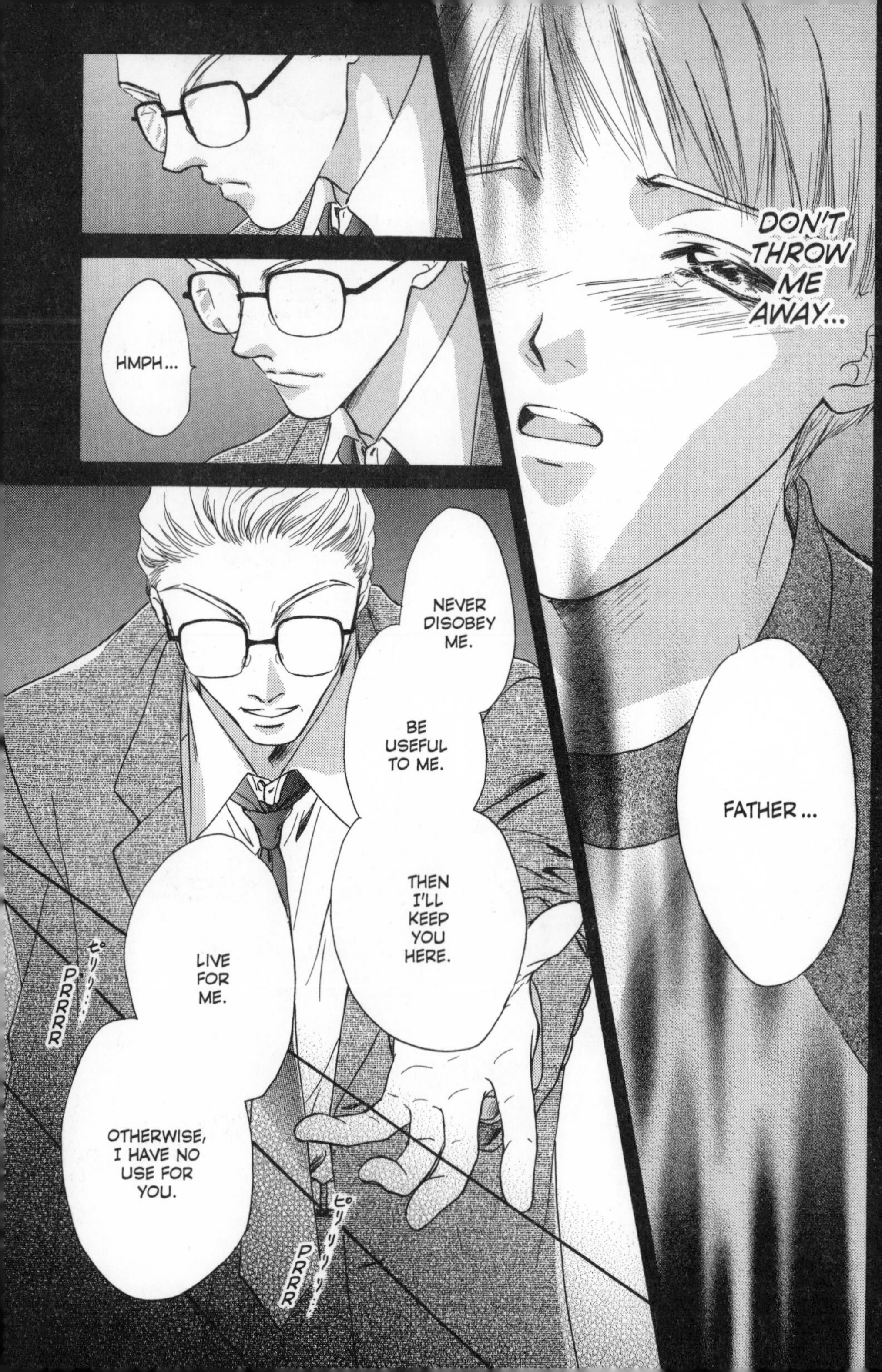
DON'T THROW ME AWAY...
FATHER...
HMPH...
NEVER DISOBEY ME.
BE USEFUL TO ME.
THEN I'LL KEEP YOU HERE.
LIVE FOR ME.
OTHERWISE, I HAVE NO USE FOR YOU.
PRRRR
PRRRR

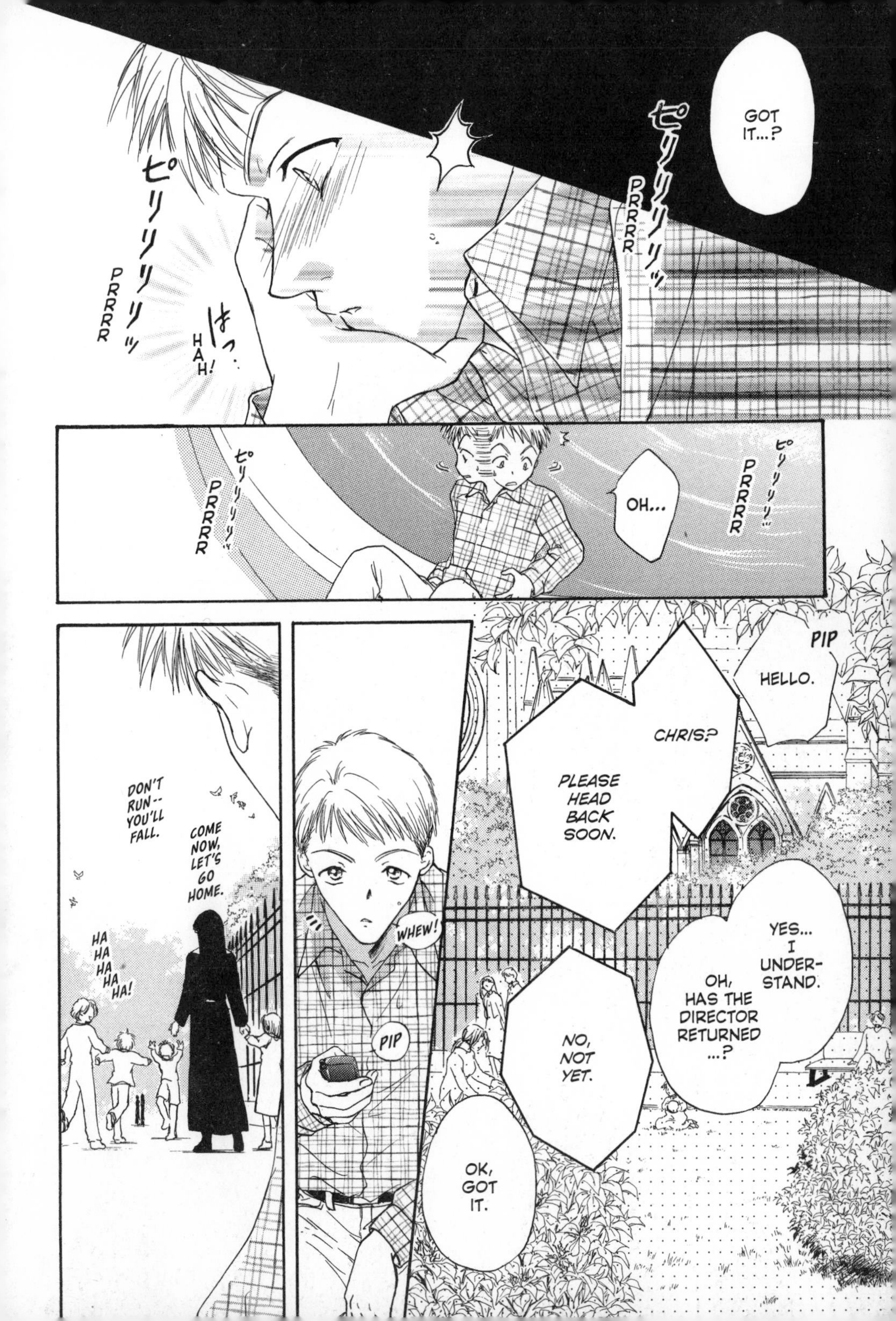
GOT IT...?
ピリリリッ
PRRRR
ピリリリッ
PRRRR
はっ
HAH!
ピリリリッ
PRRRR
OH...
ピリリリッ
PRRRR
PIP
HELLO.
CHRIS?
PLEASE HEAD BACK SOON.
YES... I UNDER-STAND.
OH, HAS THE DIRECTOR RETURNED ...?
NO, NOT YET.
OK, GOT IT.
WHEW!
PIP
COME NOW, LET'S GO HOME.
DON'T RUN-- YOU'LL FALL.
HA HA HA HA HA!

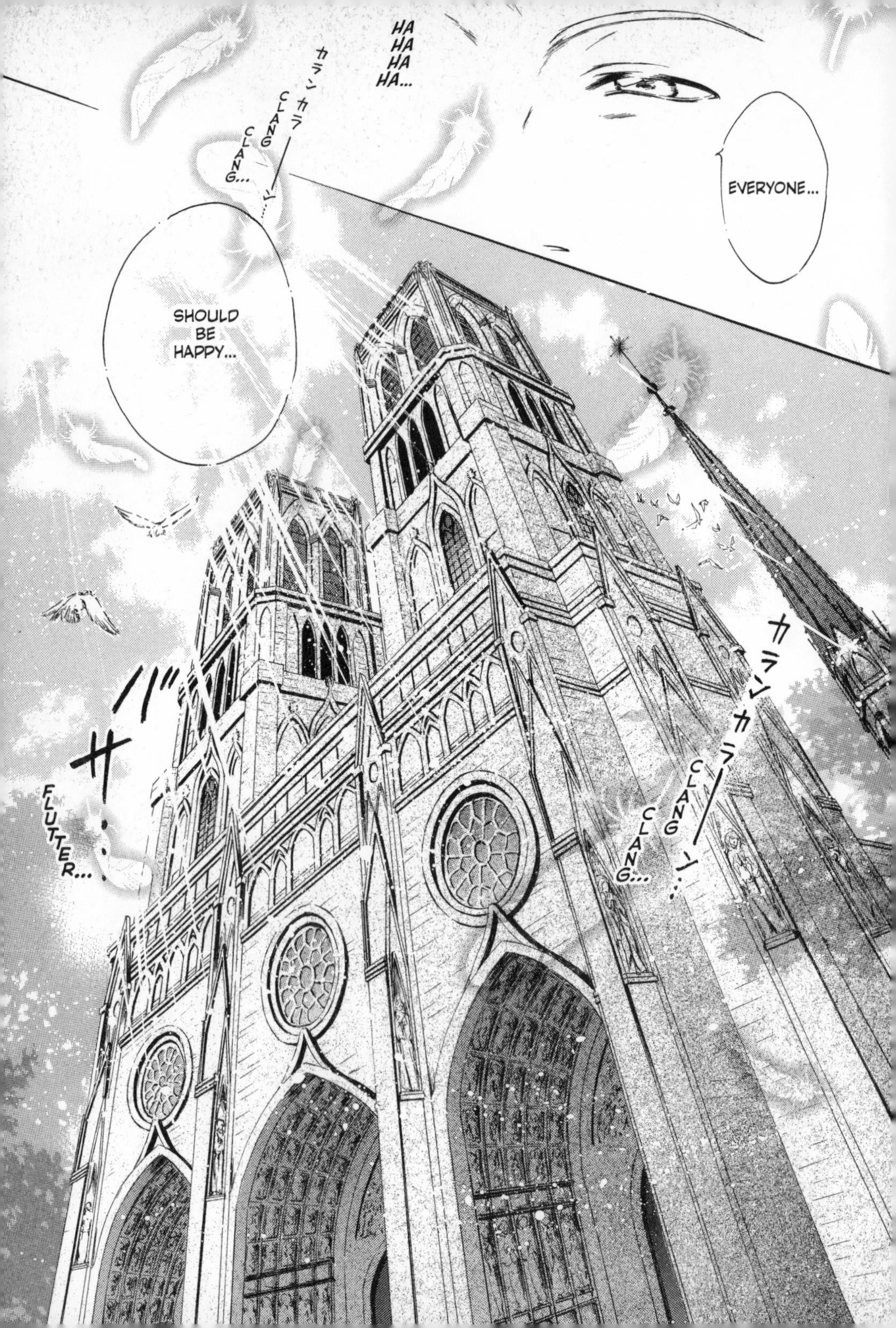
EVERYONE...
HA HA HA HA...
カラン カラ
CLANG CLANG...
SHOULD BE HAPPY...
カランカラ
CLANG CLANG...
バサ
FLUTTER...

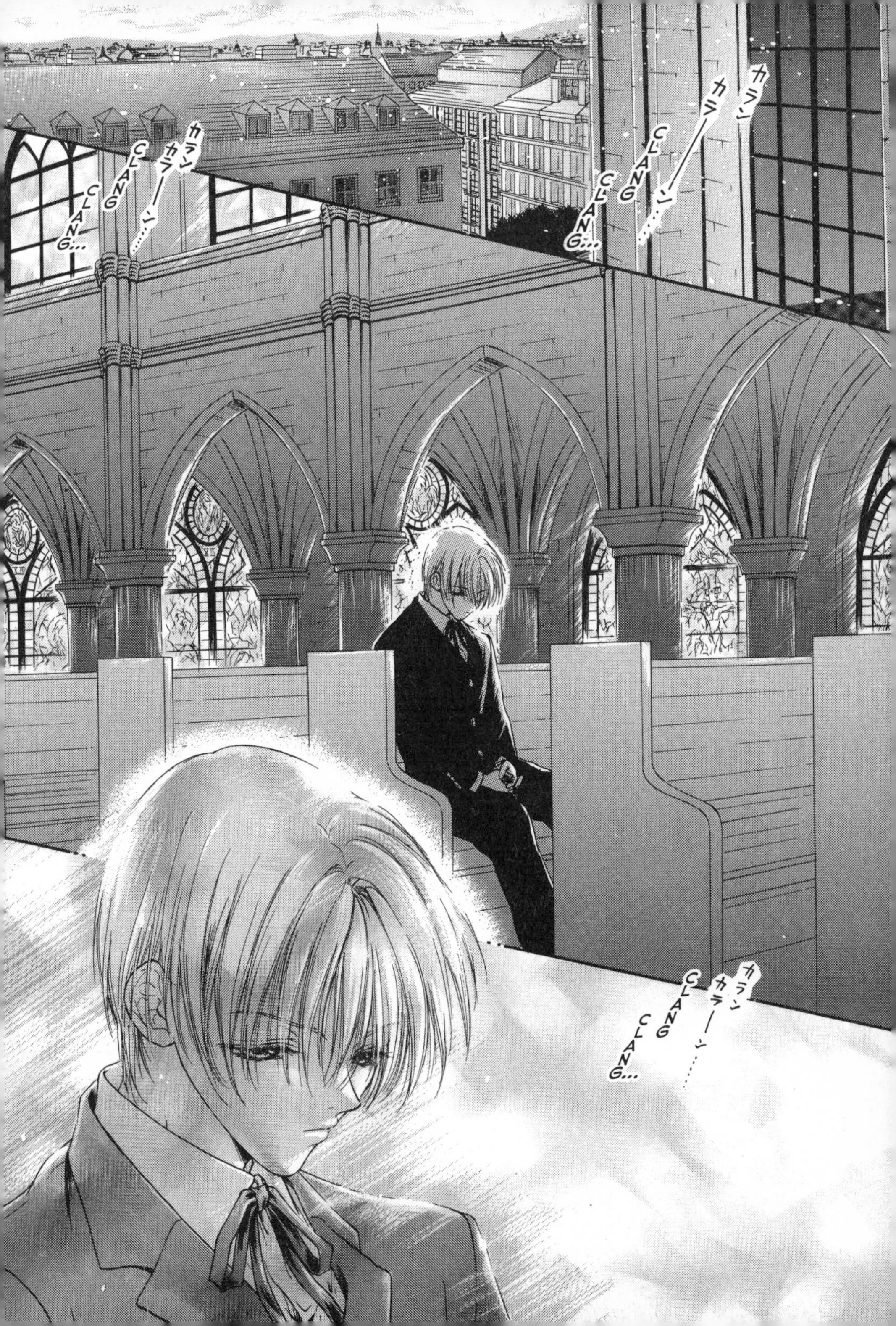
カラン
カラーン……
CLANG
CLANG...
カラン
カラーン……
CLANG
CLANG...
カラン
カラーン……
CLANG
CLANG...

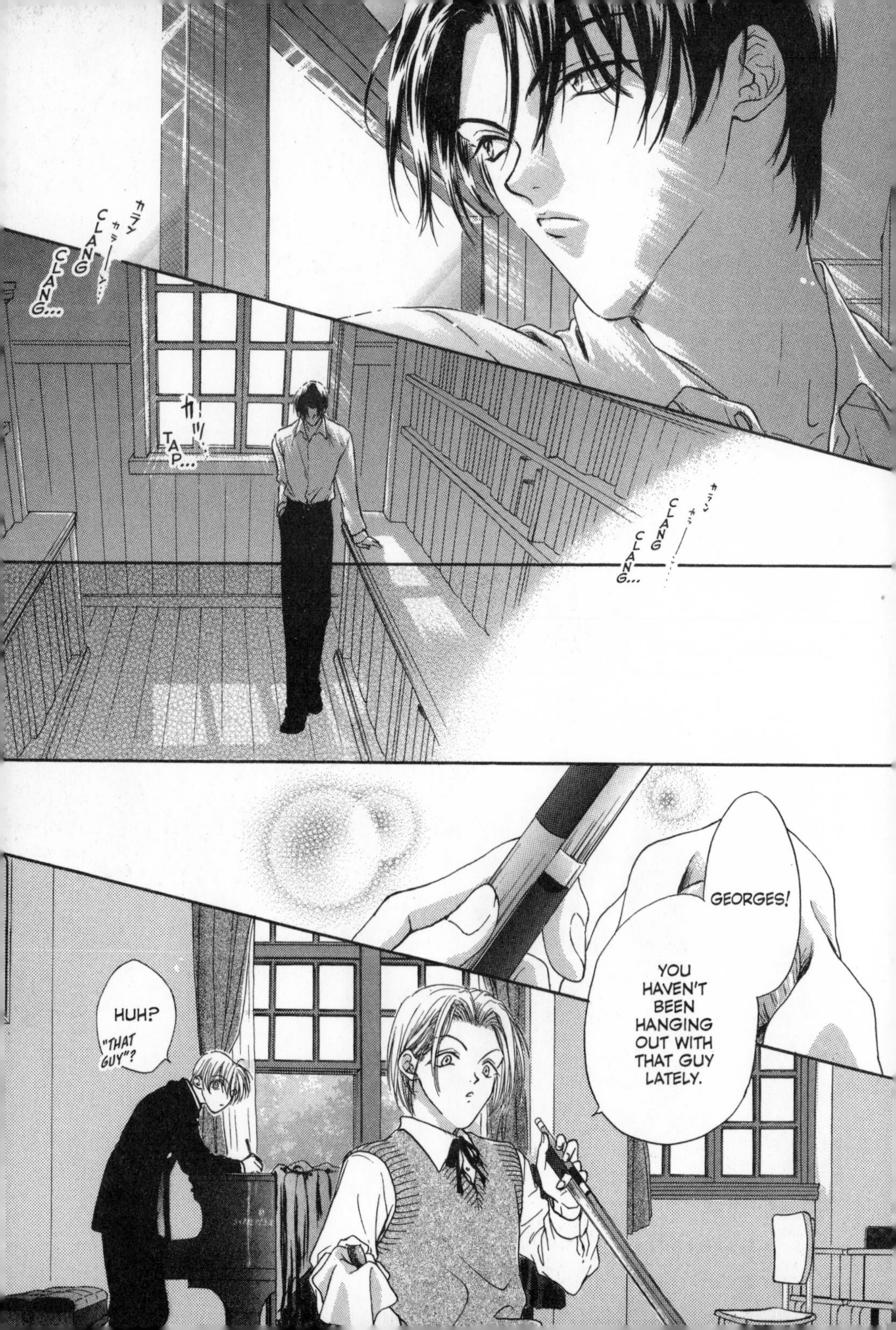

カラン カラー…
CLANG CLANG...
カツ…
TAP...
カラン カラー…
CLANG CLANG...
GEORGES!
YOU HAVEN'T BEEN HANGING OUT WITH THAT GUY LATELY.
HUH? "THAT GUY"?

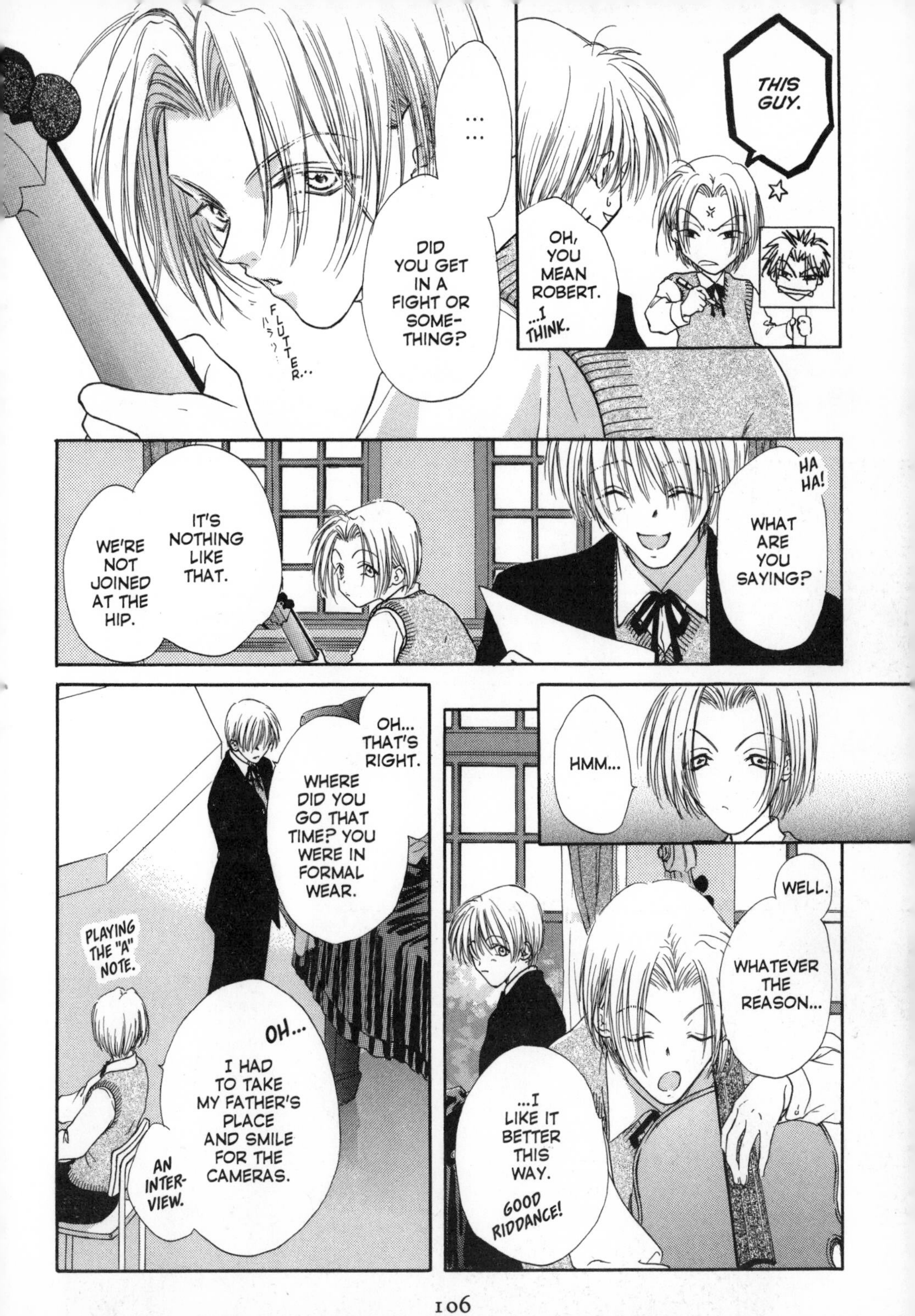
THIS GUY.
OH, YOU MEAN ROBERT. ...I THINK.
...
...
DID YOU GET IN A FIGHT OR SOMETHING?
FLUTTER...
ハラリ…
HA HA!
WHAT ARE YOU SAYING?
IT'S NOTHING LIKE THAT.
WE'RE NOT JOINED AT THE HIP.
HMM...
WELL.
WHATEVER THE REASON...
...I LIKE IT BETTER THIS WAY.
GOOD RIDDANCE!
OH... THAT'S RIGHT.
WHERE DID YOU GO THAT TIME? YOU WERE IN FORMAL WEAR.
PLAYING THE "A" NOTE.
OH...
I HAD TO TAKE MY FATHER'S PLACE AND SMILE FOR THE CAMERAS.
AN INTERVIEW.

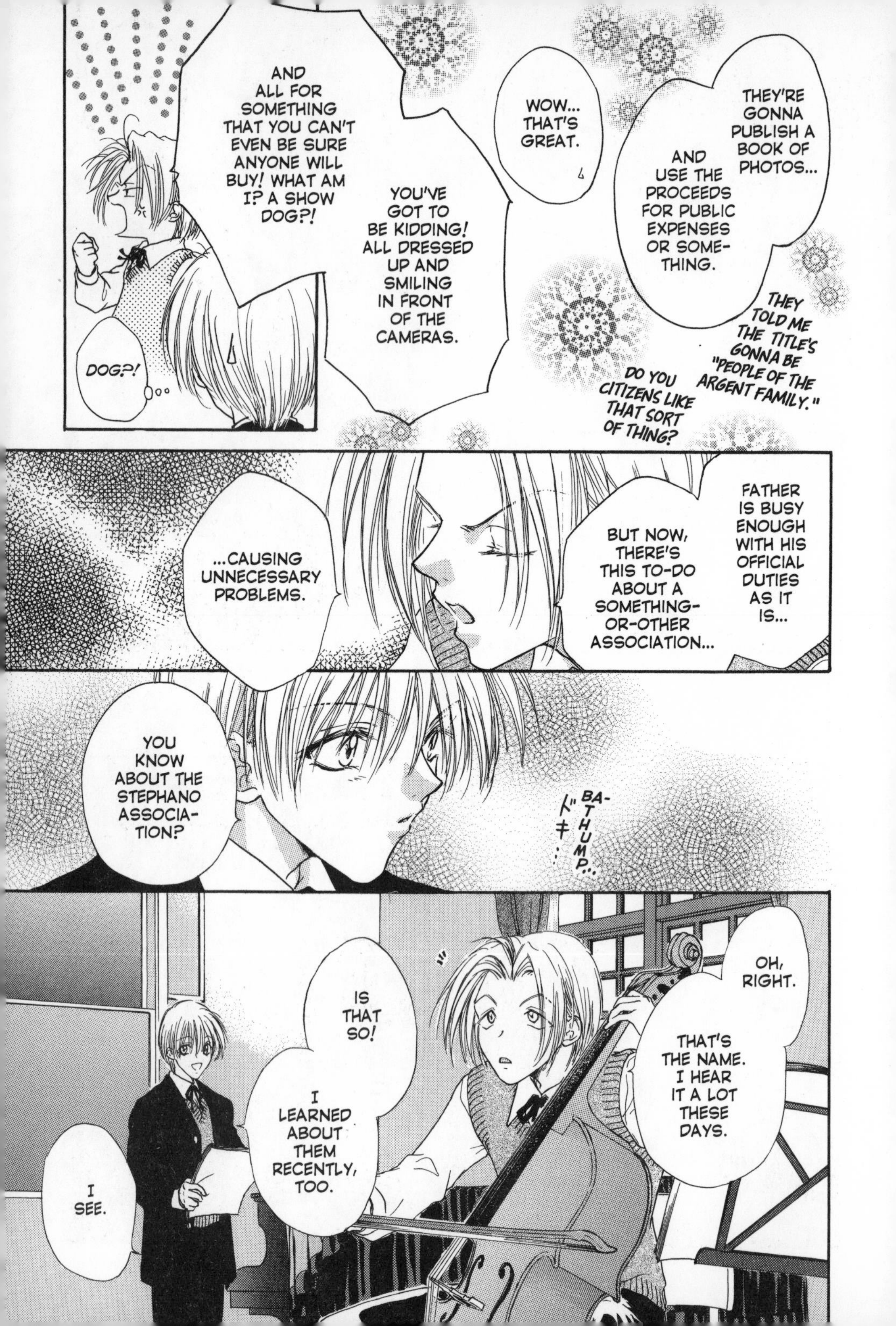
THEY'RE GONNA PUBLISH A BOOK OF PHOTOS...
AND USE THE PROCEEDS FOR PUBLIC EXPENSES OR SOME-THING.
THEY TOLD ME THE TITLE'S GONNA BE "PEOPLE OF THE ARGENT FAMILY."
DO YOU CITIZENS LIKE THAT SORT OF THING?
WOW... THAT'S GREAT.
YOU'VE GOT TO BE KIDDING! ALL DRESSED UP AND SMILING IN FRONT OF THE CAMERAS.
AND ALL FOR SOMETHING THAT YOU CAN'T EVEN BE SURE ANYONE WILL BUY! WHAT AM I? A SHOW DOG?!
DOG?!
FATHER IS BUSY ENOUGH WITH HIS OFFICIAL DUTIES AS IT IS...
BUT NOW, THERE'S THIS TO-DO ABOUT A SOMETHING-OR-OTHER ASSOCIATION...
...CAUSING UNNECESSARY PROBLEMS.
BA-THUMP...
ドキ...
YOU KNOW ABOUT THE STEPHANO ASSOCIA-TION?
OH, RIGHT.
THAT'S THE NAME. I HEAR IT A LOT THESE DAYS.
IS THAT SO!
I LEARNED ABOUT THEM RECENTLY, TOO.
I SEE.

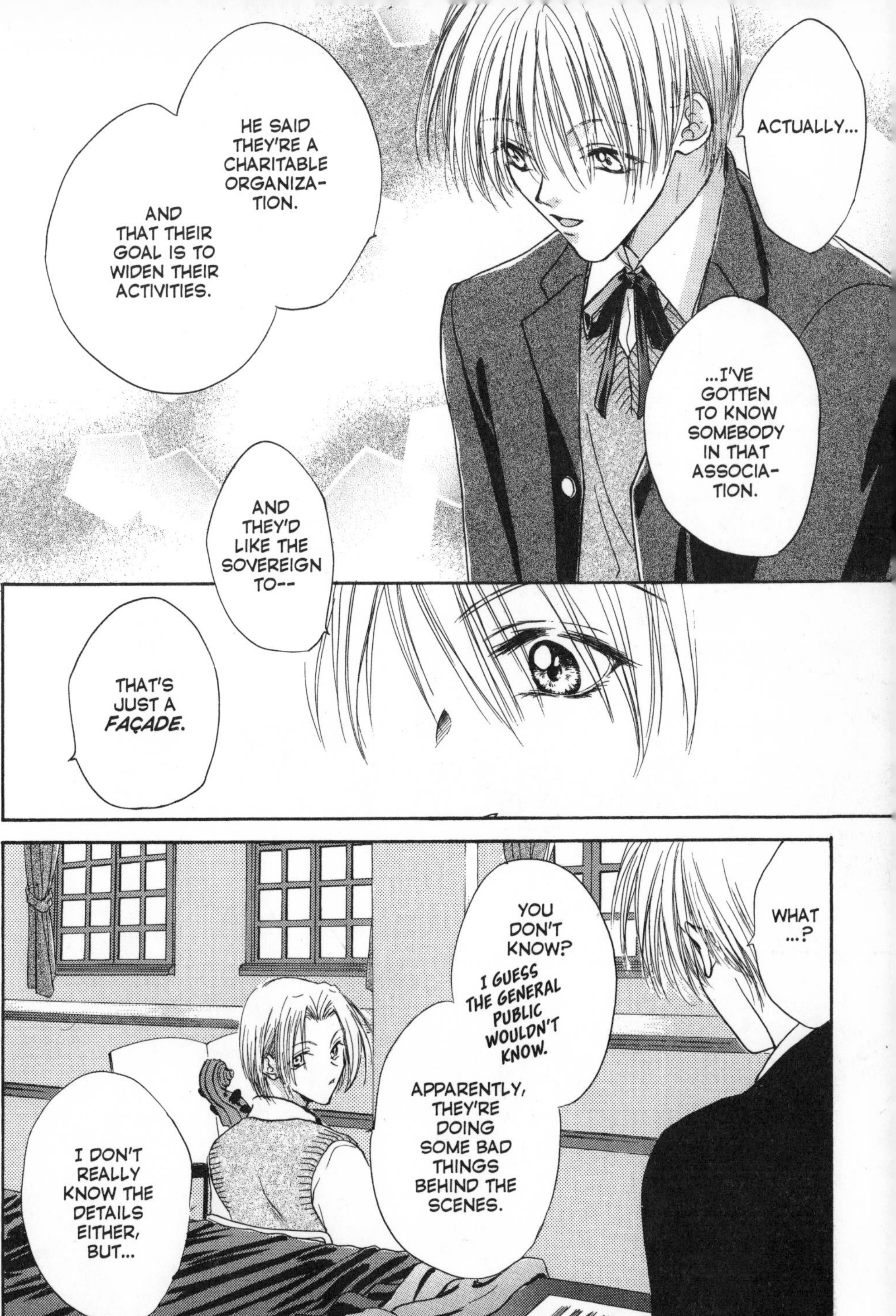
ACTUALLY...
...I'VE GOTTEN TO KNOW SOMEBODY IN THAT ASSOCIATION.
HE SAID THEY'RE A CHARITABLE ORGANIZATION.
AND THAT THEIR GOAL IS TO WIDEN THEIR ACTIVITIES.
AND THEY'D LIKE THE SOVEREIGN TO--
THAT'S JUST A *FAÇADE*.
WHAT ...?
YOU DON'T KNOW?
I GUESS THE GENERAL PUBLIC WOULDN'T KNOW.
APPARENTLY, THEY'RE DOING SOME BAD THINGS BEHIND THE SCENES.
I DON'T REALLY KNOW THE DETAILS EITHER, BUT...

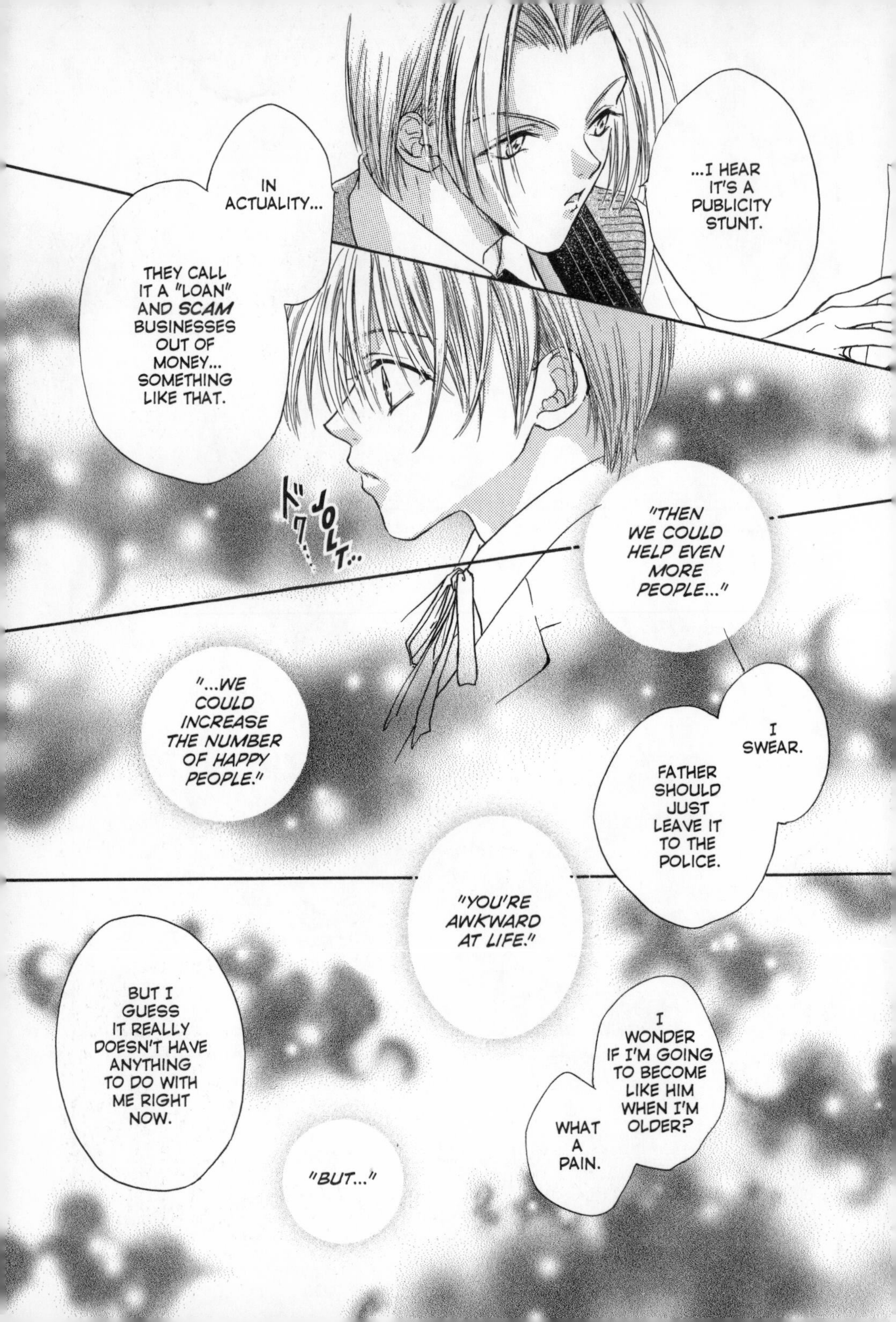
...I HEAR IT'S A PUBLICITY STUNT.
IN ACTUALITY...
THEY CALL IT A "LOAN" AND SCAM BUSINESSES OUT OF MONEY... SOMETHING LIKE THAT.
ドク... JOLT..
"THEN WE COULD HELP EVEN MORE PEOPLE..."
I SWEAR.
FATHER SHOULD JUST LEAVE IT TO THE POLICE.
"...WE COULD INCREASE THE NUMBER OF HAPPY PEOPLE."
"YOU'RE AWKWARD AT LIFE."
I WONDER IF I'M GOING TO BECOME LIKE HIM WHEN I'M OLDER?
WHAT A PAIN.
BUT I GUESS IT REALLY DOESN'T HAVE ANYTHING TO DO WITH ME RIGHT NOW.
"BUT..."

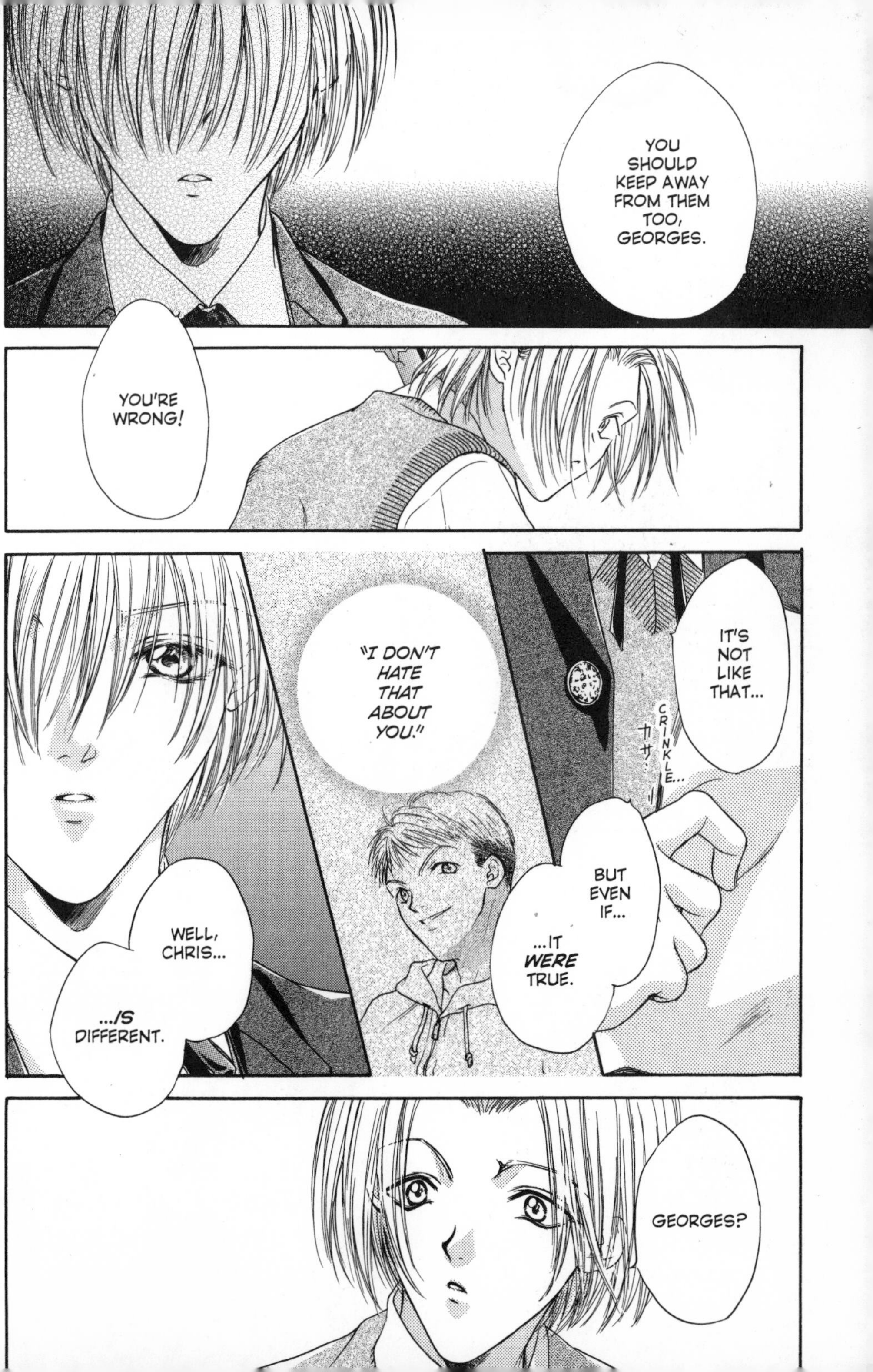
YOU SHOULD KEEP AWAY FROM THEM TOO, GEORGES.
YOU'RE WRONG!
IT'S NOT LIKE THAT...
カサ…
CRINKLE...
BUT EVEN IF...
...IT *WERE* TRUE.
"I DON'T HATE THAT ABOUT YOU."
WELL, CHRIS...
...*IS* DIFFERENT.
GEORGES?

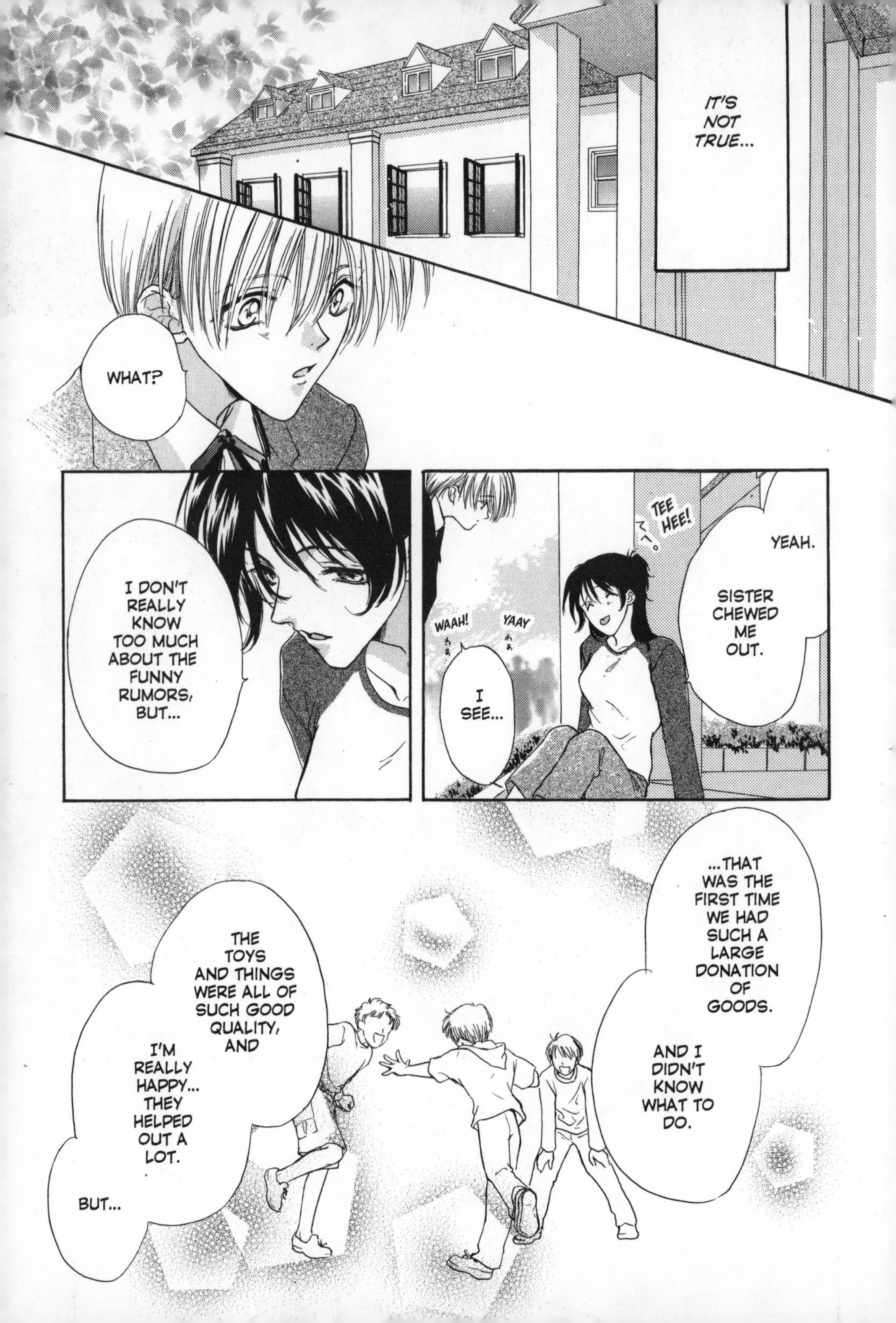
IT'S NOT TRUE...
WHAT?
TEE HEE!
YEAH.
SISTER CHEWED ME OUT.
WAAH!
YAAY
I SEE...
I DON'T REALLY KNOW TOO MUCH ABOUT THE FUNNY RUMORS, BUT...
...THAT WAS THE FIRST TIME WE HAD SUCH A LARGE DONATION OF GOODS.
AND I DIDN'T KNOW WHAT TO DO.
THE TOYS AND THINGS WERE ALL OF SUCH GOOD QUALITY, AND
I'M REALLY HAPPY... THEY HELPED OUT A LOT.
BUT...

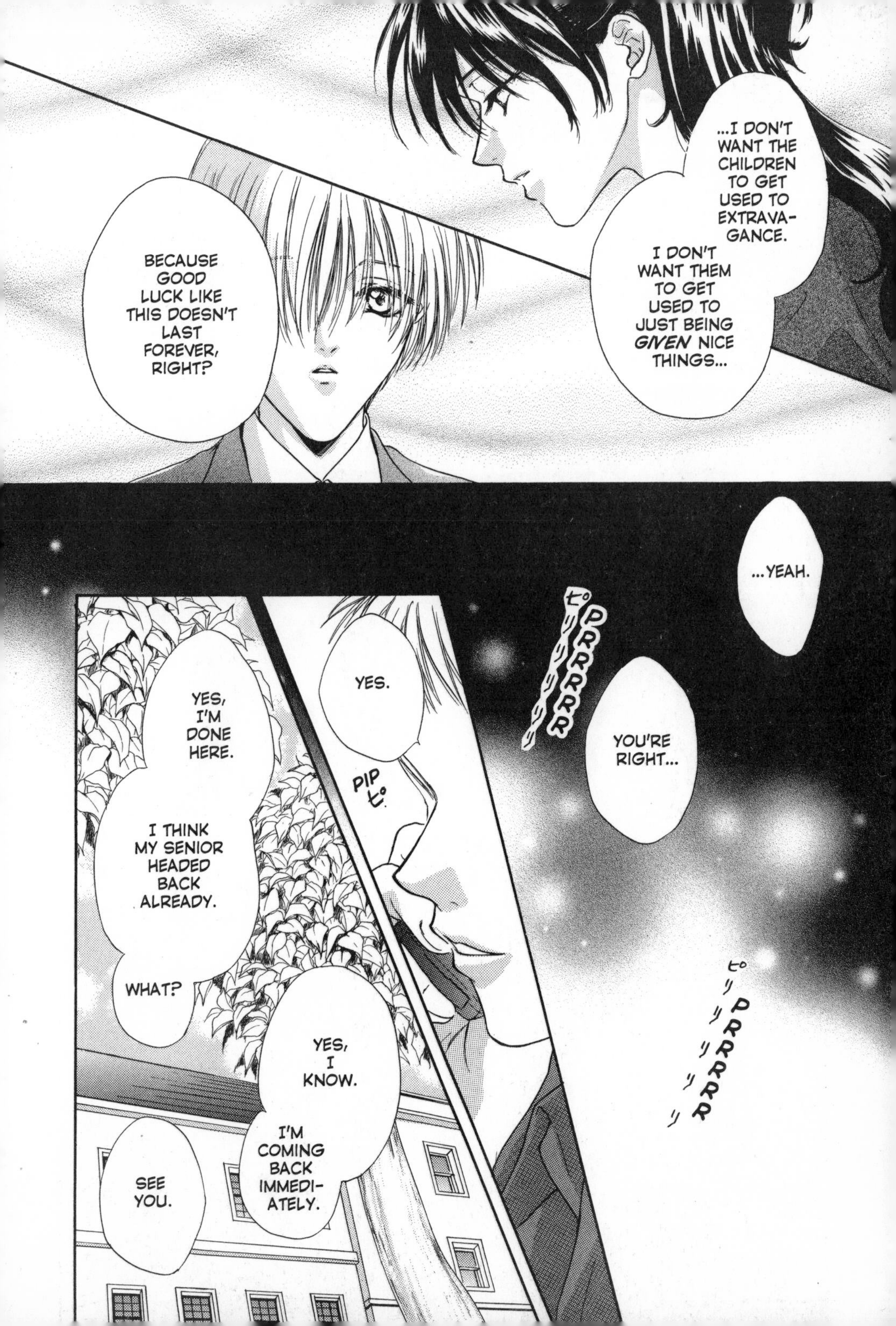
...I DON'T WANT THE CHILDREN TO GET USED TO EXTRAVAGANCE.
I DON'T WANT THEM TO GET USED TO JUST BEING *GIVEN* NICE THINGS...
BECAUSE GOOD LUCK LIKE THIS DOESN'T LAST FOREVER, RIGHT?
...YEAH.
YOU'RE RIGHT...
PRRRRR
PRRRRR
PIP
YES.
YES, I'M DONE HERE.
I THINK MY SENIOR HEADED BACK ALREADY.
WHAT?
YES, I KNOW.
I'M COMING BACK IMMEDIATELY.
SEE YOU.

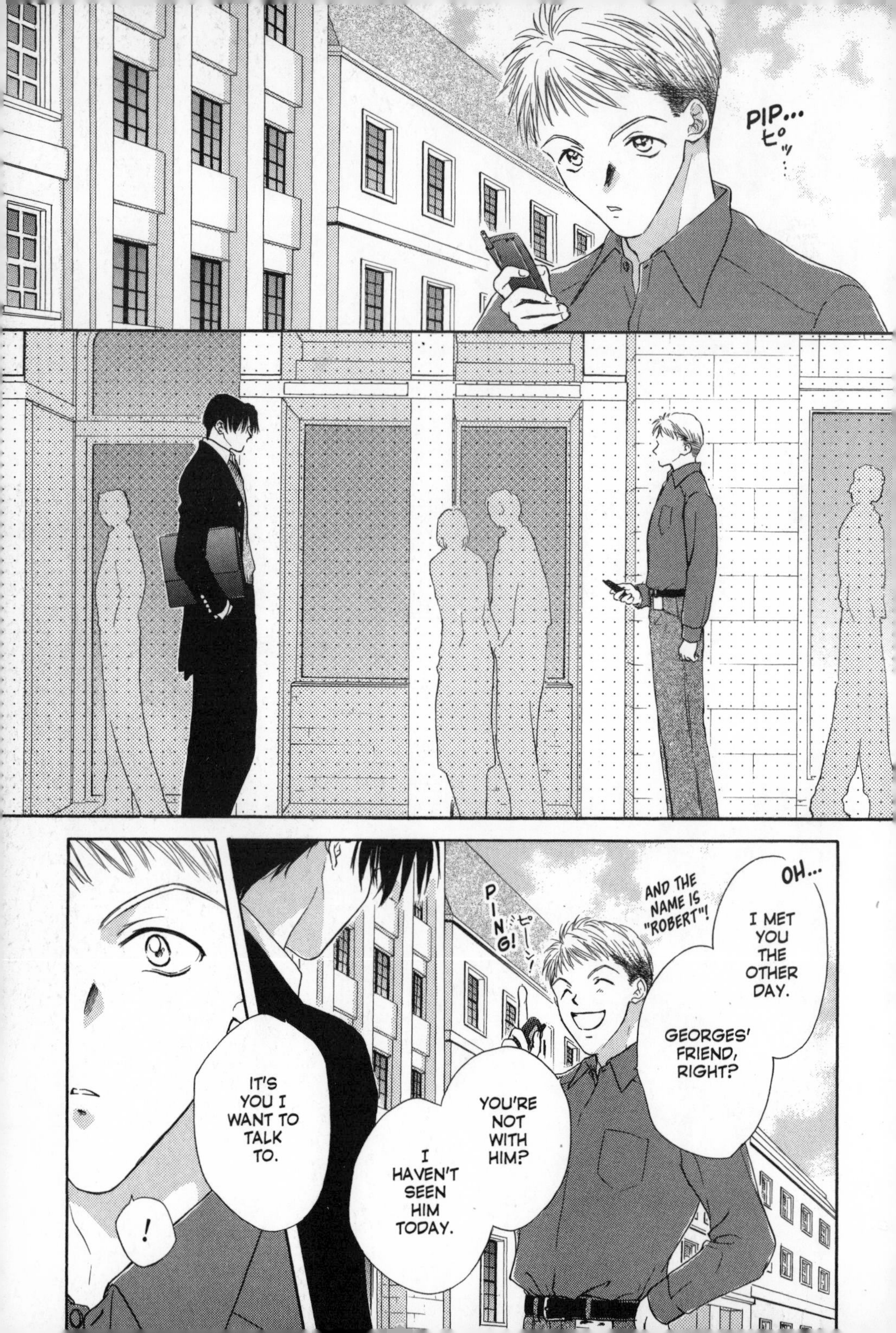
PIP...
ピッ...
OH...
I MET YOU THE OTHER DAY.
GEORGES' FRIEND, RIGHT?
AND THE NAME IS "ROBERT"!
PING!
ピーン!
YOU'RE NOT WITH HIM?
I HAVEN'T SEEN HIM TODAY.
IT'S YOU I WANT TO TALK TO.
!

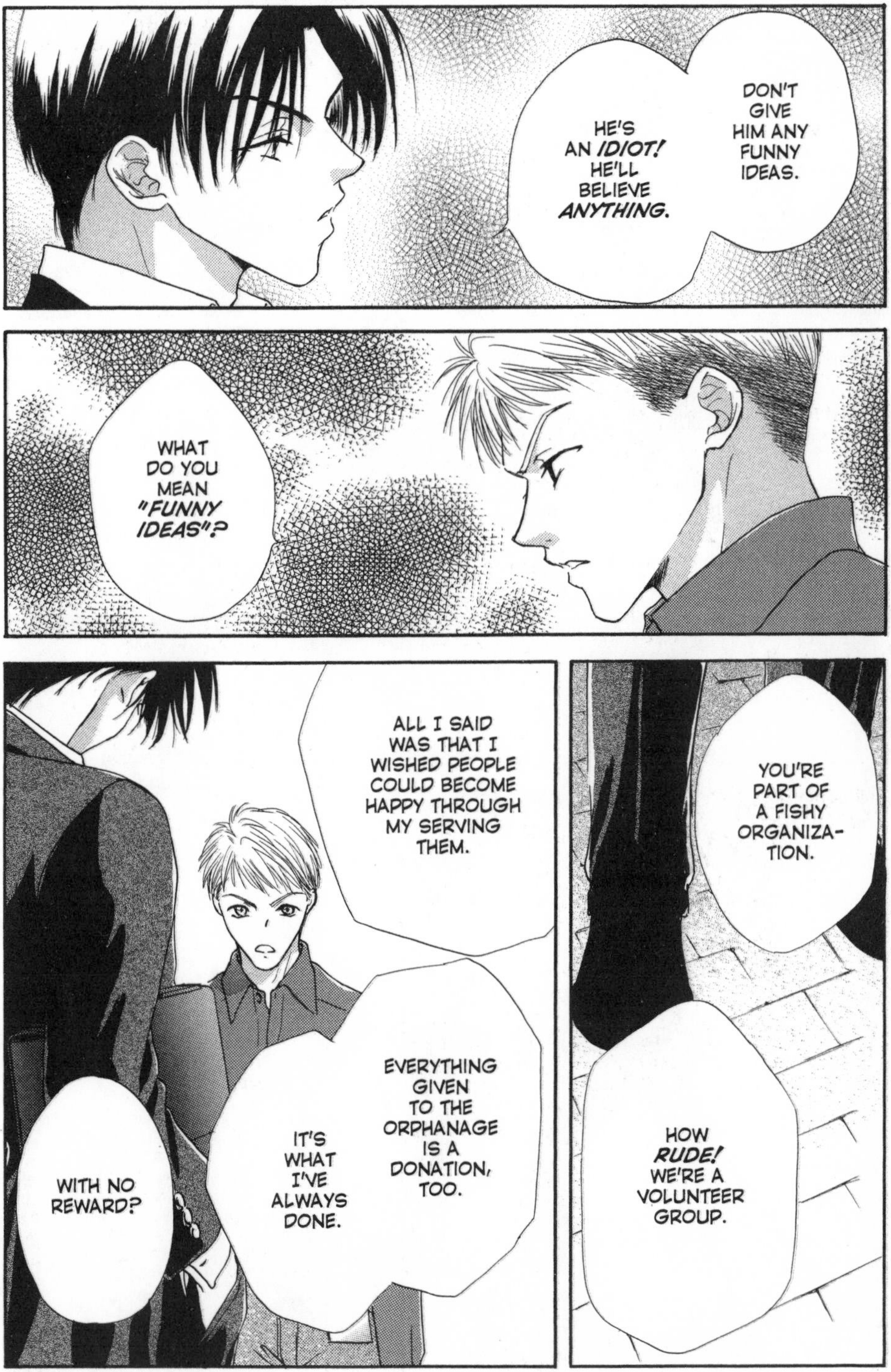
DON'T GIVE HIM ANY FUNNY IDEAS.
HE'S AN *IDIOT!* HE'LL BELIEVE *ANYTHING*.
WHAT DO YOU MEAN *"FUNNY IDEAS"*?
YOU'RE PART OF A FISHY ORGANIZA-TION.
HOW *RUDE!* WE'RE A VOLUNTEER GROUP.
ALL I SAID WAS THAT I WISHED PEOPLE COULD BECOME HAPPY THROUGH MY SERVING THEM.
EVERYTHING GIVEN TO THE ORPHANAGE IS A DONATION, TOO.
IT'S WHAT I'VE ALWAYS DONE.
WITH NO REWARD?

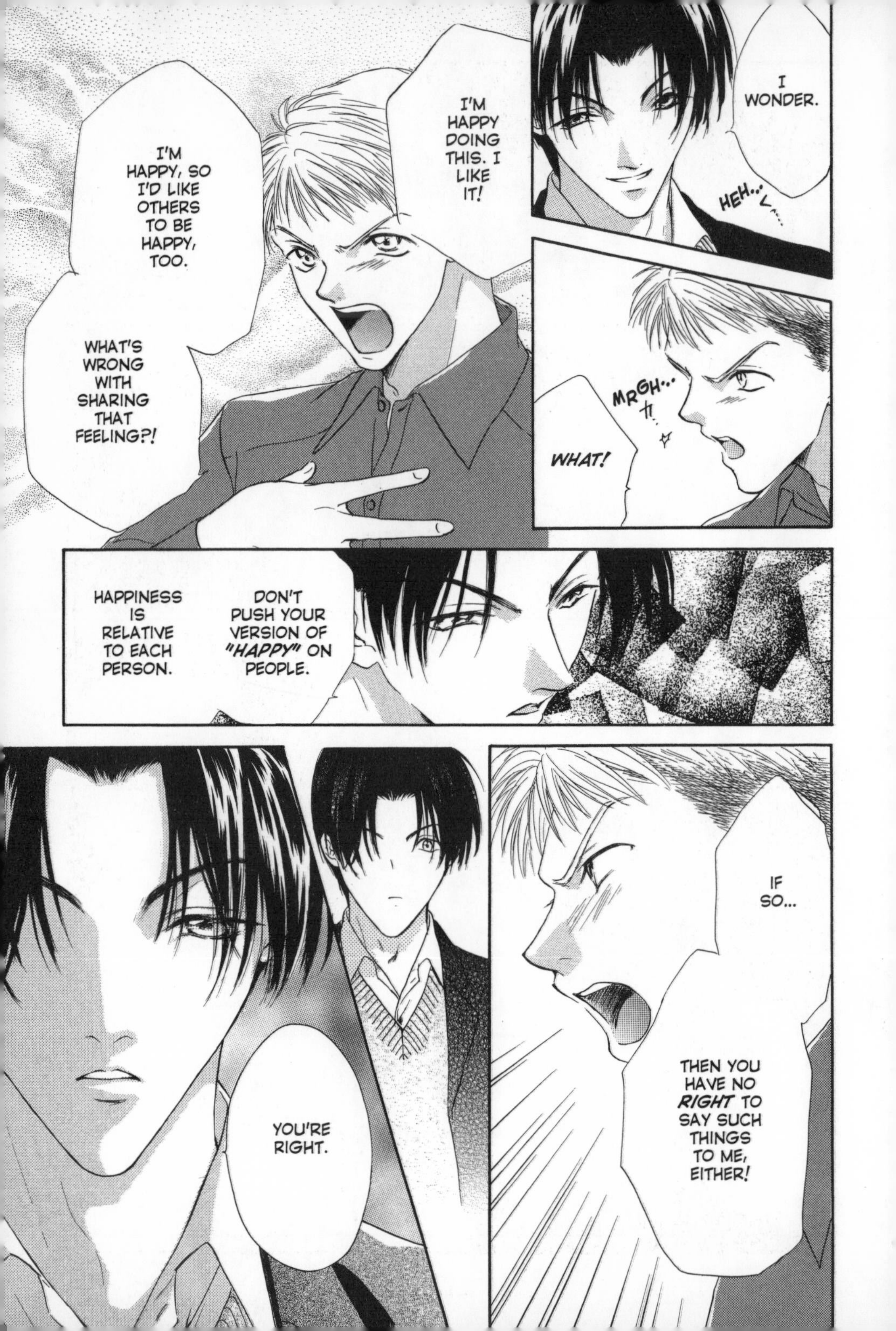
I WONDER.
HEH...
MRGH...
WHAT!
I'M HAPPY DOING THIS. I LIKE IT!
I'M HAPPY, SO I'D LIKE OTHERS TO BE HAPPY, TOO.
WHAT'S WRONG WITH SHARING THAT FEELING?!
DON'T PUSH YOUR VERSION OF "HAPPY" ON PEOPLE.
HAPPINESS IS RELATIVE TO EACH PERSON.
IF SO...
THEN YOU HAVE NO RIGHT TO SAY SUCH THINGS TO ME, EITHER!
YOU'RE RIGHT.

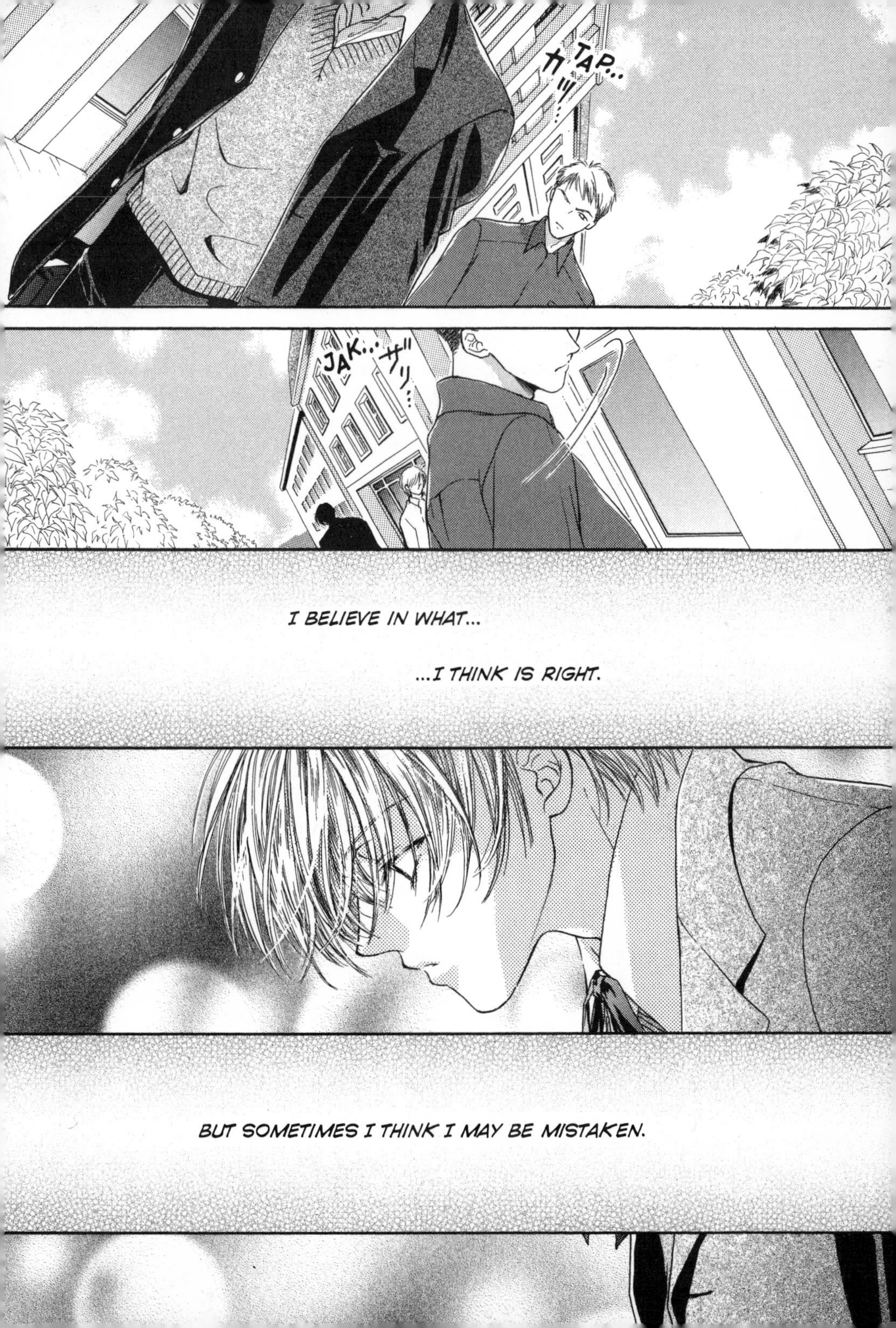
TAP...
カッ…
JAK...
ザリ…
I BELIEVE IN WHAT...
...I THINK IS RIGHT.
BUT SOMETIMES I THINK I MAY BE MISTAKEN.

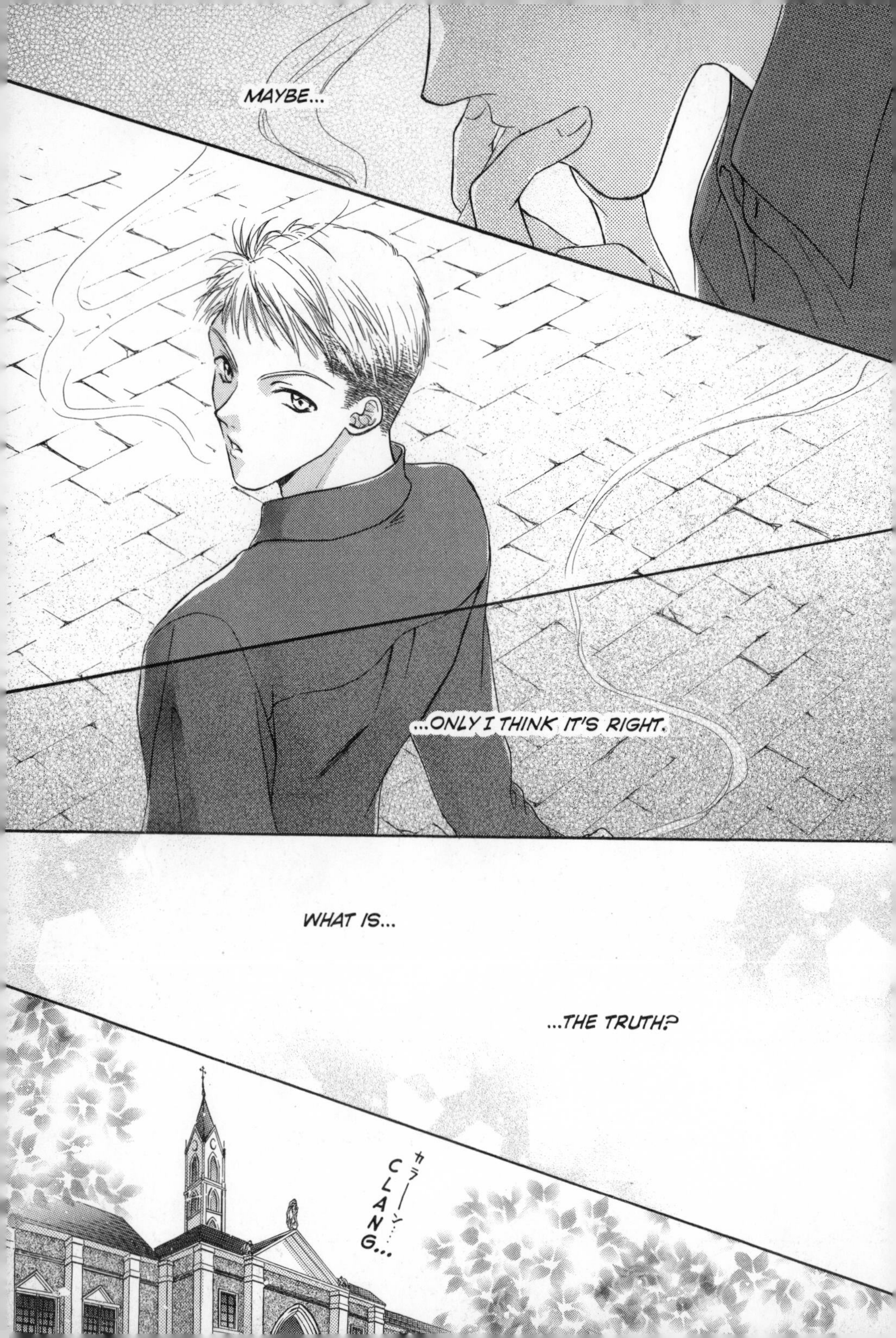
MAYBE...
...ONLY I THINK IT'S RIGHT.
WHAT IS...
...THE TRUTH?
カラーン…
CLANG...

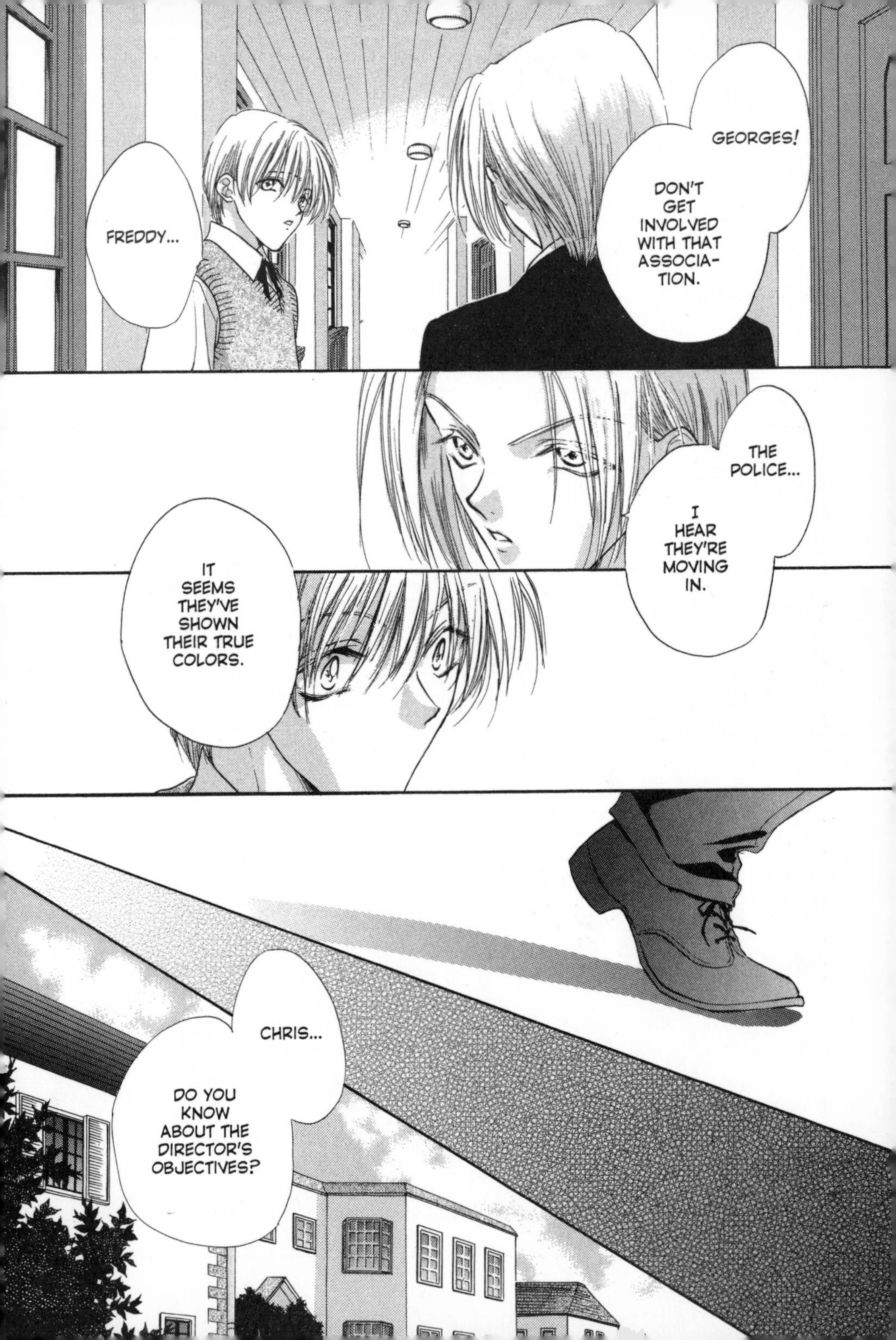
GEORGES!
DON'T GET INVOLVED WITH THAT ASSOCIA-TION.
FREDDY...
THE POLICE...
I HEAR THEY'RE MOVING IN.
IT SEEMS THEY'VE SHOWN THEIR TRUE COLORS.
CHRIS...
DO YOU KNOW ABOUT THE DIRECTOR'S OBJECTIVES?

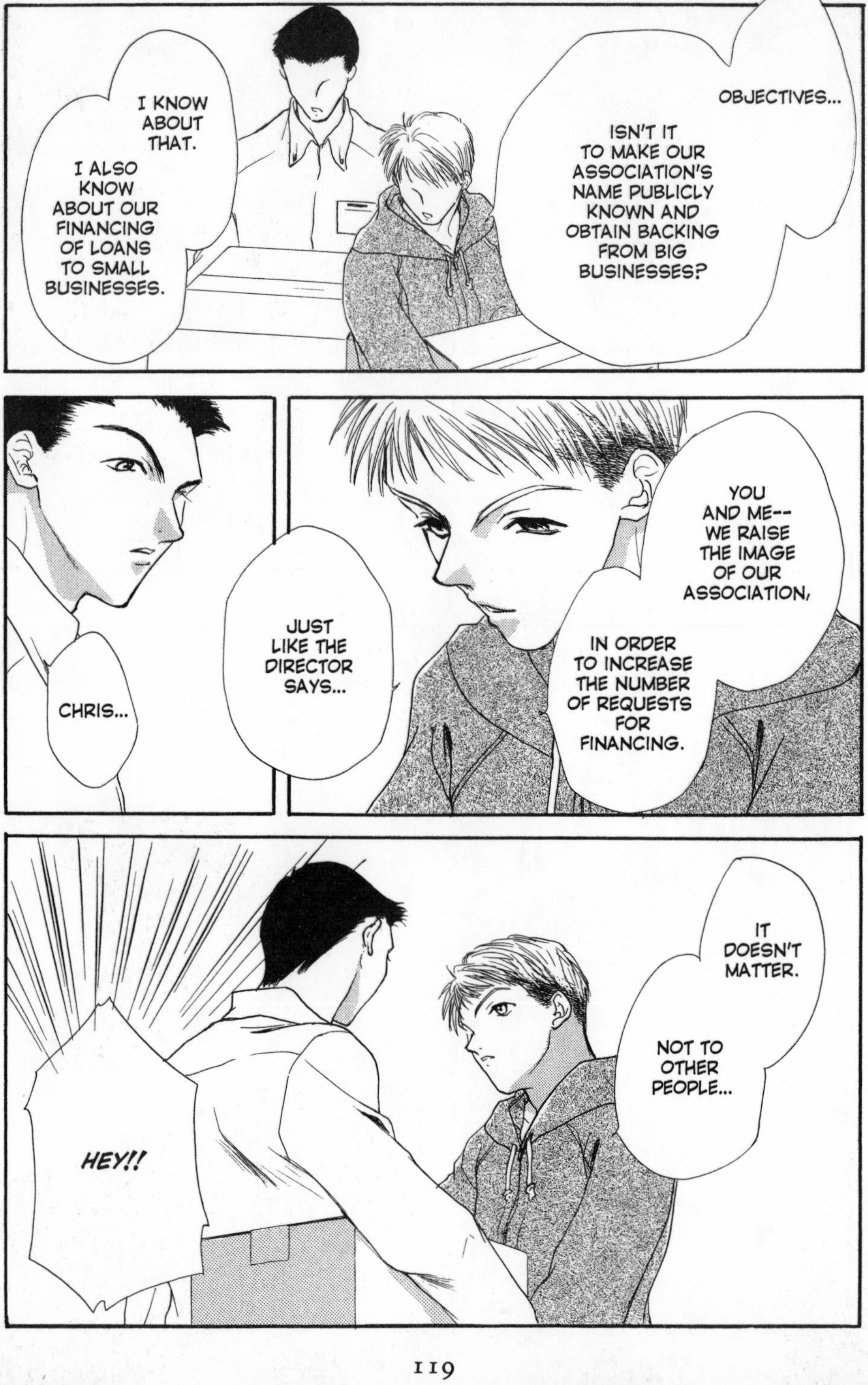
OBJECTIVES...
ISN'T IT TO MAKE OUR ASSOCIATION'S NAME PUBLICLY KNOWN AND OBTAIN BACKING FROM BIG BUSINESSES?
I KNOW ABOUT THAT.
I ALSO KNOW ABOUT OUR FINANCING OF LOANS TO SMALL BUSINESSES.
YOU AND ME-- WE RAISE THE IMAGE OF OUR ASSOCIATION,
IN ORDER TO INCREASE THE NUMBER OF REQUESTS FOR FINANCING.
JUST LIKE THE DIRECTOR SAYS...
CHRIS...
IT DOESN'T MATTER.
NOT TO OTHER PEOPLE...
HEY!!

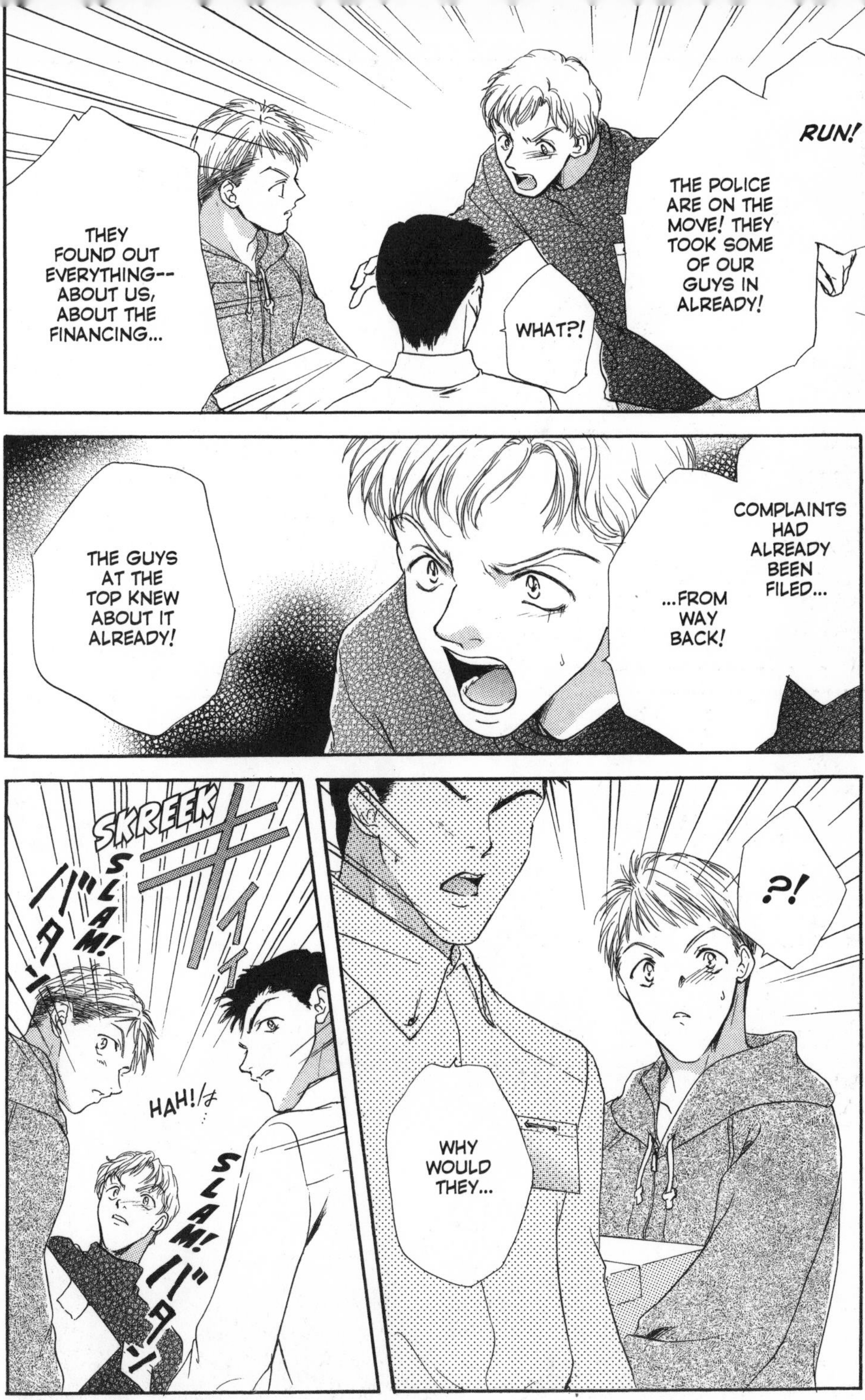
RUN!
THE POLICE ARE ON THE MOVE! THEY TOOK SOME OF OUR GUYS IN ALREADY!
WHAT?!
THEY FOUND OUT EVERYTHING-- ABOUT US, ABOUT THE FINANCING...
COMPLAINTS HAD ALREADY BEEN FILED...
...FROM WAY BACK!
THE GUYS AT THE TOP KNEW ABOUT IT ALREADY!
?!
WHY WOULD THEY...
SKREEK
SLAM!
HAH!
SLAM!

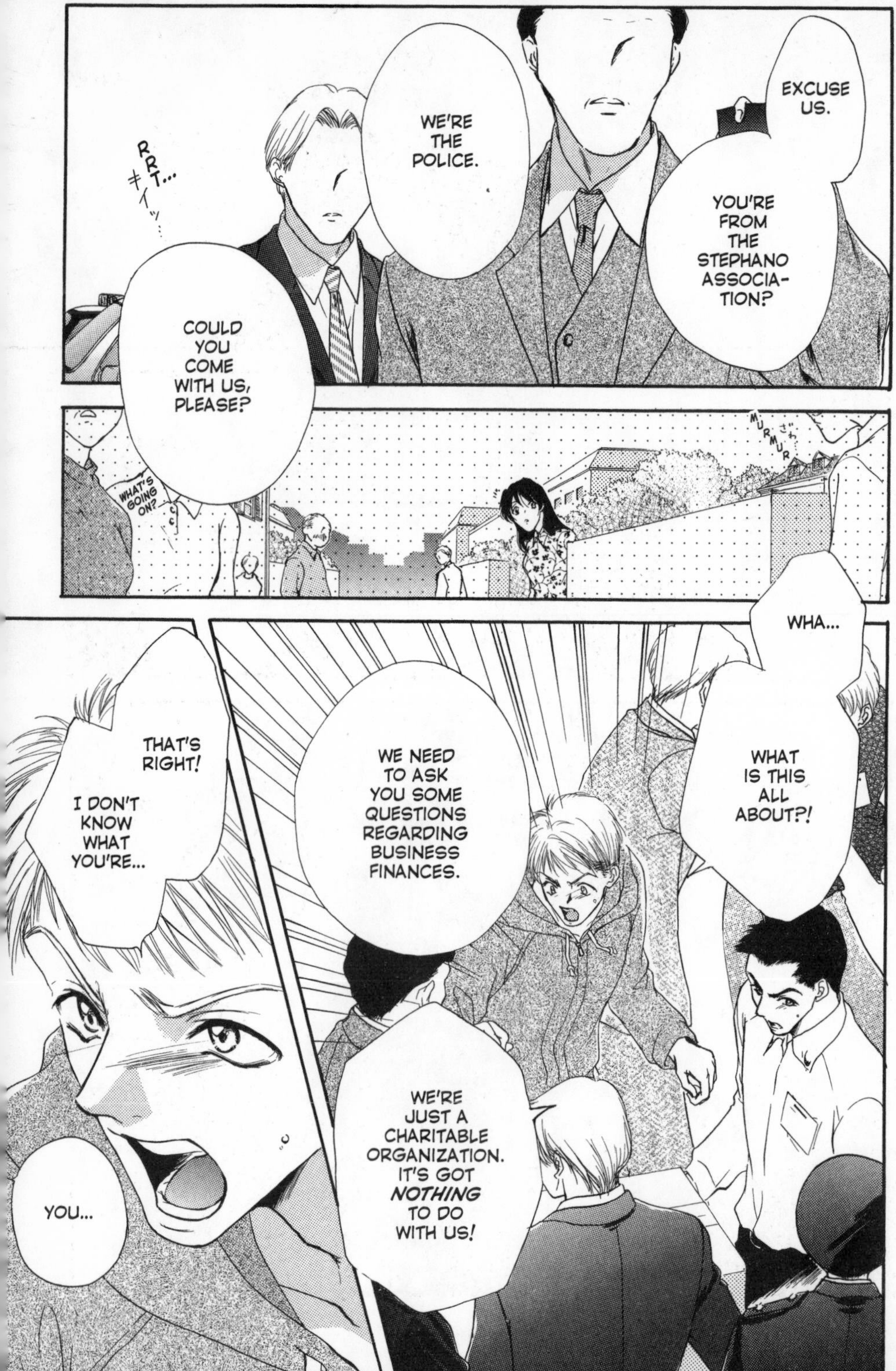
EXCUSE US.
YOU'RE FROM THE STEPHANO ASSOCIATION?
WE'RE THE POLICE.
RRT... キイッ...
COULD YOU COME WITH US, PLEASE?
MURMUR ざわ
WHAT'S GOING ON?
WHA...
WHAT IS THIS ALL ABOUT?!
WE NEED TO ASK YOU SOME QUESTIONS REGARDING BUSINESS FINANCES.
WE'RE JUST A CHARITABLE ORGANIZATION. IT'S GOT *NOTHING* TO DO WITH US!
THAT'S RIGHT!
I DON'T KNOW WHAT YOU'RE...
YOU...

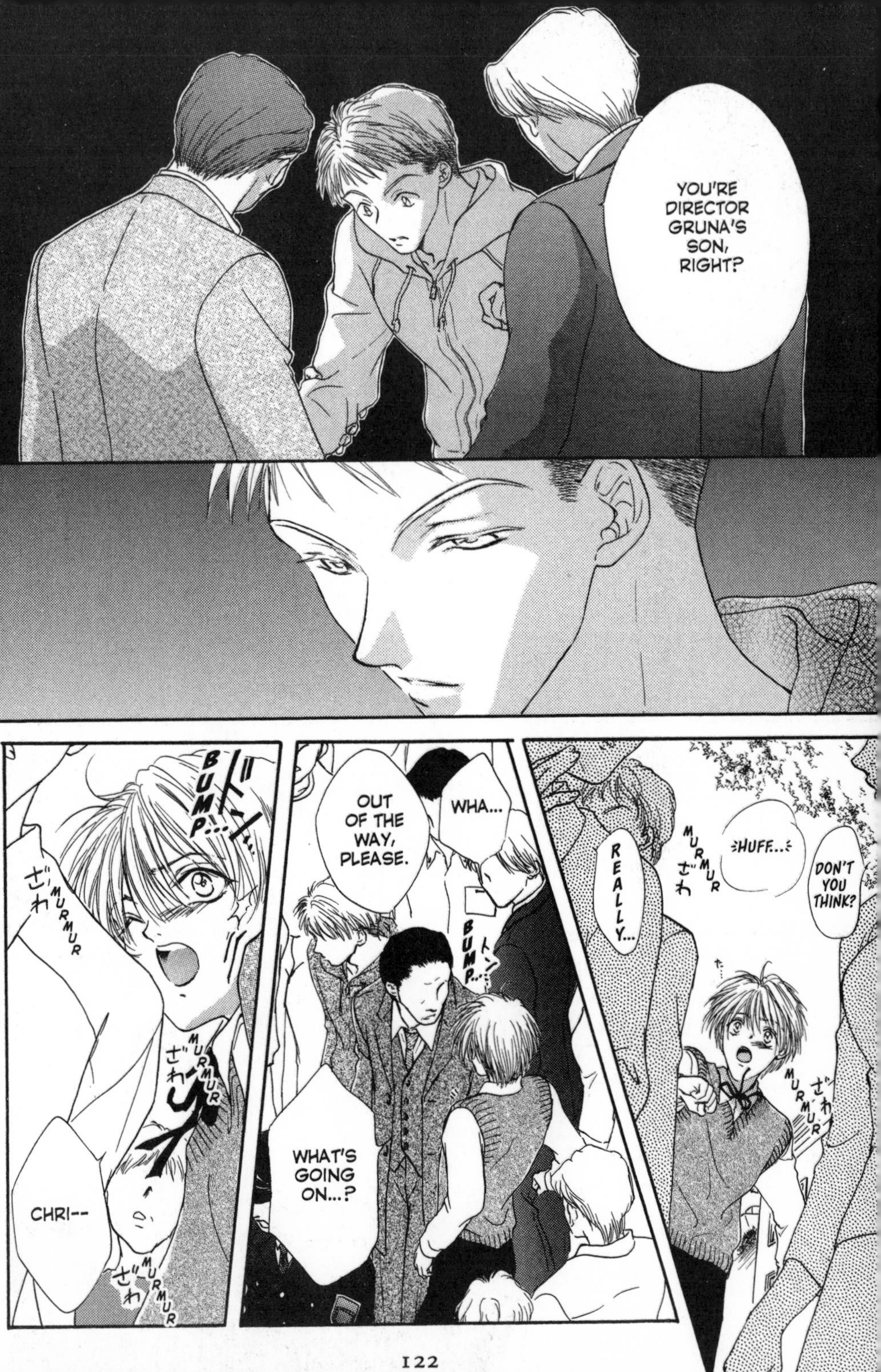
YOU'RE DIRECTOR GRUNA'S SON, RIGHT?
DON'T YOU THINK?
HUFF...
MURMUR
ざわ
REALLY...
MURMUR
ざわ
WHA...
OUT OF THE WAY, PLEASE.
BUMP...
WHAT'S GOING ON...?
BUMP...!!
MURMUR
ざわ
MURMUR
ざわ
CHRI--
MURMUR
ざわ

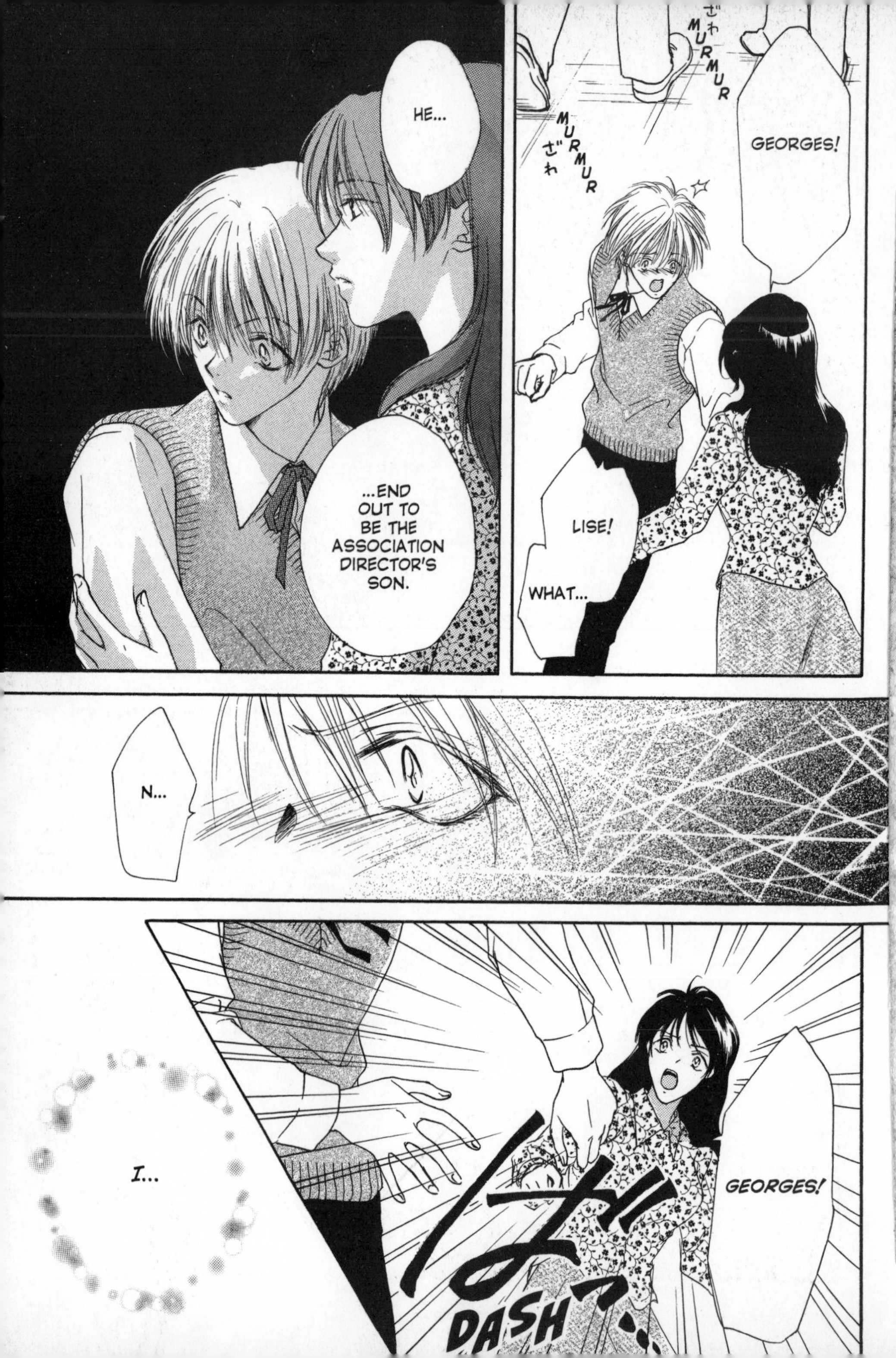
ざわ MURMUR
ざわ MURMUR
GEORGES!
LISE!
WHAT...
HE...
...END OUT TO BE THE ASSOCIATION DIRECTOR'S SON.
N...
GEORGES!
I...
DASH

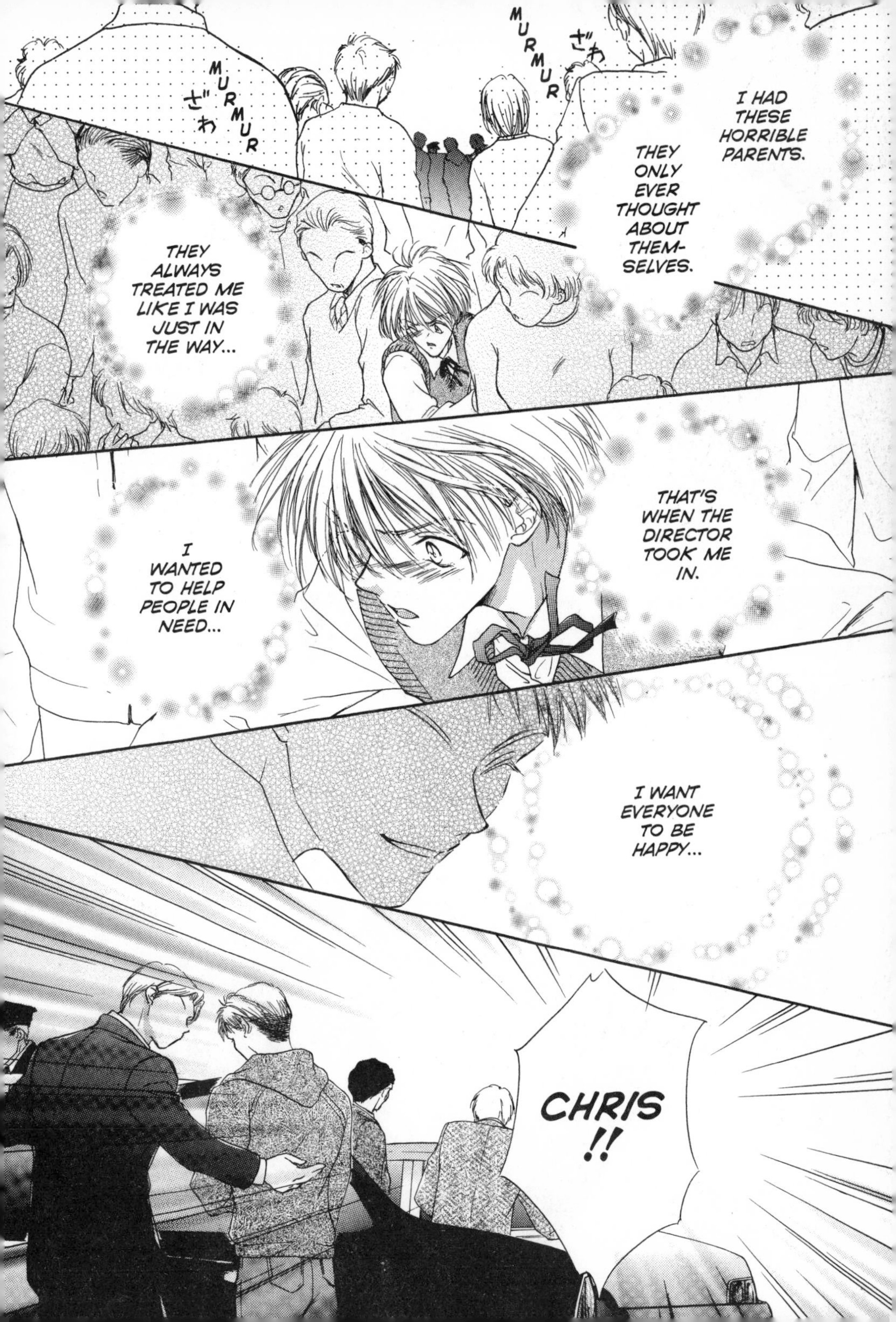
MURMUR ざわ
MURMUR ざわ
I HAD THESE HORRIBLE PARENTS.
THEY ONLY EVER THOUGHT ABOUT THEMSELVES.
THEY ALWAYS TREATED ME LIKE I WAS JUST IN THE WAY...
THAT'S WHEN THE DIRECTOR TOOK ME IN.
I WANTED TO HELP PEOPLE IN NEED...
I WANT EVERYONE TO BE HAPPY...
CHRIS !!

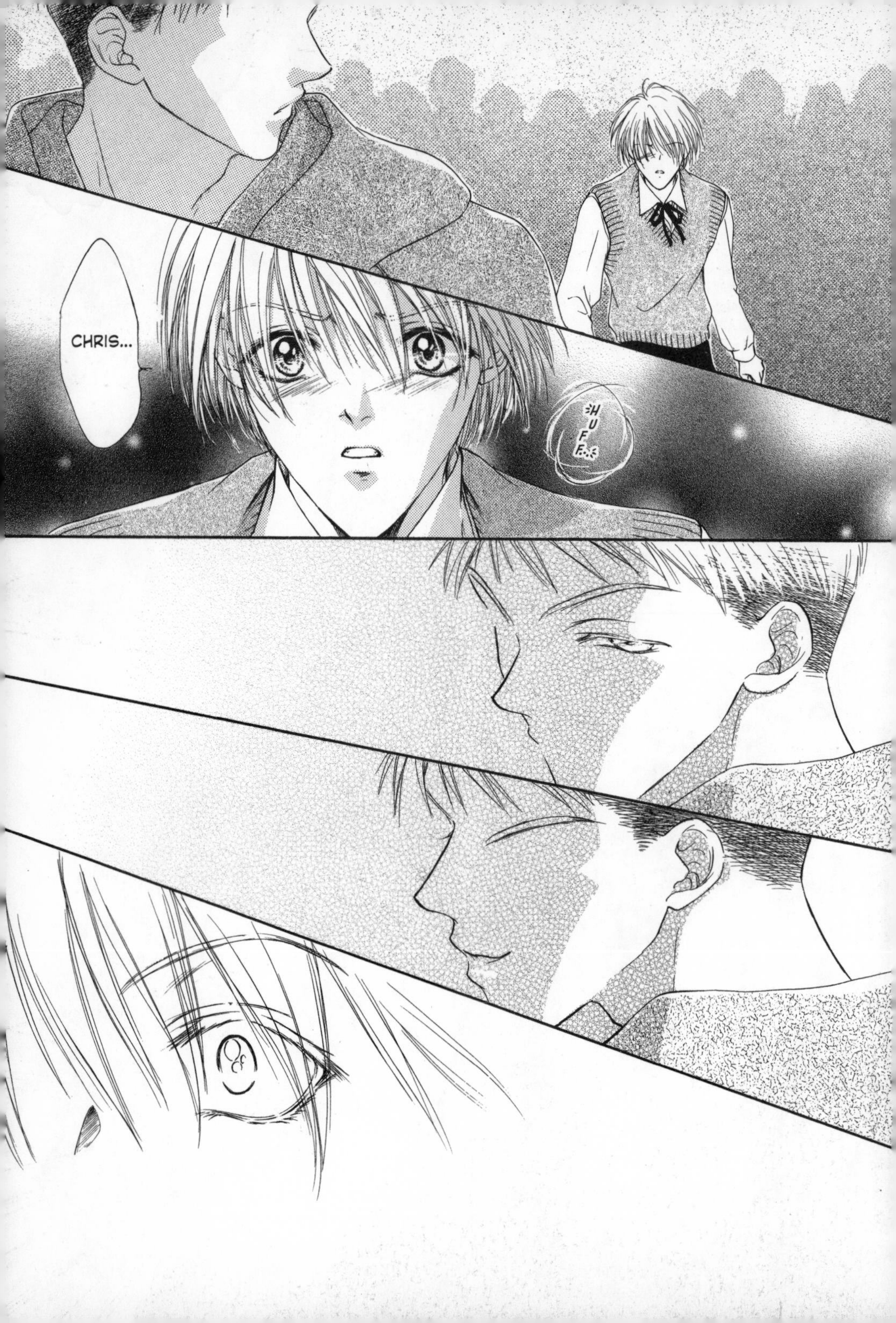
CHRIS...
HUFF...

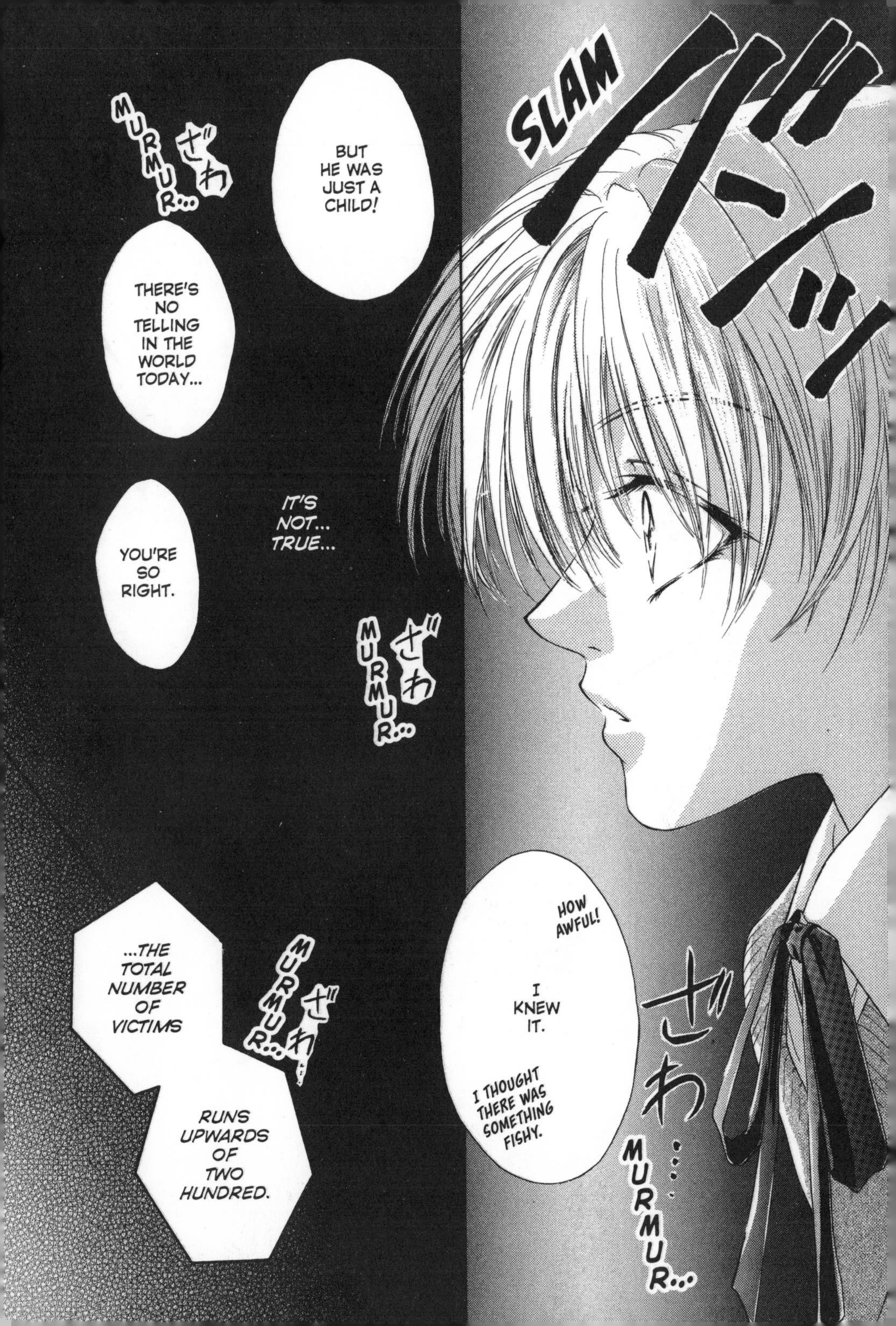
SLAM
HOW AWFUL!
I KNEW IT.
I THOUGHT THERE WAS SOMETHING FISHY.
ざわ
MURMUR...
BUT HE WAS JUST A CHILD!
ざわ
MURMUR...
THERE'S NO TELLING IN THE WORLD TODAY...
IT'S NOT... TRUE...
YOU'RE SO RIGHT.
ざわ
MURMUR...
ざわ
MURMUR...
...THE TOTAL NUMBER OF VICTIMS
RUNS UPWARDS OF TWO HUNDRED.

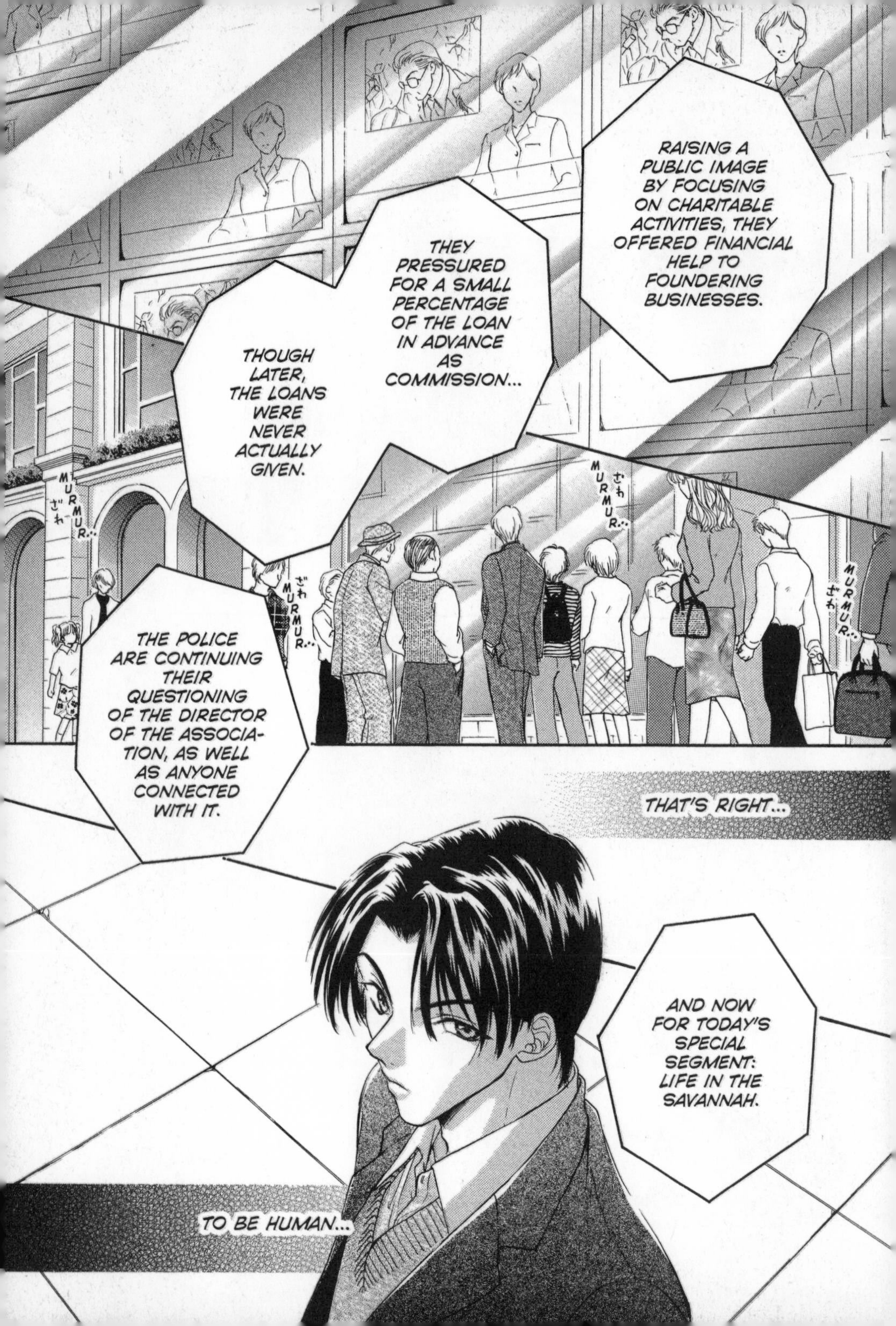
RAISING A PUBLIC IMAGE BY FOCUSING ON CHARITABLE ACTIVITIES, THEY OFFERED FINANCIAL HELP TO FOUNDERING BUSINESSES.
THEY PRESSURED FOR A SMALL PERCENTAGE OF THE LOAN IN ADVANCE AS COMMISSION...
THOUGH LATER, THE LOANS WERE NEVER ACTUALLY GIVEN.
MURMUR... ざわ
MURMUR... ざわ
MURMUR... ざわ
MURMUR... ざわ
THE POLICE ARE CONTINUING THEIR QUESTIONING OF THE DIRECTOR OF THE ASSOCIATION, AS WELL AS ANYONE CONNECTED WITH IT.
THAT'S RIGHT...
AND NOW FOR TODAY'S SPECIAL SEGMENT: LIFE IN THE SAVANNAH.
TO BE HUMAN...

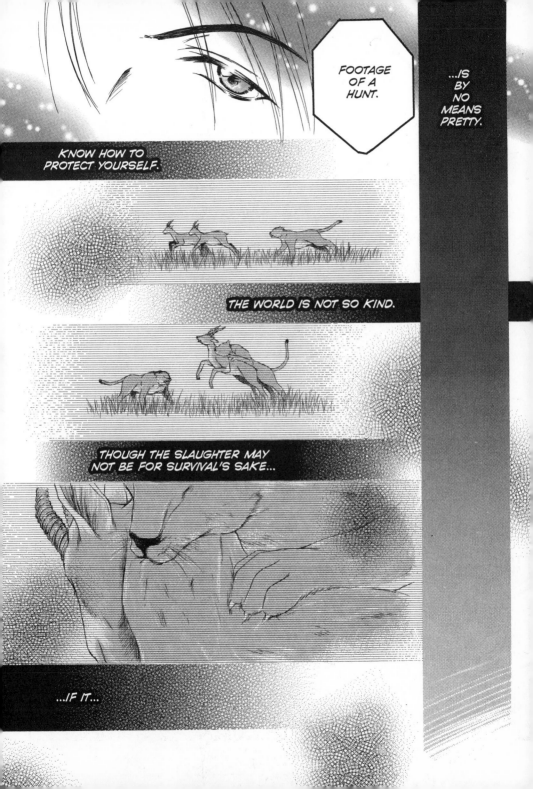

FOOTAGE
OF A
HUNT.

...IS
BY
NO
MEANS
PRETTY.

KNOW HOW TO
PROTECT YOURSELF.

THE WORLD IS NOT SO KIND.

THOUGH THE SLAUGHTER MAY
NOT BE FOR SURVIVAL'S SAKE...

...IF IT...

...VIOLATES...

...ANOTHER'S HEART.

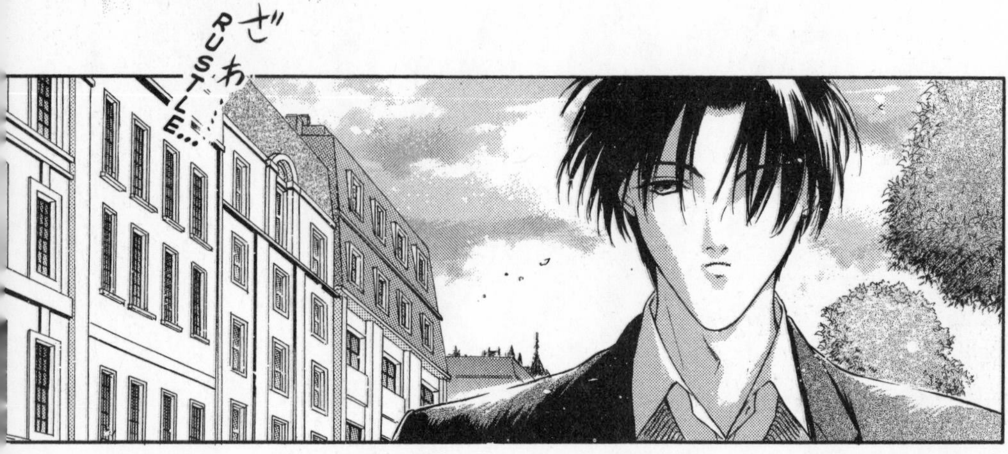
ざわ
RUSTLE...

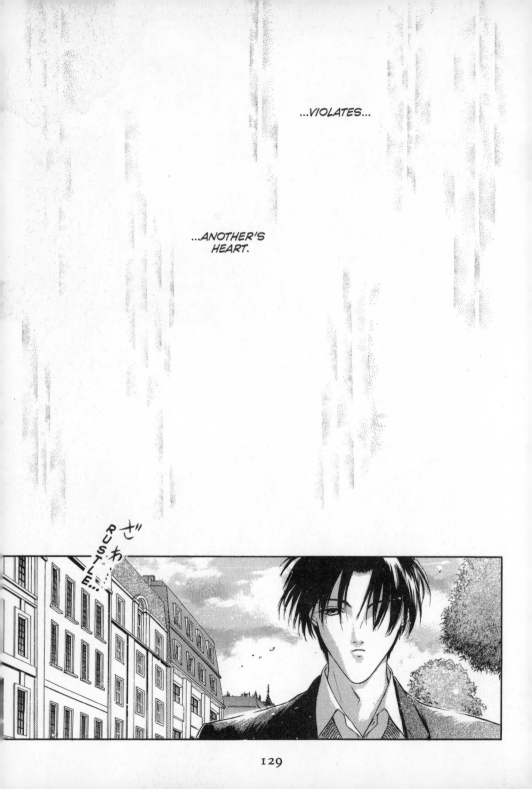

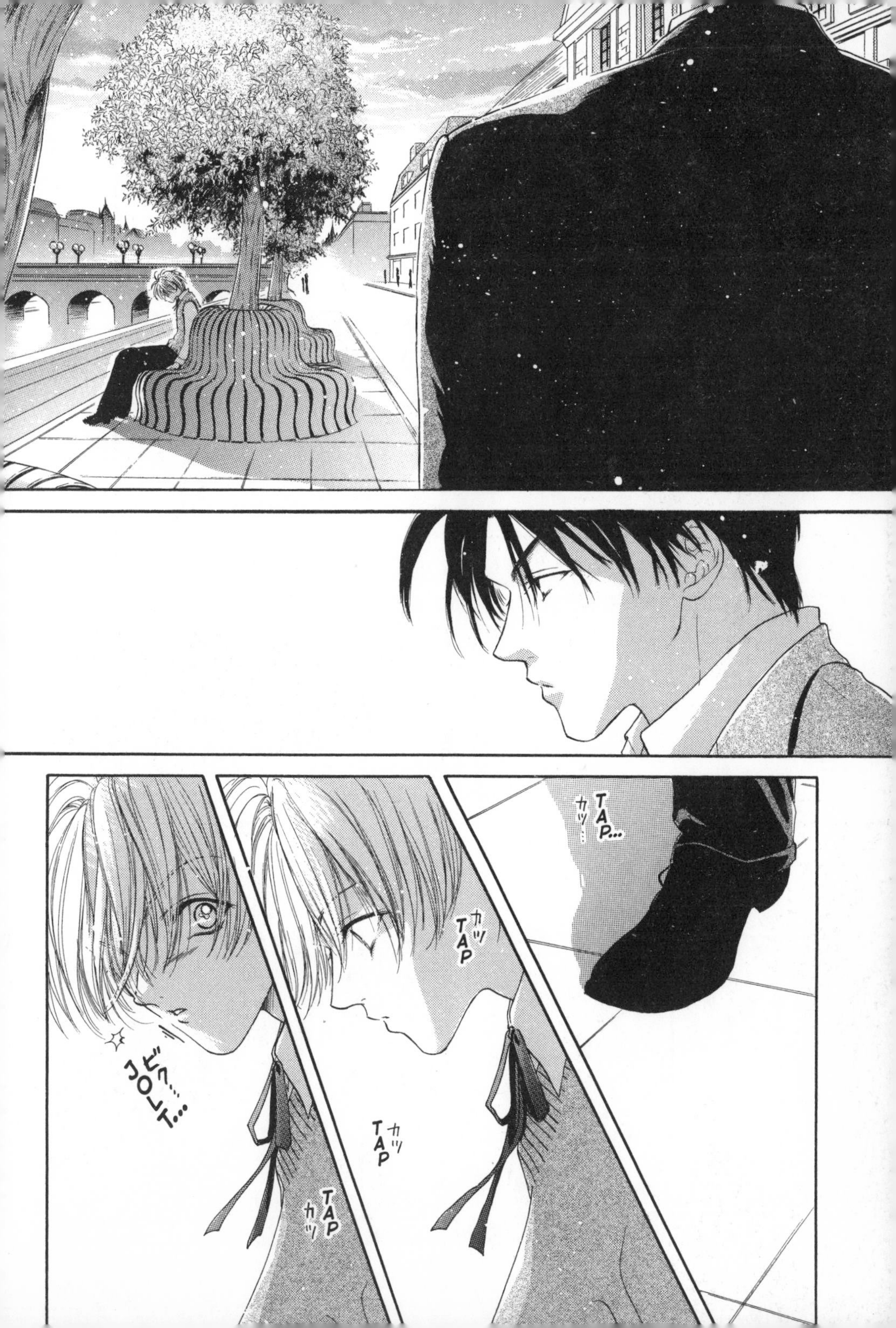

TAP...
カッ…
TAP
カッ
TAP
カッ
ビク…
JOLT...
TAP
カッ

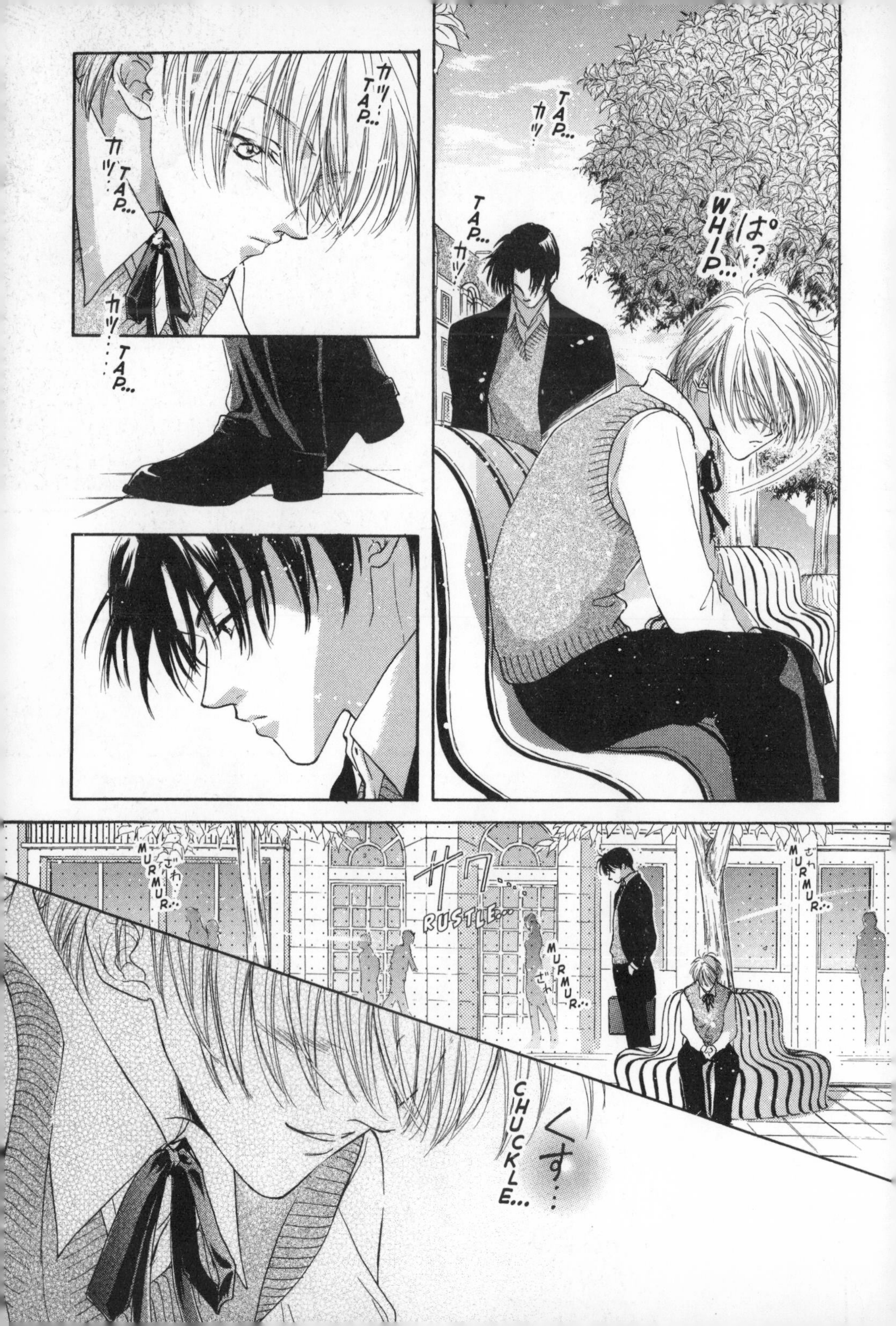
TAP... カッ
TAP... カッ
WHIP... ぱっ...
カッ... TAP...
カッ... TAP...
カッ... TAP...
MURMUR... ざわ
RUSTLE... サワ...
MURMUR... ざわ
MURMUR... ざわ
CHUCKLE... くす...

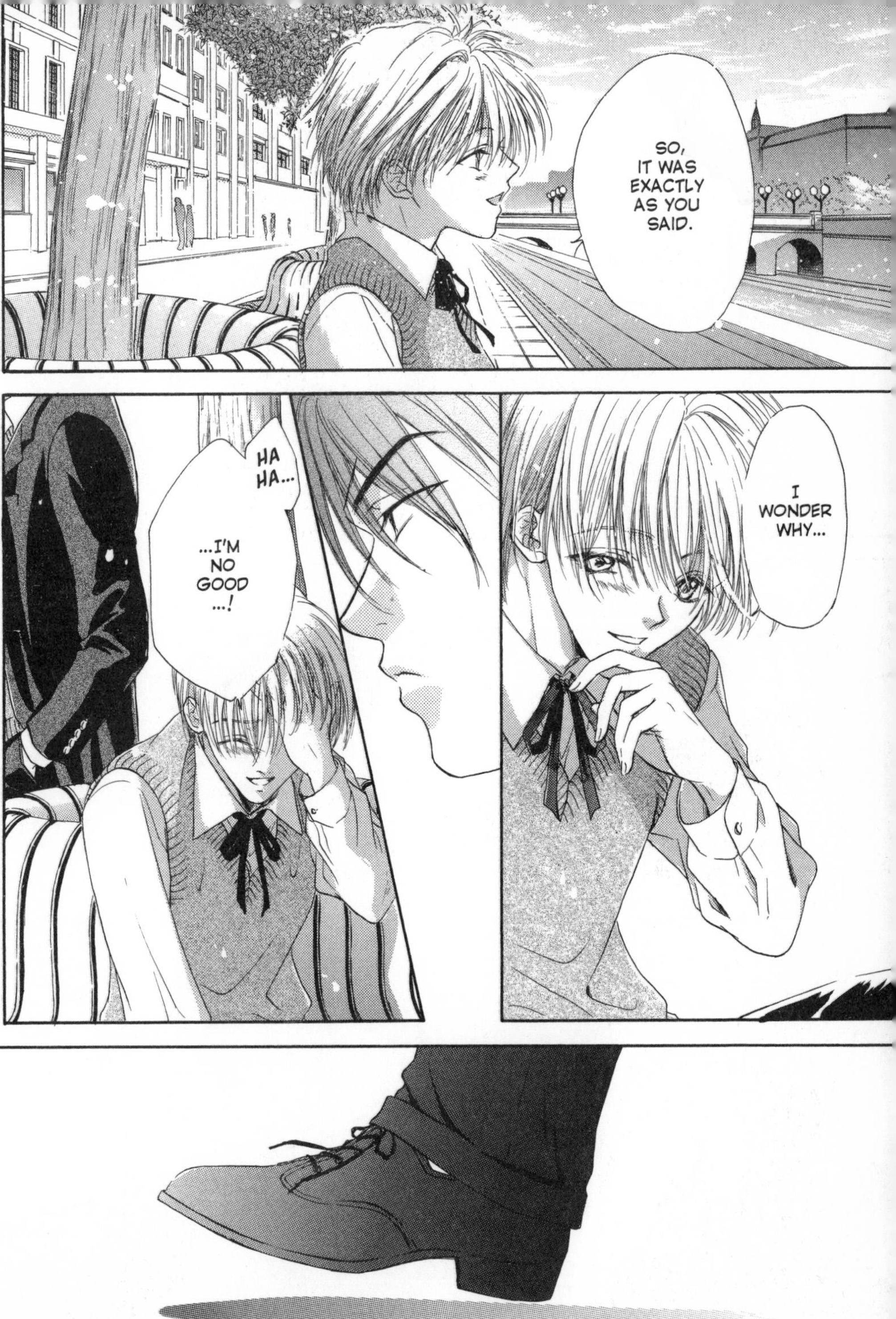
SO, IT WAS EXACTLY AS YOU SAID.
I WONDER WHY...
HA HA...
...I'M NO GOOD ...!

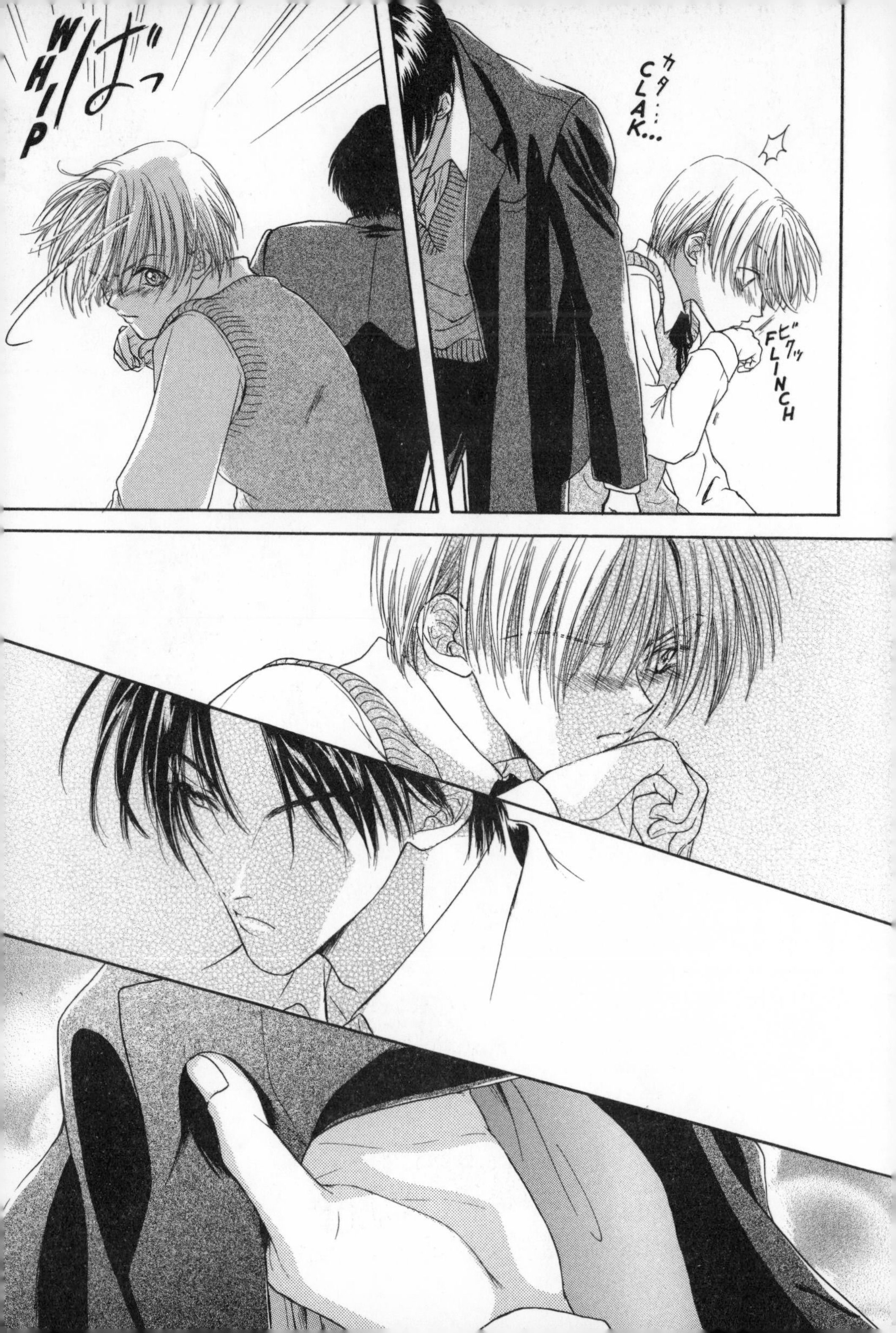
カタ…
CLAK...
ビクッ
FLINCH
ばっ
WHIP

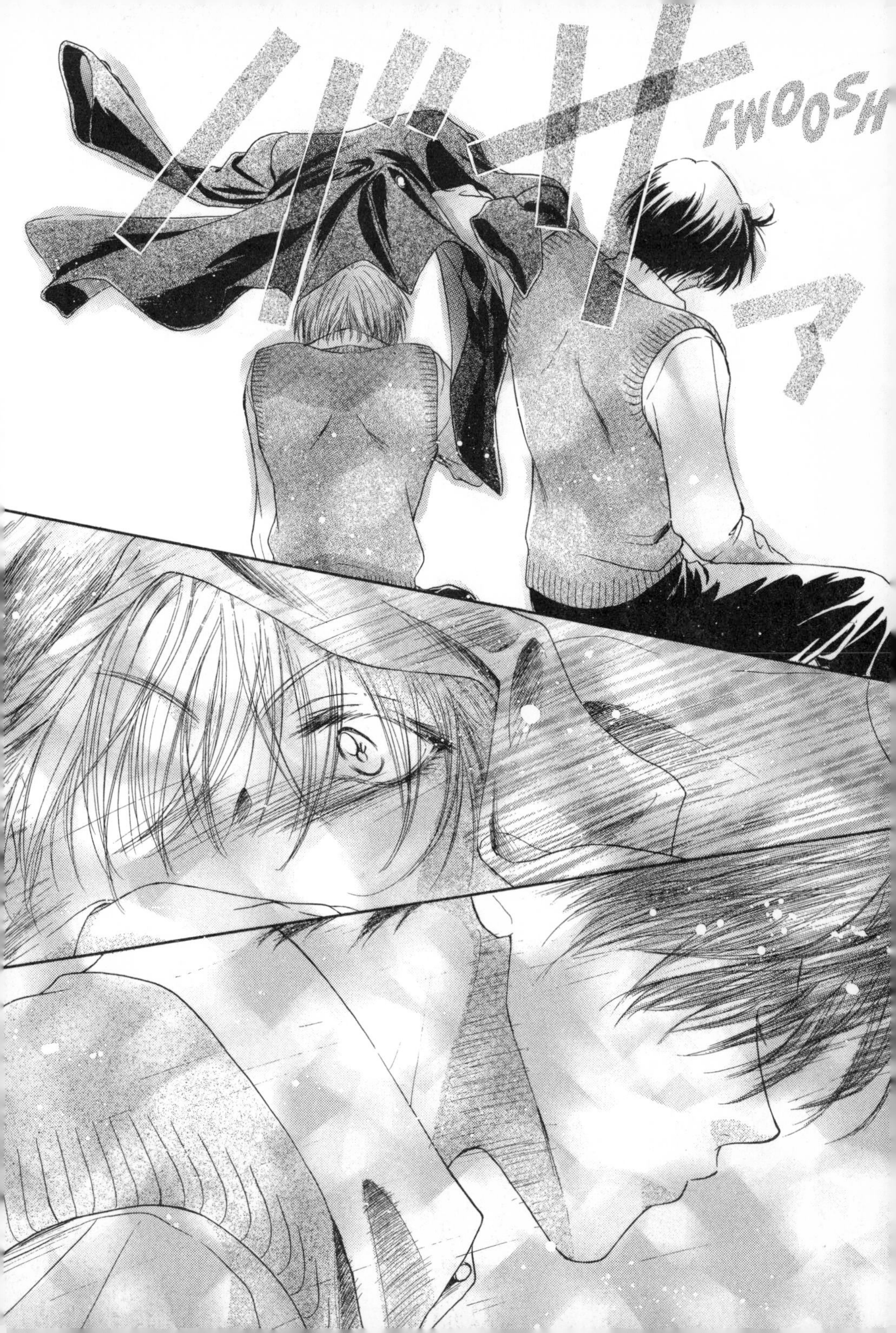
FWOOSH

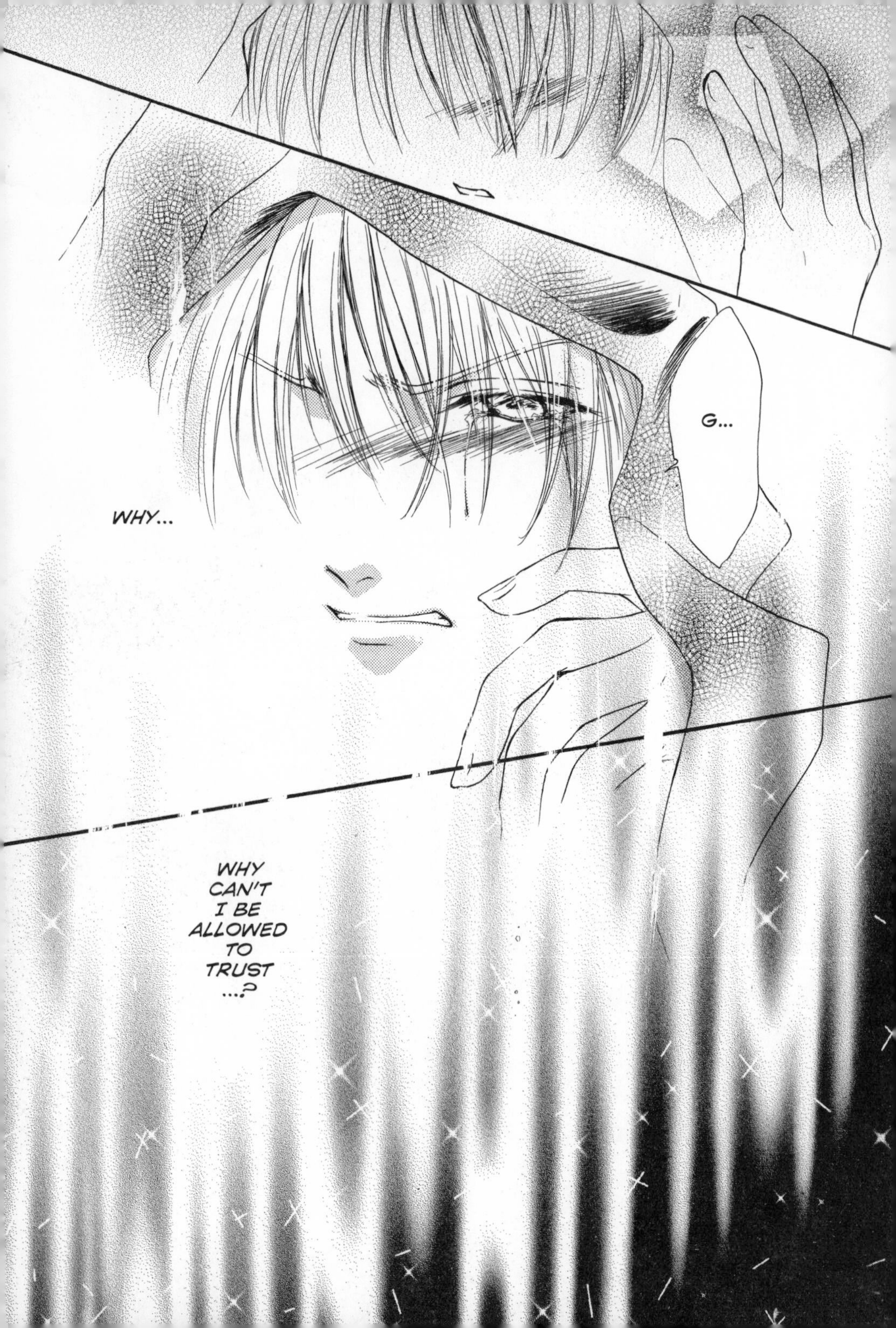
G...
WHY...
WHY CAN'T I BE ALLOWED TO TRUST ...?

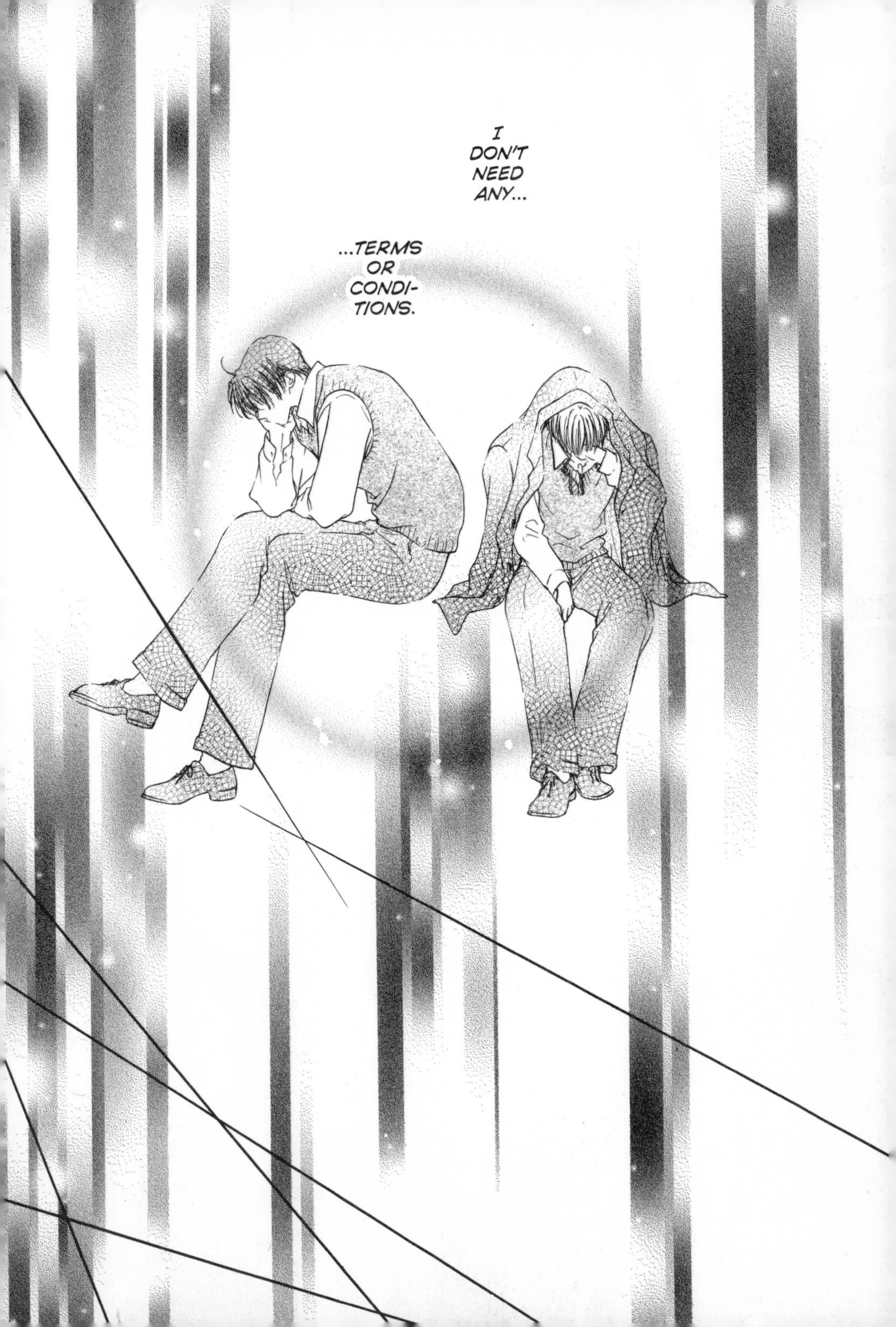
I DON'T NEED ANY...
...TERMS OR CONDITIONS.

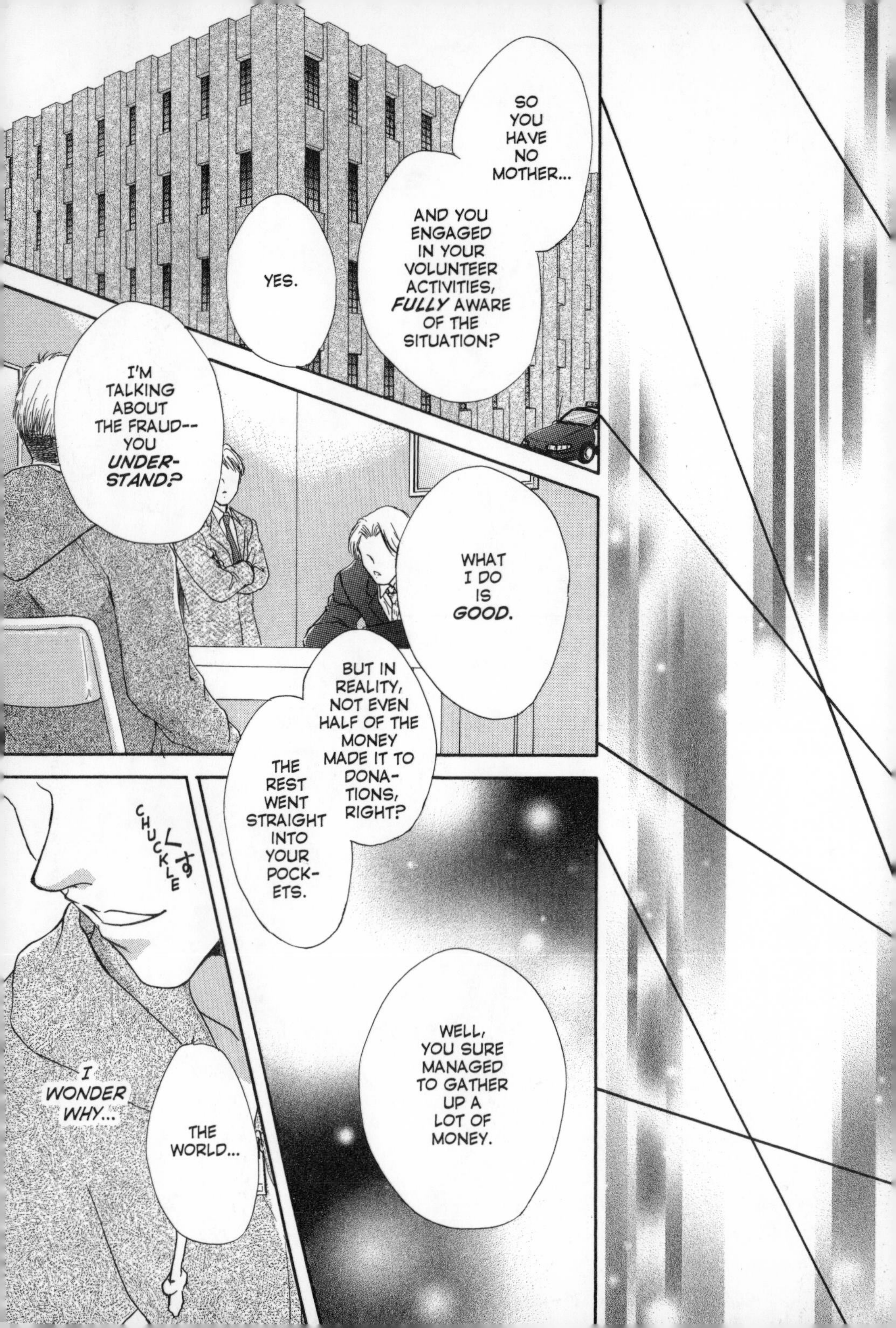
SO YOU HAVE NO MOTHER...
AND YOU ENGAGED IN YOUR VOLUNTEER ACTIVITIES, *FULLY* AWARE OF THE SITUATION?
YES.
I'M TALKING ABOUT THE FRAUD--YOU *UNDERSTAND?*
WHAT I DO IS *GOOD.*
BUT IN REALITY, NOT EVEN HALF OF THE MONEY MADE IT TO DONATIONS, RIGHT?
THE REST WENT STRAIGHT INTO YOUR POCKETS.
WELL, YOU SURE MANAGED TO GATHER UP A LOT OF MONEY.
CHUCKLE くす
THE WORLD...
I WONDER WHY...

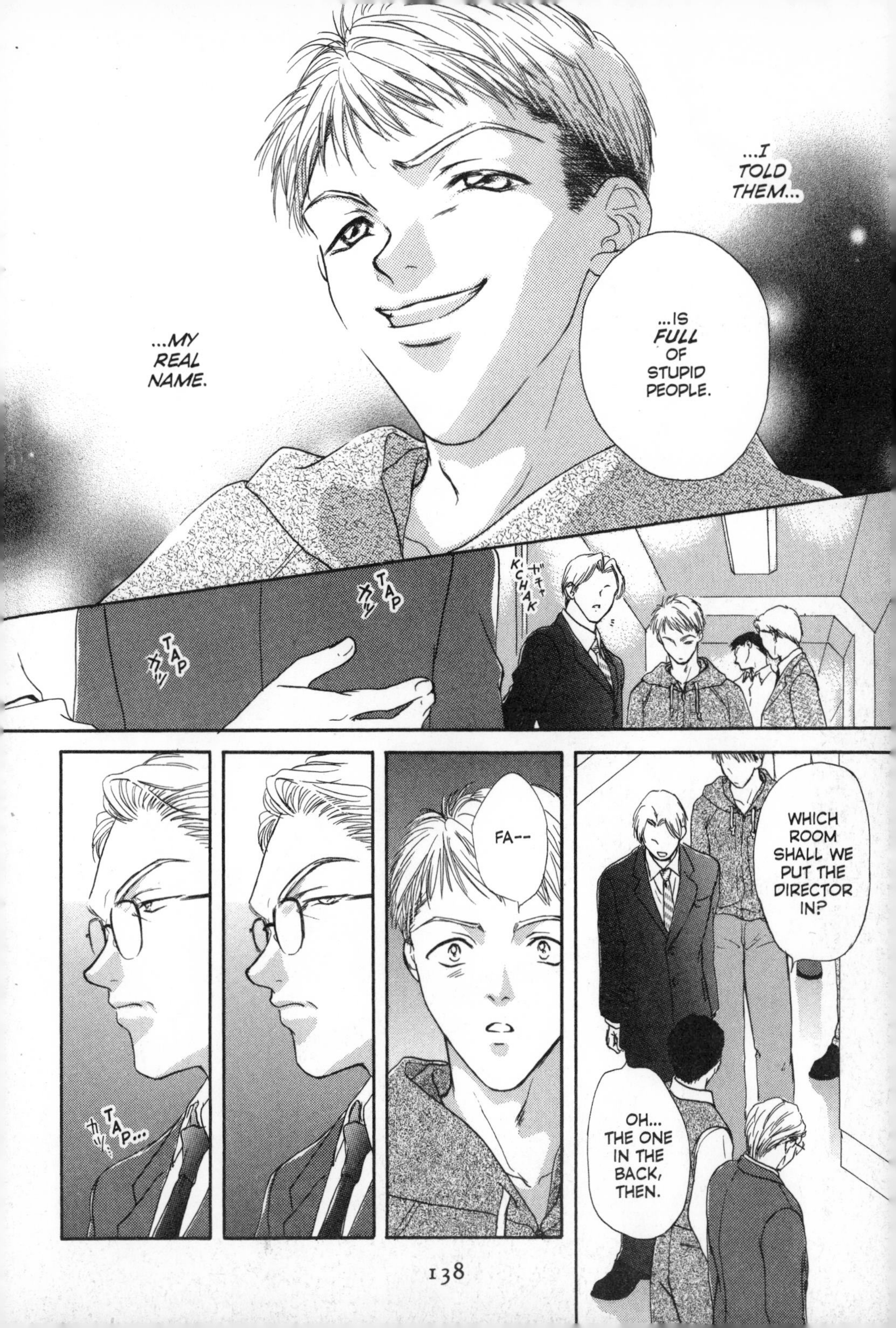
...I TOLD THEM...
...IS FULL OF STUPID PEOPLE.
...MY REAL NAME.
KCHAK
TAP
TAP
WHICH ROOM SHALL WE PUT THE DIRECTOR IN?
OH... THE ONE IN THE BACK, THEN.
FA--
TAP...

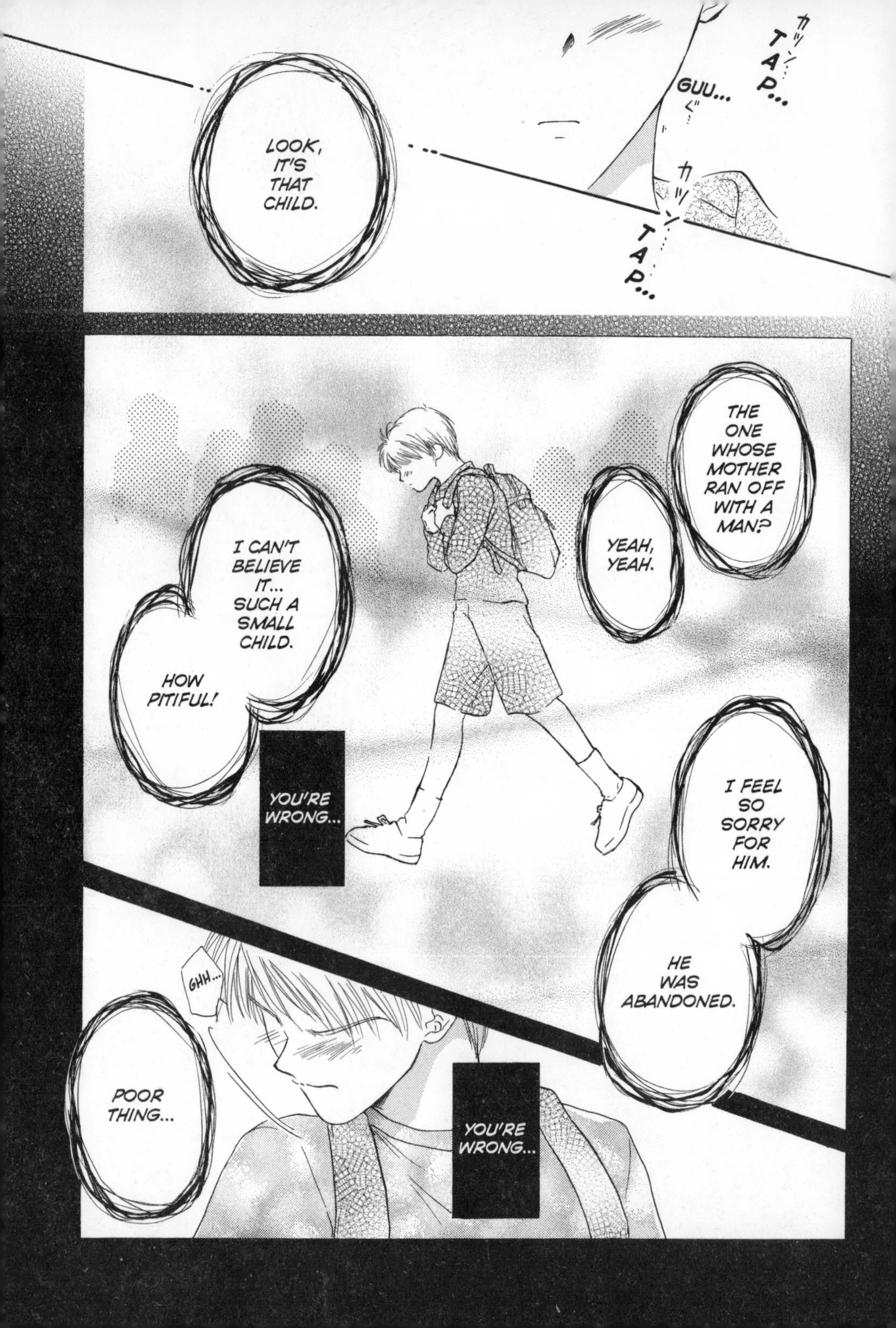
TAP...
GUU...
TAP...
LOOK, IT'S THAT CHILD.
THE ONE WHOSE MOTHER RAN OFF WITH A MAN?
YEAH, YEAH.
I CAN'T BELIEVE IT... SUCH A SMALL CHILD.
HOW PITIFUL!
I FEEL SO SORRY FOR HIM.
HE WAS ABANDONED.
YOU'RE WRONG...
YOU'RE WRONG...
GHH...
POOR THING...

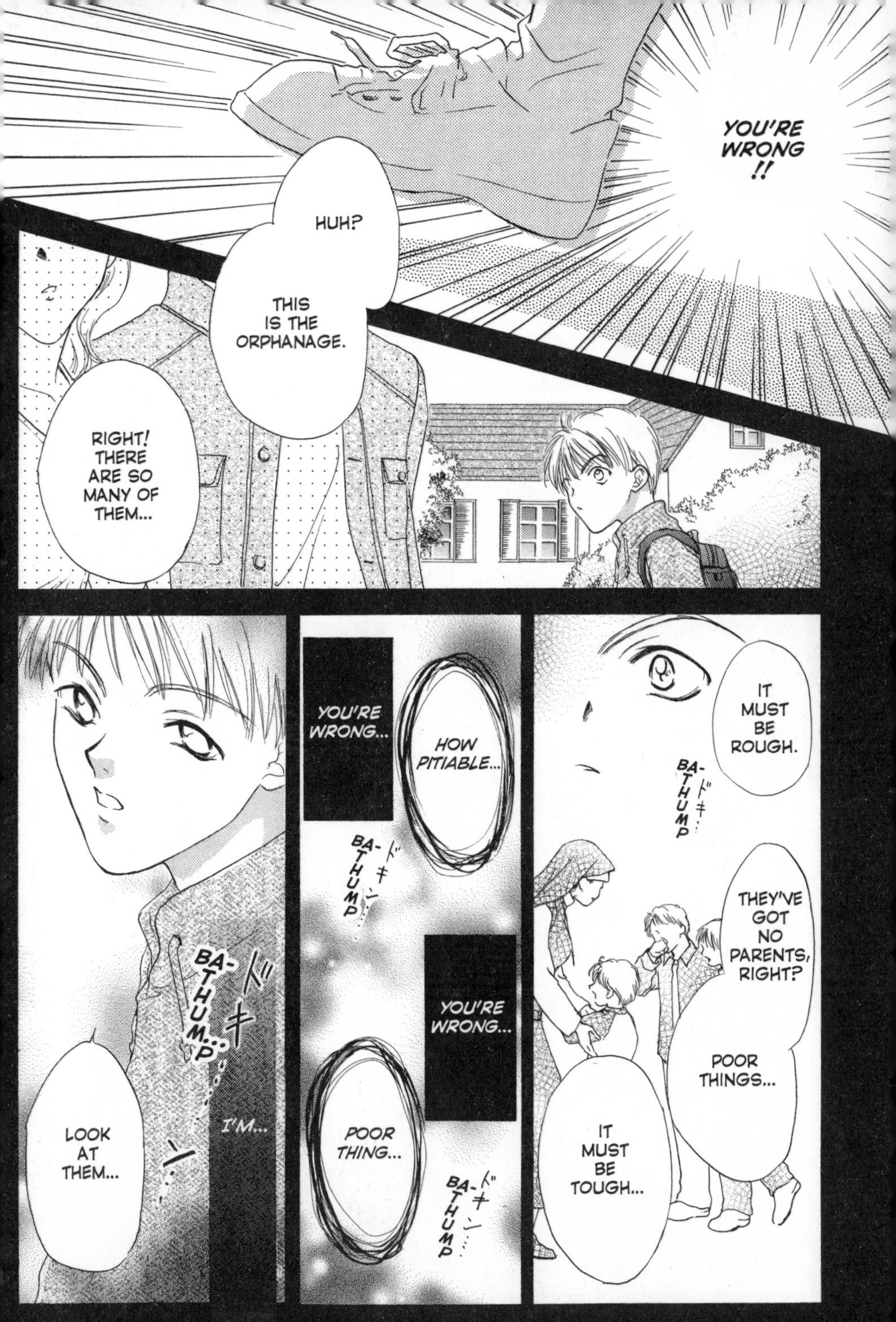
YOU'RE WRONG !!
HUH?
THIS IS THE ORPHANAGE.
RIGHT! THERE ARE SO MANY OF THEM...
IT MUST BE ROUGH.
BA-THUMP ドキ...
THEY'VE GOT NO PARENTS, RIGHT?
POOR THINGS...
IT MUST BE TOUGH...
HOW PITIABLE...
YOU'RE WRONG...
BA-THUMP ドキン...
YOU'RE WRONG...
POOR THING...
BA-THUMP ドキン...
BA-THUMP... ドキ...ン...
I'M...
LOOK AT THEM...

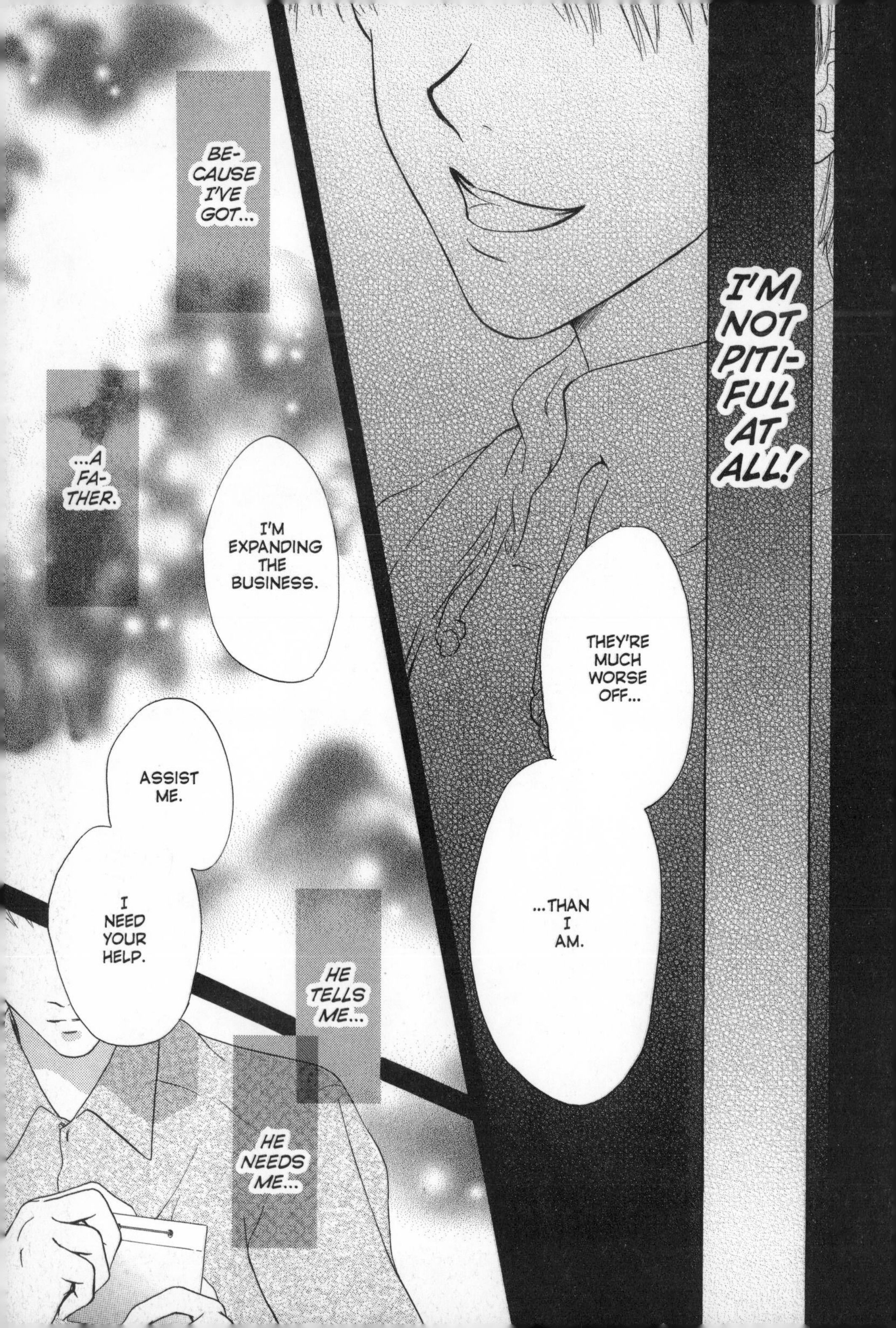
I'M NOT PITI-FUL AT ALL!
THEY'RE MUCH WORSE OFF...
...THAN I AM.
BE-CAUSE I'VE GOT...
...A FA-THER.
I'M EXPANDING THE BUSINESS.
ASSIST ME.
I NEED YOUR HELP.
HE TELLS ME...
HE NEEDS ME...

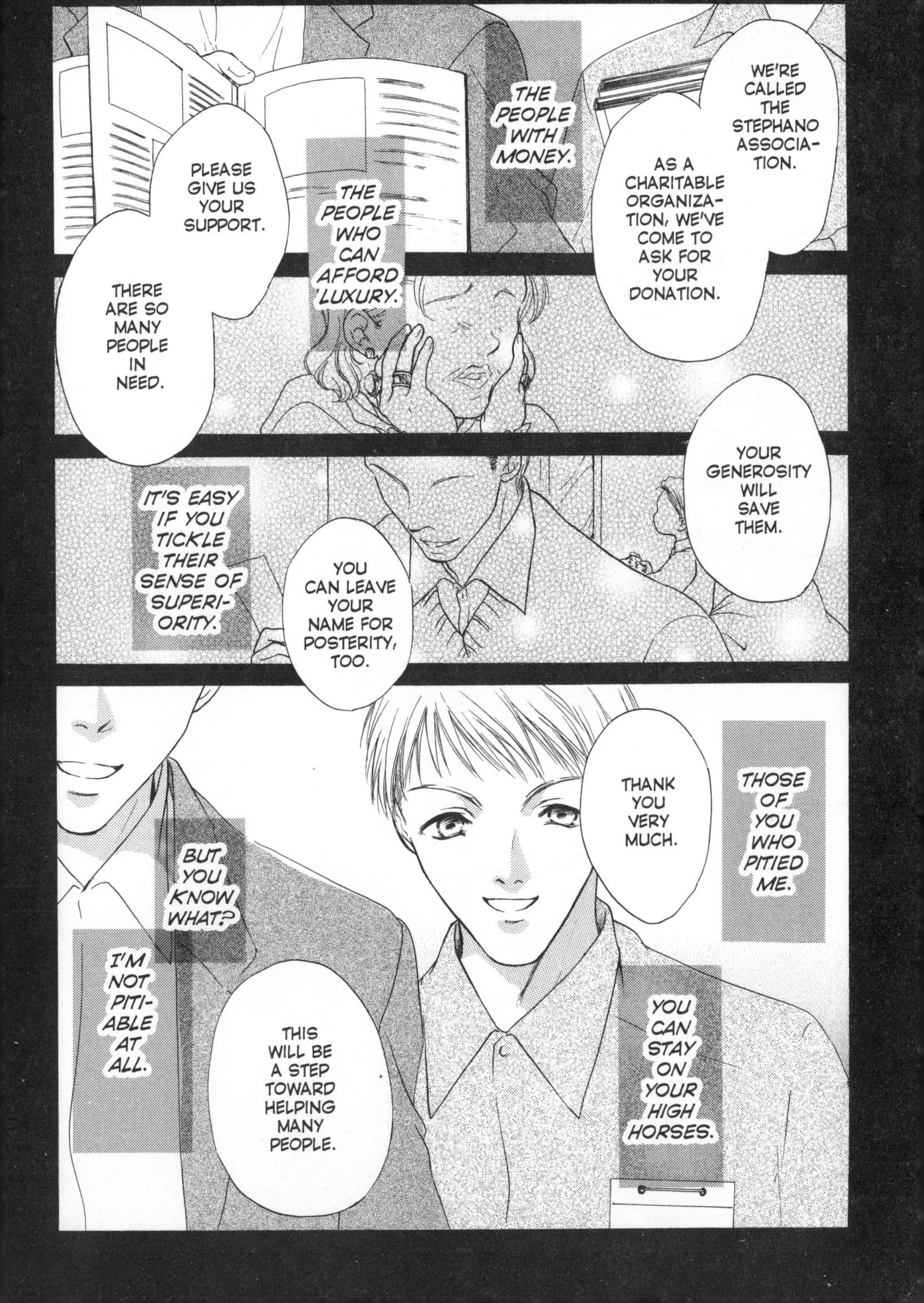
WE'RE CALLED THE STEPHANO ASSOCIATION.
AS A CHARITABLE ORGANIZATION, WE'VE COME TO ASK FOR YOUR DONATION.
THE PEOPLE WITH MONEY.
THE PEOPLE WHO CAN AFFORD LUXURY.
PLEASE GIVE US YOUR SUPPORT.
THERE ARE SO MANY PEOPLE IN NEED.
YOUR GENEROSITY WILL SAVE THEM.
YOU CAN LEAVE YOUR NAME FOR POSTERITY, TOO.
IT'S EASY IF YOU TICKLE THEIR SENSE OF SUPERIORITY.
THOSE OF YOU WHO PITIED ME.
THANK YOU VERY MUCH.
YOU CAN STAY ON YOUR HIGH HORSES.
BUT YOU KNOW WHAT?
THIS WILL BE A STEP TOWARD HELPING MANY PEOPLE.
I'M NOT PITIABLE AT ALL.

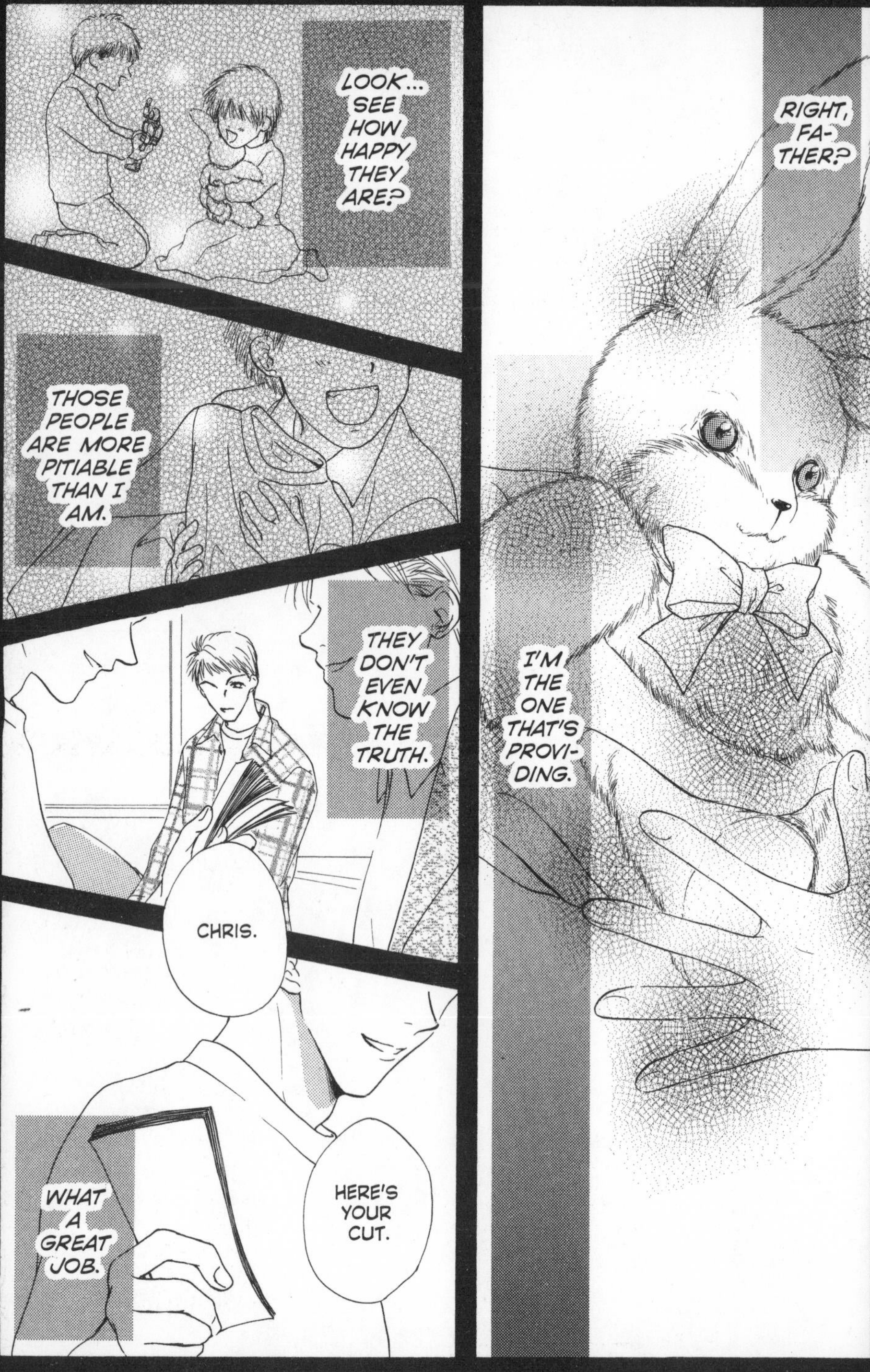
RIGHT, FA-THER?
I'M THE ONE THAT'S PROVI-DING.
LOOK... SEE HOW HAPPY THEY ARE?
THOSE PEOPLE ARE MORE PITIABLE THAN I AM.
THEY DON'T EVEN KNOW THE TRUTH.
CHRIS.
HERE'S YOUR CUT.
WHAT A GREAT JOB.

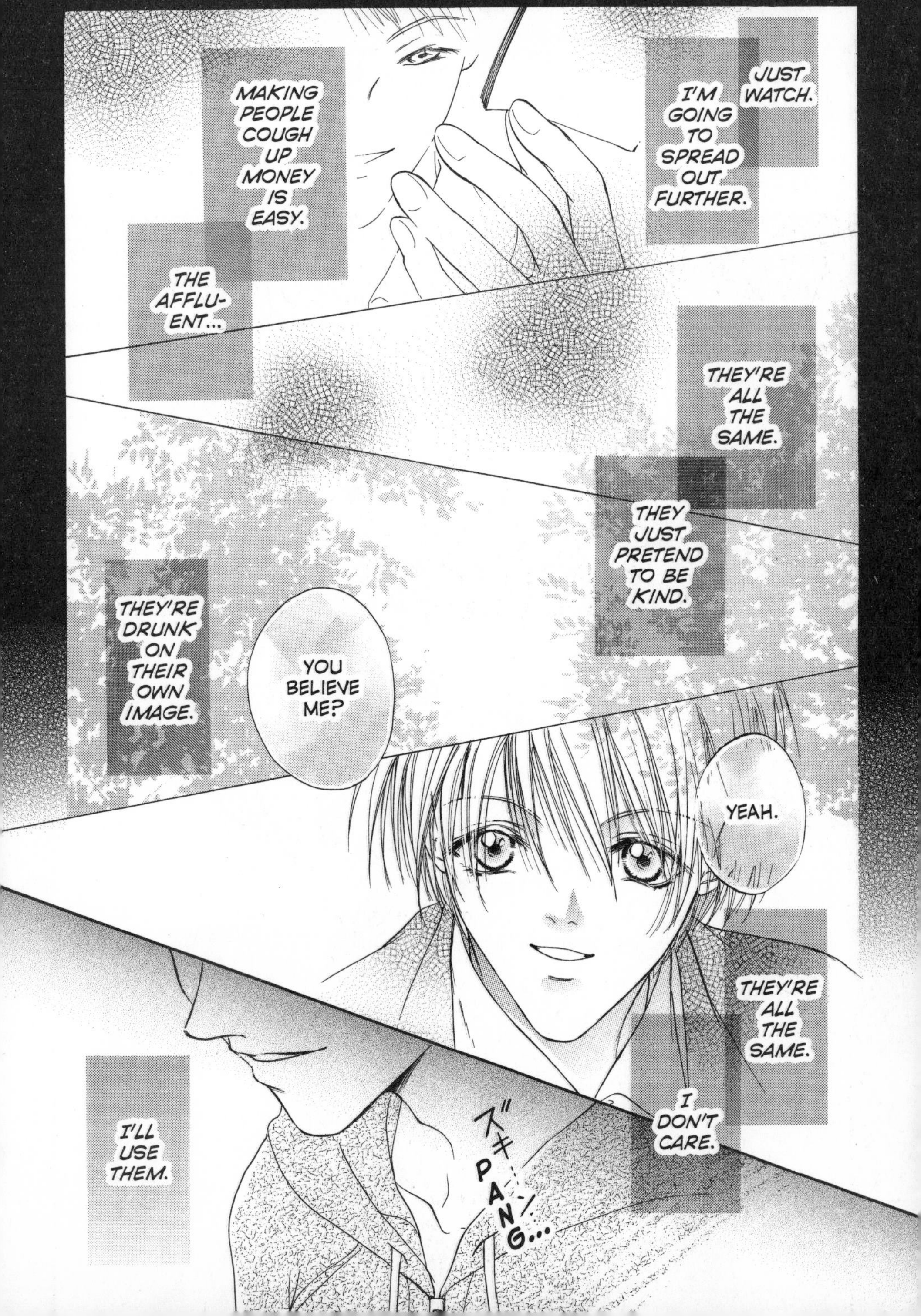
JUST WATCH.
I'M GOING TO SPREAD OUT FURTHER.
MAKING PEOPLE COUGH UP MONEY IS EASY.
THE AFFLU-ENT...
THEY'RE ALL THE SAME.
THEY JUST PRETEND TO BE KIND.
THEY'RE DRUNK ON THEIR OWN IMAGE.
YOU BELIEVE ME?
YEAH.
THEY'RE ALL THE SAME.
I DON'T CARE.
ズキ
PANG...
I'LL USE THEM.

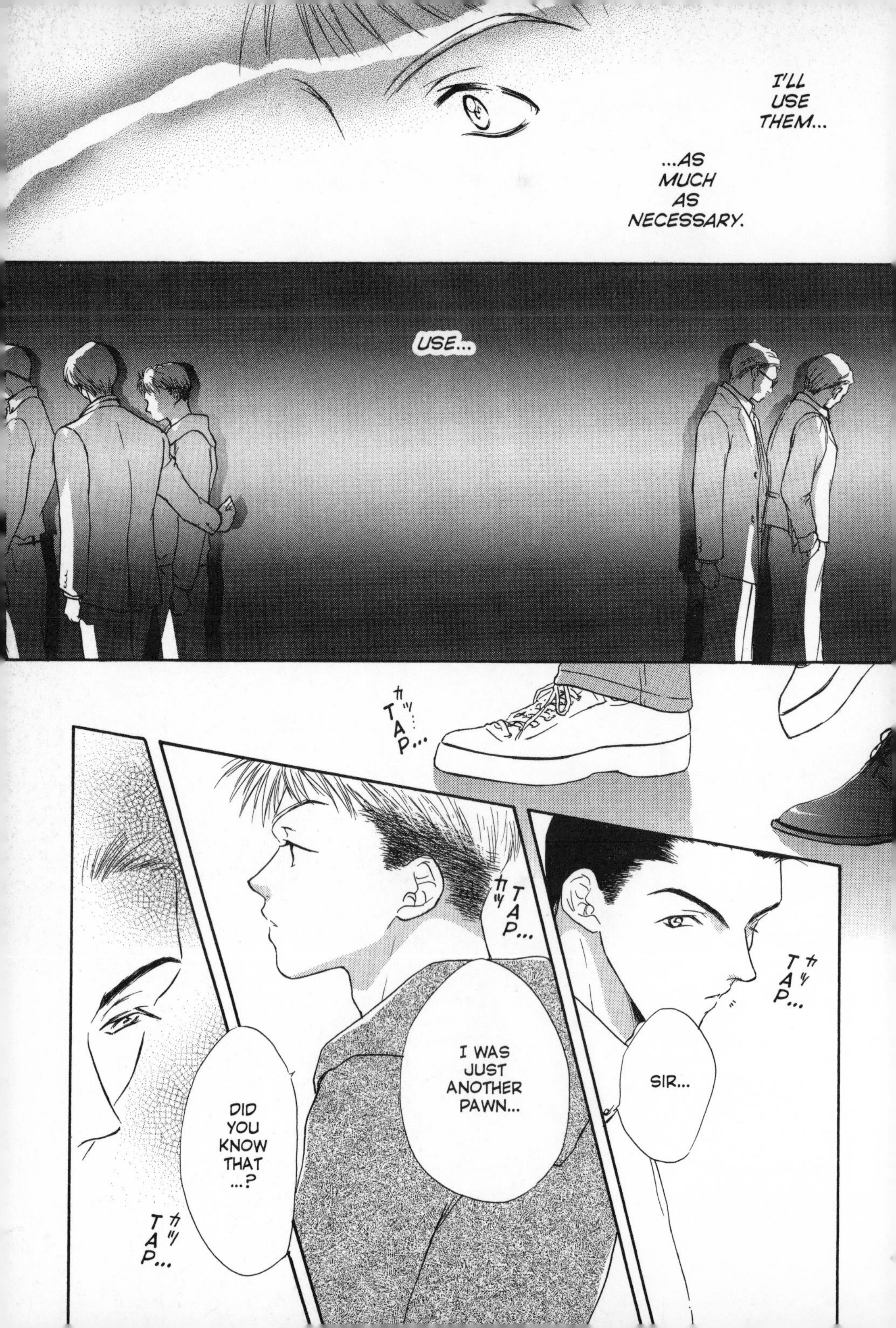
I'LL USE THEM...
...AS MUCH AS NECESSARY.
USE...
TAP...
TAP...
SIR...
TAP...
I WAS JUST ANOTHER PAWN...
DID YOU KNOW THAT ...?
TAP...

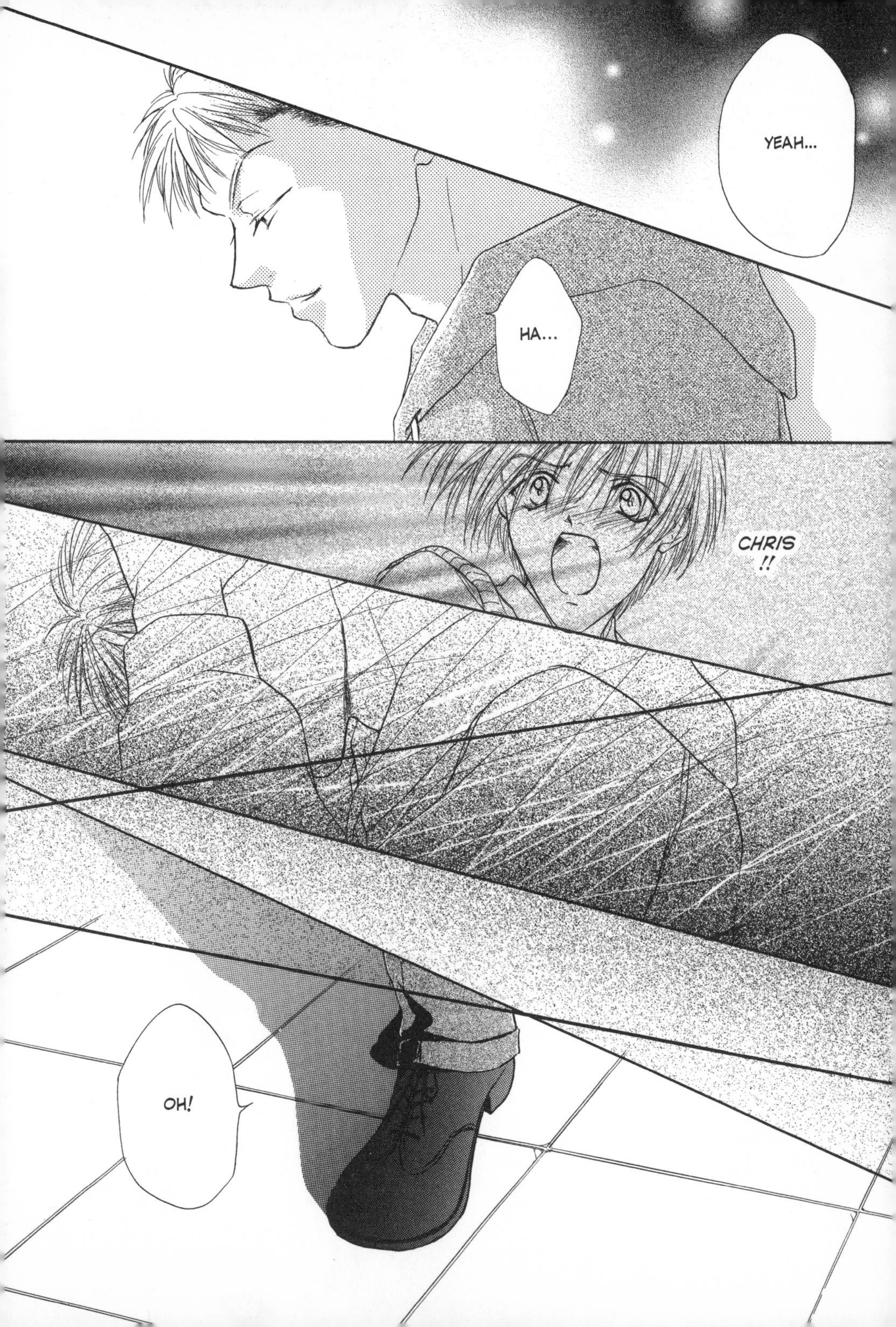
YEAH...
HA...
CHRIS !!
OH!

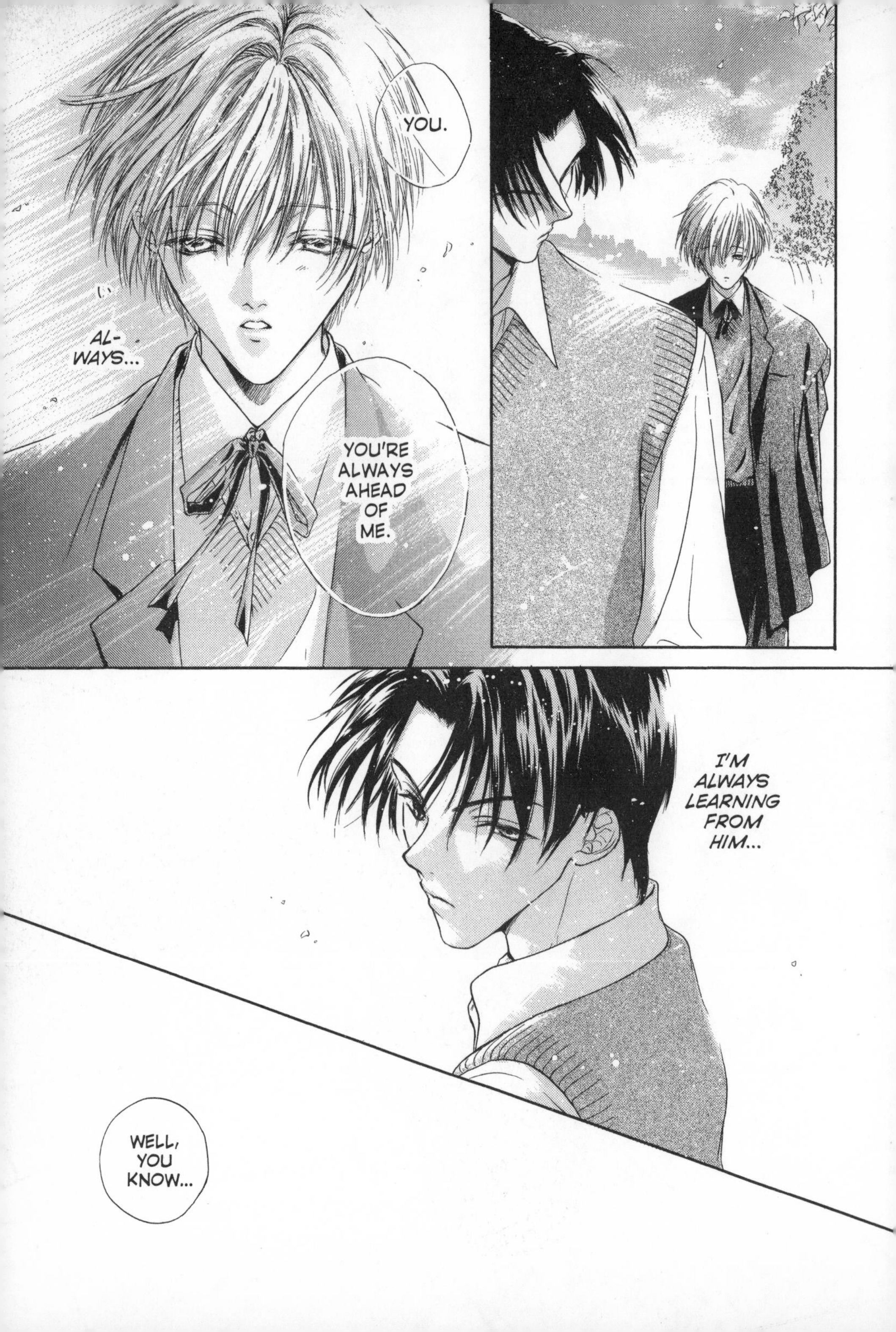
YOU.
AL-WAYS...
YOU'RE ALWAYS AHEAD OF ME.
I'M ALWAYS LEARNING FROM HIM...
WELL, YOU KNOW...

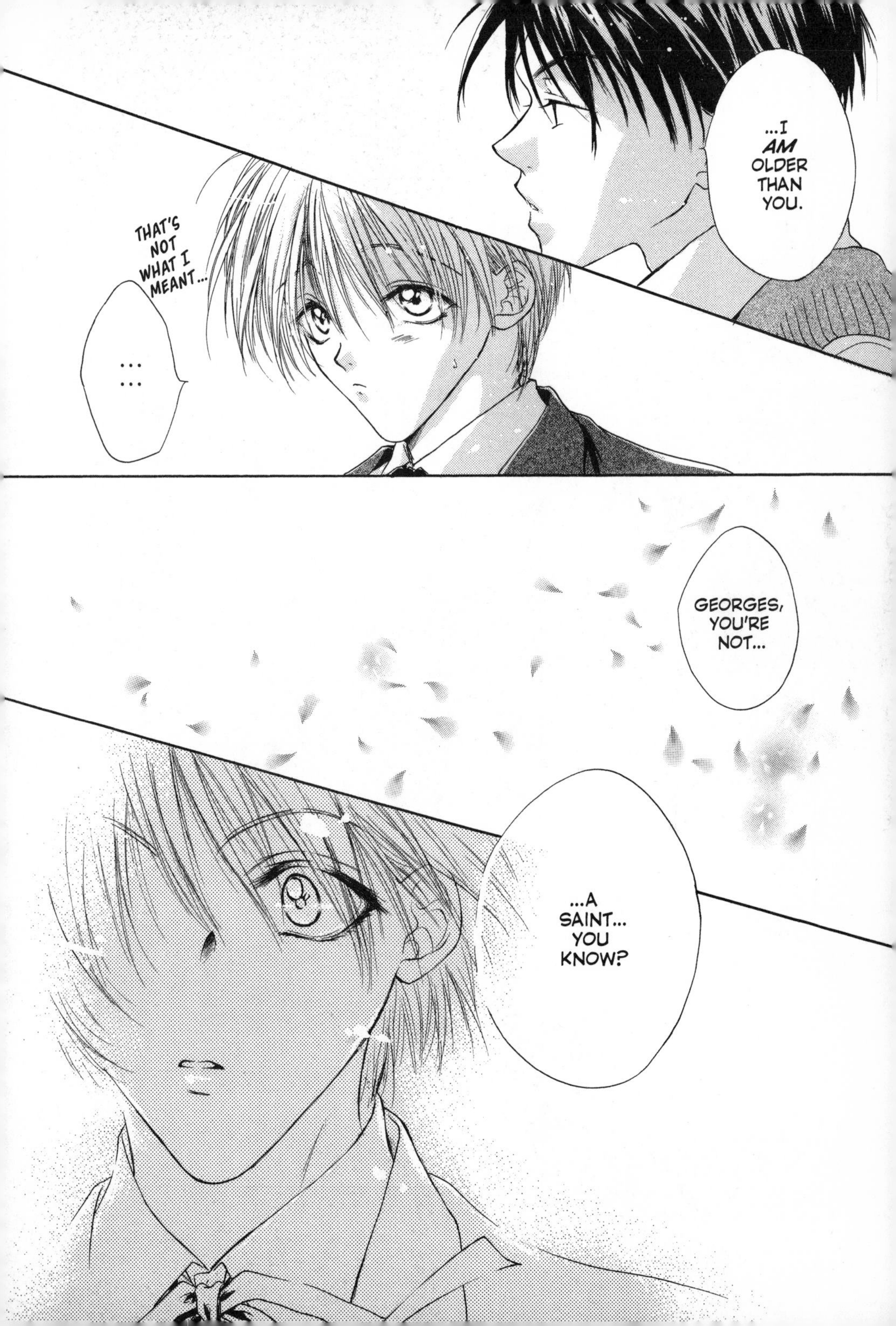
...I *AM* OLDER THAN YOU.
THAT'S NOT WHAT I MEANT...
......
GEORGES, YOU'RE NOT...
...A SAINT... YOU KNOW?

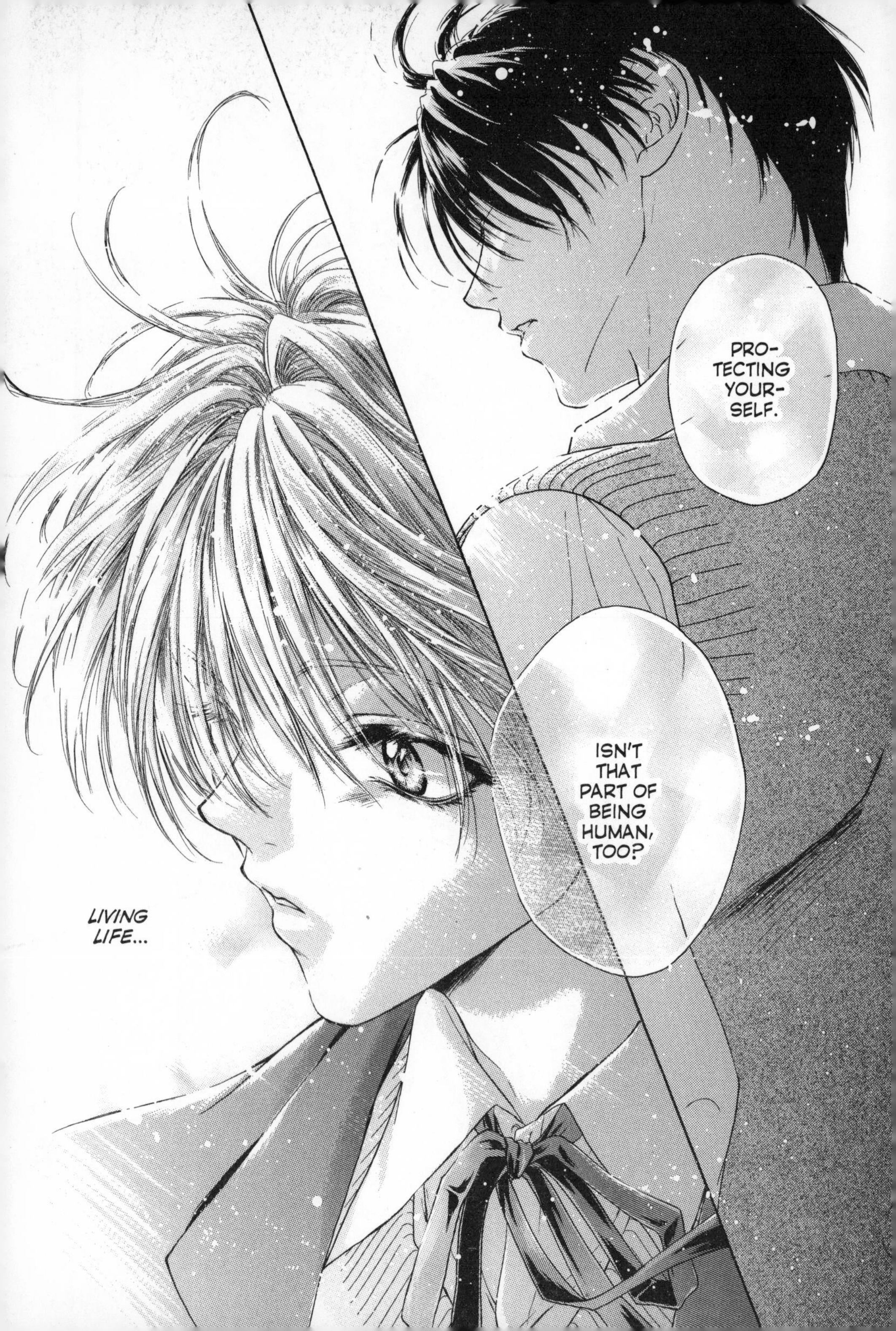
PRO-TECTING YOUR-SELF.
ISN'T THAT PART OF BEING HUMAN, TOO?
LIVING LIFE...

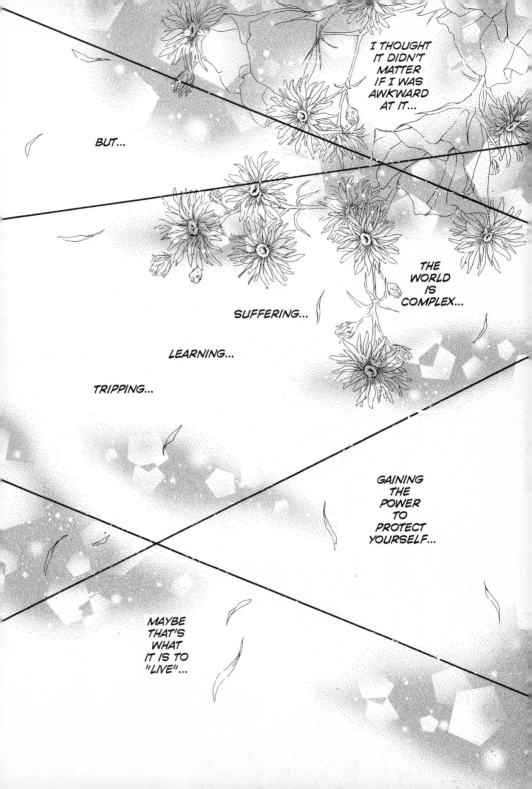

I THOUGHT IT DIDN'T MATTER IF I WAS AWKWARD AT IT...

BUT...

THE WORLD IS COMPLEX...

SUFFERING...

LEARNING...

TRIPPING...

GAINING THE POWER TO PROTECT YOURSELF...

MAYBE THAT'S WHAT IT IS TO "LIVE"...

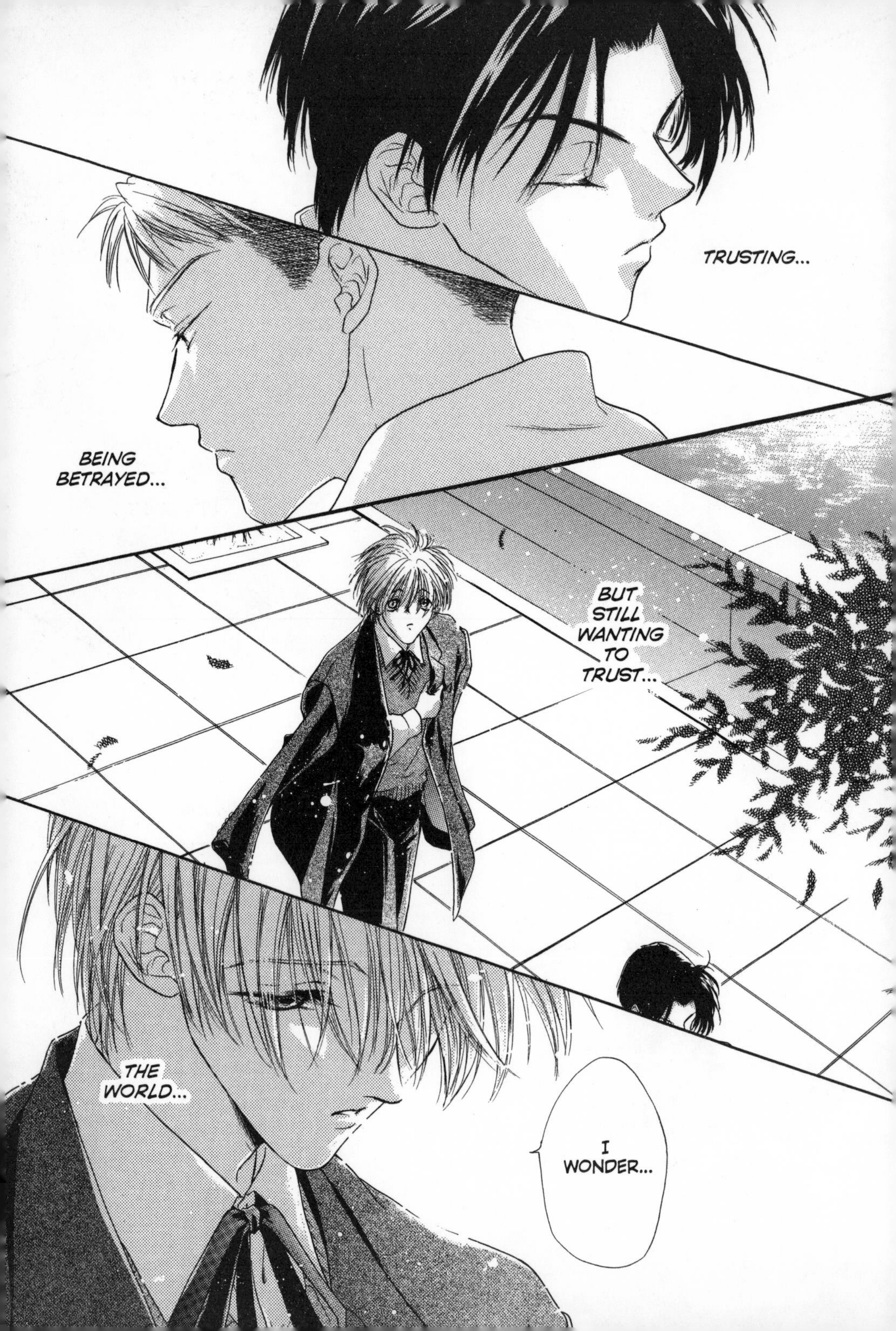
TRUSTING...
BEING BETRAYED...
BUT STILL WANTING TO TRUST...
THE WORLD...
I WONDER...

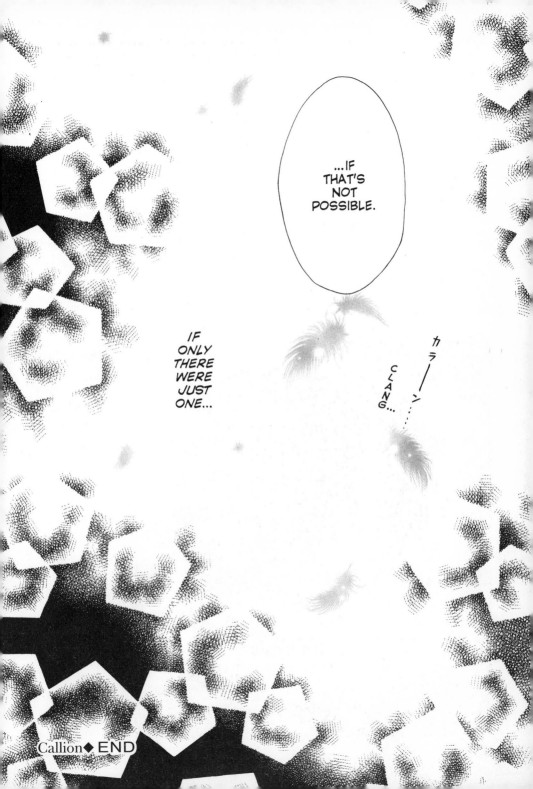

...IF
THAT'S
NOT
POSSIBLE.

IF
ONLY
THERE
WERE
JUST
ONE...

カラ―ン......

CLANG...

Callion◆END

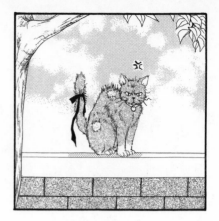

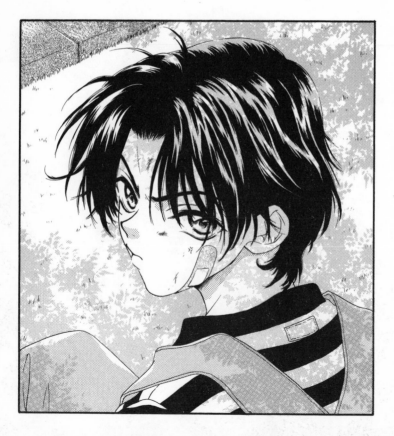

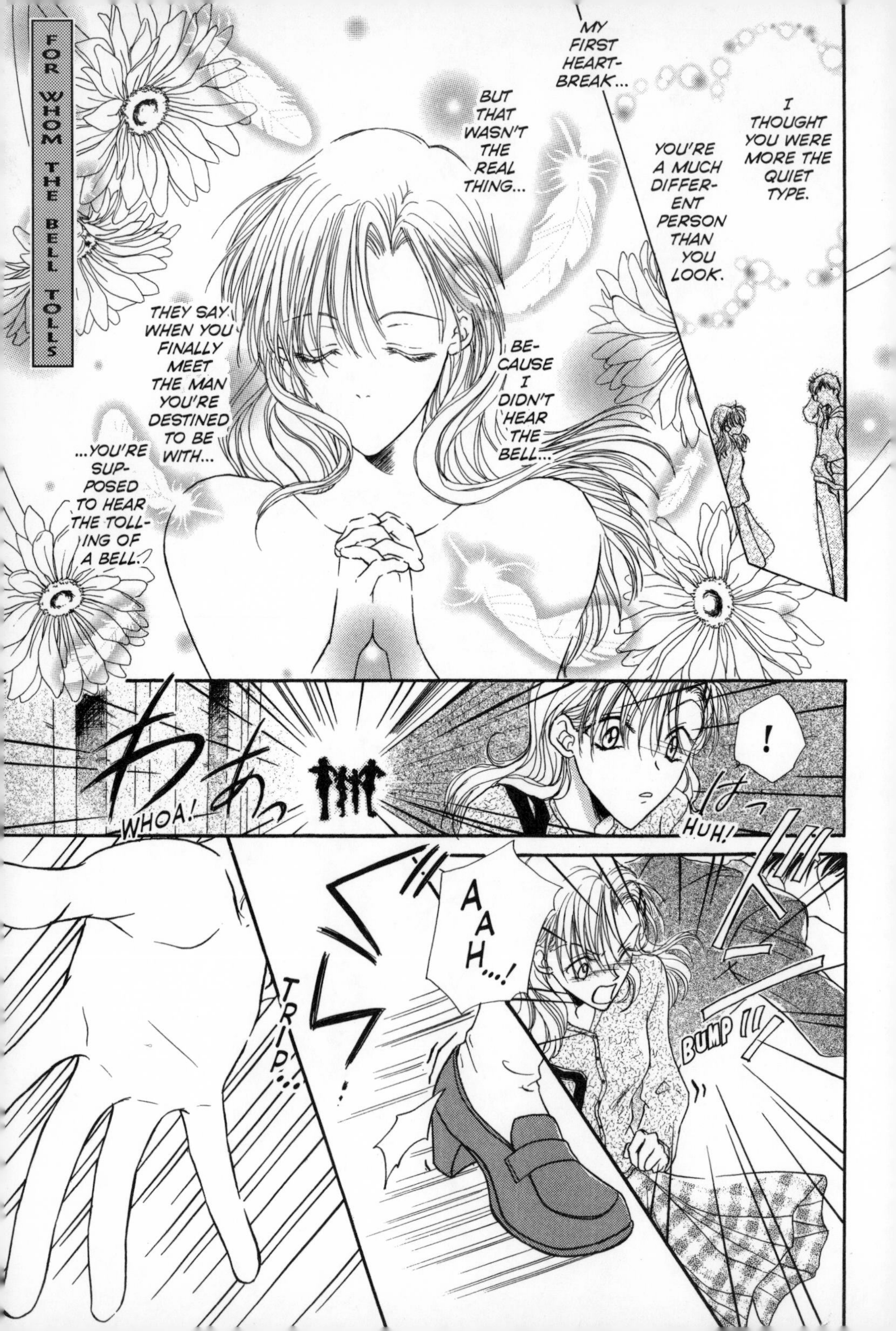
I THOUGHT YOU WERE MORE THE QUIET TYPE.
YOU'RE A MUCH DIFFERENT PERSON THAN YOU LOOK.
MY FIRST HEARTBREAK...
BUT THAT WASN'T THE REAL THING...
BECAUSE I DIDN'T HEAR THE BELL...
THEY SAY WHEN YOU FINALLY MEET THE MAN YOU'RE DESTINED TO BE WITH...
...YOU'RE SUPPOSED TO HEAR THE TOLLING OF A BELL.
!
はっ
HUH!
わぁっ
WHOA!
BUMP!!
AAH...!
TRIP...!

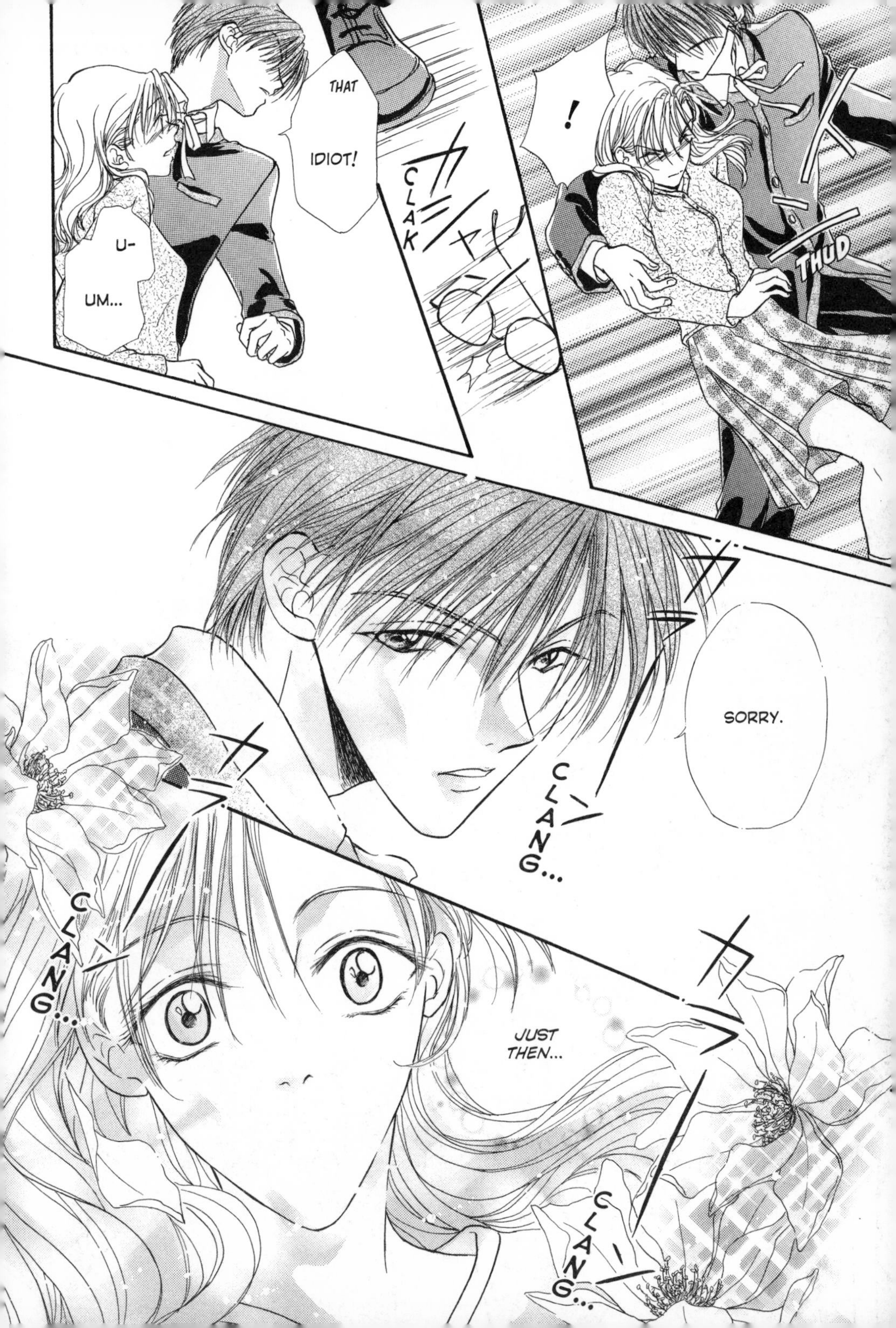
!
THUD
CLAK
THAT IDIOT!
U- UM...
SORRY.
CLANG...
CLANG...
JUST THEN...
CLANG...

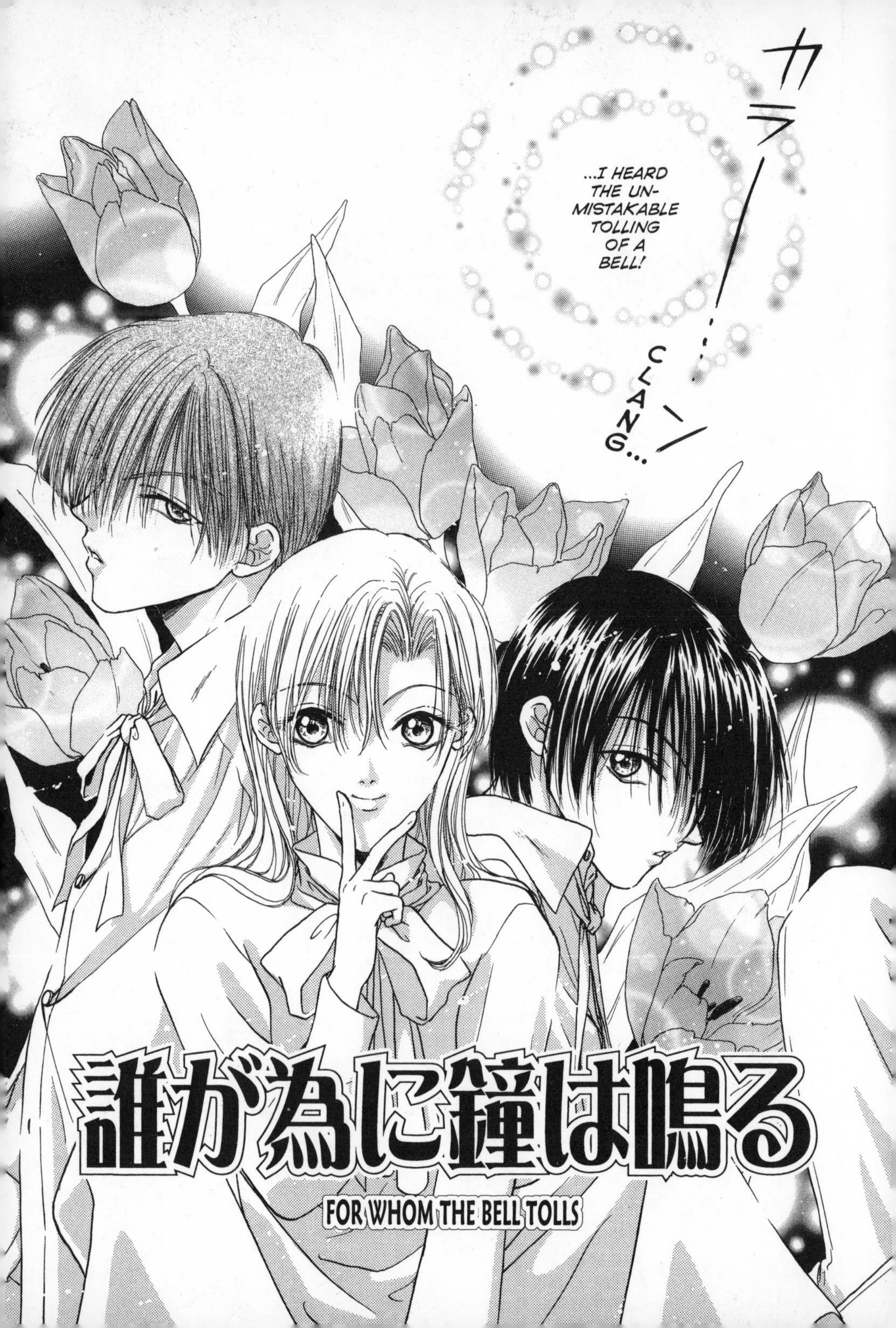
カラ－－－…
...I HEARD THE UN-MISTAKABLE TOLLING OF A BELL!
CLANG...
誰が為に鐘は鳴る
FOR WHOM THE BELL TOLLS

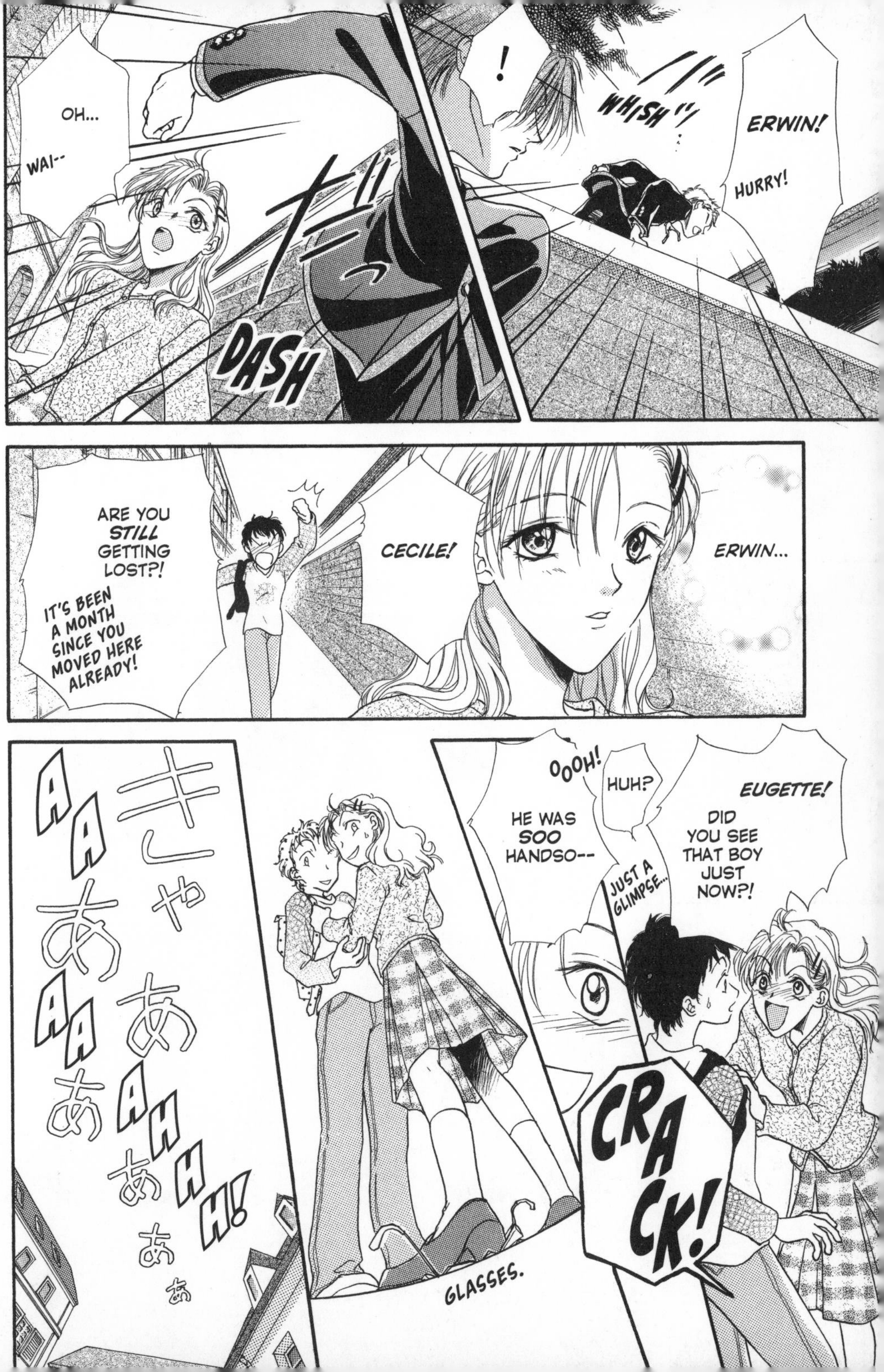
!
WHISH
ERWIN!
HURRY!
OH...
WAI--
DASH
ERWIN...
CECILE!
ARE YOU STILL GETTING LOST?!
IT'S BEEN A MONTH SINCE YOU MOVED HERE ALREADY!
EUGETTE!
DID YOU SEE THAT BOY JUST NOW?!
HUH?
JUST A GLIMPSE...
OOOH!
HE WAS SOO HANDSO--
CRACK!
GLASSES.
AAAAAAHHHHH!

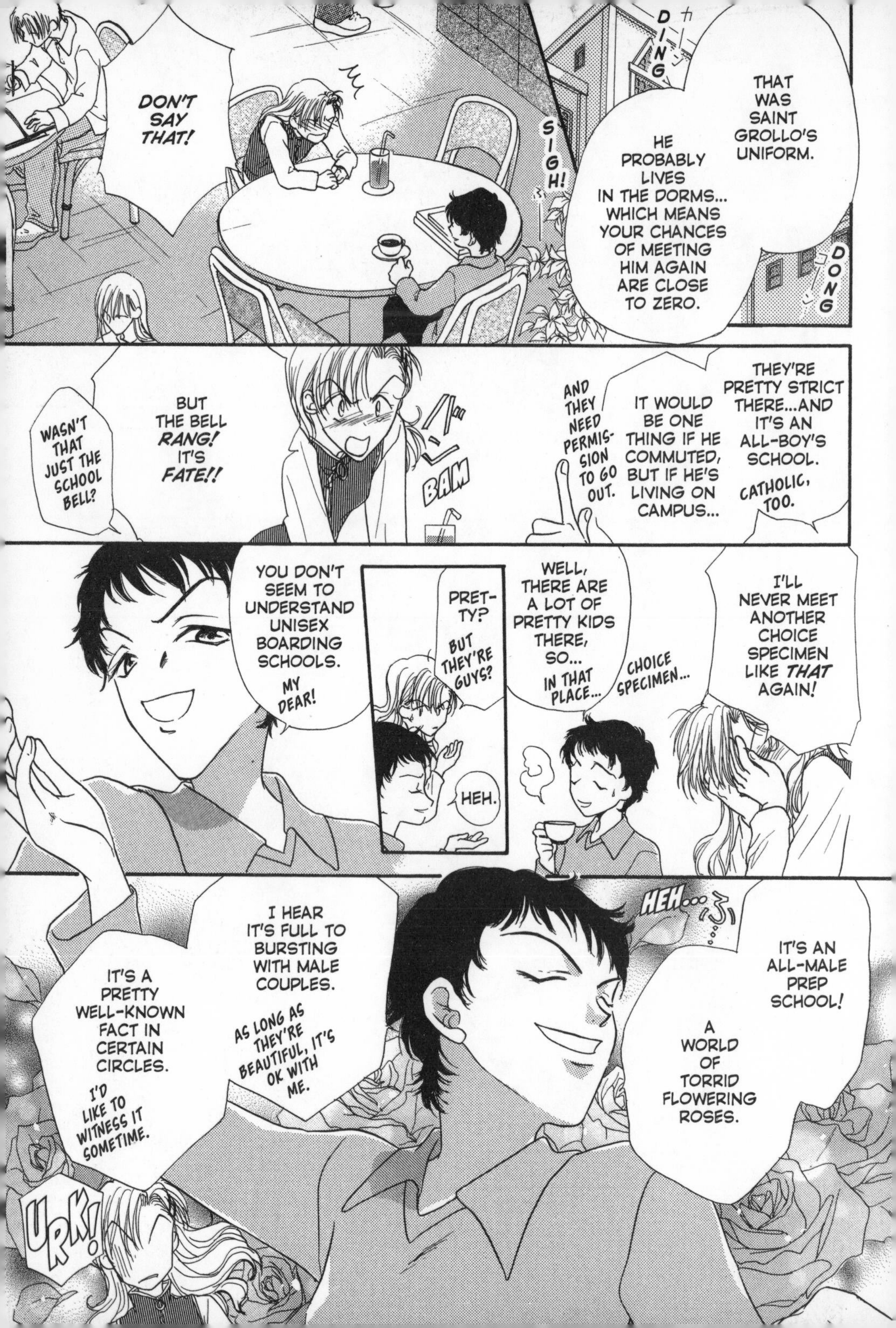
DING DONG
THAT WAS SAINT GROLLO'S UNIFORM.
HE PROBABLY LIVES IN THE DORMS... WHICH MEANS YOUR CHANCES OF MEETING HIM AGAIN ARE CLOSE TO ZERO.
SIGH!
DON'T SAY THAT!
THEY'RE PRETTY STRICT THERE...AND IT'S AN ALL-BOY'S SCHOOL.
CATHOLIC, TOO.
IT WOULD BE ONE THING IF HE COMMUTED, BUT IF HE'S LIVING ON CAMPUS...
AND THEY NEED PERMIS-SION TO GO OUT.
BAM
BUT THE BELL RANG! IT'S FATE!!
WASN'T THAT JUST THE SCHOOL BELL?
I'LL NEVER MEET ANOTHER CHOICE SPECIMEN LIKE THAT AGAIN!
CHOICE SPECIMEN...
WELL, THERE ARE A LOT OF PRETTY KIDS THERE, SO...
IN THAT PLACE...
PRET-TY?
BUT THEY'RE GUYS?
HEH.
YOU DON'T SEEM TO UNDERSTAND UNISEX BOARDING SCHOOLS.
MY DEAR!
HEH...
IT'S AN ALL-MALE PREP SCHOOL!
A WORLD OF TORRID FLOWERING ROSES.
I HEAR IT'S FULL TO BURSTING WITH MALE COUPLES.
AS LONG AS THEY'RE BEAUTIFUL, IT'S OK WITH ME.
IT'S A PRETTY WELL-KNOWN FACT IN CERTAIN CIRCLES.
I'D LIKE TO WITNESS IT SOMETIME.
URK!

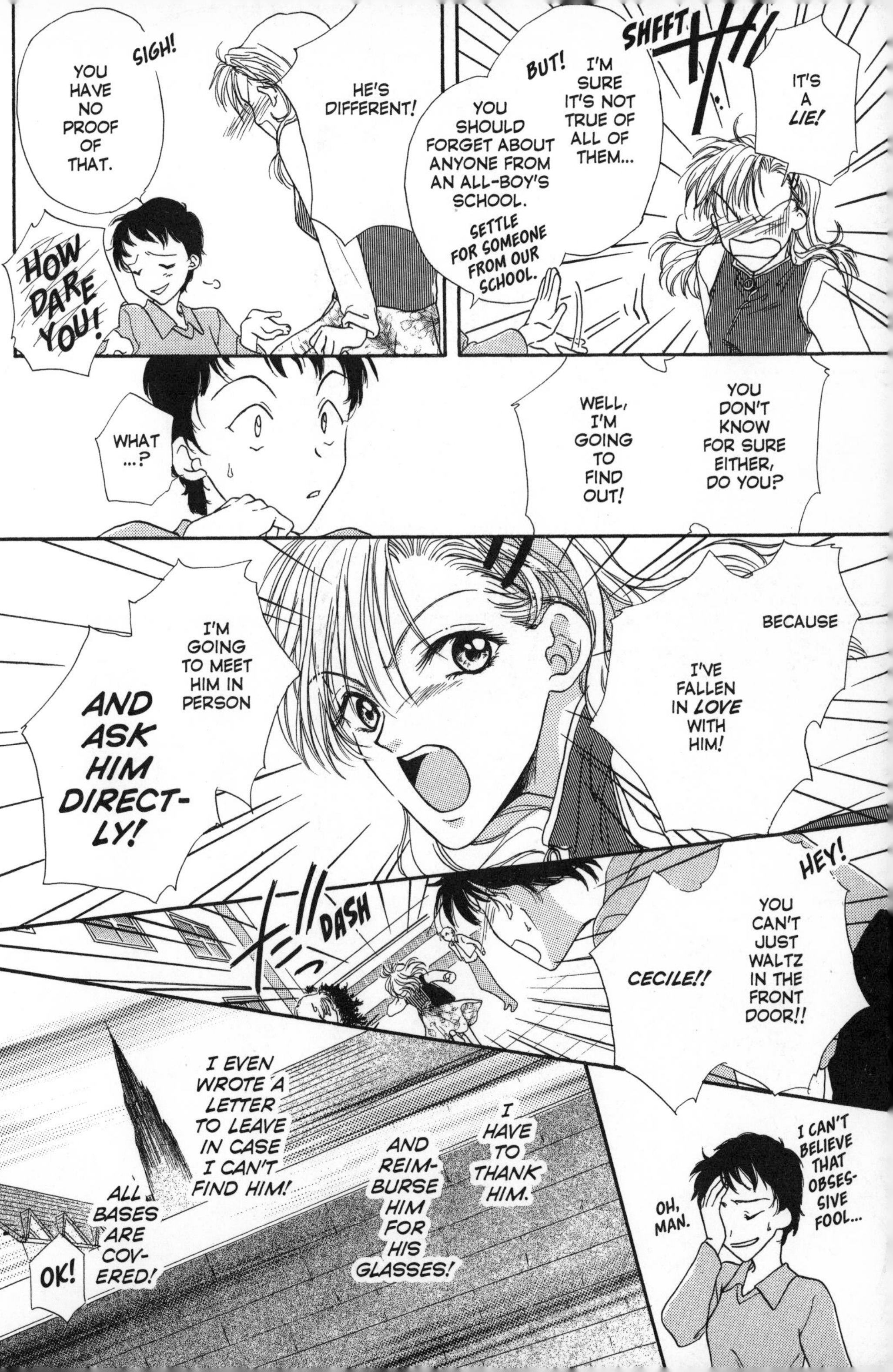
SHFFT
IT'S A LIE!
I'M SURE IT'S NOT TRUE OF ALL OF THEM...
BUT!
YOU SHOULD FORGET ABOUT ANYONE FROM AN ALL-BOY'S SCHOOL.
SETTLE FOR SOMEONE FROM OUR SCHOOL.
HE'S DIFFERENT!
SIGH!
YOU HAVE NO PROOF OF THAT.
HOW DARE YOU!
YOU DON'T KNOW FOR SURE EITHER, DO YOU?
WELL, I'M GOING TO FIND OUT!
WHAT ...?
BECAUSE
I'VE FALLEN IN LOVE WITH HIM!
I'M GOING TO MEET HIM IN PERSON
AND ASK HIM DIRECTLY!
HEY!
YOU CAN'T JUST WALTZ IN THE FRONT DOOR!!
CECILE!!
DASH
I CAN'T BELIEVE THAT OBSESSIVE FOOL...
OH, MAN.
I HAVE TO THANK HIM.
AND REIMBURSE HIM FOR HIS GLASSES!
I EVEN WROTE A LETTER TO LEAVE IN CASE I CAN'T FIND HIM!
ALL BASES ARE COVERED!
OK!

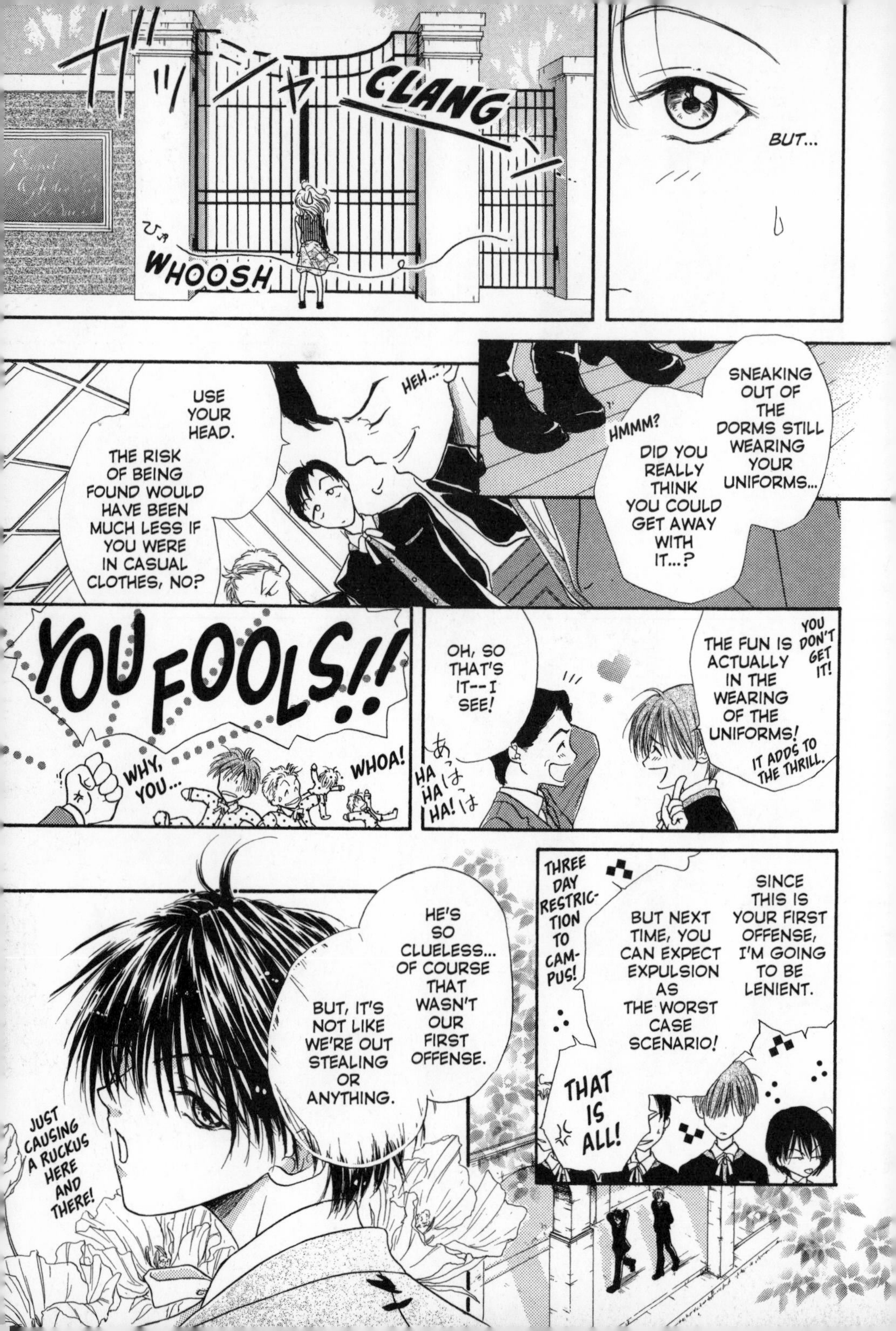
BUT...
CLANG
WHOOSH
SNEAKING OUT OF THE DORMS STILL WEARING YOUR UNIFORMS...
HMMM?
DID YOU REALLY THINK YOU COULD GET AWAY WITH IT...?
HEH...
USE YOUR HEAD.
THE RISK OF BEING FOUND WOULD HAVE BEEN MUCH LESS IF YOU WERE IN CASUAL CLOTHES, NO?
THE FUN IS ACTUALLY IN THE WEARING OF THE UNIFORMS!
YOU DON'T GET IT!
IT ADDS TO THE THRILL.
OH, SO THAT'S IT--I SEE!
HA HA HA!
YOU FOOLS!!
WHY, YOU...
WHOA!
SINCE THIS IS YOUR FIRST OFFENSE, I'M GOING TO BE LENIENT.
BUT NEXT TIME, YOU CAN EXPECT EXPULSION AS THE WORST CASE SCENARIO!
THREE DAY RESTRICTION TO CAMPUS!
THAT IS ALL!
HE'S SO CLUELESS... OF COURSE THAT WASN'T OUR FIRST OFFENSE.
BUT, IT'S NOT LIKE WE'RE OUT STEALING OR ANYTHING.
JUST CAUSING A RUCKUS HERE AND THERE!

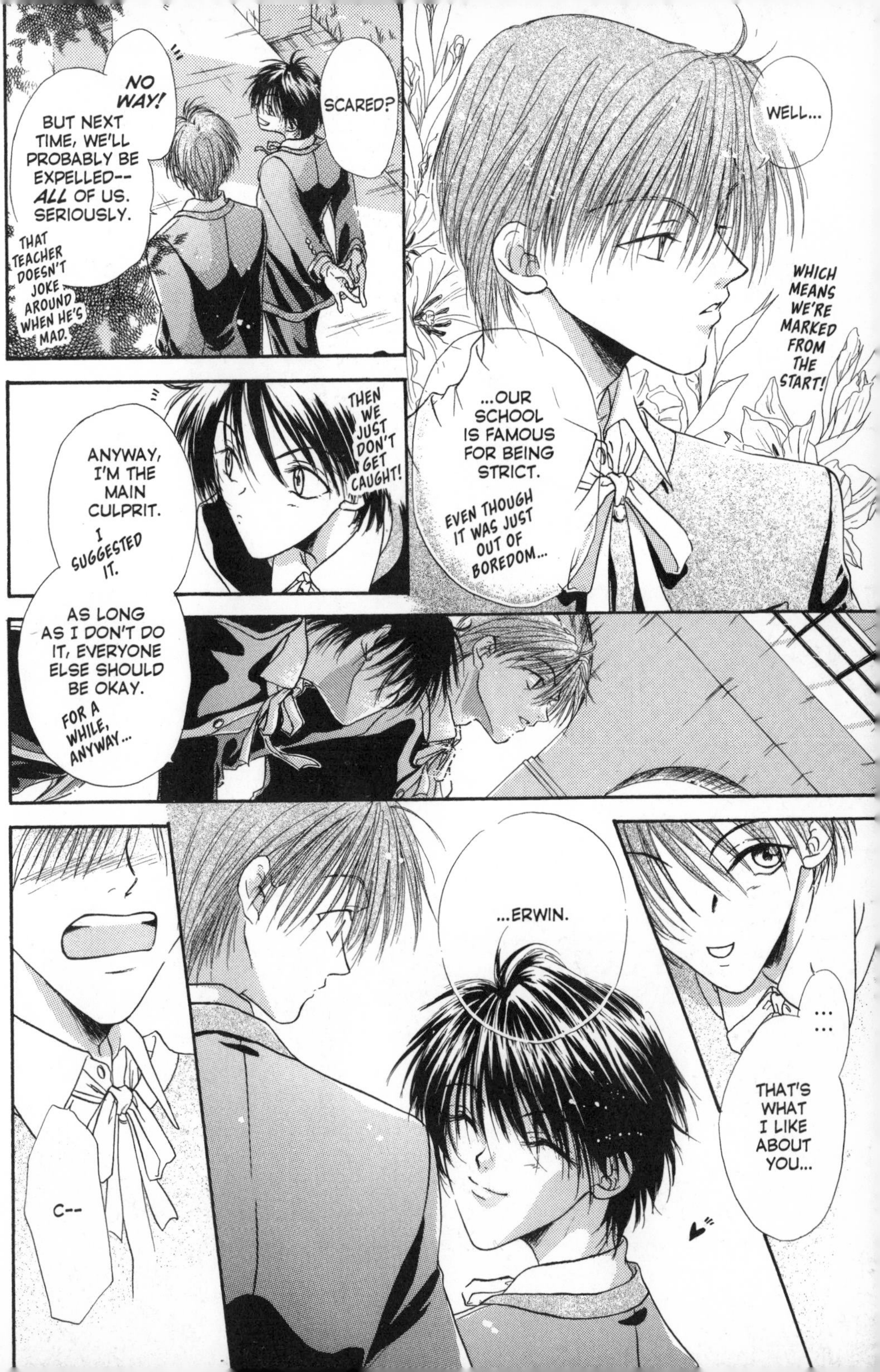
WELL...
WHICH MEANS WE'RE MARKED FROM THE START!
...OUR SCHOOL IS FAMOUS FOR BEING STRICT.
EVEN THOUGH IT WAS JUST OUT OF BOREDOM...
SCARED?
NO WAY! BUT NEXT TIME, WE'LL PROBABLY BE EXPELLED-- ALL OF US. SERIOUSLY.
THAT TEACHER DOESN'T JOKE AROUND WHEN HE'S MAD.
THEN WE JUST DON'T GET CAUGHT!
ANYWAY, I'M THE MAIN CULPRIT.
I SUGGESTED IT.
AS LONG AS I DON'T DO IT, EVERYONE ELSE SHOULD BE OKAY.
FOR A WHILE, ANYWAY...
......
THAT'S WHAT I LIKE ABOUT YOU...
...ERWIN.
C--

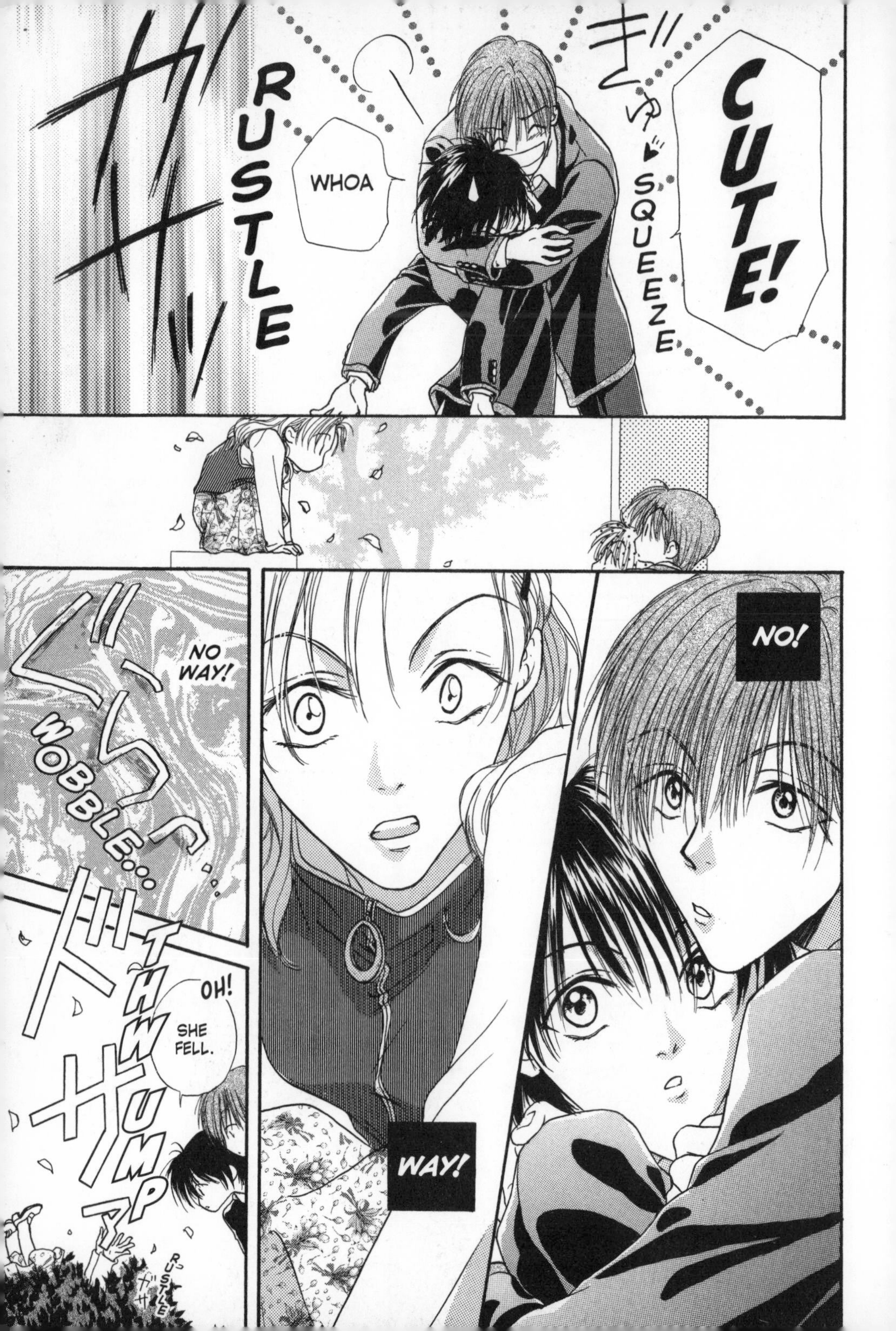

CUTE!
ぎゅ
SQUEEZE
WHOA
RUSTLE
NO!
WAY!
NO WAY!
WOBBLE...
THWUMP
OH!
SHE FELL.
RUSTLE

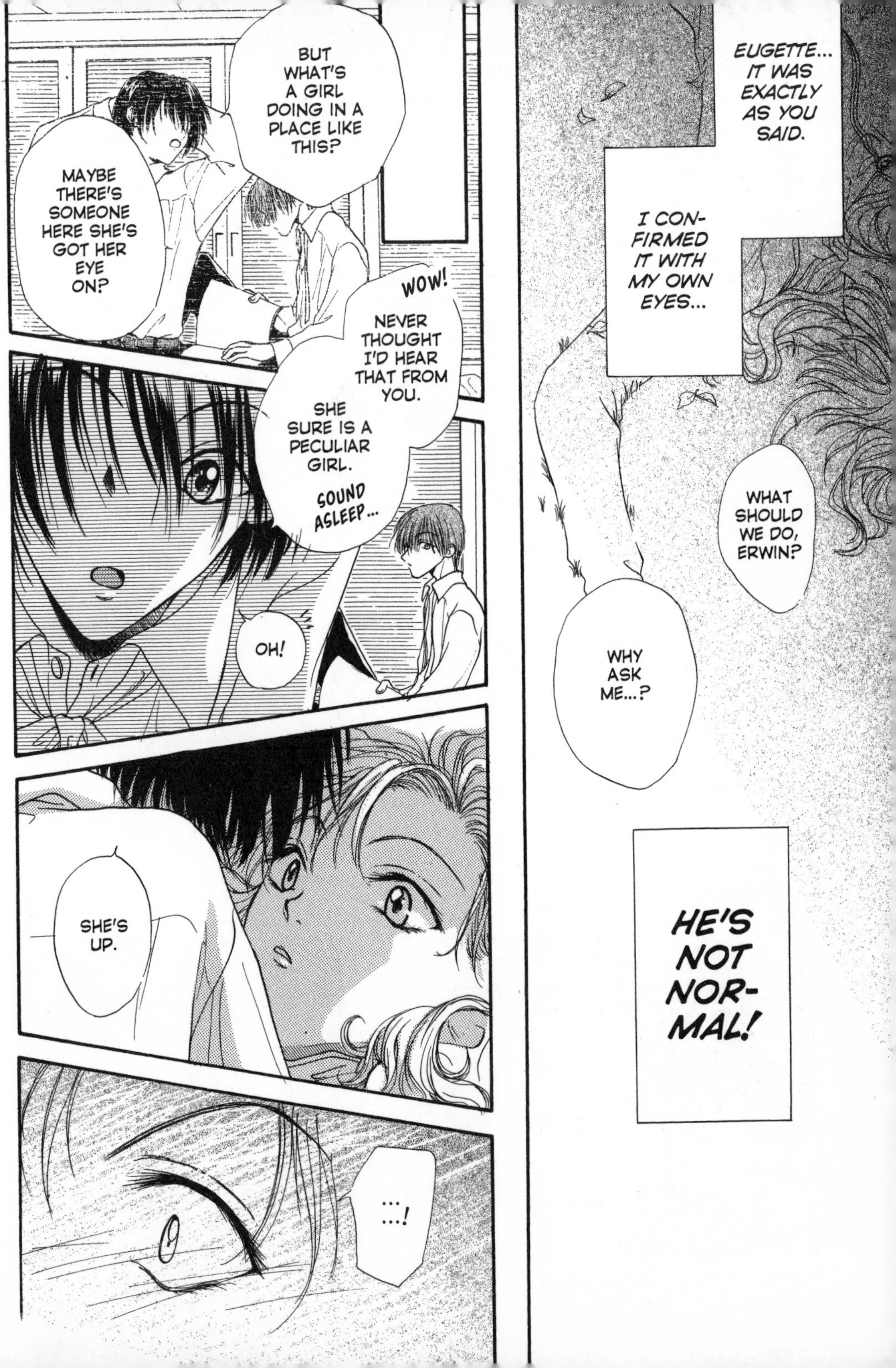
EUGETTE... IT WAS EXACTLY AS YOU SAID.
I CONFIRMED IT WITH MY OWN EYES...
WHAT SHOULD WE DO, ERWIN?
WHY ASK ME...?
HE'S NOT NORMAL!
BUT WHAT'S A GIRL DOING IN A PLACE LIKE THIS?
MAYBE THERE'S SOMEONE HERE SHE'S GOT HER EYE ON?
WOW!
NEVER THOUGHT I'D HEAR THAT FROM YOU.
SHE SURE IS A PECULIAR GIRL.
SOUND ASLEEP...
OH!
SHE'S UP.
... ...!

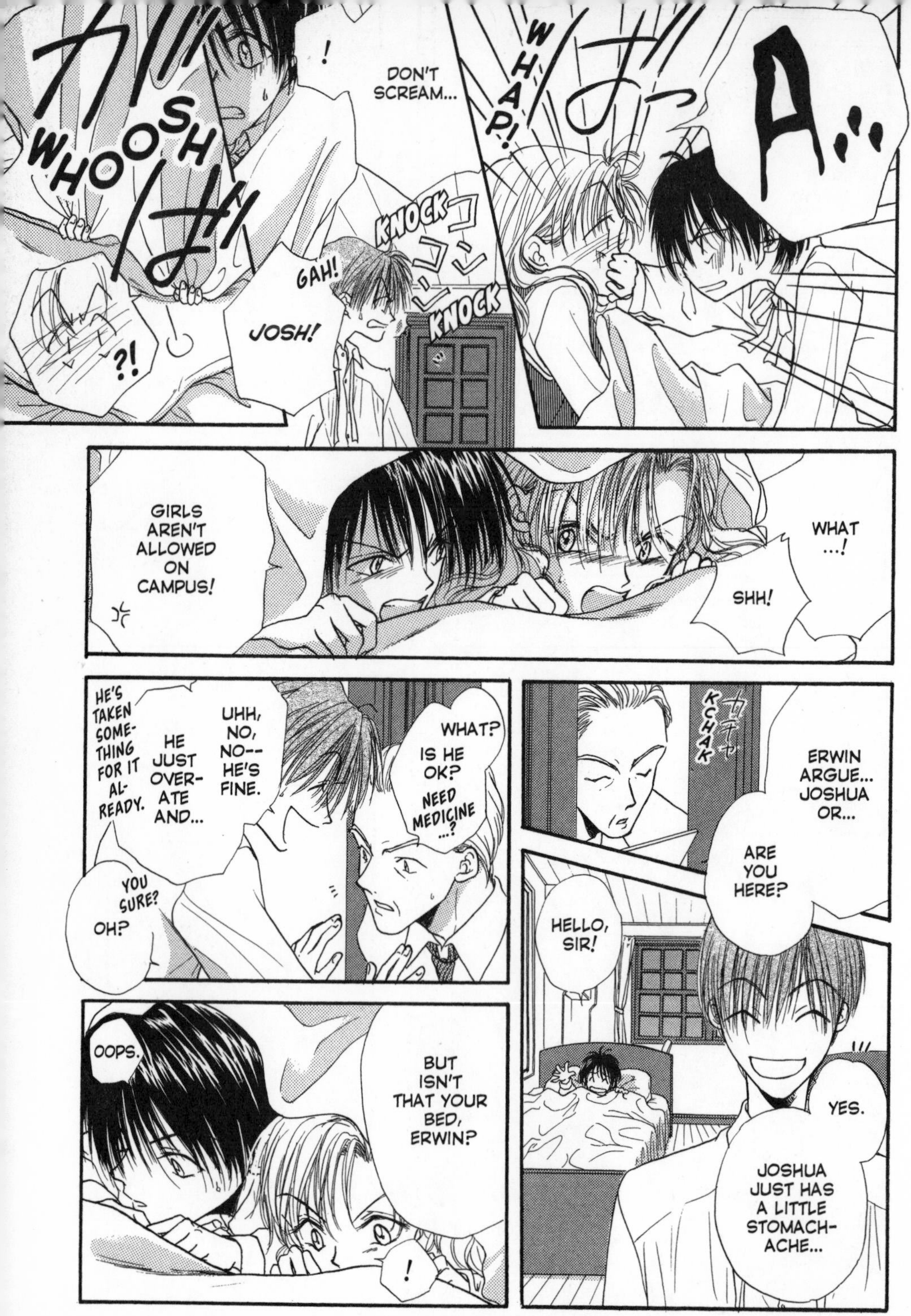
WHAP!
A...
!
DON'T SCREAM...
WHOOSH
KNOCK
KNOCK
GAH!
JOSH!
?!
WHAT ...!
SHH!
GIRLS AREN'T ALLOWED ON CAMPUS!
KCHAK
ERWIN ARGUE... JOSHUA OR...
ARE YOU HERE?
HELLO, SIR!
YES.
JOSHUA JUST HAS A LITTLE STOMACH-ACHE...
WHAT? IS HE OK?
NEED MEDICINE ...?
UHH, NO, NO-- HE'S FINE.
HE JUST OVER-ATE AND...
HE'S TAKEN SOME-THING FOR IT AL-READY.
YOU SURE?
OH?
BUT ISN'T THAT YOUR BED, ERWIN?
OOPS.
!

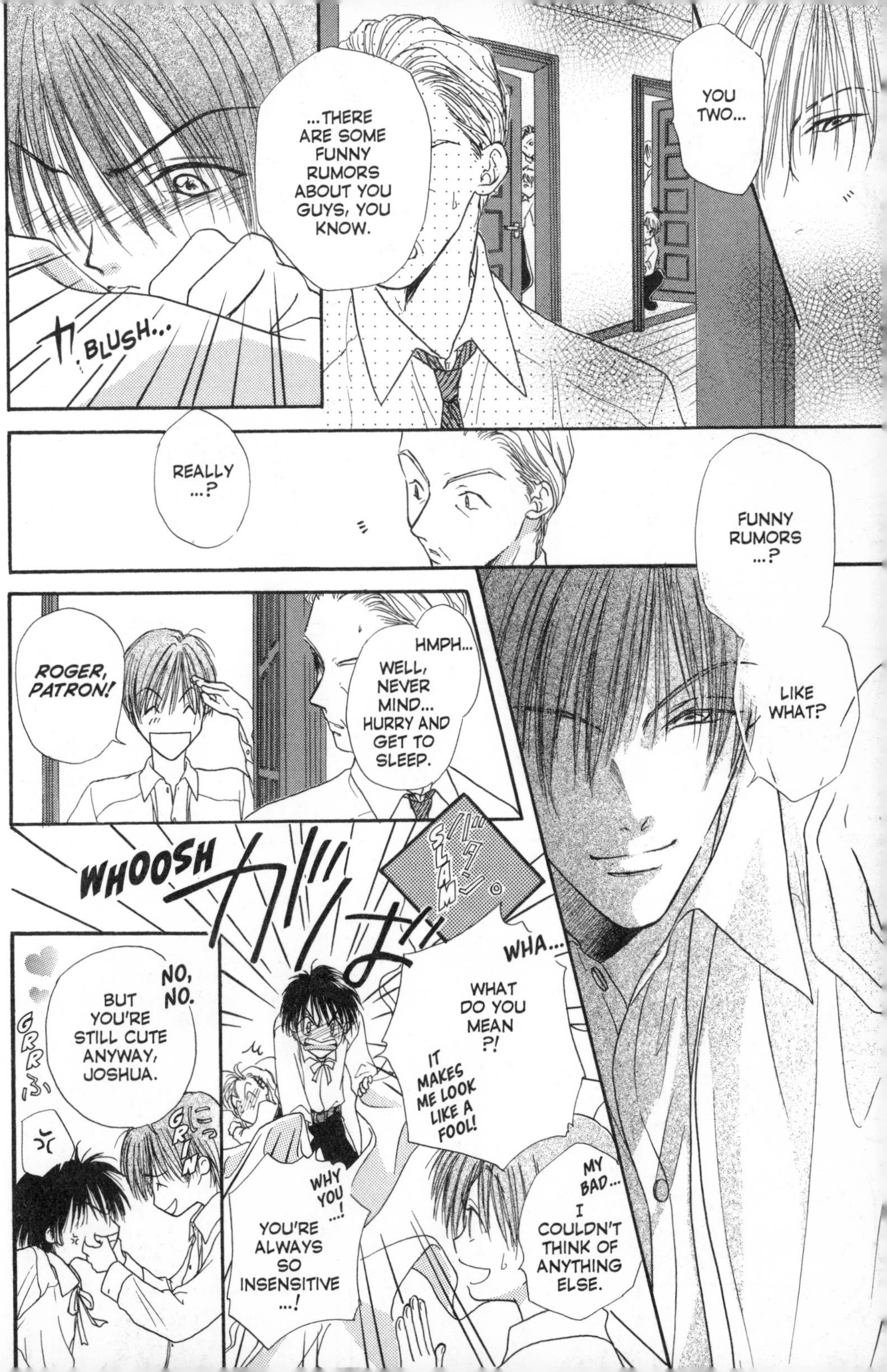
YOU TWO...
...THERE ARE SOME FUNNY RUMORS ABOUT YOU GUYS, YOU KNOW.
BLUSH...
REALLY ...?
FUNNY RUMORS ...?
LIKE WHAT?
HMPH... WELL, NEVER MIND... HURRY AND GET TO SLEEP.
ROGER, PATRON!
SLAM
WHOOSH
WHA...
WHAT DO YOU MEAN ?!
IT MAKES ME LOOK LIKE A FOOL!
MY BAD... I COULDN'T THINK OF ANYTHING ELSE.
WHY YOU ...!
YOU'RE ALWAYS SO INSENSITIVE ...!
NO, NO.
BUT YOU'RE STILL CUTE ANYWAY, JOSHUA.
GRIN
GRR

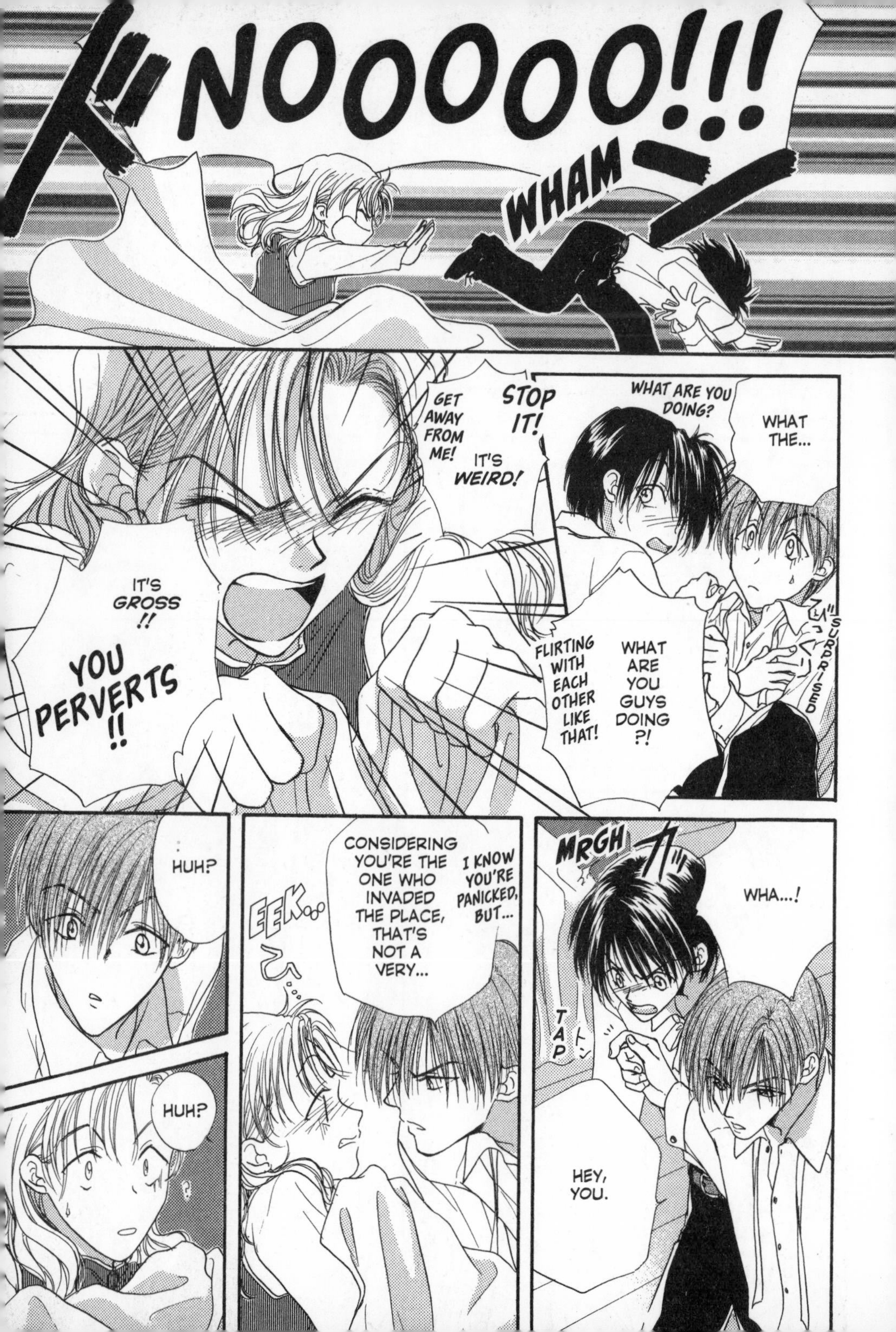
NOOOOO!!!
WHAM
WHAT THE...
WHAT ARE YOU DOING?
SURPRISED
STOP IT!
GET AWAY FROM ME!
IT'S WEIRD!
WHAT ARE YOU GUYS DOING?!
FLIRTING WITH EACH OTHER LIKE THAT!
IT'S GROSS!!
YOU PERVERTS!!
MRGH
WHA...!
TAP
HEY, YOU.
I KNOW YOU'RE PANICKED, BUT...
CONSIDERING YOU'RE THE ONE WHO INVADED THE PLACE, THAT'S NOT A VERY...
EEK
HUH?
HUH?

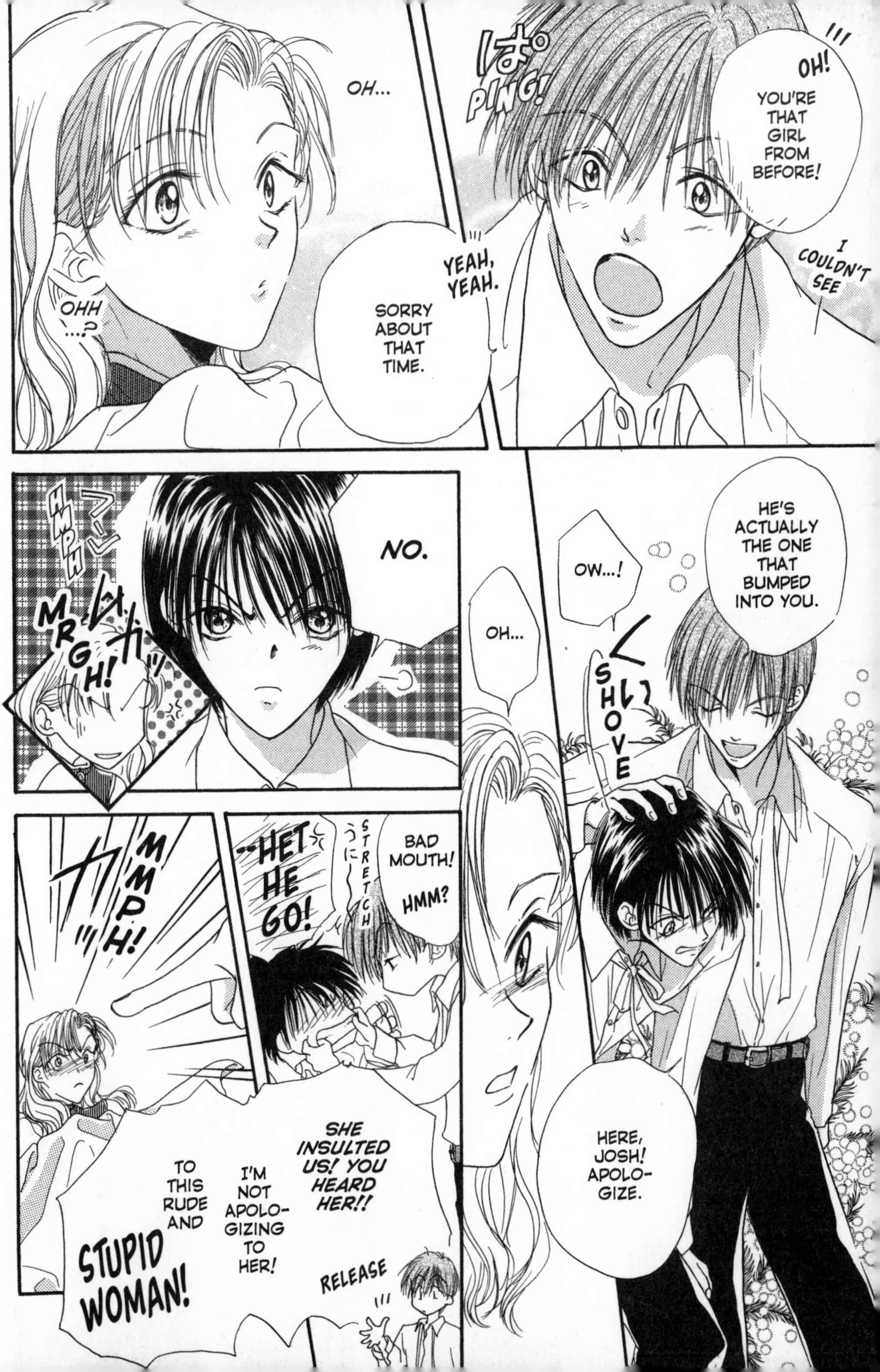
ぱ PING!
OH!
YOU'RE THAT GIRL FROM BEFORE!
I COULDN'T SEE
OH...
YEAH, YEAH.
SORRY ABOUT THAT TIME.
OHH ...?
HE'S ACTUALLY THE ONE THAT BUMPED INTO YOU.
OW...!
OH...
SHOVE
HERE, JOSH! APOLOGIZE.
NO.
HMPH
MRGH!
BAD MOUTH!
HMM?
STRETCH
...HET HE GO!
MMMPH!
SHE INSULTED US! YOU HEARD HER!!
I'M NOT APOLOGIZING TO HER!
TO THIS RUDE AND STUPID WOMAN!
RELEASE

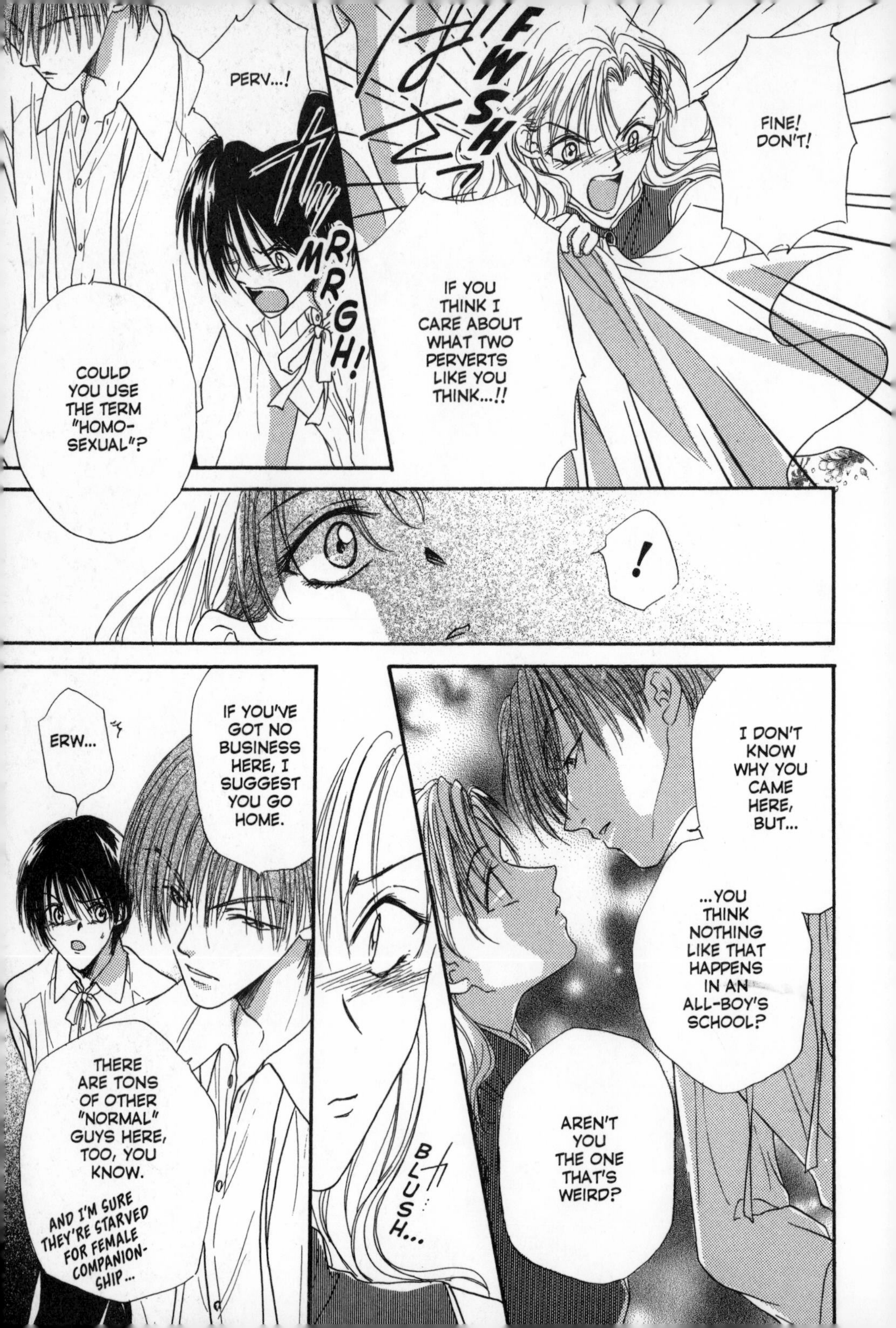
FWSH
FINE! DON'T!
IF YOU THINK I CARE ABOUT WHAT TWO PERVERTS LIKE YOU THINK...!!
PERV...!
MRRGH!
COULD YOU USE THE TERM "HOMO-SEXUAL"?
!
I DON'T KNOW WHY YOU CAME HERE, BUT...
...YOU THINK NOTHING LIKE THAT HAPPENS IN AN ALL-BOY'S SCHOOL?
AREN'T YOU THE ONE THAT'S WEIRD?
BLUSH...
IF YOU'VE GOT NO BUSINESS HERE, I SUGGEST YOU GO HOME.
ERW...
THERE ARE TONS OF OTHER "NORMAL" GUYS HERE, TOO, YOU KNOW.
AND I'M SURE THEY'RE STARVED FOR FEMALE COMPANION-SHIP...

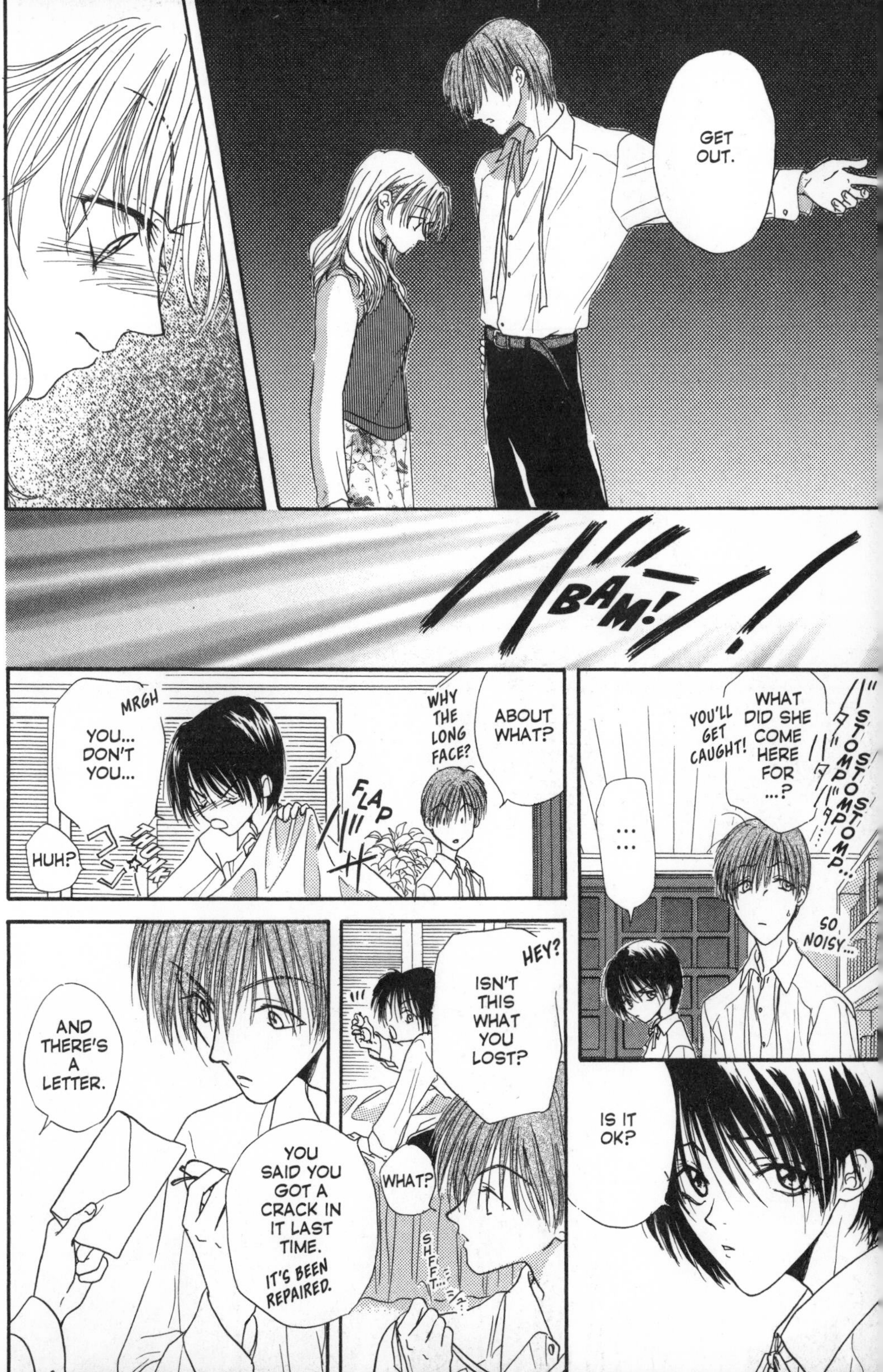
GET OUT.
BAM!
STOMP STOMP STOMP...
WHAT DID SHE COME HERE FOR ...?
YOU'LL GET CAUGHT!
......
SO NOISY...
ABOUT WHAT?
WHY THE LONG FACE?
FLAP
MRGH
YOU... DON'T YOU...
THUNK
HUH?
IS IT OK?
HEY?
ISN'T THIS WHAT YOU LOST?
WHAT?
SHFFT...
YOU SAID YOU GOT A CRACK IN IT LAST TIME. IT'S BEEN REPAIRED.
AND THERE'S A LETTER.

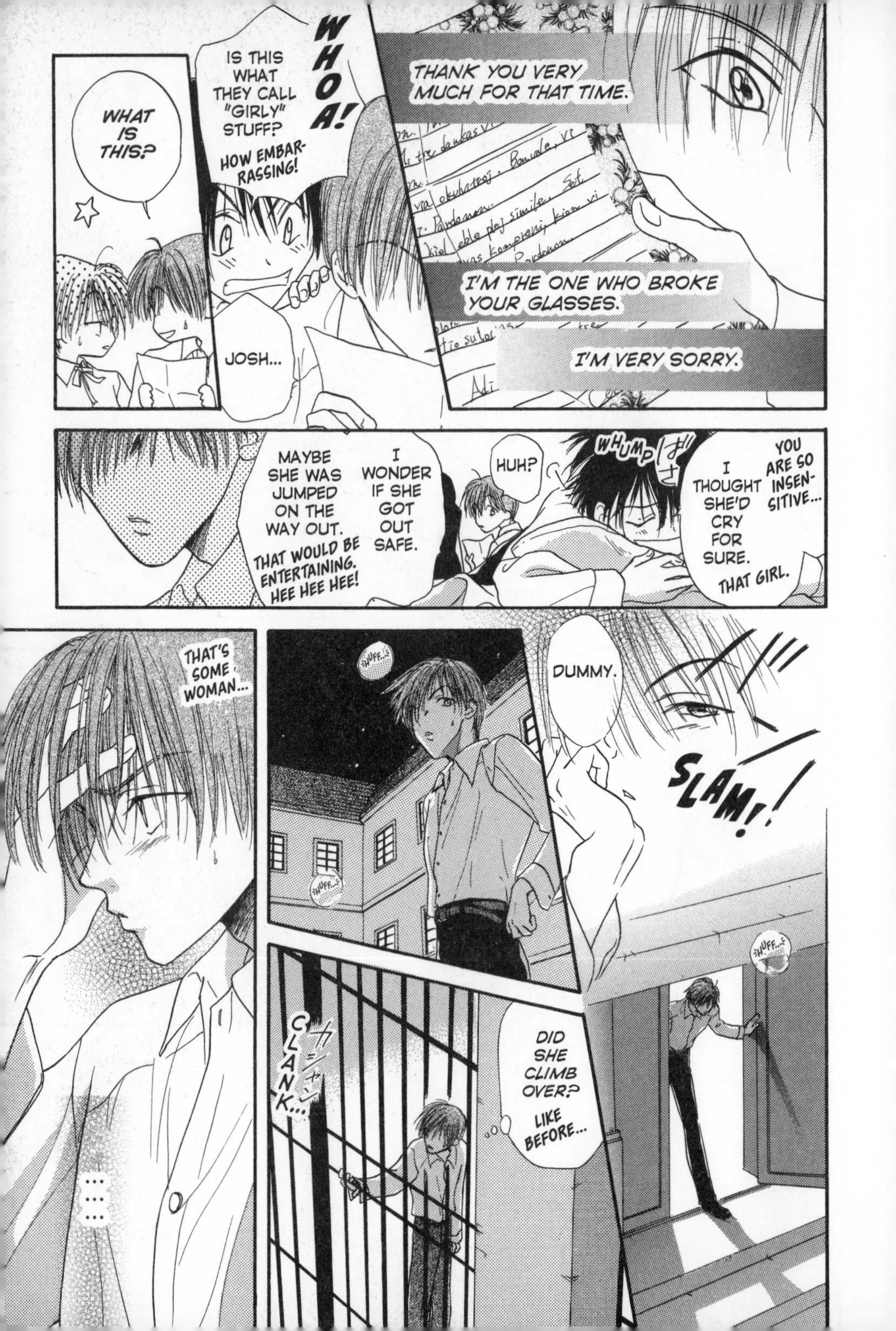
THANK YOU VERY MUCH FOR THAT TIME.
I'M THE ONE WHO BROKE YOUR GLASSES.
I'M VERY SORRY.
WHOA!
IS THIS WHAT THEY CALL "GIRLY" STUFF?
HOW EMBARRASSING!
JOSH...
WHAT IS THIS?
WHUMP
YOU ARE SO INSENSITIVE...
I THOUGHT SHE'D CRY FOR SURE.
THAT GIRL.
HUH?
I WONDER IF SHE GOT OUT SAFE.
MAYBE SHE WAS JUMPED ON THE WAY OUT.
THAT WOULD BE ENTERTAINING. HEE HEE HEE!
DUMMY.
SLAM!!
HUFF...
HUFF...
HUFF...
CLANK...
DID SHE CLIMB OVER?
LIKE BEFORE...
THAT'S SOME WOMAN...
......

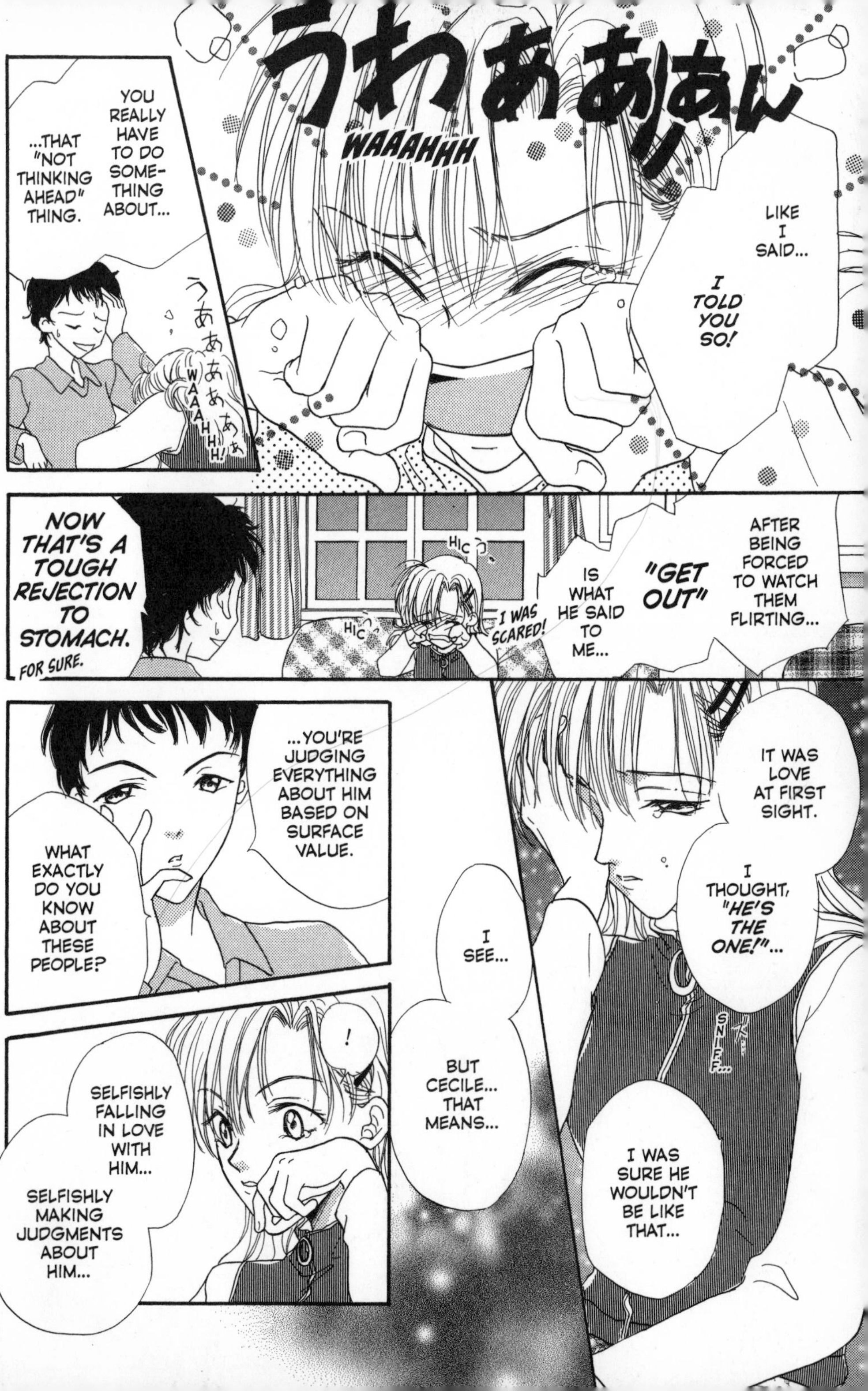
うわあああん
WAAAHHH
LIKE I SAID...
I TOLD YOU SO!
YOU REALLY HAVE TO DO SOME-THING ABOUT...
...THAT "NOT THINKING AHEAD" THING.
うああああ
WAAAHH!
AFTER BEING FORCED TO WATCH THEM FLIRTING...
"GET OUT"
IS WHAT HE SAID TO ME...
I WAS SCARED!
HIC
HIC
NOW THAT'S A TOUGH REJECTION TO STOMACH.
FOR SURE.
IT WAS LOVE AT FIRST SIGHT.
I THOUGHT, "HE'S THE ONE!"...
SNIFF...
I WAS SURE HE WOULDN'T BE LIKE THAT...
I SEE...
BUT CECILE... THAT MEANS...
...YOU'RE JUDGING EVERYTHING ABOUT HIM BASED ON SURFACE VALUE.
WHAT EXACTLY DO YOU KNOW ABOUT THESE PEOPLE?
!
SELFISHLY FALLING IN LOVE WITH HIM...
SELFISHLY MAKING JUDGMENTS ABOUT HIM...

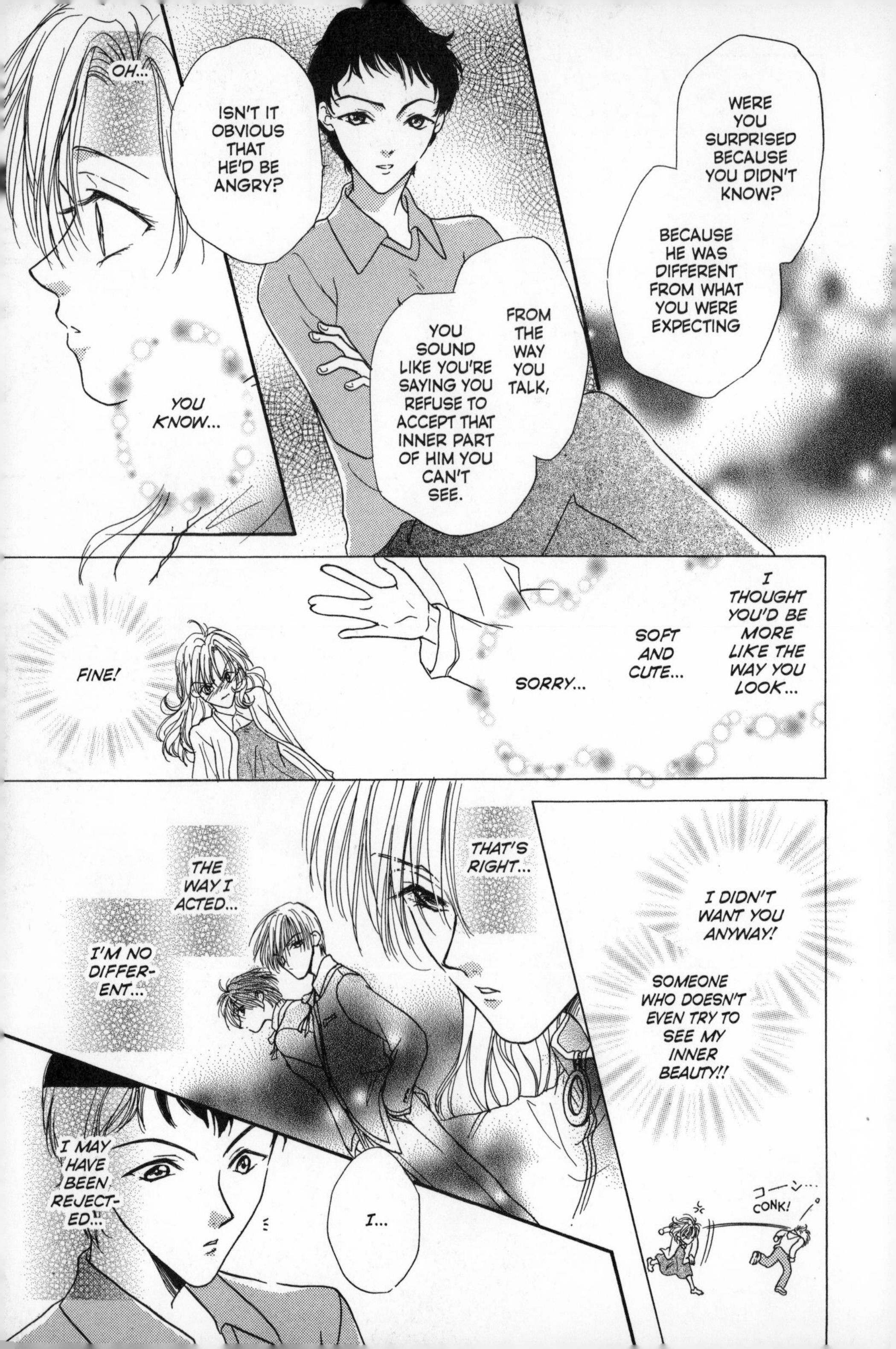
WERE YOU SURPRISED BECAUSE YOU DIDN'T KNOW?
BECAUSE HE WAS DIFFERENT FROM WHAT YOU WERE EXPECTING
FROM THE WAY YOU TALK,
YOU SOUND LIKE YOU'RE SAYING YOU REFUSE TO ACCEPT THAT INNER PART OF HIM YOU CAN'T SEE.
ISN'T IT OBVIOUS THAT HE'D BE ANGRY?
OH...
YOU KNOW...
I THOUGHT YOU'D BE MORE LIKE THE WAY YOU LOOK...
SOFT AND CUTE...
SORRY...
FINE!
I DIDN'T WANT YOU ANYWAY!
SOMEONE WHO DOESN'T EVEN TRY TO SEE MY INNER BEAUTY!!
コーン…
CONK!
THAT'S RIGHT...
THE WAY I ACTED...
I'M NO DIFFER-ENT...
I...
I MAY HAVE BEEN REJECT-ED...

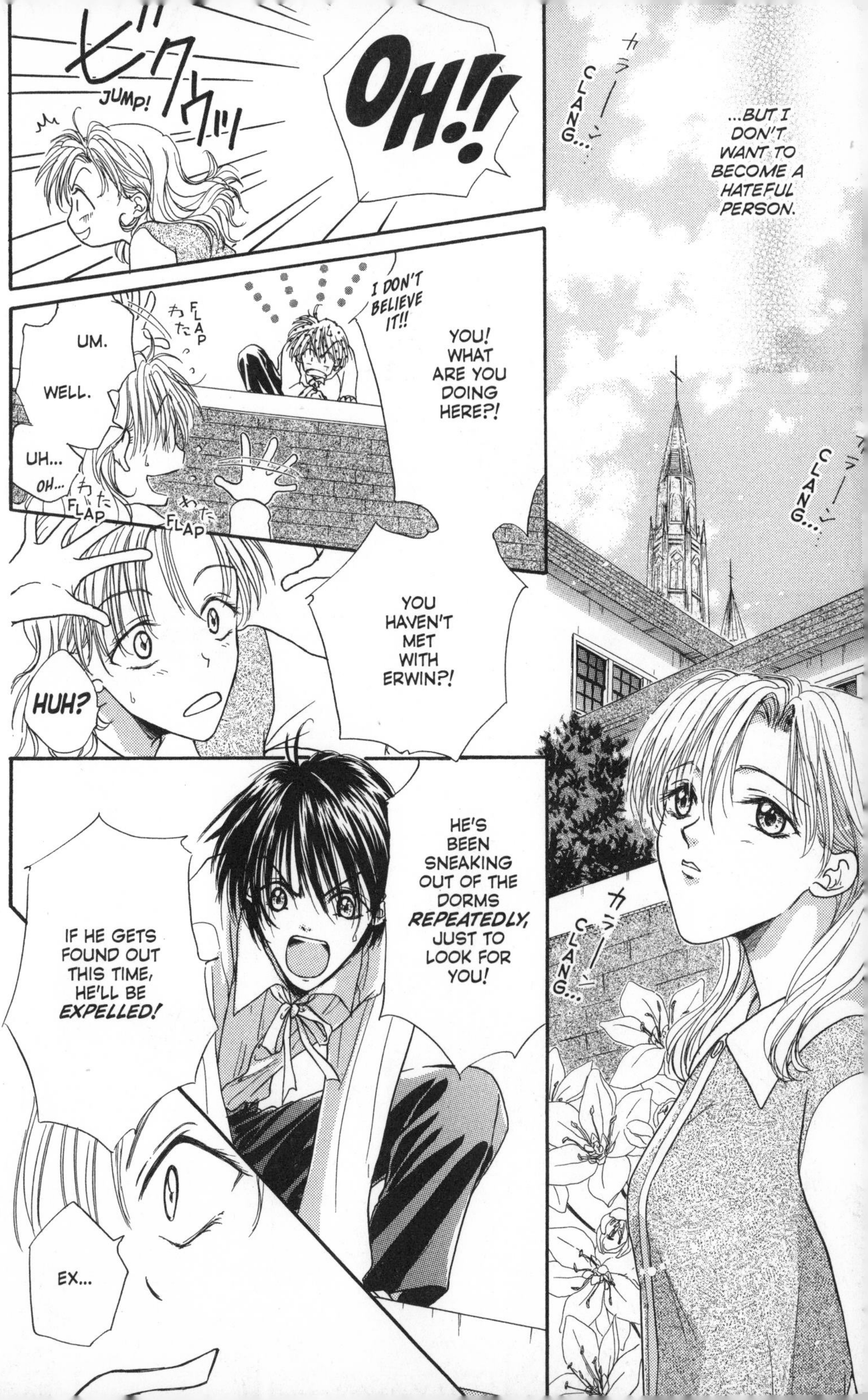

CLANG...
...BUT I DON'T WANT TO BECOME A HATEFUL PERSON.
CLANG...
CLANG...
OH!!
JUMP!
I DON'T BELIEVE IT!!
FLAP
UM.
WELL.
UH...
OH...
FLAP
FLAP
YOU! WHAT ARE YOU DOING HERE?!
YOU HAVEN'T MET WITH ERWIN?!
HUH?
HE'S BEEN SNEAKING OUT OF THE DORMS REPEATEDLY, JUST TO LOOK FOR YOU!
IF HE GETS FOUND OUT THIS TIME, HE'LL BE EXPELLED!
EX...

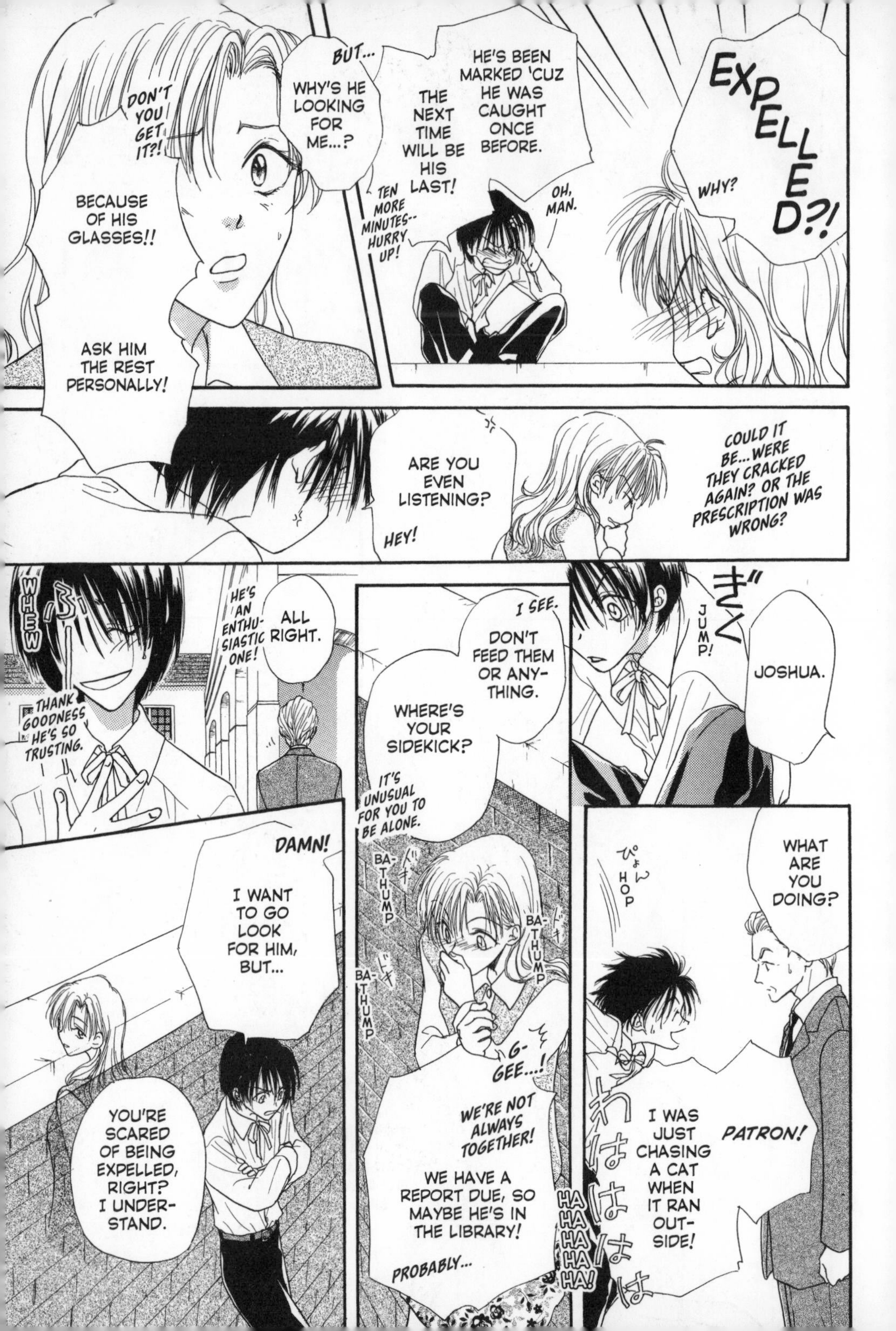
EXPELLED?!
WHY?
HE'S BEEN MARKED 'CUZ HE WAS CAUGHT ONCE BEFORE.
THE NEXT TIME WILL BE HIS LAST!
OH, MAN.
TEN MORE MINUTES--HURRY UP!
BUT... WHY'S HE LOOKING FOR ME...?
DON'T YOU GET IT?!
BECAUSE OF HIS GLASSES!!
ASK HIM THE REST PERSONALLY!
COULD IT BE...WERE THEY CRACKED AGAIN? OR THE PRESCRIPTION WAS WRONG?
ARE YOU EVEN LISTENING?
HEY!
ぎく
JUMP!
JOSHUA.
WHAT ARE YOU DOING?
ぴょん
HOP
I WAS JUST CHASING A CAT WHEN IT RAN OUTSIDE!
PATRON!
わははははは
HA HA HA HA HA!
I SEE.
DON'T FEED THEM OR ANYTHING.
WHERE'S YOUR SIDEKICK?
IT'S UNUSUAL FOR YOU TO BE ALONE.
ドキ
BA-THUMP
ドキ
BA-THUMP
ドキ
BA-THUMP
G-GEE...!
WE'RE NOT ALWAYS TOGETHER!
WE HAVE A REPORT DUE, SO MAYBE HE'S IN THE LIBRARY!
PROBABLY...
ALL RIGHT.
HE'S AN ENTHUSIASTIC ONE!
ふ
WHEW
THANK GOODNESS HE'S SO TRUSTING.
DAMN!
I WANT TO GO LOOK FOR HIM, BUT...
YOU'RE SCARED OF BEING EXPELLED, RIGHT? I UNDERSTAND.

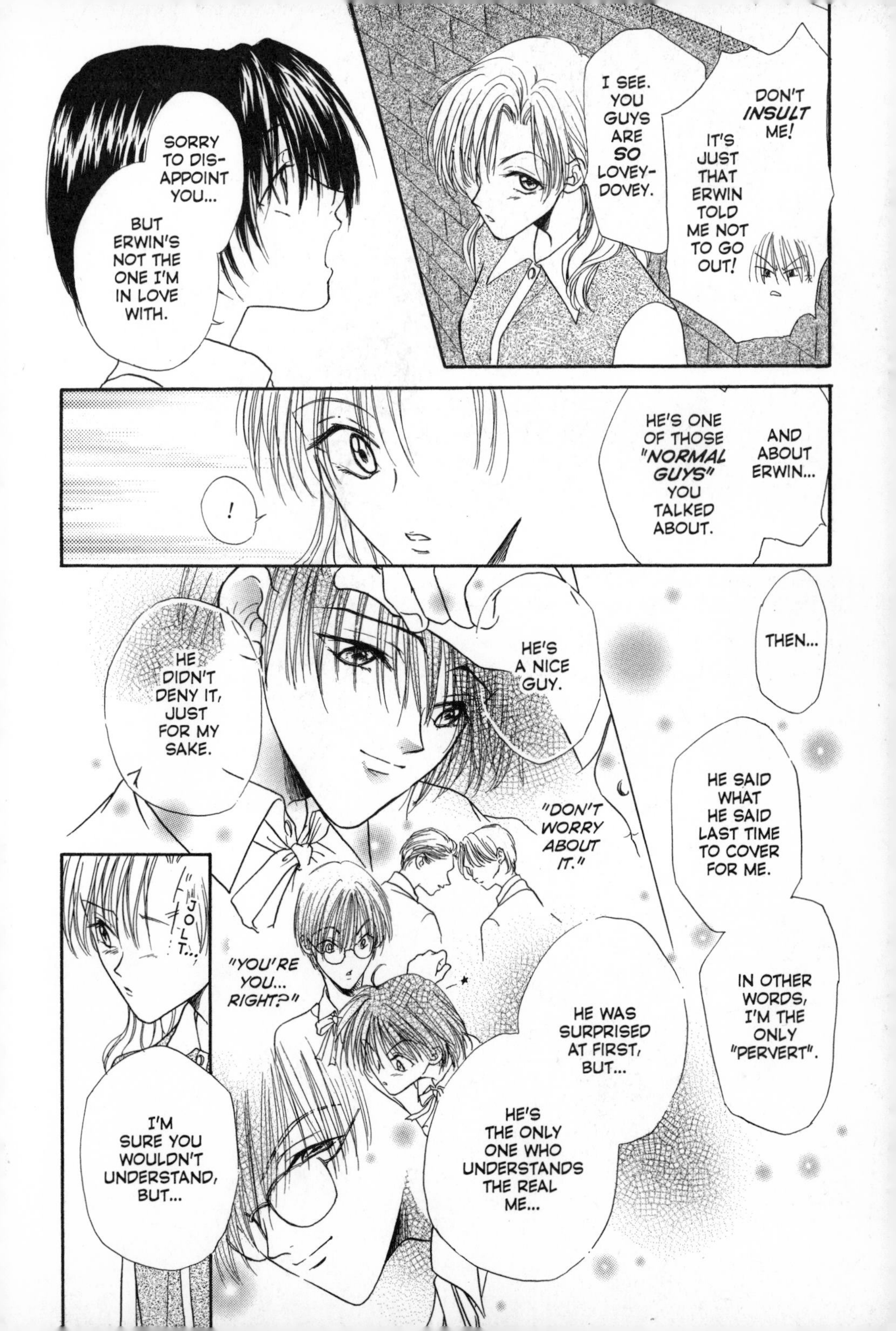
DON'T INSULT ME!
IT'S JUST THAT ERWIN TOLD ME NOT TO GO OUT!
I SEE. YOU GUYS ARE SO LOVEY-DOVEY.
SORRY TO DIS-APPOINT YOU...
BUT ERWIN'S NOT THE ONE I'M IN LOVE WITH.
AND ABOUT ERWIN...
HE'S ONE OF THOSE "NORMAL GUYS" YOU TALKED ABOUT.
!
THEN...
HE SAID WHAT HE SAID LAST TIME TO COVER FOR ME.
IN OTHER WORDS, I'M THE ONLY "PERVERT".
HE'S A NICE GUY.
HE DIDN'T DENY IT, JUST FOR MY SAKE.
"DON'T WORRY ABOUT IT."
HE WAS SURPRISED AT FIRST, BUT...
HE'S THE ONLY ONE WHO UNDERSTANDS THE REAL ME...
"YOU'RE YOU... RIGHT?"
JOLT...
I'M SURE YOU WOULDN'T UNDERSTAND, BUT...

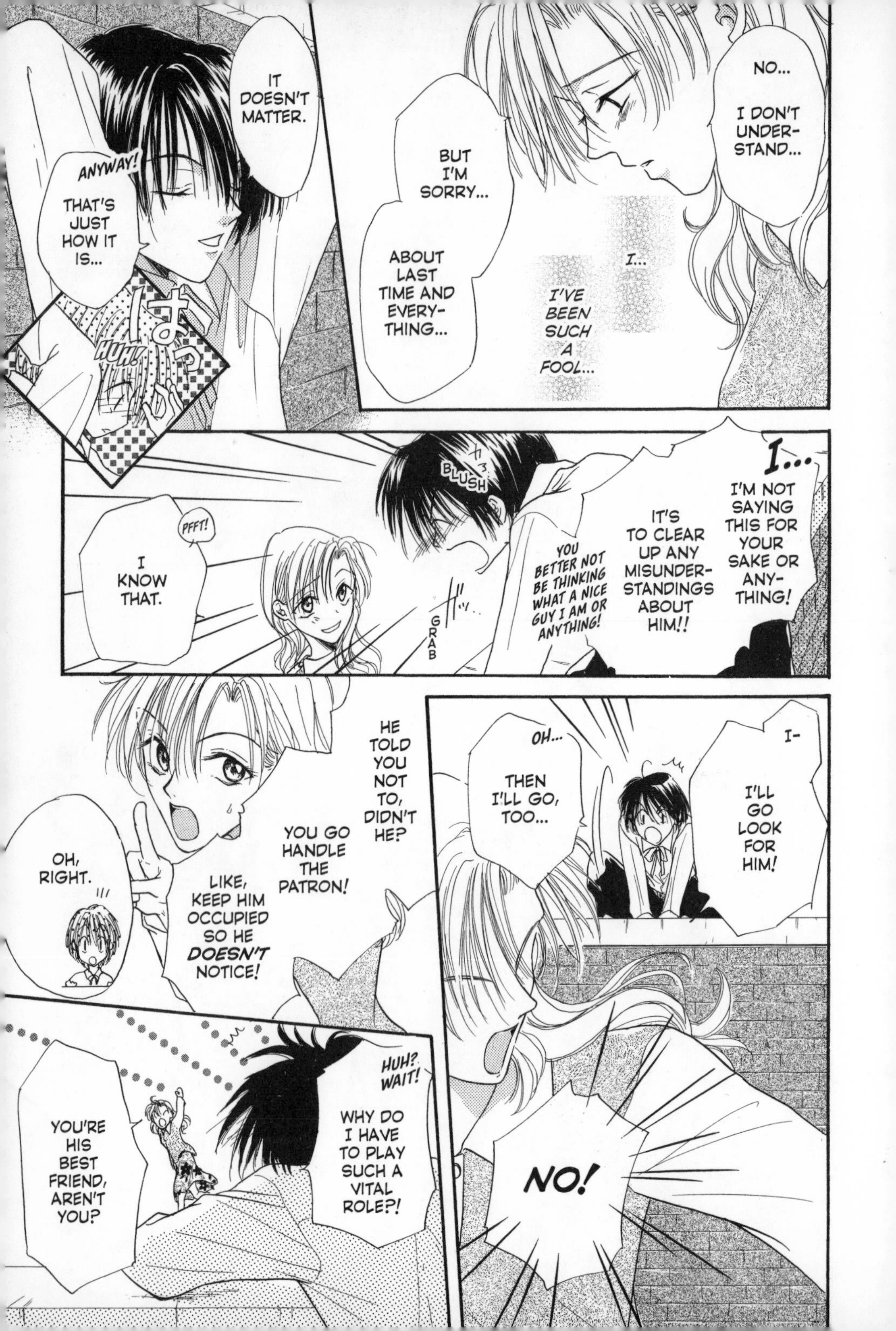
NO...
I DON'T UNDERSTAND...
I...
I'VE BEEN SUCH A FOOL...
BUT I'M SORRY...
ABOUT LAST TIME AND EVERYTHING...
IT DOESN'T MATTER.
ANYWAY!
THAT'S JUST HOW IT IS...
はっ
HUH!
I...
I'M NOT SAYING THIS FOR YOUR SAKE OR ANYTHING!
IT'S TO CLEAR UP ANY MISUNDERSTANDINGS ABOUT HIM!!
YOU BETTER NOT BE THINKING WHAT A NICE GUY I AM OR ANYTHING!
BLUSH
GRAB
PFFT!
I KNOW THAT.
I-
I'LL GO LOOK FOR HIM!
OH...
THEN I'LL GO, TOO...
NO!
HE TOLD YOU NOT TO, DIDN'T HE?
YOU GO HANDLE THE PATRON!
LIKE, KEEP HIM OCCUPIED SO HE DOESN'T NOTICE!
OH, RIGHT.
HUH? WAIT!
WHY DO I HAVE TO PLAY SUCH A VITAL ROLE?!
YOU'RE HIS BEST FRIEND, AREN'T YOU?

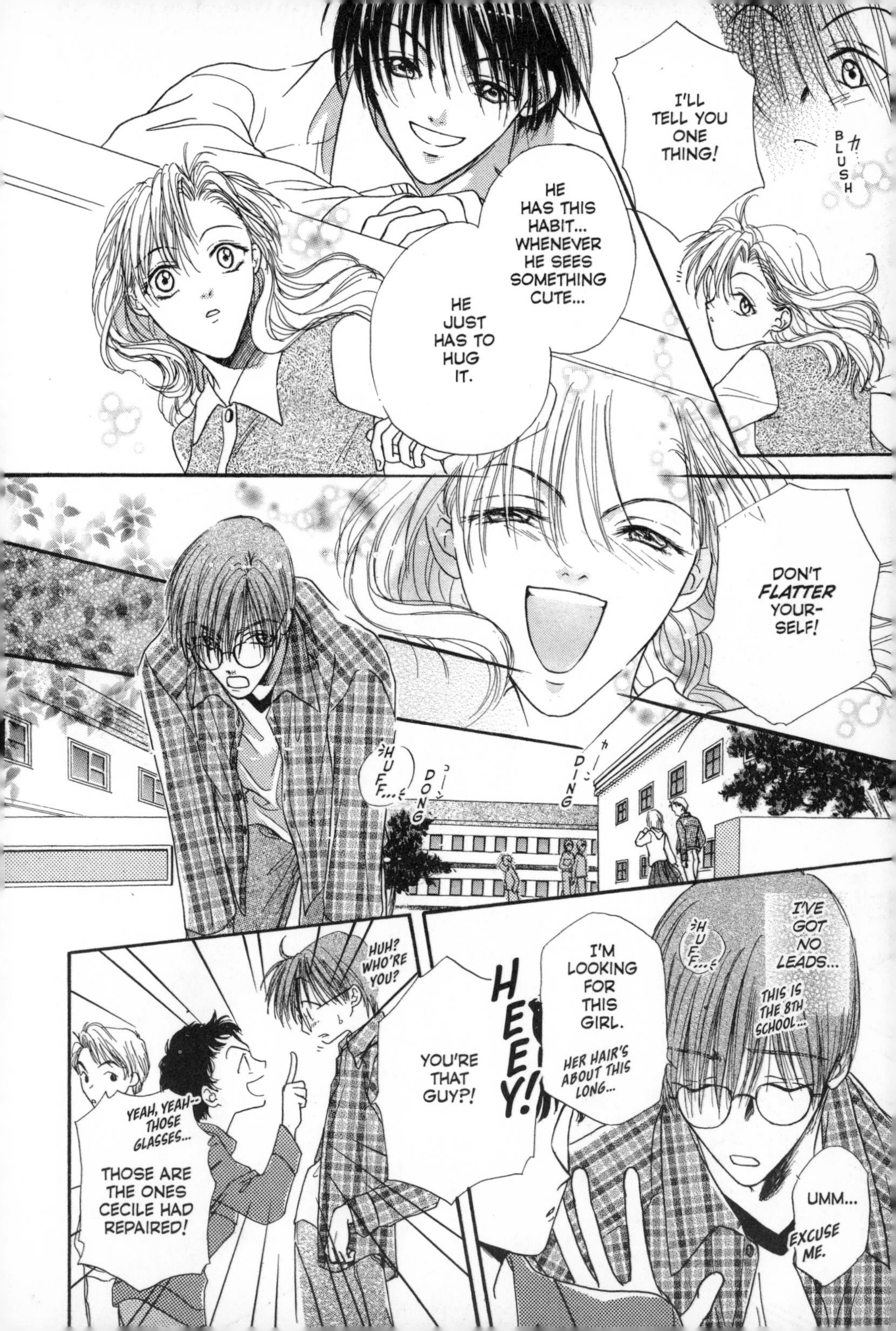

I'LL TELL YOU ONE THING!
BLUSH
HE HAS THIS HABIT... WHENEVER HE SEES SOMETHING CUTE...
HE JUST HAS TO HUG IT.
DON'T *FLATTER* YOURSELF!
DING
DONG
HUFF...
I'VE GOT NO LEADS...
THIS IS THE 8TH SCHOOL...
HUFF...
UMM...
EXCUSE ME.
I'M LOOKING FOR THIS GIRL.
HER HAIR'S ABOUT THIS LONG...
HEEEY!
YOU'RE THAT GUY?!
HUH? WHO'RE YOU?
YEAH, YEAH-- THOSE GLASSES...
THOSE ARE THE ONES CECILE HAD REPAIRED!

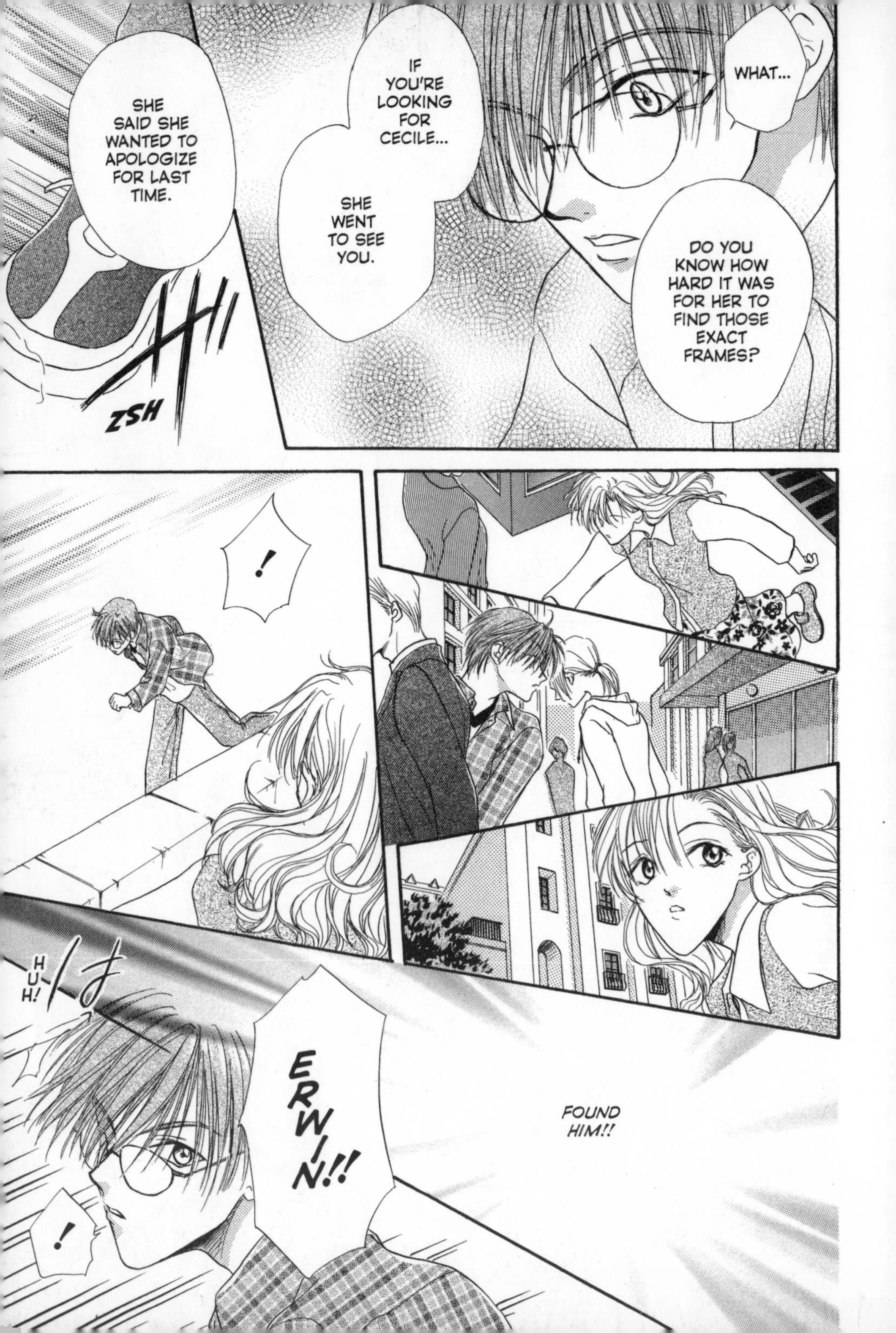
WHAT...
DO YOU KNOW HOW HARD IT WAS FOR HER TO FIND THOSE EXACT FRAMES?
IF YOU'RE LOOKING FOR CECILE...
SHE WENT TO SEE YOU.
SHE SAID SHE WANTED TO APOLOGIZE FOR LAST TIME.
ZSH
!
FOUND HIM!!
ERWIN!!
HUH!
!

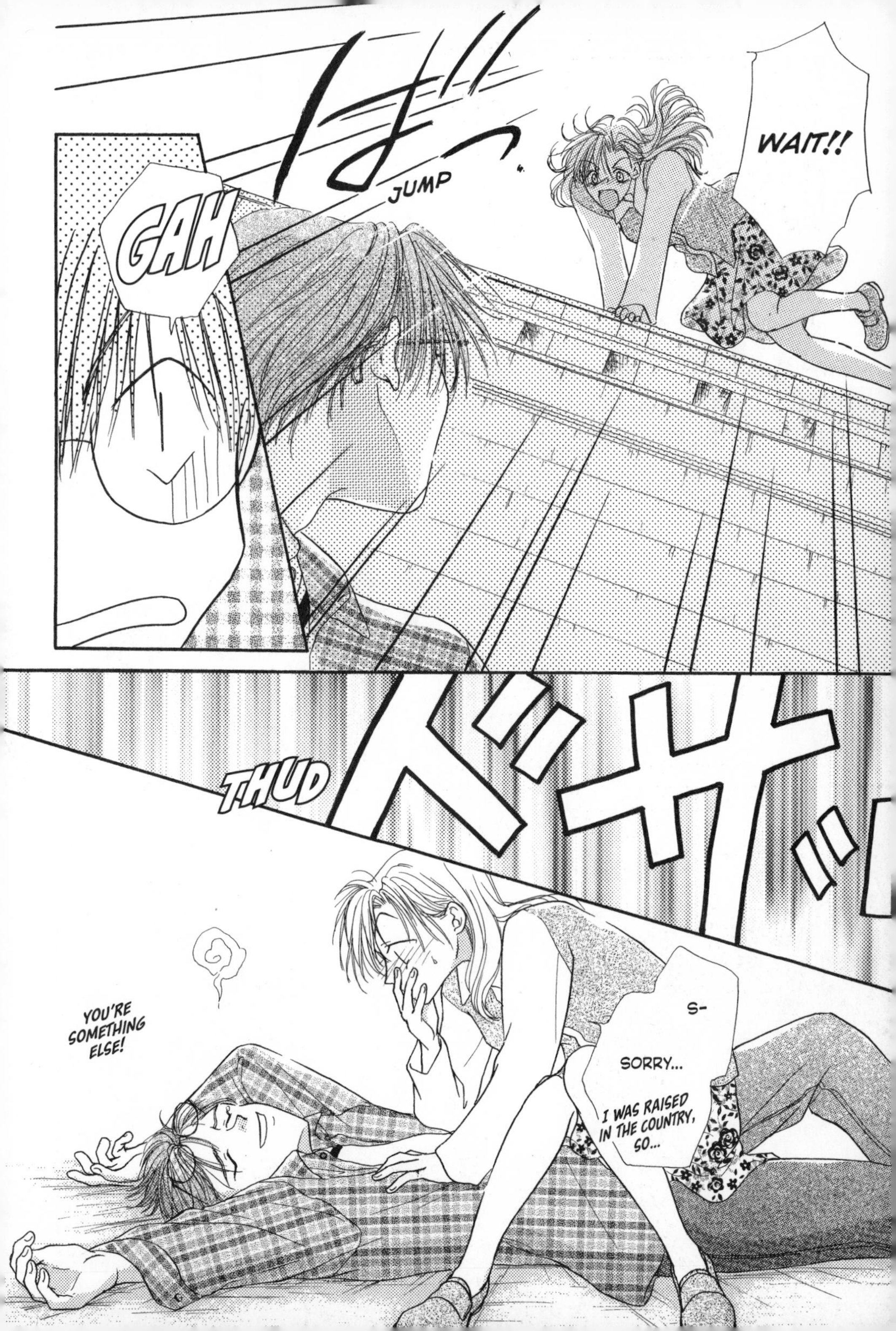
WAIT!!
ぱっ
JUMP
GAH
ドサッ
THUD
S-
SORRY...
I WAS RAISED IN THE COUNTRY, SO...
YOU'RE SOMETHING ELSE!

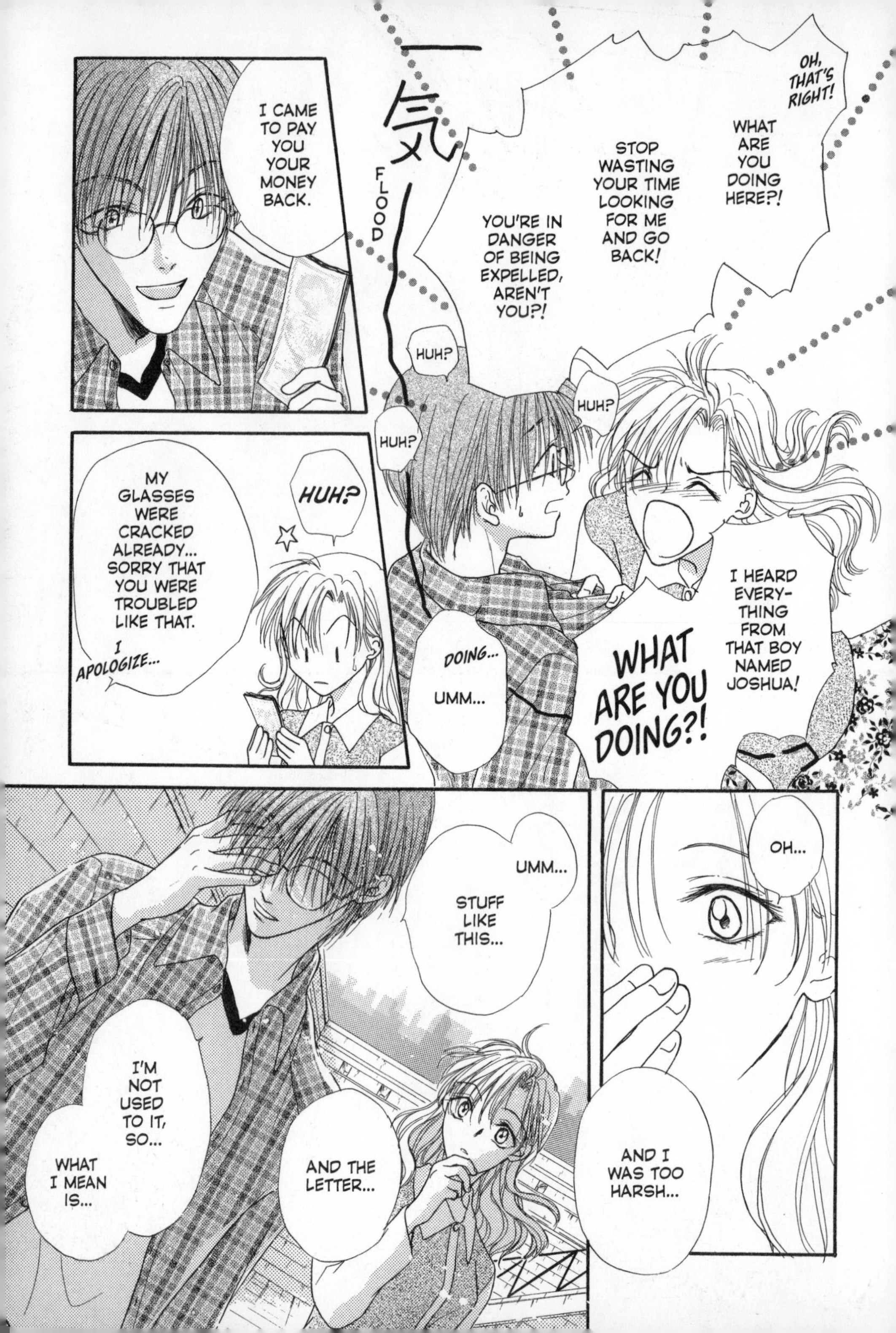
OH, THAT'S RIGHT!
WHAT ARE YOU DOING HERE?!
STOP WASTING YOUR TIME LOOKING FOR ME AND GO BACK!
YOU'RE IN DANGER OF BEING EXPELLED, AREN'T YOU?!
HUH?
HUH?
HUH?
I HEARD EVERYTHING FROM THAT BOY NAMED JOSHUA!
WHAT ARE YOU DOING?!
DOING... UMM...
一気
FLOOD
I CAME TO PAY YOU YOUR MONEY BACK.
HUH?
MY GLASSES WERE CRACKED ALREADY... SORRY THAT YOU WERE TROUBLED LIKE THAT.
I APOLOGIZE...
OH...
AND I WAS TOO HARSH...
UMM...
STUFF LIKE THIS...
AND THE LETTER...
I'M NOT USED TO IT, SO...
WHAT I MEAN IS...

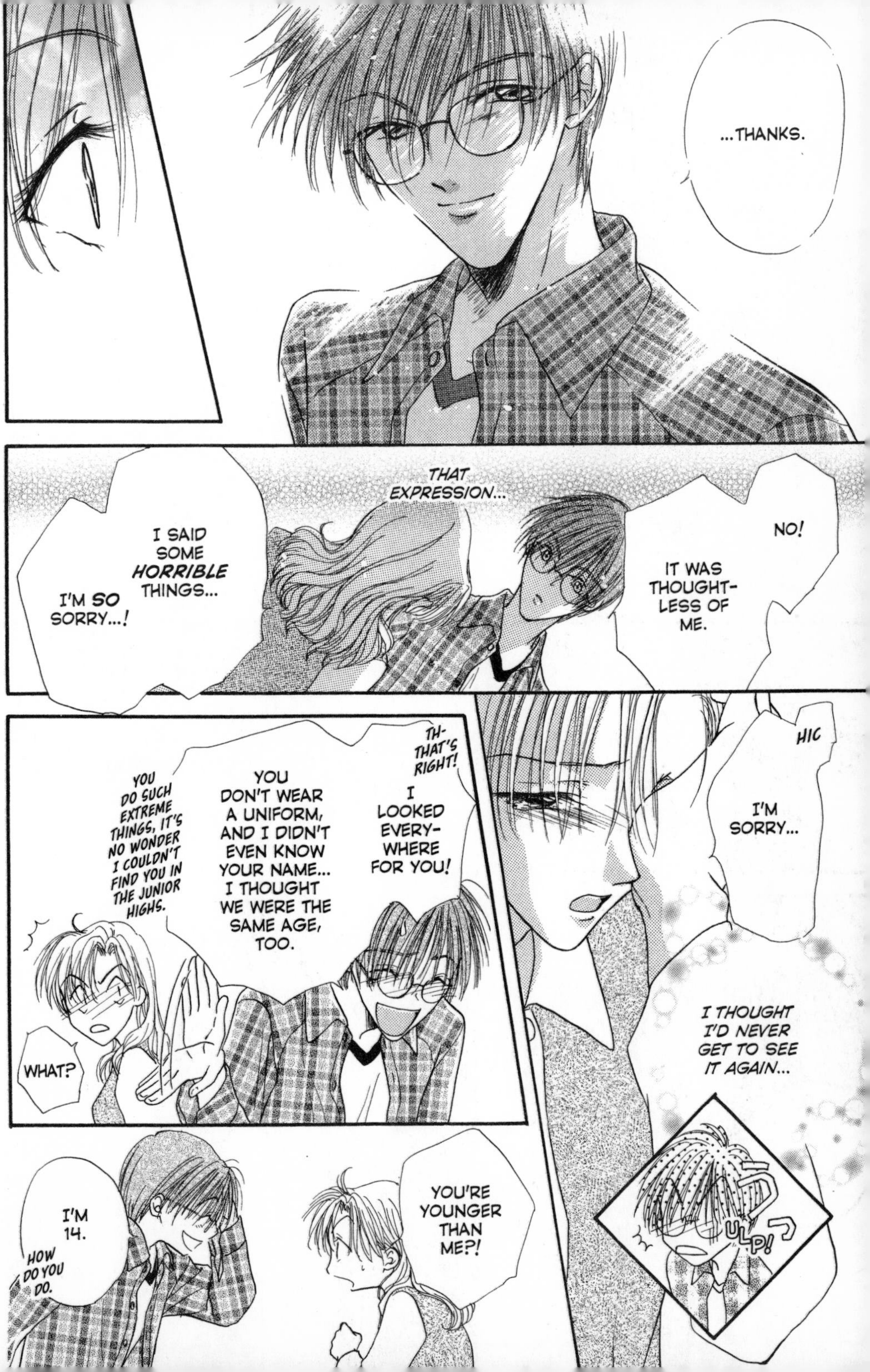
...THANKS.
NO!
IT WAS THOUGHT-LESS OF ME.
THAT EXPRESSION...
I SAID SOME HORRIBLE THINGS...
I'M SO SORRY...!
HIC
I'M SORRY...
I THOUGHT I'D NEVER GET TO SEE IT AGAIN...
ULP!
TH-THAT'S RIGHT!
I LOOKED EVERY-WHERE FOR YOU!
YOU DON'T WEAR A UNIFORM, AND I DIDN'T EVEN KNOW YOUR NAME... I THOUGHT WE WERE THE SAME AGE, TOO.
YOU DO SUCH EXTREME THINGS, IT'S NO WONDER I COULDN'T FIND YOU IN THE JUNIOR HIGHS.
WHAT?
YOU'RE YOUNGER THAN ME?!
I'M 14.
HOW DO YOU DO.

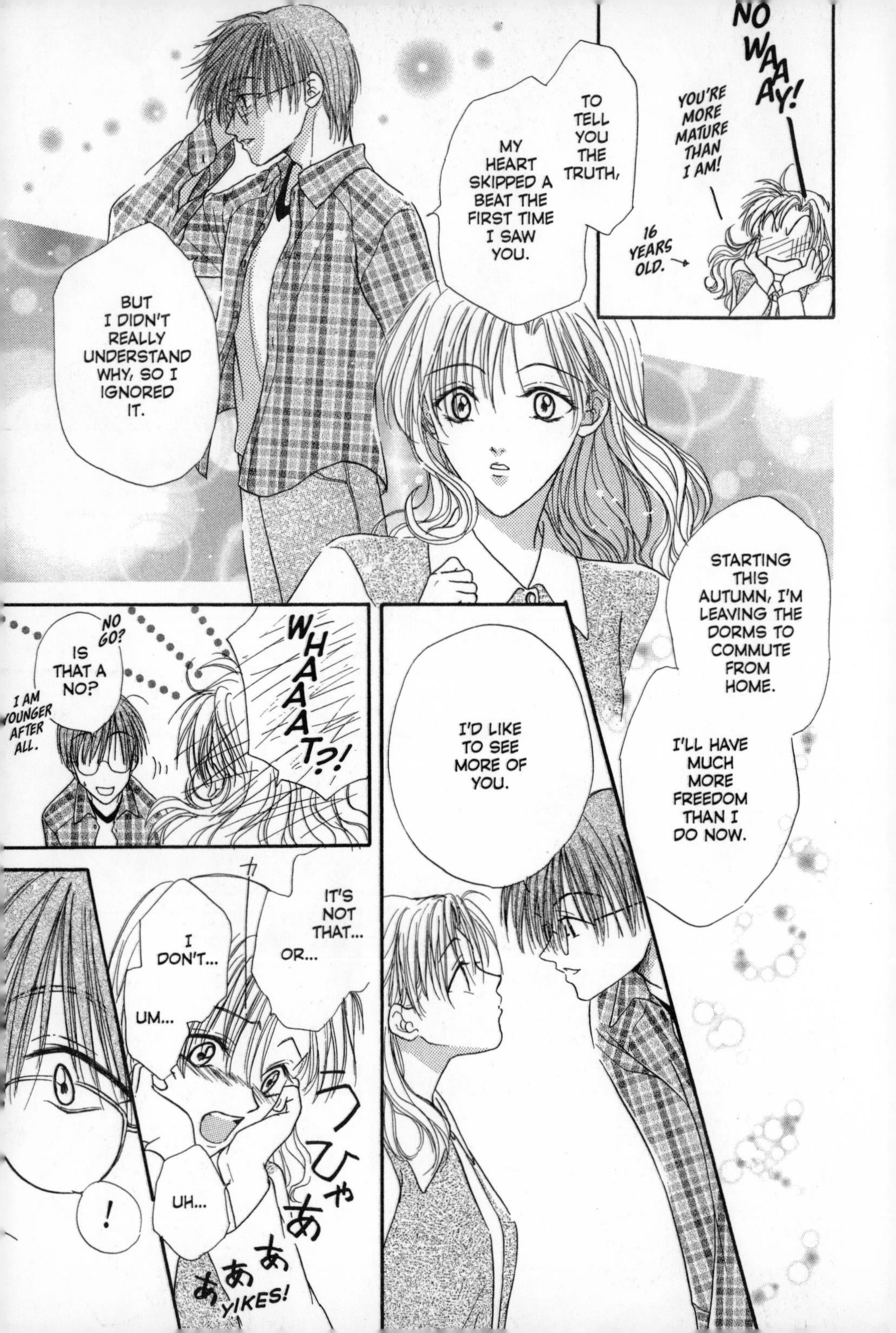
NO WAAAY!
YOU'RE MORE MATURE THAN I AM!
16 YEARS OLD.
TO TELL YOU THE TRUTH,
MY HEART SKIPPED A BEAT THE FIRST TIME I SAW YOU.
BUT I DIDN'T REALLY UNDERSTAND WHY, SO I IGNORED IT.
STARTING THIS AUTUMN, I'M LEAVING THE DORMS TO COMMUTE FROM HOME.
I'LL HAVE MUCH MORE FREEDOM THAN I DO NOW.
I'D LIKE TO SEE MORE OF YOU.
WHAAAAT?!
IS THAT A NO?
NO GO?
I AM YOUNGER AFTER ALL.
IT'S NOT THAT...
OR...
I DON'T...
UM...
UH...
!
ひゃあああ
YIKES!

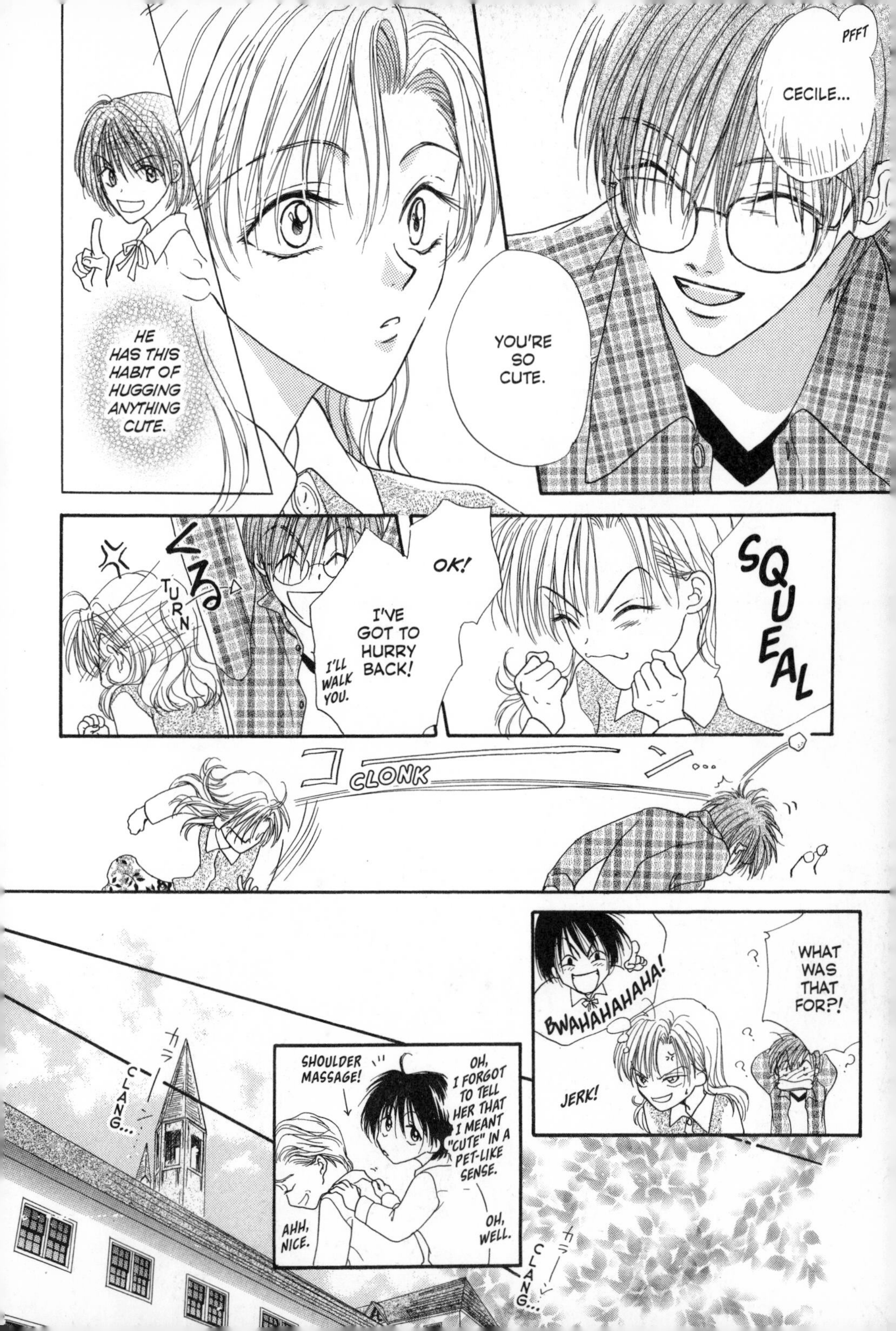
PFFT
CECILE...
YOU'RE SO CUTE.
HE HAS THIS HABIT OF HUGGING ANYTHING CUTE.
SQUEAL
OK!
I'VE GOT TO HURRY BACK!
I'LL WALK YOU.
くる
TURN
CLONK
WHAT WAS THAT FOR?!
BWAHAHAHAHA!
JERK!
OH, I FORGOT TO TELL HER THAT I MEANT "CUTE" IN A PET-LIKE SENSE.
SHOULDER MASSAGE!
OH, WELL.
AHH, NICE.
CLANG...
CLANG...

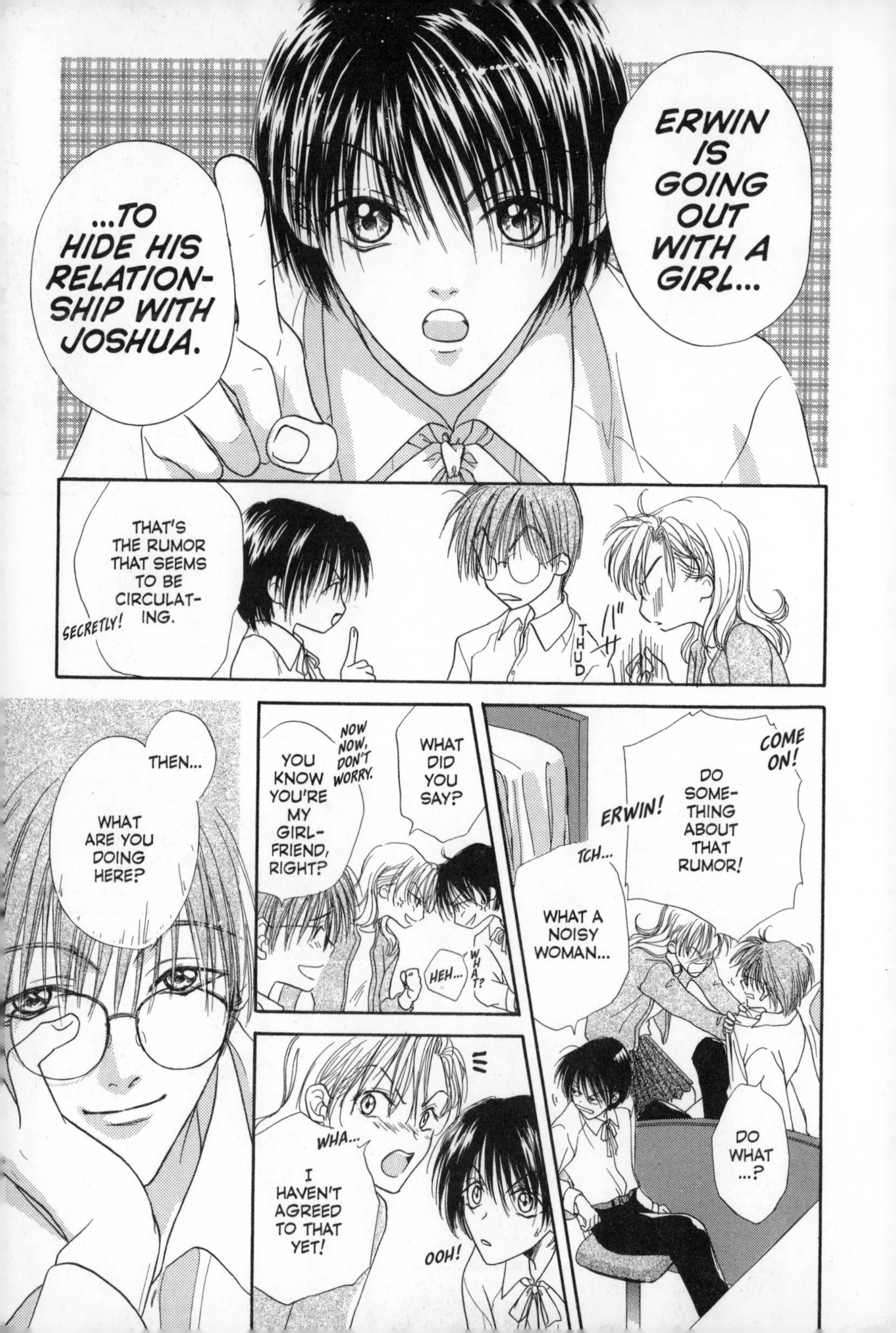
ERWIN IS GOING OUT WITH A GIRL...
...TO HIDE HIS RELATION-SHIP WITH JOSHUA.
THAT'S THE RUMOR THAT SEEMS TO BE CIRCULAT-ING.
SECRETLY!
THUD
COME ON!
ERWIN!
DO SOME-THING ABOUT THAT RUMOR!
TCH...
WHAT A NOISY WOMAN...
DO WHAT ...?
WHAT DID YOU SAY?
NOW NOW, DON'T WORRY.
YOU KNOW YOU'RE MY GIRL-FRIEND, RIGHT?
WHAT?
HEH...
WHA...
I HAVEN'T AGREED TO THAT YET!
OOH!
THEN...
WHAT ARE YOU DOING HERE?

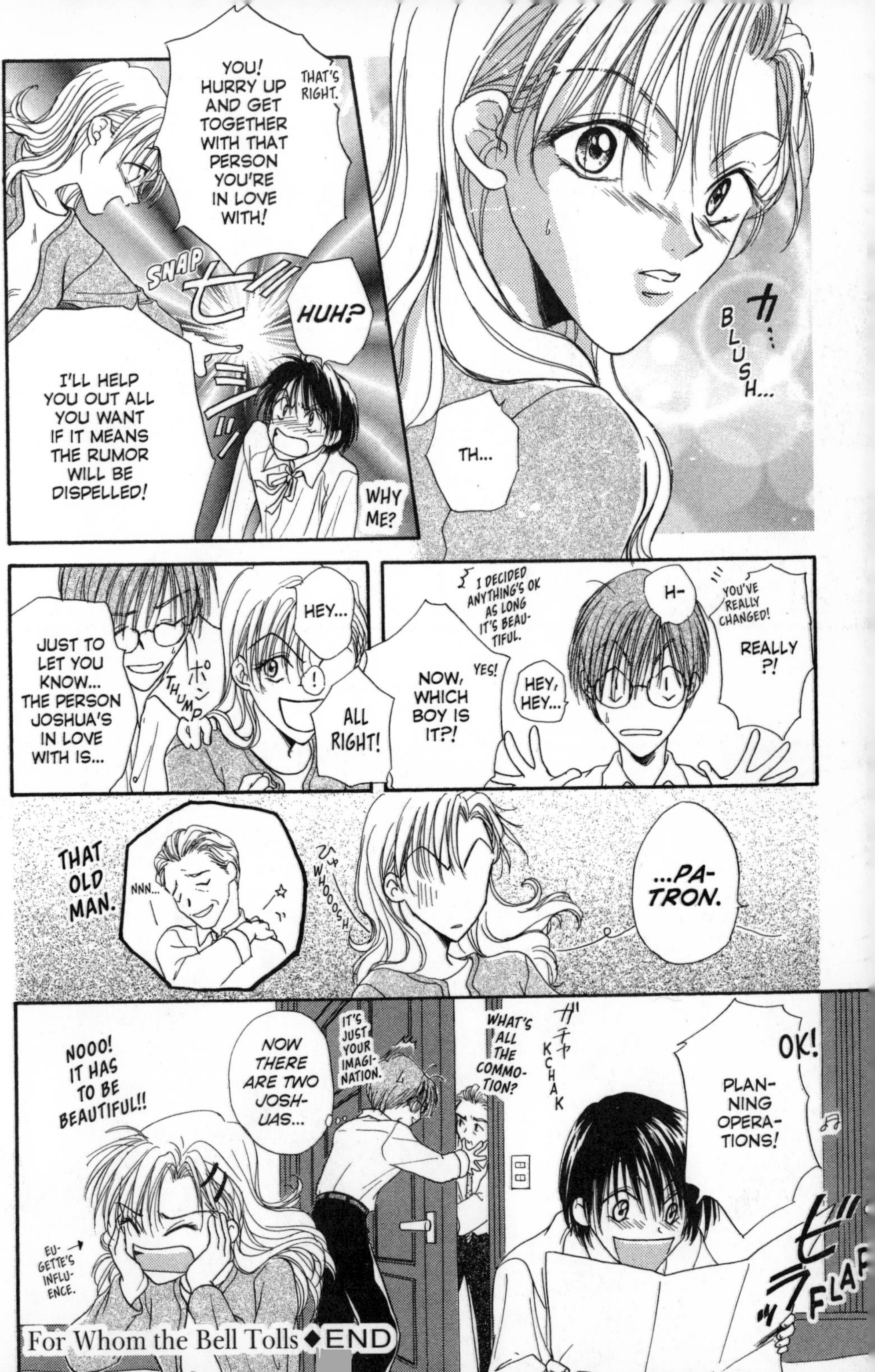
BLUSH...
TH...
YOU! HURRY UP AND GET TOGETHER WITH THAT PERSON YOU'RE IN LOVE WITH!
THAT'S RIGHT.
SNAP
HUH?
I'LL HELP YOU OUT ALL YOU WANT IF IT MEANS THE RUMOR WILL BE DISPELLED!
WHY ME?
YOU'VE REALLY CHANGED!
H-
I DECIDED ANYTHING'S OK AS LONG IT'S BEAU-TIFUL.
REALLY ?!
HEY, HEY...
YES!
NOW, WHICH BOY IS IT?!
HEY...
JUST TO LET YOU KNOW... THE PERSON JOSHUA'S IN LOVE WITH IS...
THUMP
ALL RIGHT!
...PA-TRON.
WHOOOSH
THAT OLD MAN.
NNN...
OK!
PLAN-NING OPERA-TIONS!
FLAP
KCHAK
WHAT'S ALL THE COMMO-TION?
IT'S JUST YOUR IMAGI-NATION.
NOW THERE ARE TWO JOSH-UAS...
NOOO! IT HAS TO BE BEAUTIFUL!!
EU-GETTE'S INFLU-ENCE.
For Whom the Bell Tolls ◆END

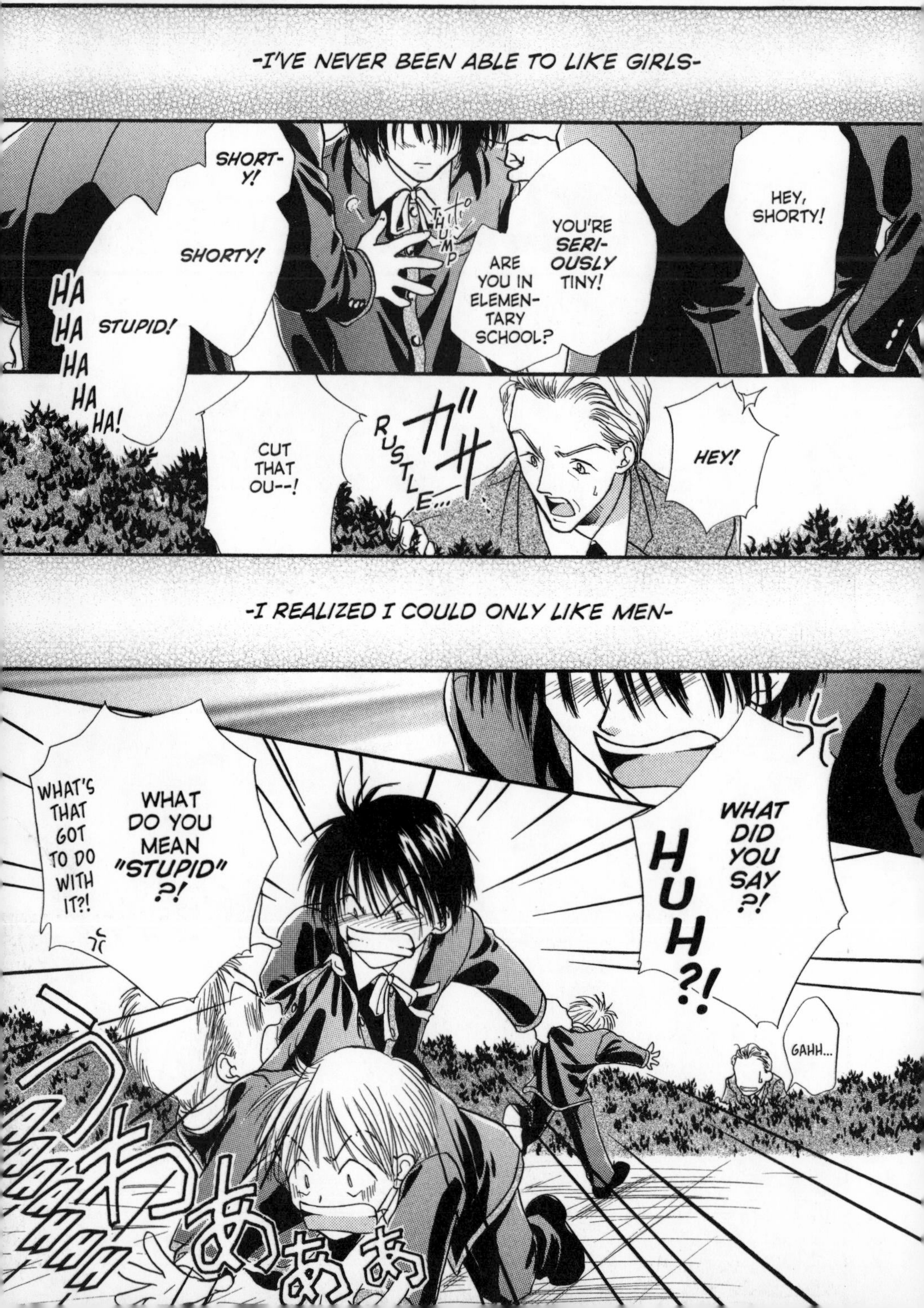
-I'VE NEVER BEEN ABLE TO LIKE GIRLS-
HEY, SHORTY!
YOU'RE SERIOUSLY TINY!
ARE YOU IN ELEMENTARY SCHOOL?
THUMP
SHORTY!
SHORTY!
STUPID!
HA HA HA HA HA!
HEY!
ガサ
RUSTLE...
CUT THAT OU--!
-I REALIZED I COULD ONLY LIKE MEN-
WHAT DID YOU SAY?!
HUH?!
GAHH...
WHAT DO YOU MEAN "STUPID"?!
WHAT'S THAT GOT TO DO WITH IT?!
うわあああ

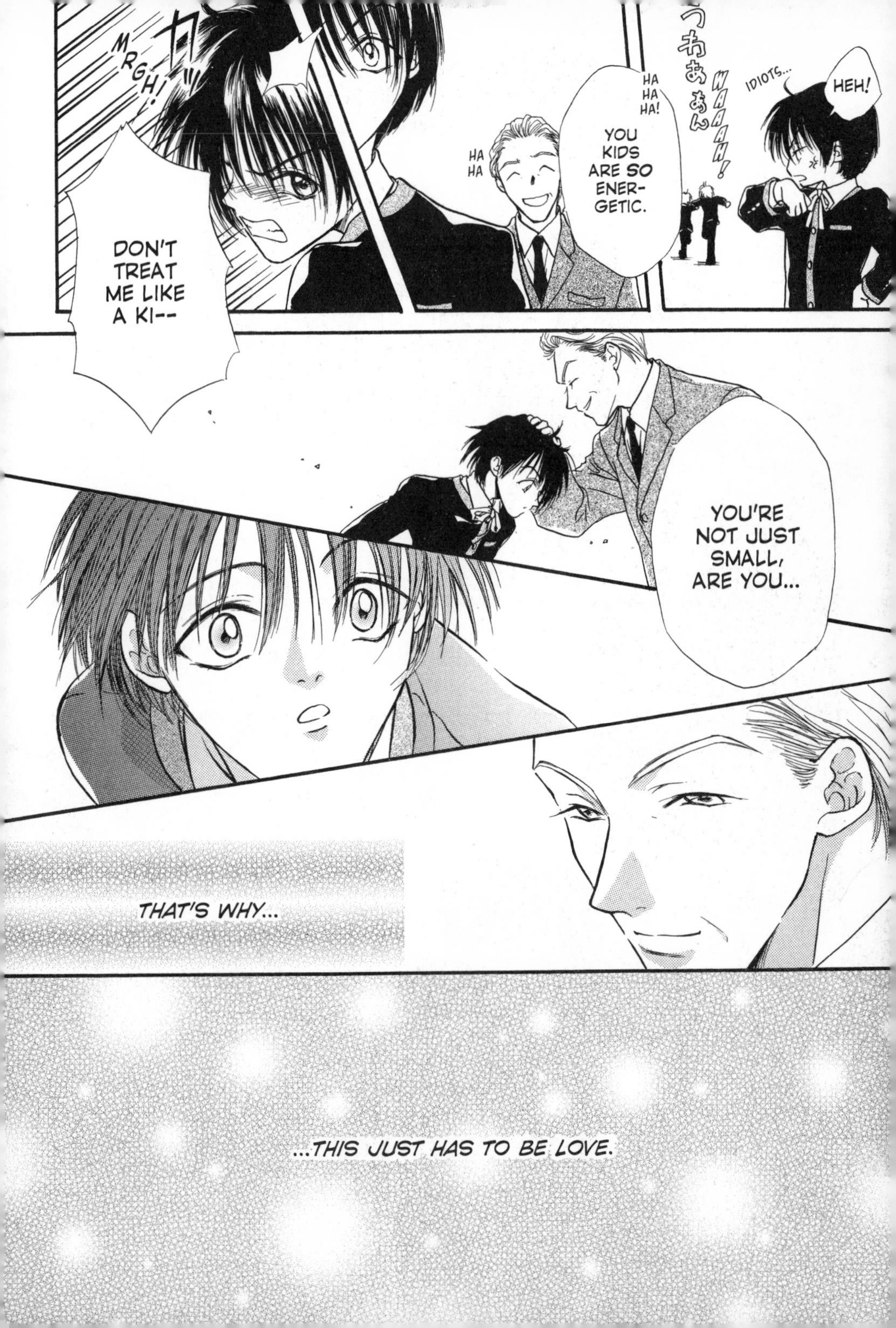
IDIOTS...
HEH!
うわああん
WAAAAH!
HA HA HA!
YOU KIDS ARE SO ENERGETIC.
HA HA
カッ
MRGH!
DON'T TREAT ME LIKE A KI--
YOU'RE NOT JUST SMALL, ARE YOU...
THAT'S WHY...
...THIS JUST HAS TO BE LOVE.

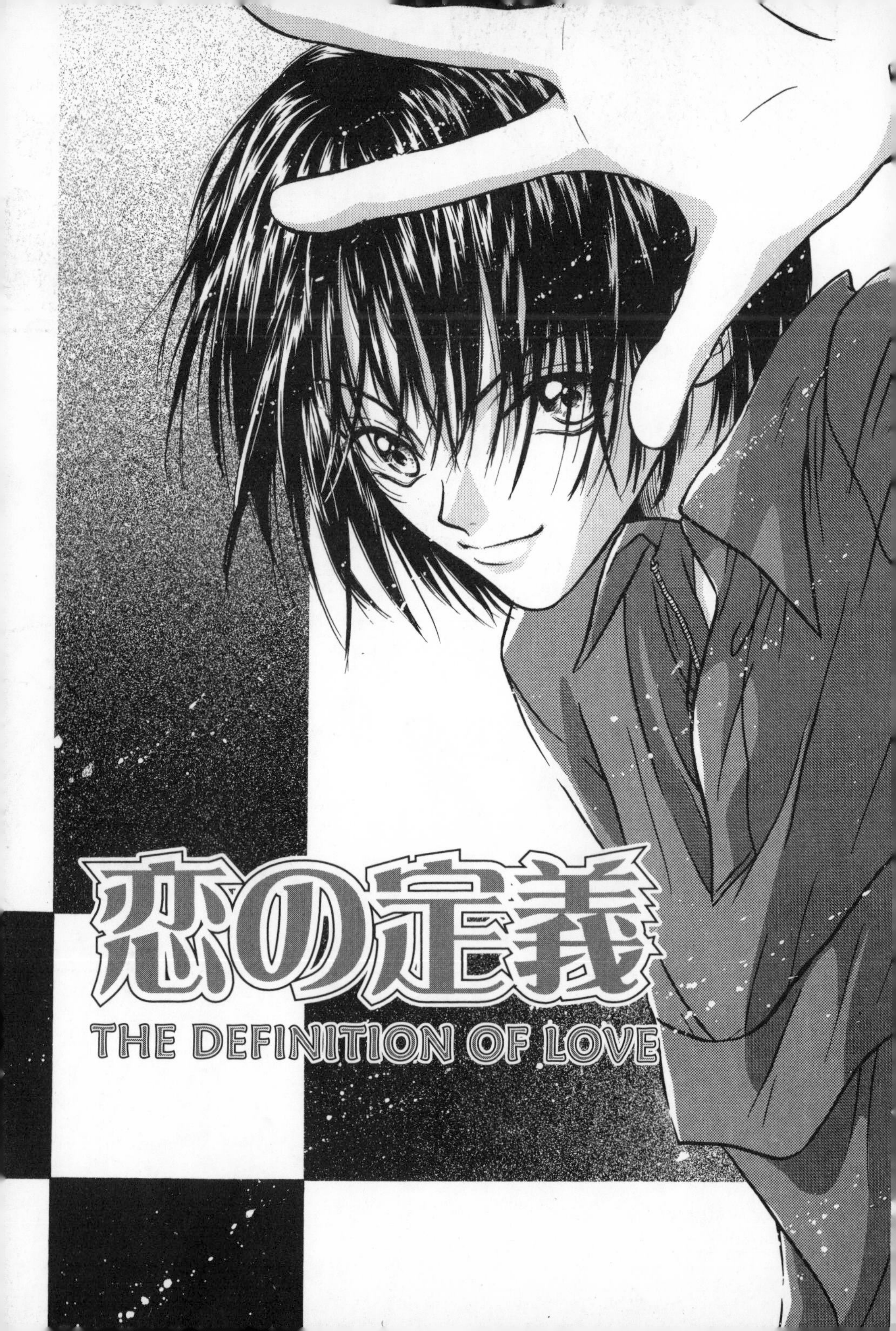

恋の定義
THE DEFINITION OF LOVE

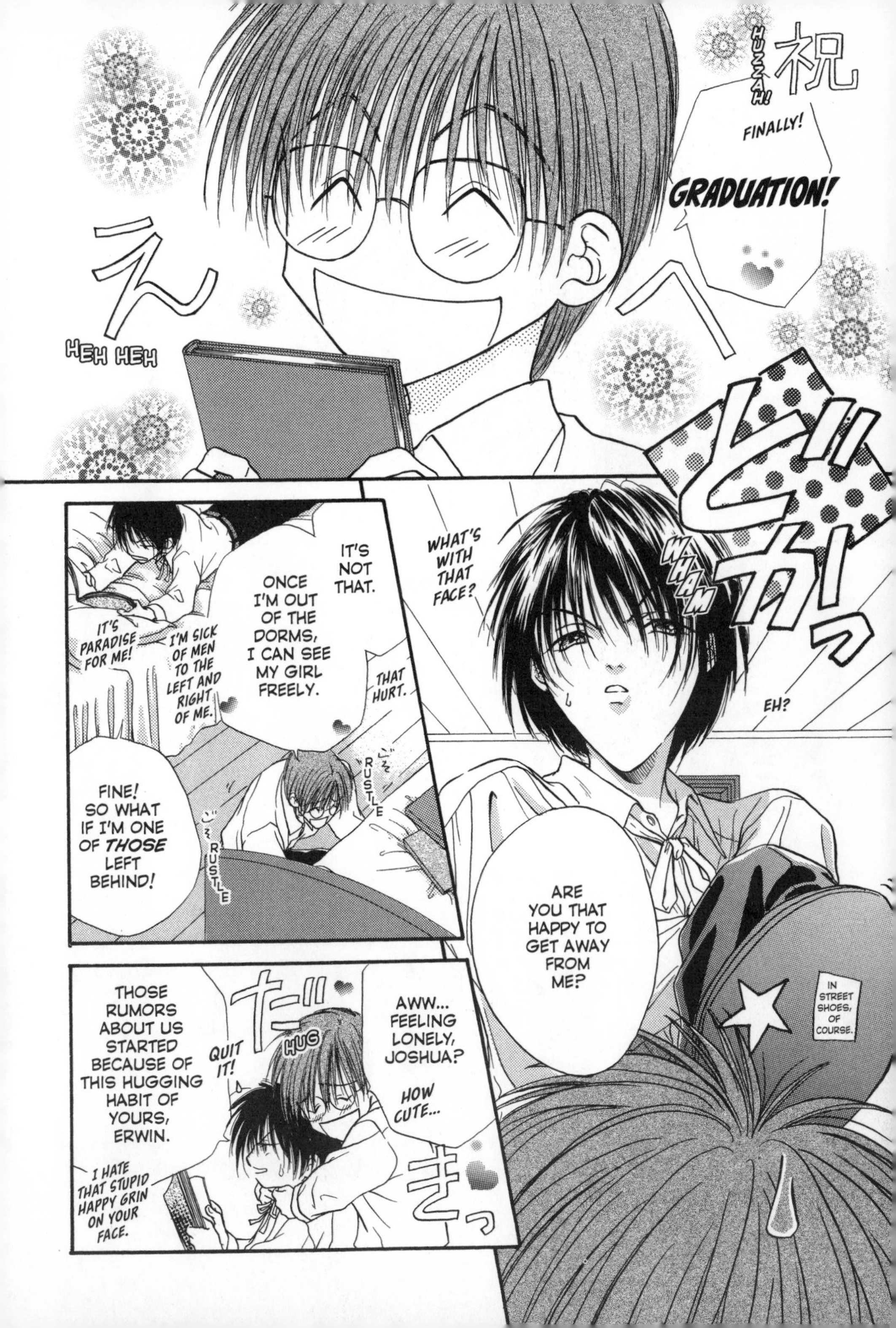
HUZZAH!
祝
FINALLY!
GRADUATION!
え
へ
HEH HEH
どかっ
WHAM
WHAT'S WITH THAT FACE?
EH?
ARE YOU THAT HAPPY TO GET AWAY FROM ME?
IN STREET SHOES, OF COURSE.
IT'S NOT THAT.
ONCE I'M OUT OF THE DORMS, I CAN SEE MY GIRL FREELY.
THAT HURT.
IT'S PARADISE FOR ME!
I'M SICK OF MEN TO THE LEFT AND RIGHT OF ME.
RUSTLE
FINE! SO WHAT IF I'M ONE OF *THOSE* LEFT BEHIND!
RUSTLE
AWW... FEELING LONELY, JOSHUA?
HOW CUTE...
たーッ
HUG
QUIT IT!
THOSE RUMORS ABOUT US STARTED BECAUSE OF THIS HUGGING HABIT OF YOURS, ERWIN.
I HATE THAT STUPID HAPPY GRIN ON YOUR FACE.
きっ

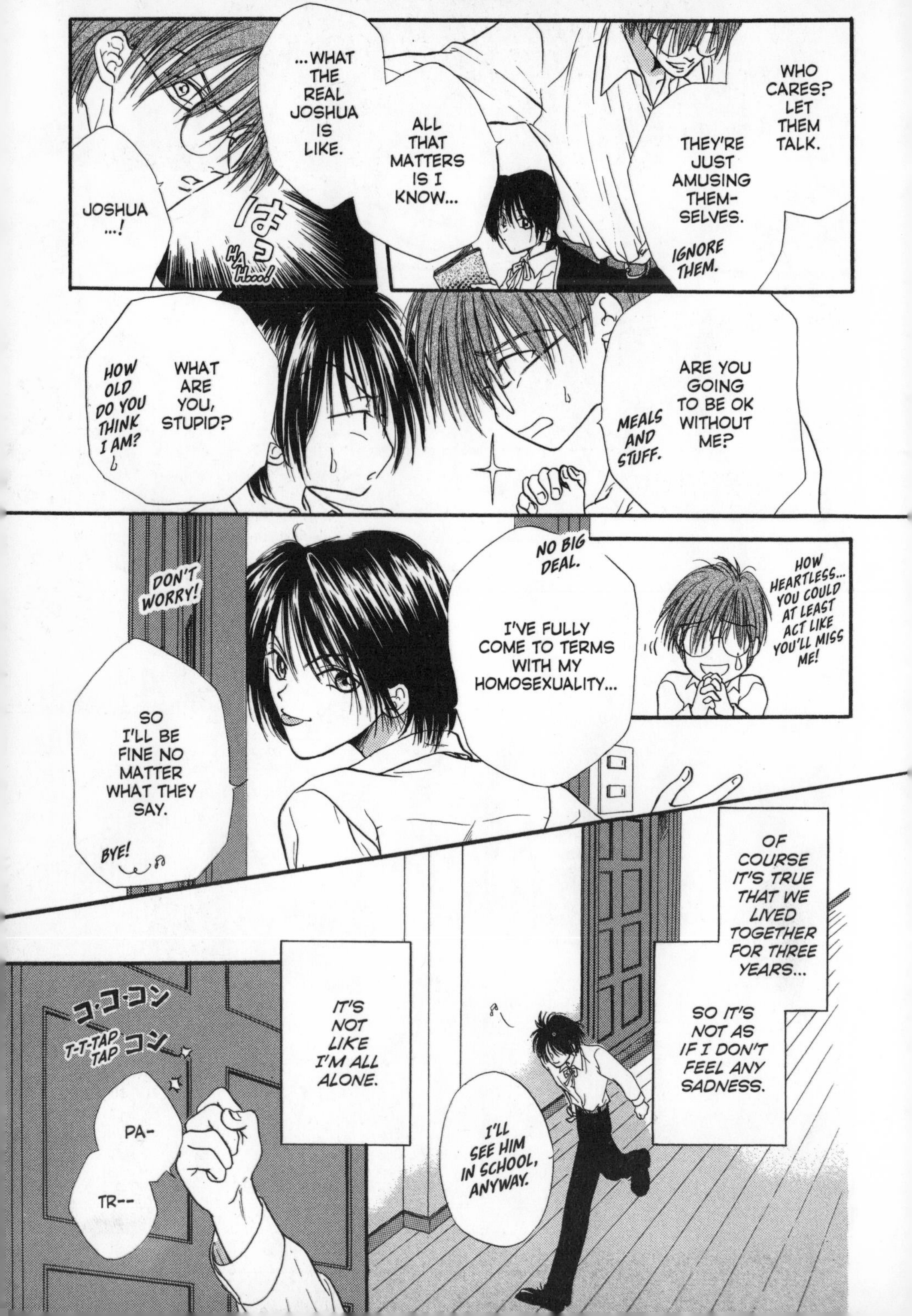
WHO CARES? LET THEM TALK.
THEY'RE JUST AMUSING THEM-SELVES.
IGNORE THEM.
ALL THAT MATTERS IS I KNOW...
...WHAT THE REAL JOSHUA IS LIKE.
JOSHUA ...!
はっ
HAHooo!
ARE YOU GOING TO BE OK WITHOUT ME?
MEALS AND STUFF.
WHAT ARE YOU, STUPID?
HOW OLD DO YOU THINK I AM?
HOW HEARTLESS... YOU COULD AT LEAST ACT LIKE YOU'LL MISS ME!
NO BIG DEAL.
I'VE FULLY COME TO TERMS WITH MY HOMOSEXUALITY...
DON'T WORRY!
SO I'LL BE FINE NO MATTER WHAT THEY SAY.
BYE!
OF COURSE IT'S TRUE THAT WE LIVED TOGETHER FOR THREE YEARS...
SO IT'S NOT AS IF I DON'T FEEL ANY SADNESS.
IT'S NOT LIKE I'M ALL ALONE.
I'LL SEE HIM IN SCHOOL, ANYWAY.
コ・コ・コン
T-T-TAP TAP
コン
PA-
TR--

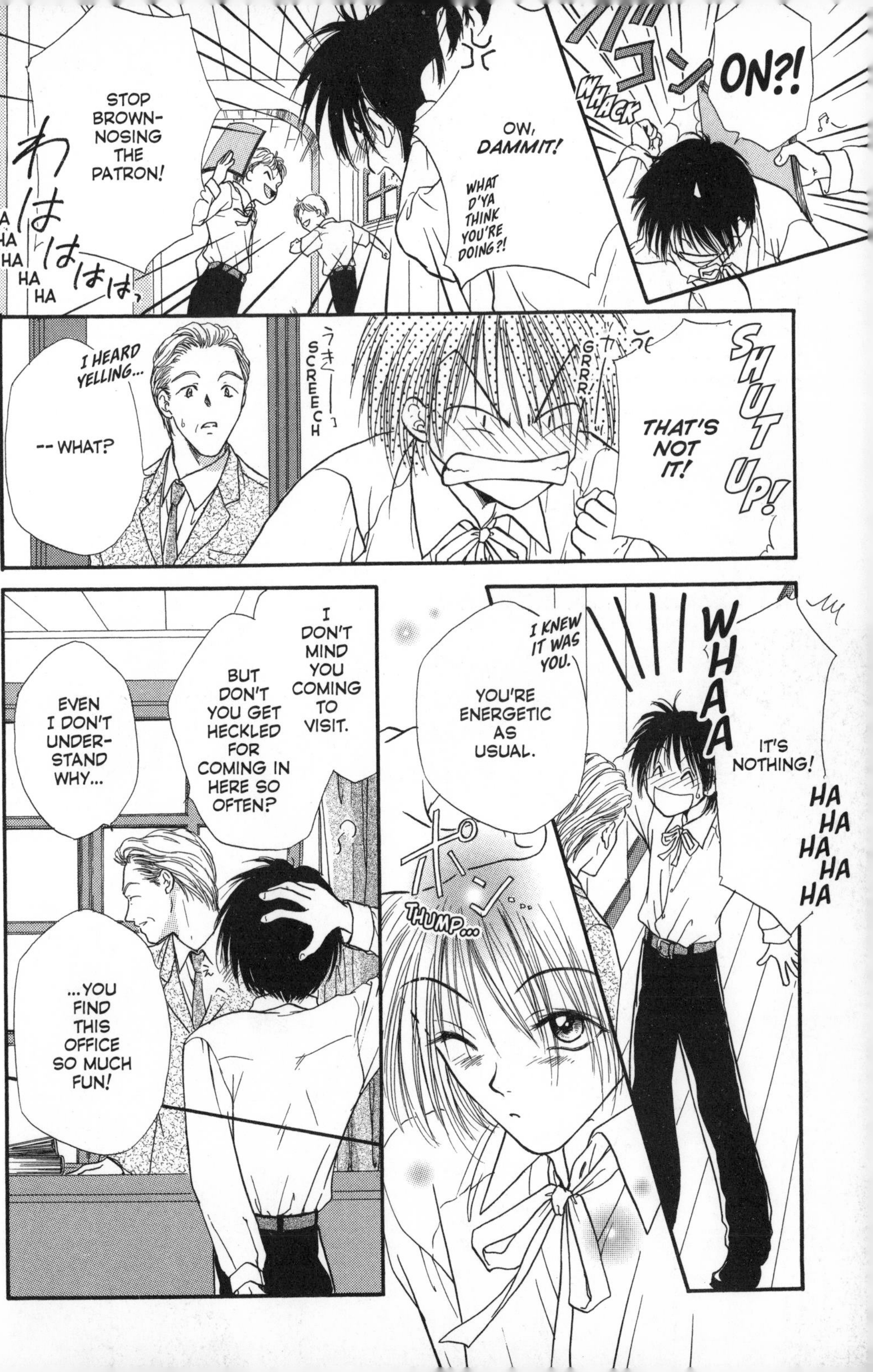
ON?!
WHACK
OW, DAMMIT!
WHAT D'YA THINK YOU'RE DOING?!
STOP BROWN-NOSING THE PATRON!
HA HA HA HA HA
SHUT UP!
THAT'S NOT IT!
GRRR
SCREECH
I HEARD YELLING...
-- WHAT?
WHAAA
IT'S NOTHING!
HA HA HA HA HA HA
I KNEW IT WAS YOU.
YOU'RE ENERGETIC AS USUAL.
THUMP...
I DON'T MIND YOU COMING TO VISIT.
BUT DON'T YOU GET HECKLED FOR COMING IN HERE SO OFTEN?
EVEN I DON'T UNDERSTAND WHY...
...YOU FIND THIS OFFICE SO MUCH FUN!

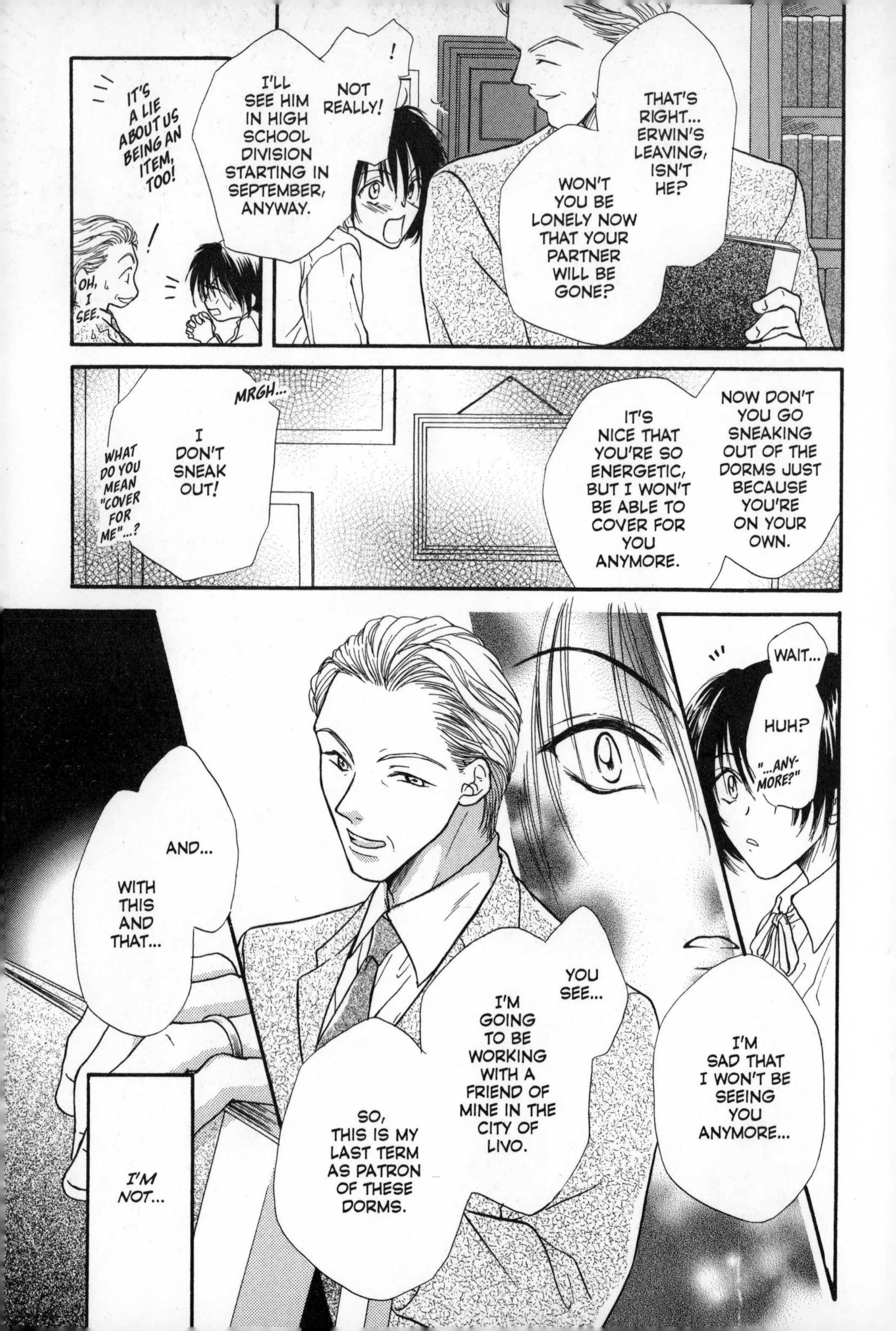
THAT'S RIGHT... ERWIN'S LEAVING, ISN'T HE?
WON'T YOU BE LONELY NOW THAT YOUR PARTNER WILL BE GONE?
!
NOT REALLY!
I'LL SEE HIM IN HIGH SCHOOL DIVISION STARTING IN SEPTEMBER, ANYWAY.
IT'S A LIE ABOUT US BEING AN ITEM, TOO!
!
OH, I SEE.
NOW DON'T YOU GO SNEAKING OUT OF THE DORMS JUST BECAUSE YOU'RE ON YOUR OWN.
IT'S NICE THAT YOU'RE SO ENERGETIC, BUT I WON'T BE ABLE TO COVER FOR YOU ANYMORE.
MRGH...
I DON'T SNEAK OUT!
WHAT DO YOU MEAN "COVER FOR ME"...?
WAIT...
HUH?
"...ANY-MORE?"
I'M SAD THAT I WON'T BE SEEING YOU ANYMORE...
YOU SEE...
I'M GOING TO BE WORKING WITH A FRIEND OF MINE IN THE CITY OF LIVO.
SO, THIS IS MY LAST TERM AS PATRON OF THESE DORMS.
AND...
WITH THIS AND THAT...
I'M NOT...

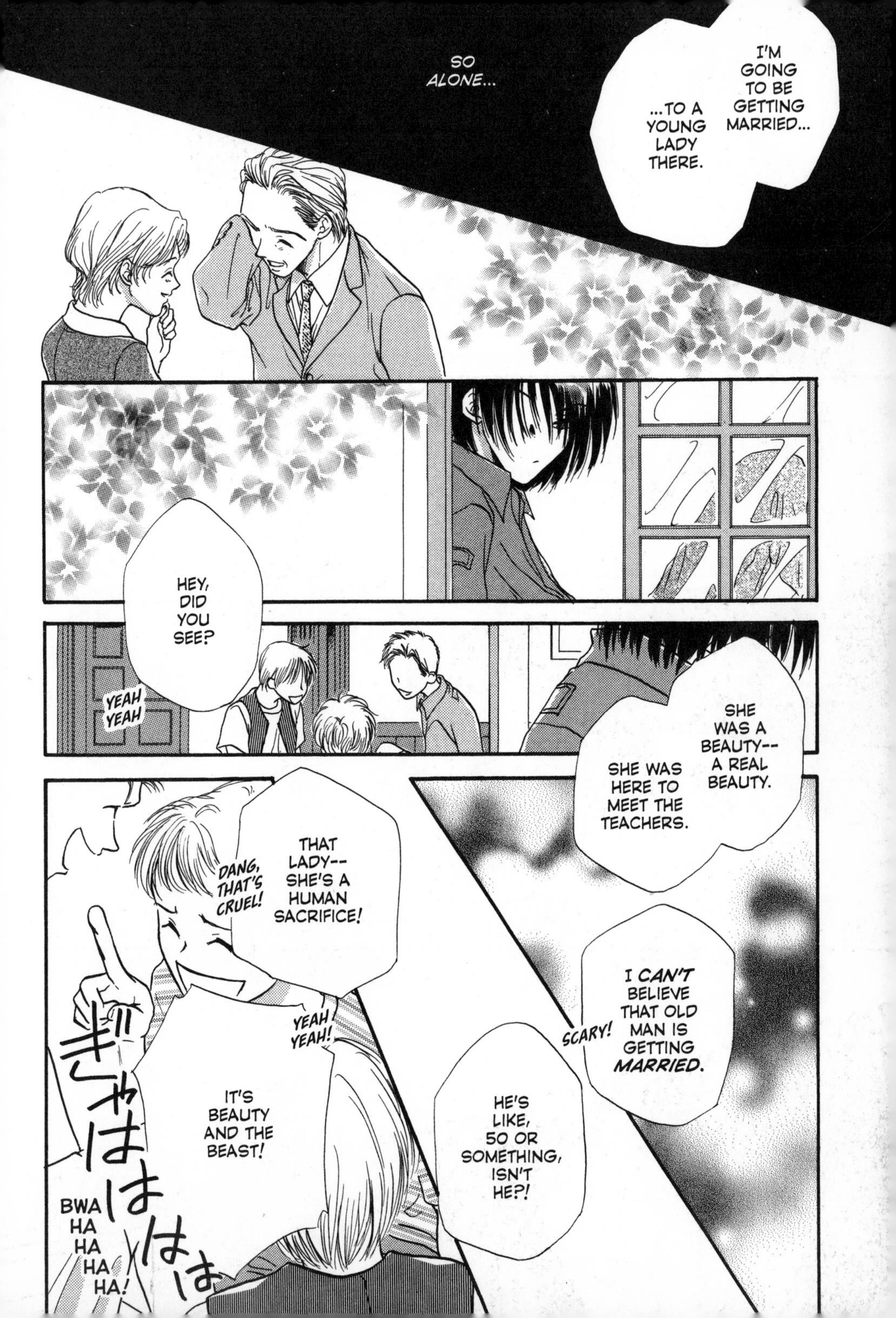
I'M GOING TO BE GETTING MARRIED...
...TO A YOUNG LADY THERE.
SO ALONE...
HEY, DID YOU SEE?
YEAH YEAH
SHE WAS A BEAUTY-- A REAL BEAUTY.
SHE WAS HERE TO MEET THE TEACHERS.
I CAN'T BELIEVE THAT OLD MAN IS GETTING MARRIED.
SCARY!
HE'S LIKE, 50 OR SOMETHING, ISN'T HE?!
THAT LADY-- SHE'S A HUMAN SACRIFICE!
DANG, THAT'S CRUEL!
YEAH YEAH!
IT'S BEAUTY AND THE BEAST!
ぎゃははは
BWA HA HA HA HA!

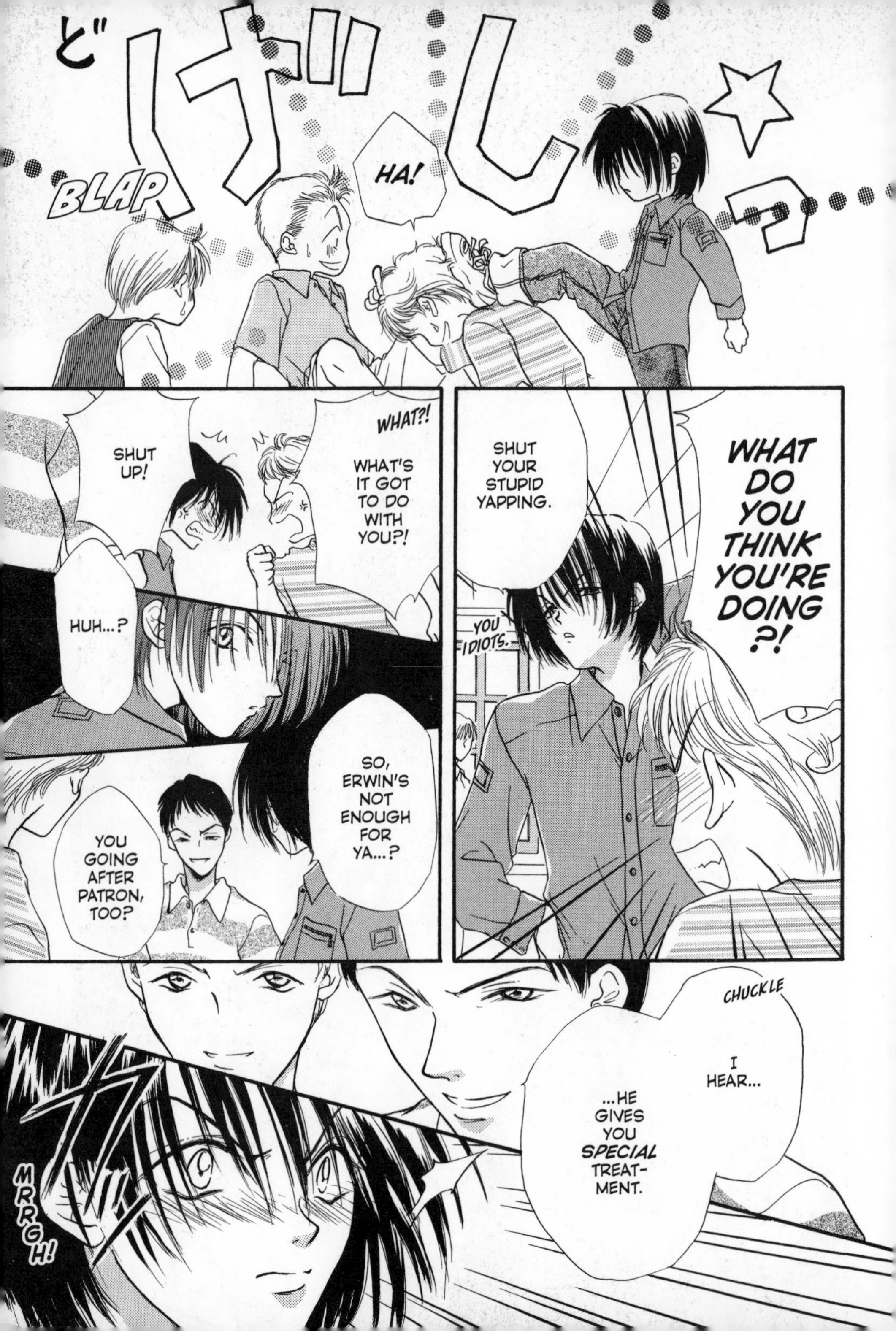
どげしっ☆
HA!
BLAP
WHAT DO YOU THINK YOU'RE DOING?!
SHUT YOUR STUPID YAPPING.
YOU IDIOTS.
WHAT?!
WHAT'S IT GOT TO DO WITH YOU?!
SHUT UP!
HUH...?
SO, ERWIN'S NOT ENOUGH FOR YA...?
YOU GOING AFTER PATRON, TOO?
CHUCKLE
I HEAR...
...HE GIVES YOU SPECIAL TREATMENT.
MRRGH!

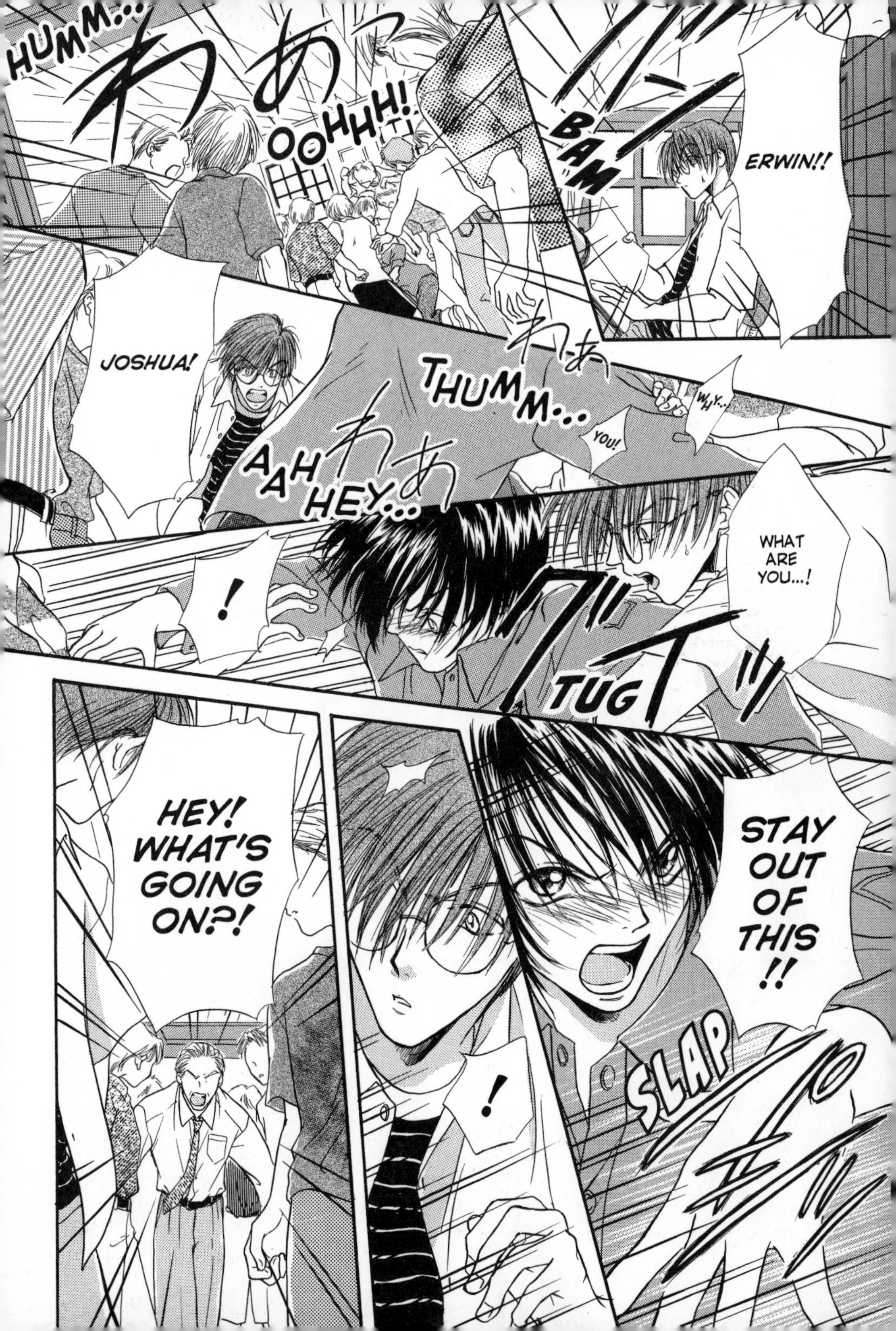
BAM
ERWIN!!
HUMM...
わあっ
OOHHH!
WHY..
YOU!
JOSHUA!
THUMM...
AAH
HEY...
WHAT ARE YOU...!
TUG
!
STAY OUT OF THIS!!
SLAP
!
HEY! WHAT'S GOING ON?!

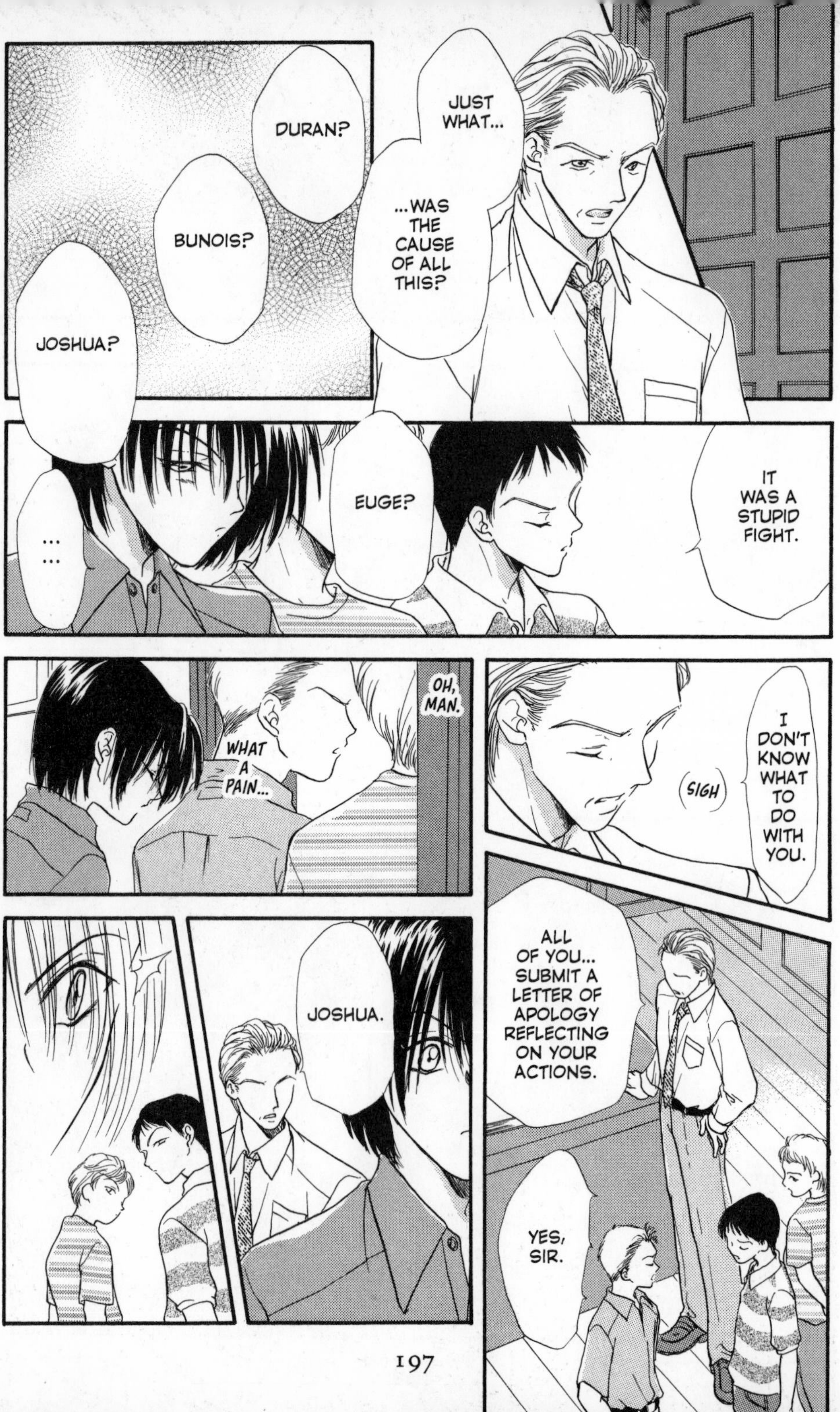
JUST WHAT...
...WAS THE CAUSE OF ALL THIS?
DURAN?
BUNOIS?
JOSHUA?
IT WAS A STUPID FIGHT.
EUGE?
......
I DON'T KNOW WHAT TO DO WITH YOU.
(SIGH)
OH, MAN.
WHAT A PAIN...
ALL OF YOU... SUBMIT A LETTER OF APOLOGY REFLECTING ON YOUR ACTIONS.
YES, SIR.
JOSHUA.

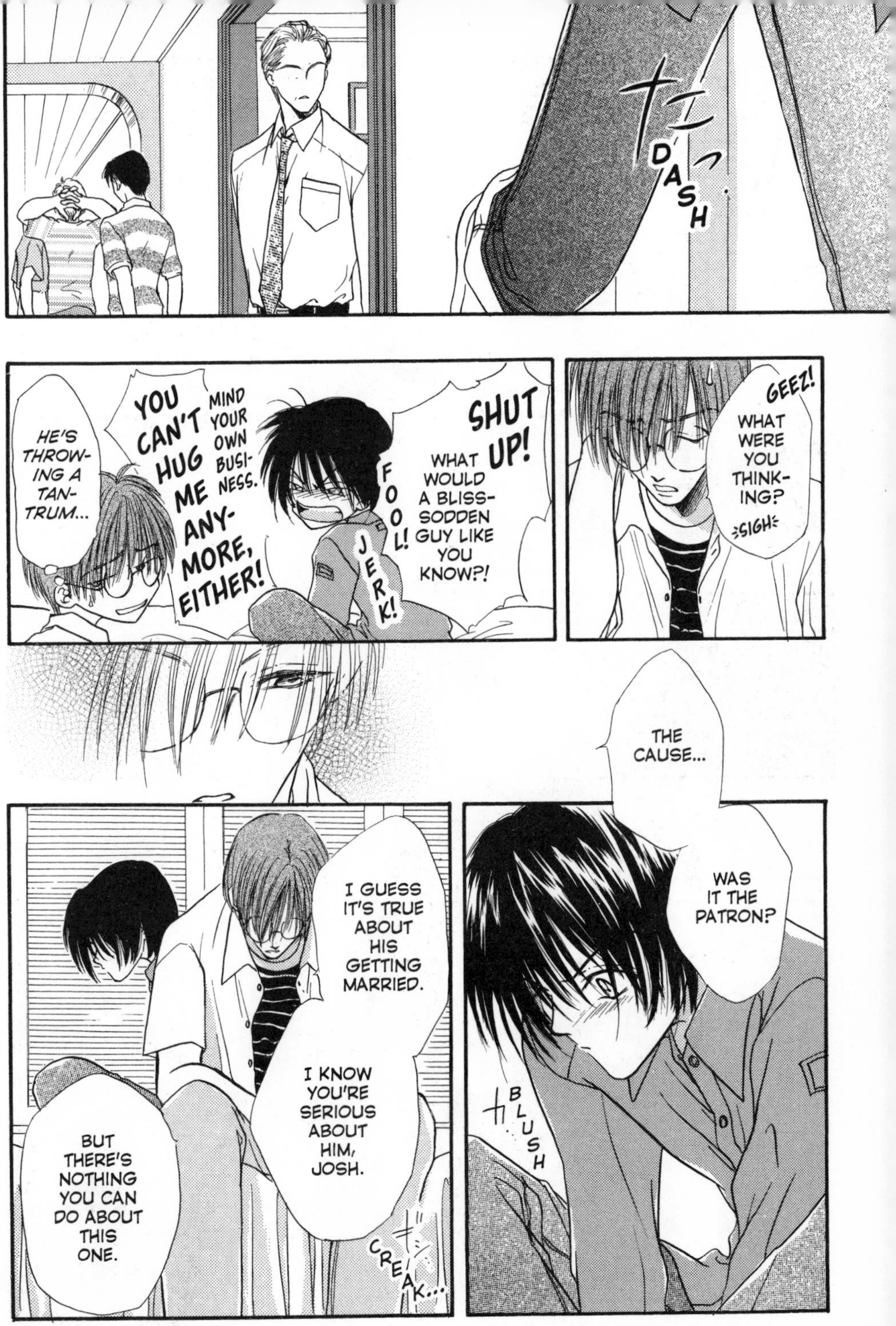
DASH
GEEZ! WHAT WERE YOU THINKING?
SIGH
SHUT UP! WHAT WOULD A BLISS-SODDEN GUY LIKE YOU KNOW?!
FOOL!
JERK!
MIND YOUR OWN BUSINESS.
YOU CAN'T HUG ME ANYMORE, EITHER!
HE'S THROWING A TANTRUM...
THE CAUSE...
WAS IT THE PATRON?
BLUSH
I GUESS IT'S TRUE ABOUT HIS GETTING MARRIED.
I KNOW YOU'RE SERIOUS ABOUT HIM, JOSH.
BUT THERE'S NOTHING YOU CAN DO ABOUT THIS ONE.
CREAK...

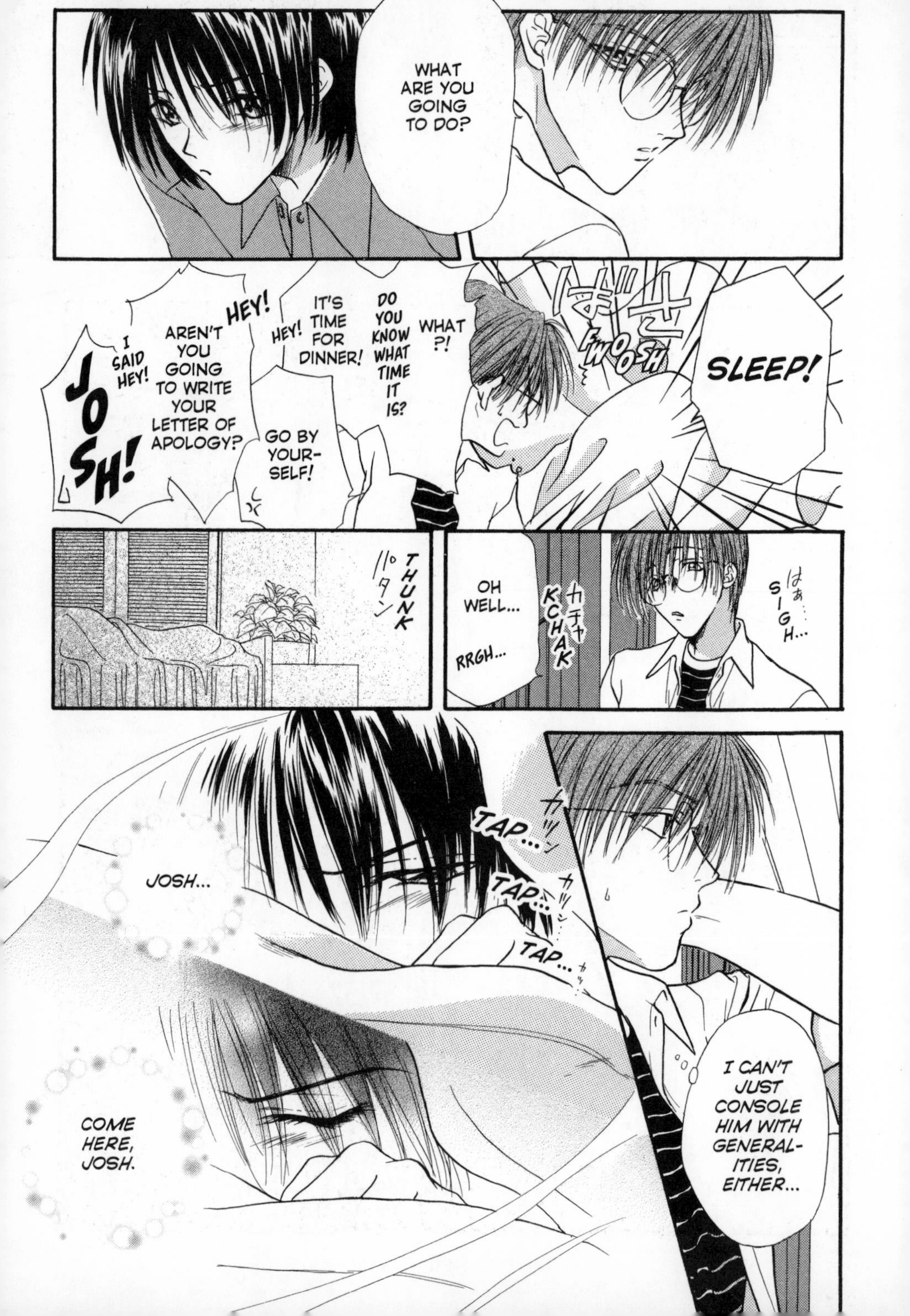

WHAT ARE YOU GOING TO DO?
SLEEP!
FWOOSH
WHAT?!
DO YOU KNOW WHAT TIME IT IS?
IT'S TIME FOR DINNER!
HEY!
GO BY YOURSELF!
HEY!
AREN'T YOU GOING TO WRITE YOUR LETTER OF APOLOGY?
I SAID HEY!
JOSH!
はぁ…
SIGH...
OH WELL...
カチャ
KCHAK
RRGH...
パタン
THUNK
TAP...
TAP...
TAP...
I CAN'T JUST CONSOLE HIM WITH GENERALITIES, EITHER...
JOSH...
COME HERE, JOSH.

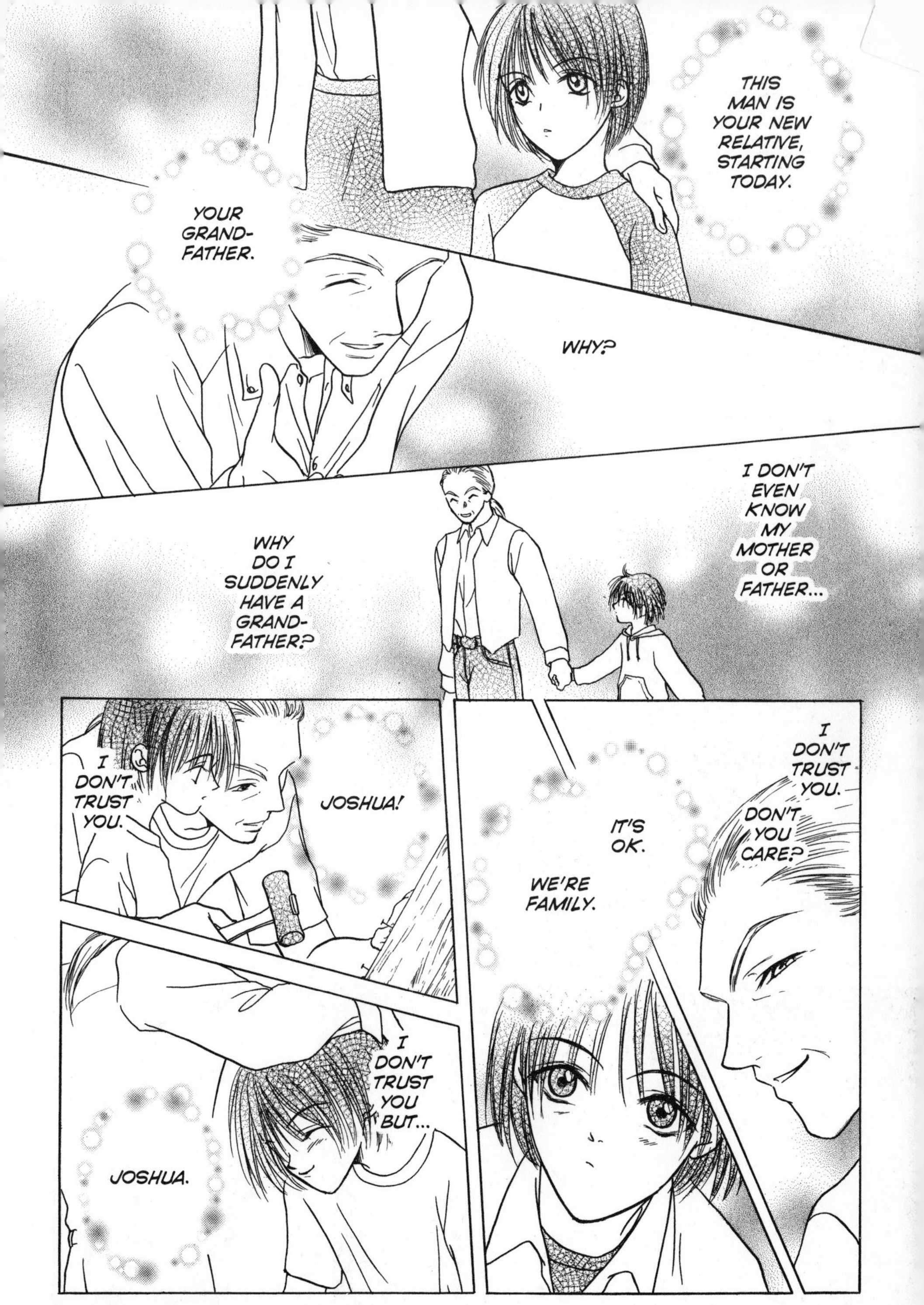
THIS MAN IS YOUR NEW RELATIVE, STARTING TODAY.
YOUR GRAND-FATHER.
WHY?
I DON'T EVEN KNOW MY MOTHER OR FATHER...
WHY DO I SUDDENLY HAVE A GRAND-FATHER?
I DON'T TRUST YOU.
DON'T YOU CARE?
IT'S OK.
WE'RE FAMILY.
JOSHUA!
I DON'T TRUST YOU.
I DON'T TRUST YOU BUT...
JOSHUA.

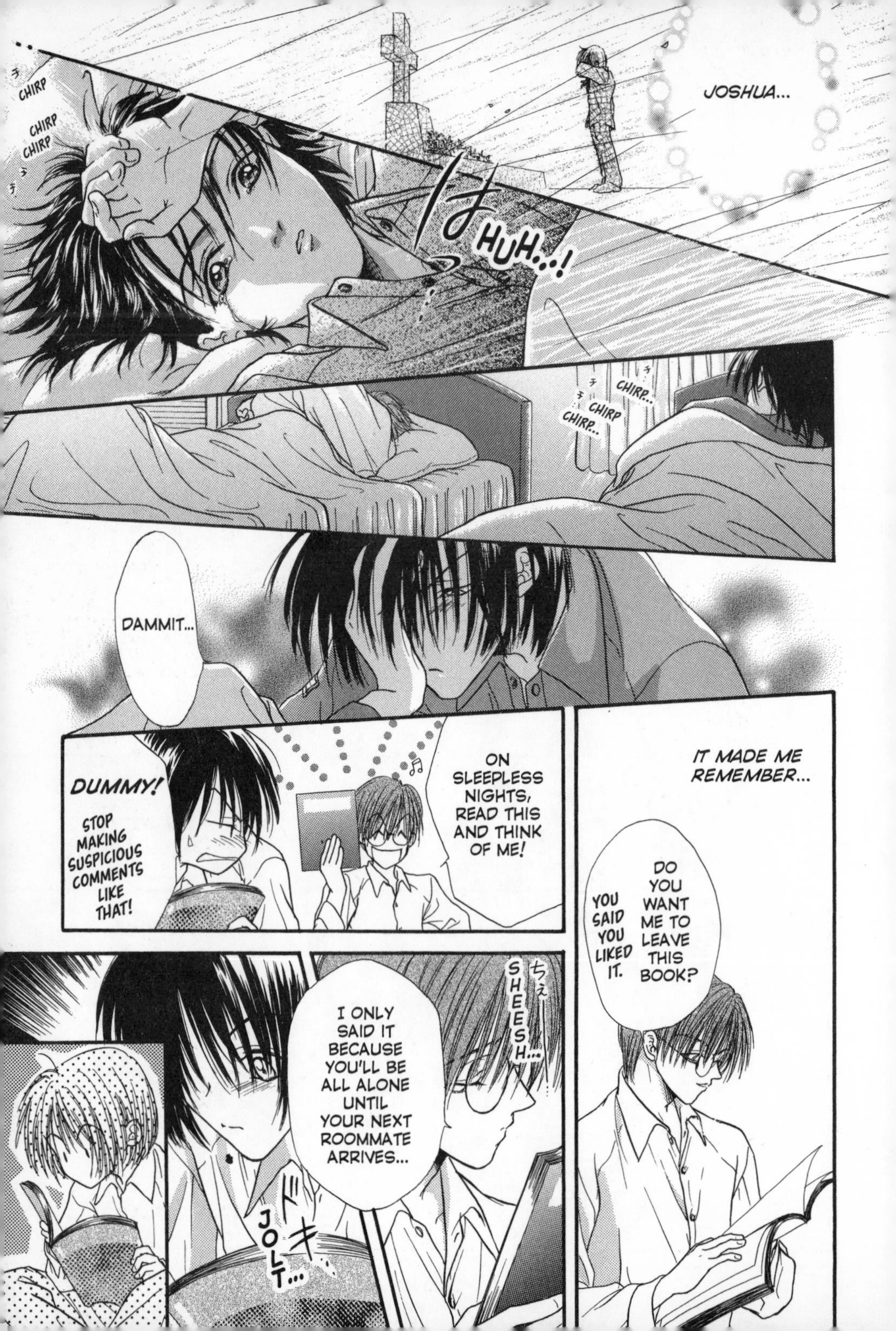
JOSHUA...
は HUH...!
チ CHIRP
CHIRP CHIRP
ぅ チ
チ CHIRP...
チ CHIRP
チ CHIRP...
DAMMIT...
IT MADE ME REMEMBER...
DO YOU WANT ME TO LEAVE THIS BOOK?
YOU SAID YOU LIKED IT.
ON SLEEPLESS NIGHTS, READ THIS AND THINK OF ME!
DUMMY!
STOP MAKING SUSPICIOUS COMMENTS LIKE THAT!
ちぇ SHEESH...
I ONLY SAID IT BECAUSE YOU'LL BE ALL ALONE UNTIL YOUR NEXT ROOMMATE ARRIVES...
ドキ JOLT...

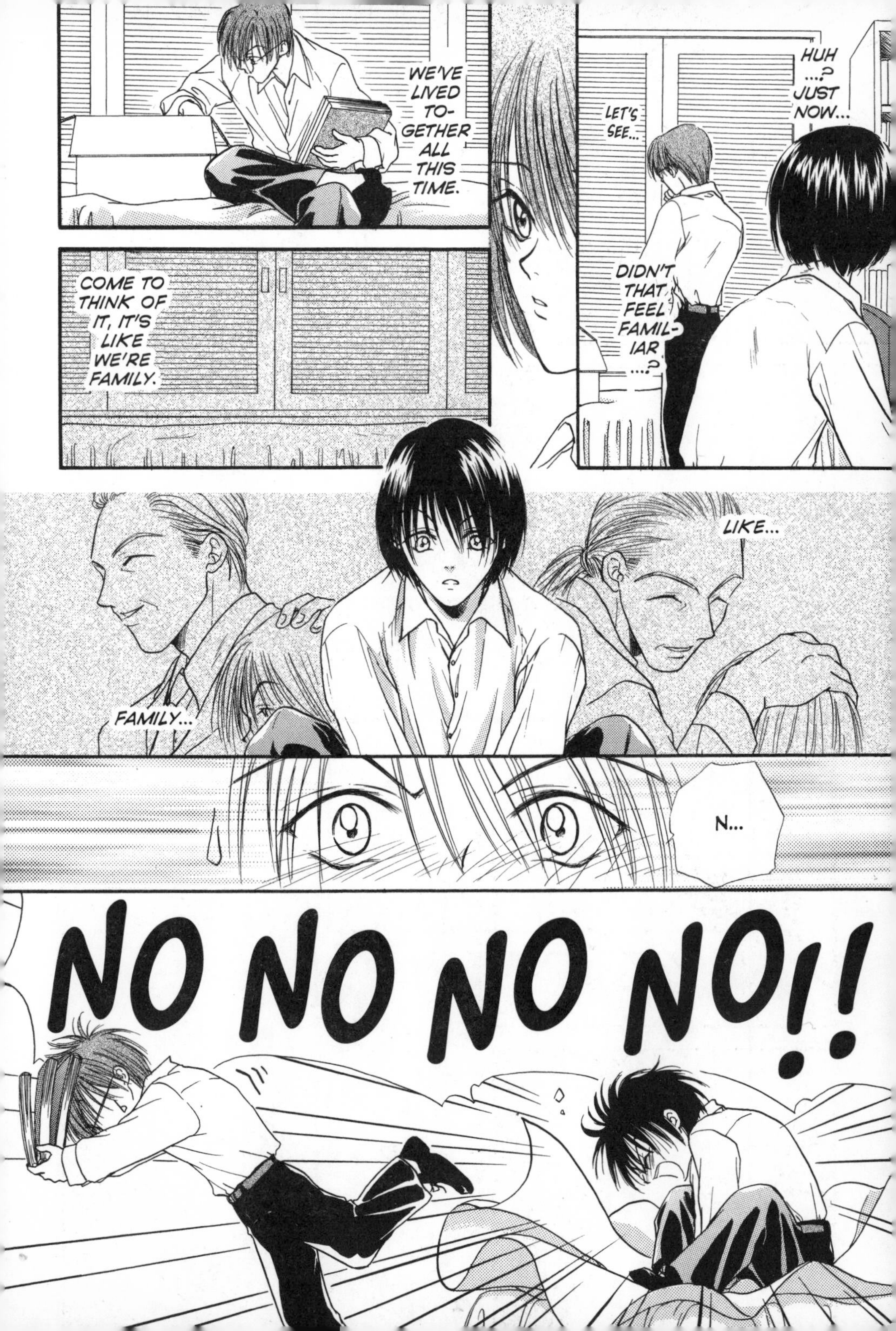
HUH ...? JUST NOW...
LET'S SEE...
DIDN'T THAT FEEL FAMIL-IAR ...?
WE'VE LIVED TO-GETHER ALL THIS TIME.
COME TO THINK OF IT, IT'S LIKE WE'RE FAMILY.
LIKE...
FAMILY...
N...
NO NO NO NO NO!!

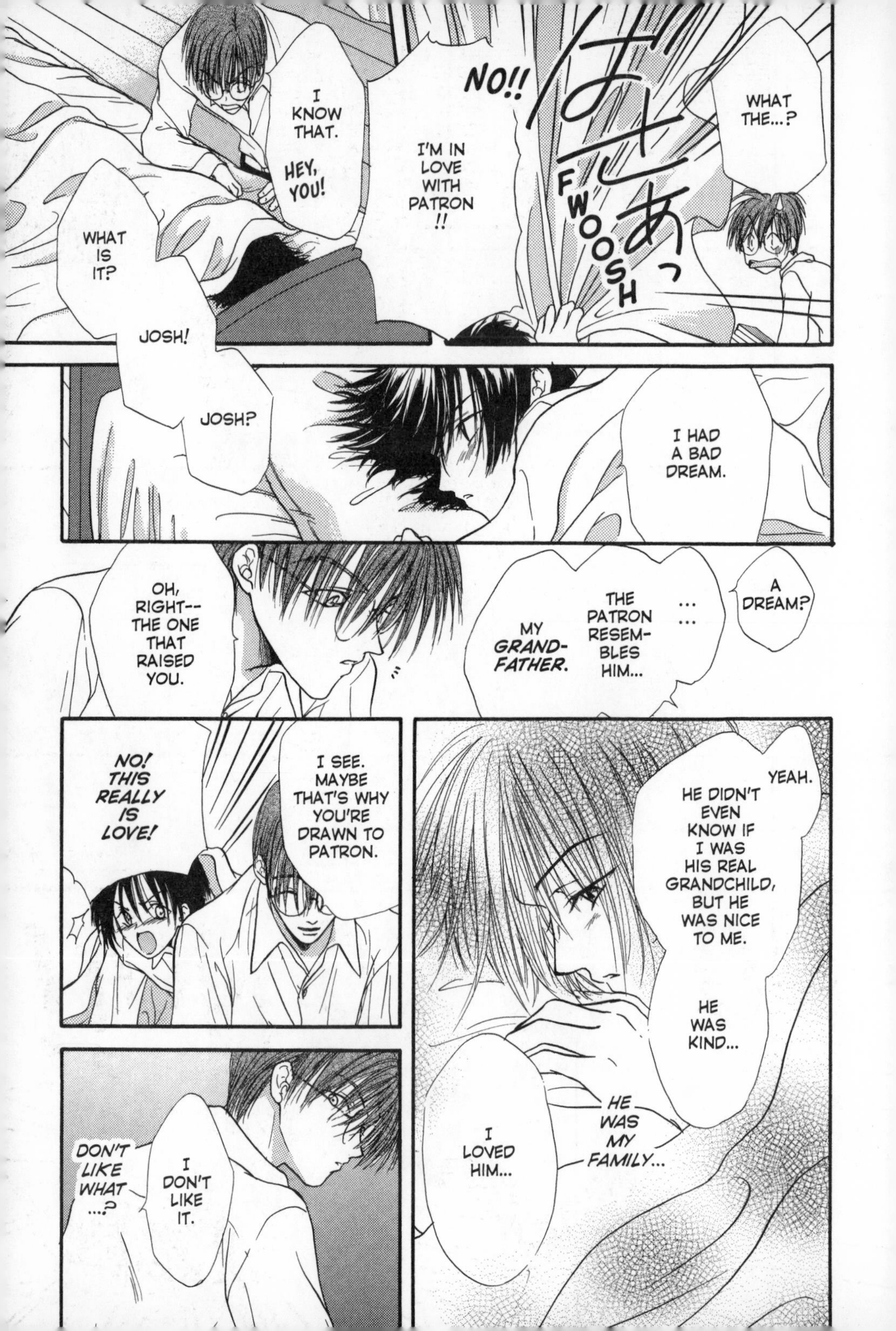
WHAT THE...?
ばさあっ
FWOOSH
NO!!
I'M IN LOVE WITH PATRON !!
I KNOW THAT.
HEY, YOU!
WHAT IS IT?
JOSH!
I HAD A BAD DREAM.
JOSH?
A DREAM?
......
THE PATRON RESEMBLES HIM...
MY GRANDFATHER.
OH, RIGHT-- THE ONE THAT RAISED YOU.
YEAH.
HE DIDN'T EVEN KNOW IF I WAS HIS REAL GRANDCHILD, BUT HE WAS NICE TO ME.
HE WAS KIND...
HE WAS MY FAMILY...
I LOVED HIM...
I SEE. MAYBE THAT'S WHY YOU'RE DRAWN TO PATRON.
NO! THIS REALLY IS LOVE!
I DON'T LIKE IT.
DON'T LIKE WHAT ...?

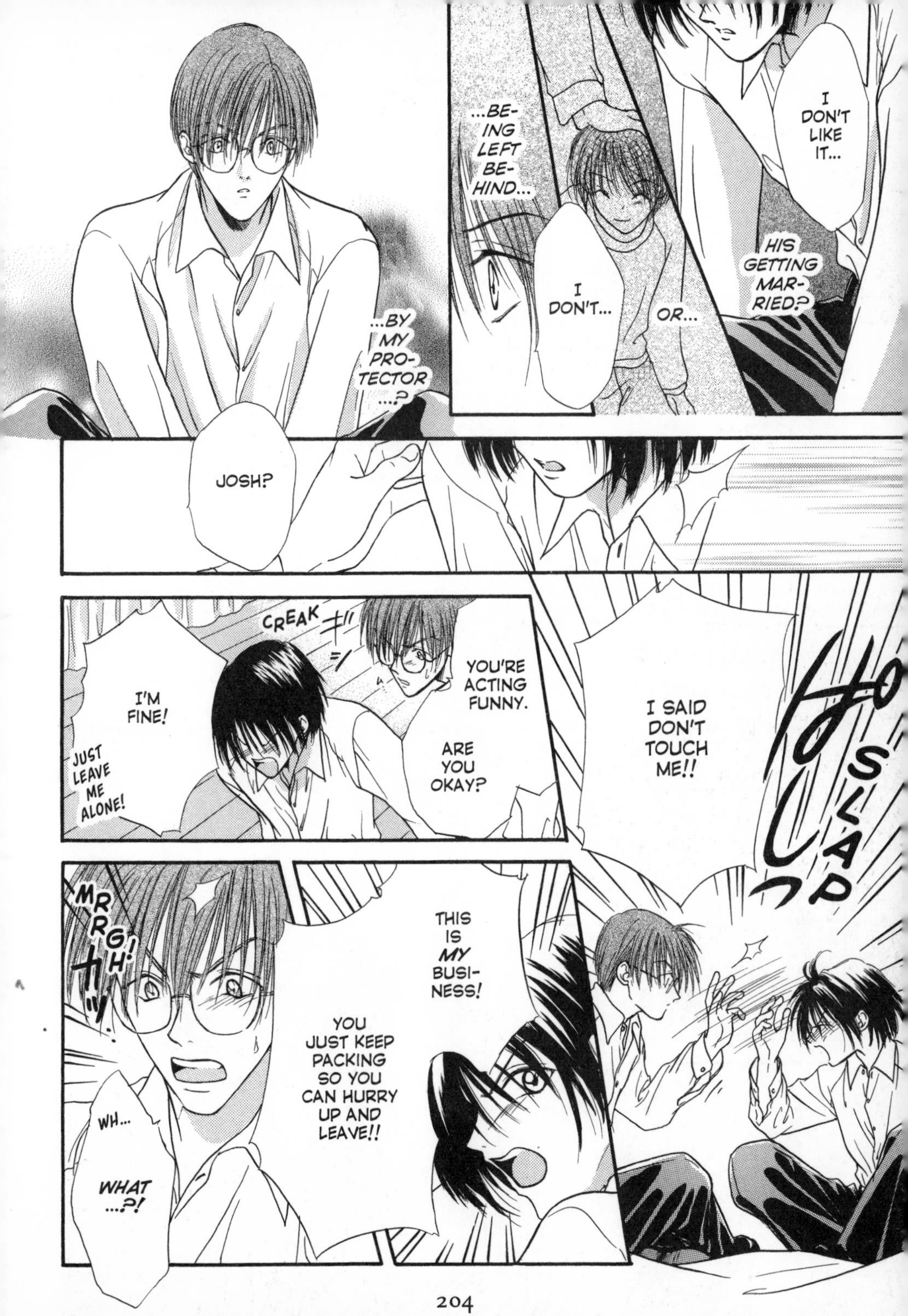
I DON'T LIKE IT...
HIS GETTING MAR-RIED?
OR...
I DON'T...
...BE-ING LEFT BE-HIND...
...BY MY PRO-TECTOR ...?
JOSH?
I SAID DON'T TOUCH ME!!
SLAP
CREAK
YOU'RE ACTING FUNNY.
ARE YOU OKAY?
I'M FINE!
JUST LEAVE ME ALONE!
THIS IS MY BUSI-NESS!
YOU JUST KEEP PACKING SO YOU CAN HURRY UP AND LEAVE!!
MRRGH!
WH...
WHAT ...?!

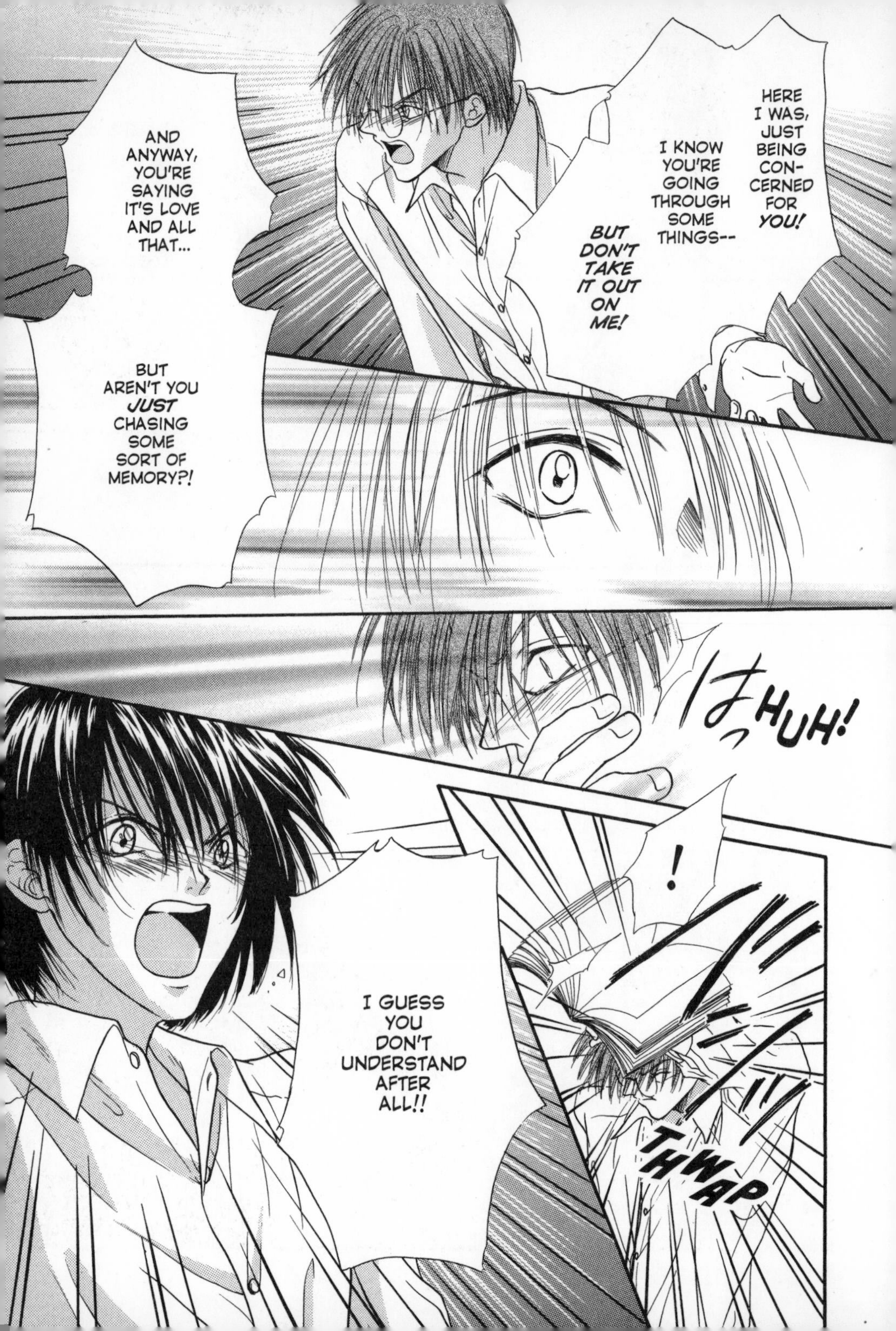
HERE I WAS, JUST BEING CON-CERNED FOR *YOU!*
I KNOW YOU'RE GOING THROUGH SOME THINGS--
BUT DON'T TAKE IT OUT ON ME!
AND ANYWAY, YOU'RE SAYING IT'S LOVE AND ALL THAT...
BUT AREN'T YOU *JUST* CHASING SOME SORT OF MEMORY?!
はっ HUH!
!
THWAP
I GUESS YOU DON'T UNDERSTAND AFTER ALL!!

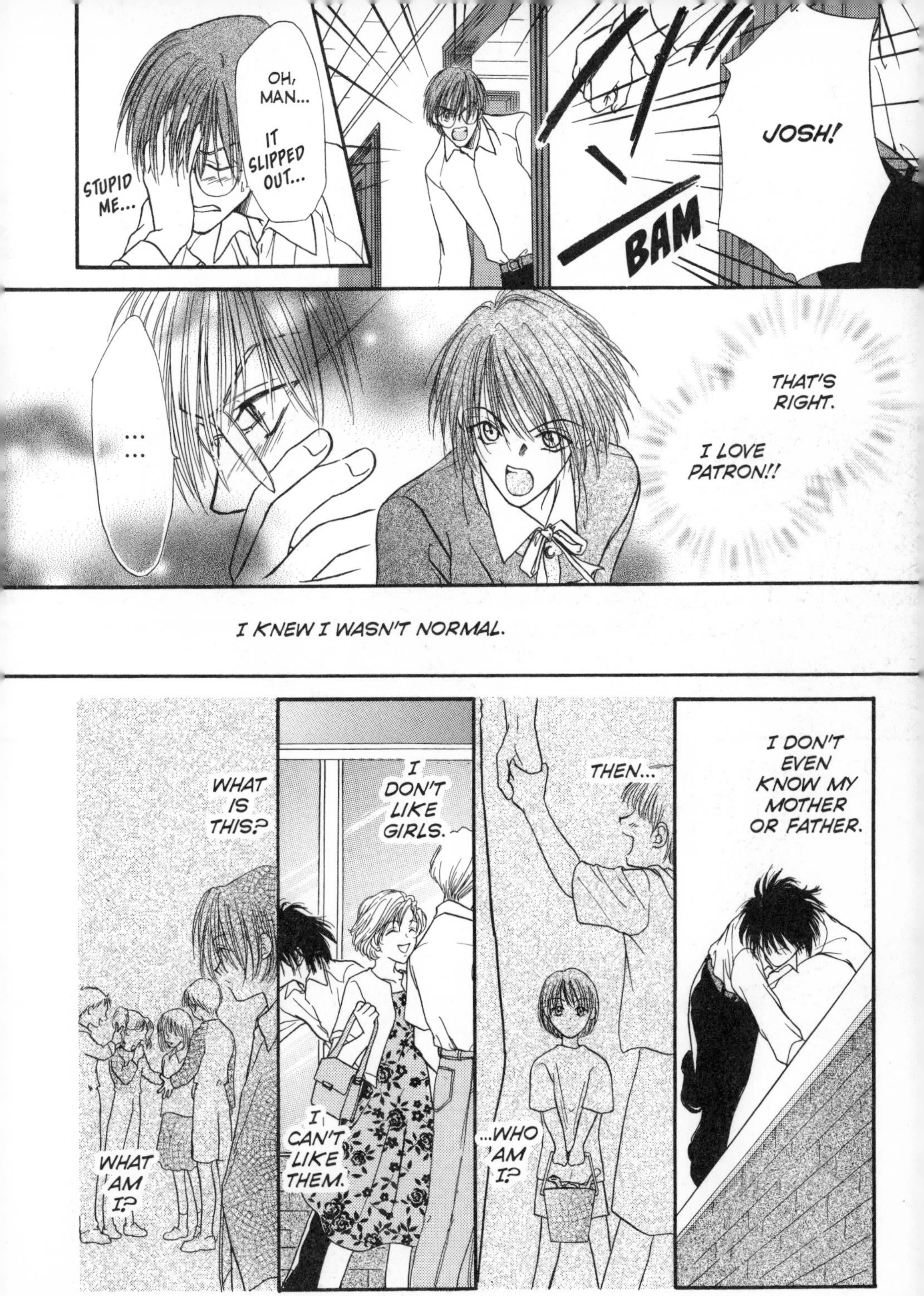
JOSH!
BAM
OH, MAN...
IT SLIPPED OUT...
STUPID ME...
THAT'S RIGHT.
I LOVE PATRON!!
......
I KNEW I WASN'T NORMAL.
I DON'T EVEN KNOW MY MOTHER OR FATHER.
THEN...
...WHO AM I?
I DON'T LIKE GIRLS.
I CAN'T LIKE THEM.
WHAT IS THIS?
WHAT AM I?

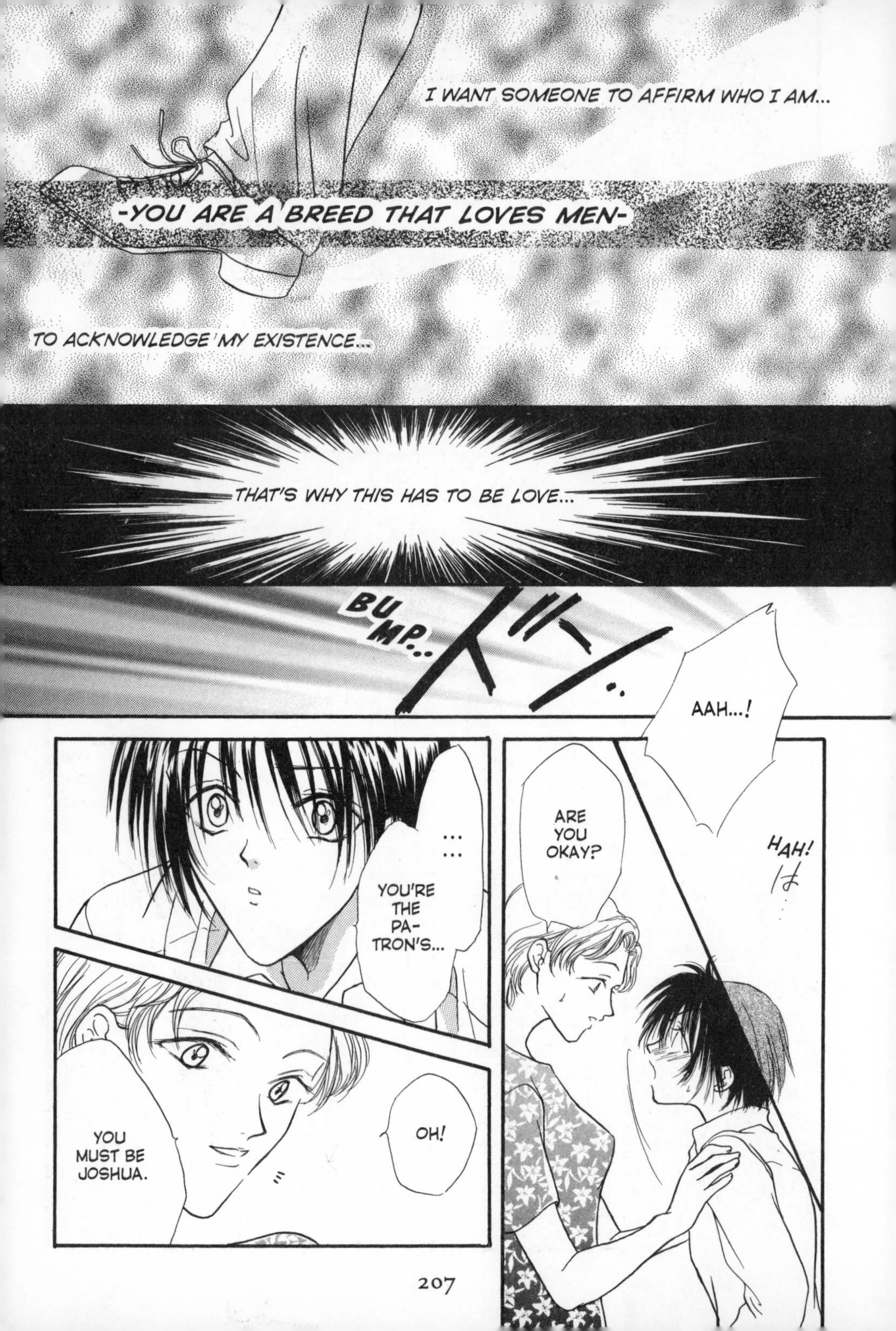
I WANT SOMEONE TO AFFIRM WHO I AM...
-YOU ARE A BREED THAT LOVES MEN-
TO ACKNOWLEDGE MY EXISTENCE...
THAT'S WHY THIS HAS TO BE LOVE...
BUMP...
AAH...!
HAH!
は
ARE YOU OKAY?
... ...
YOU'RE THE PA-TRON'S...
OH!
YOU MUST BE JOSHUA.

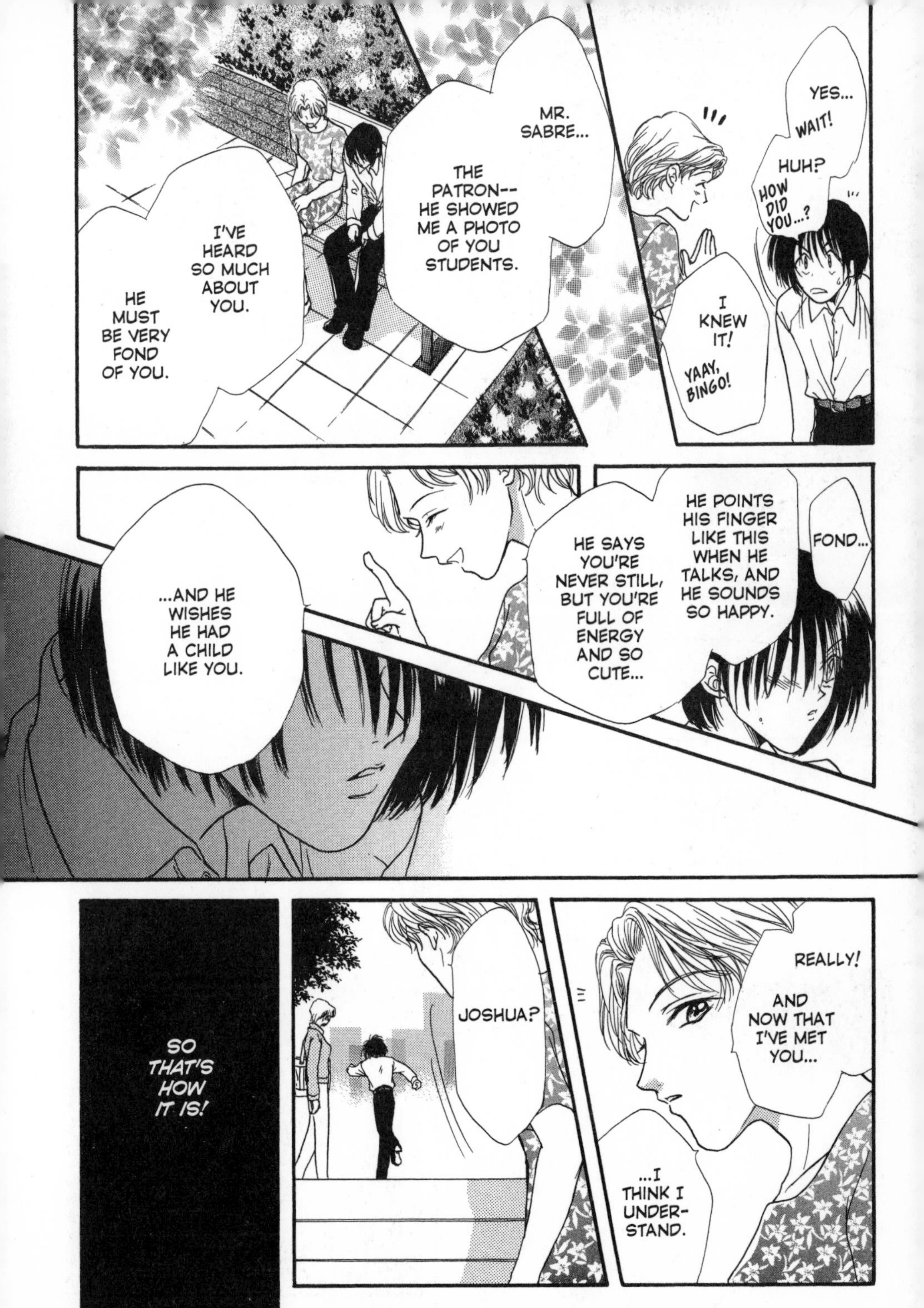
YES...
WAIT!
HUH?
HOW DID YOU...?
I KNEW IT!
YAAY, BINGO!
MR. SABRE...
THE PATRON-- HE SHOWED ME A PHOTO OF YOU STUDENTS.
I'VE HEARD SO MUCH ABOUT YOU.
HE MUST BE VERY FOND OF YOU.
FOND...
HE POINTS HIS FINGER LIKE THIS WHEN HE TALKS, AND HE SOUNDS SO HAPPY.
HE SAYS YOU'RE NEVER STILL, BUT YOU'RE FULL OF ENERGY AND SO CUTE...
...AND HE WISHES HE HAD A CHILD LIKE YOU.
REALLY!
AND NOW THAT I'VE MET YOU...
...I THINK I UNDERSTAND.
JOSHUA?
SO THAT'S HOW IT IS!

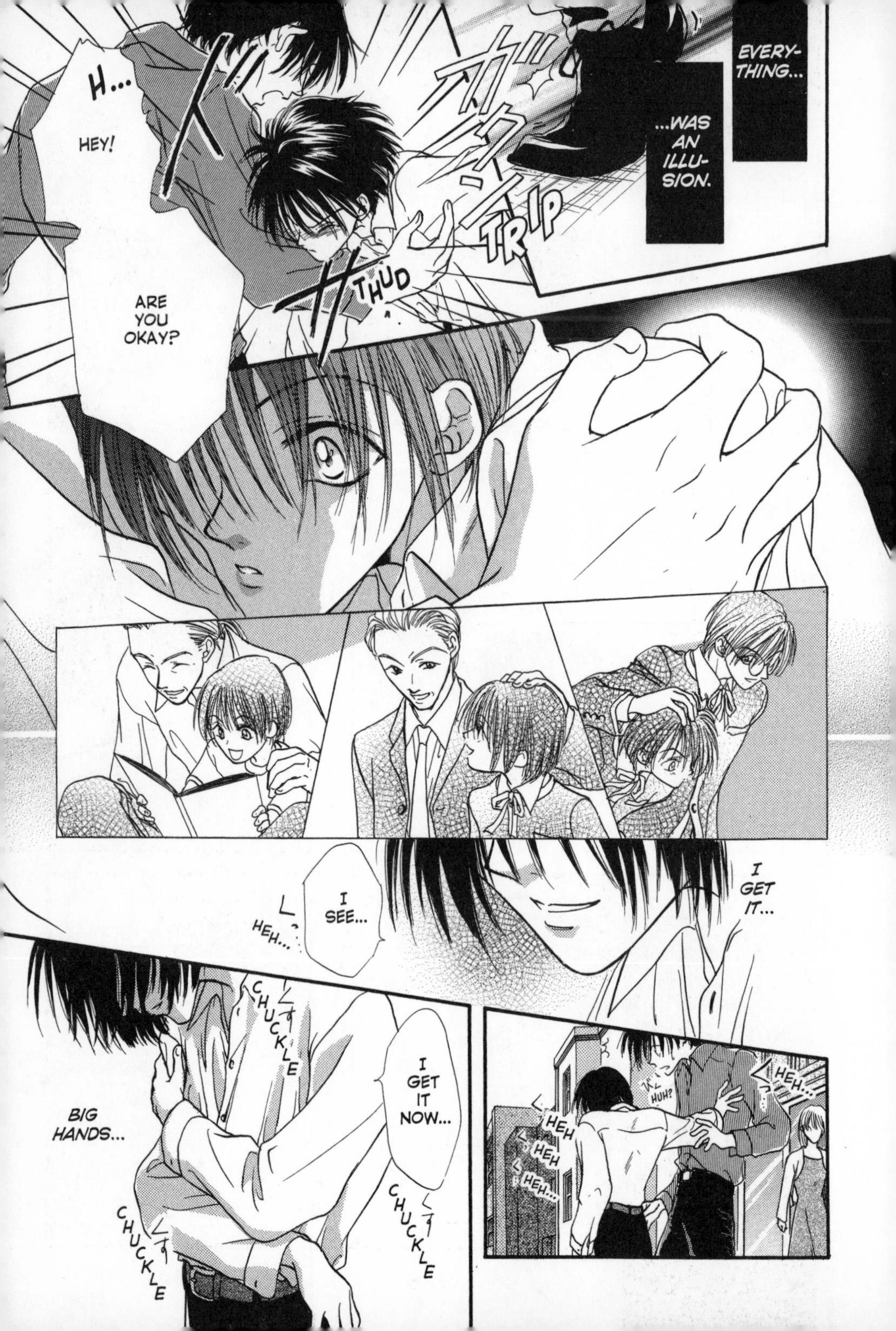
EVERY-THING...
...WAS AN ILLUSION.
TRIP
THUD
H...
HEY!
ARE YOU OKAY?
I GET IT...
I SEE...
HEH...
HEH...
HUH?
HEH
HEH
HEH...
CHUCKLE
I GET IT NOW...
CHUCKLE
BIG HANDS...
CHUCKLE

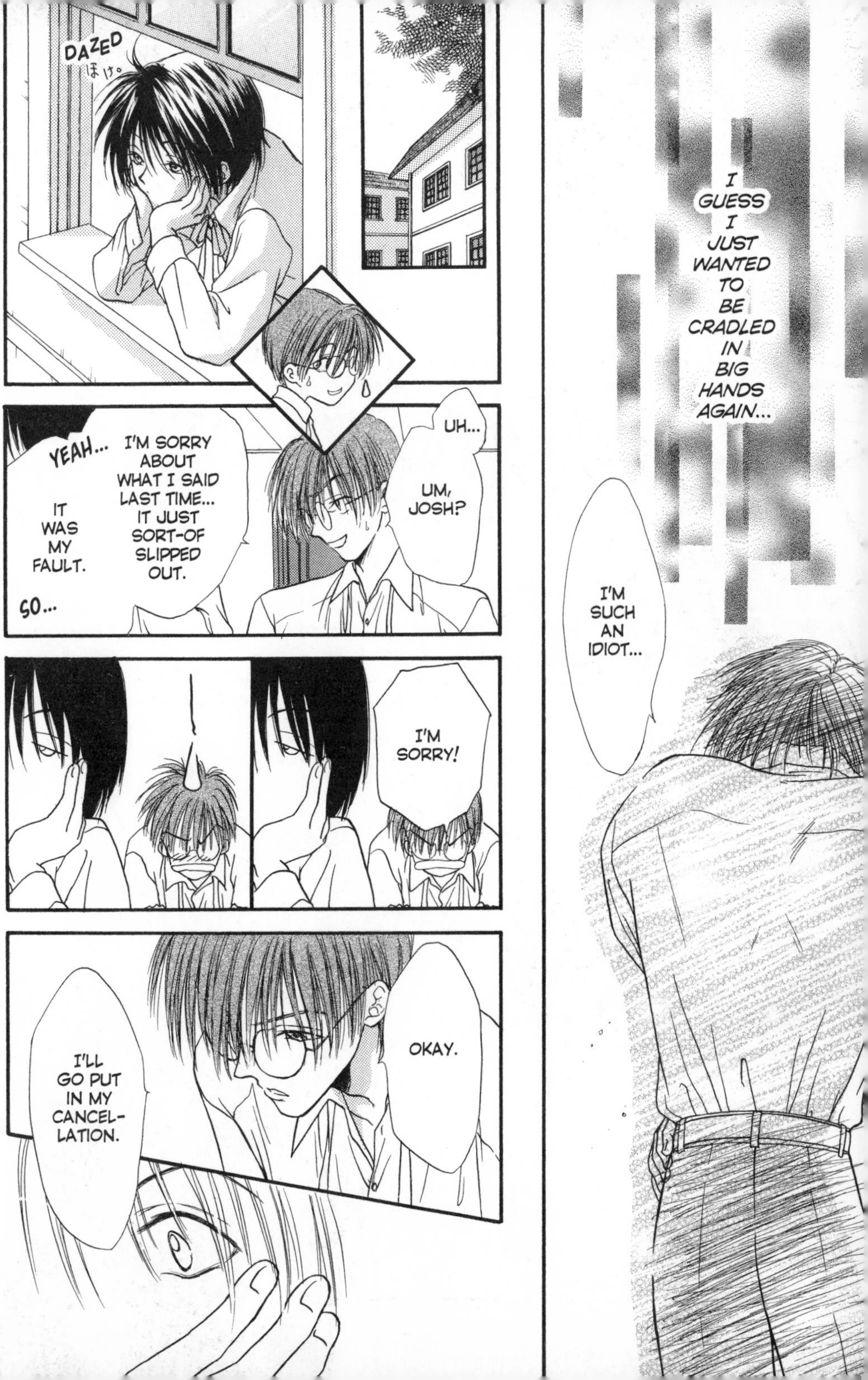
I GUESS I JUST WANTED TO BE CRADLED IN BIG HANDS AGAIN...
I'M SUCH AN IDIOT...
DAZED
ほけ。
UH...
UM, JOSH?
YEAH...
I'M SORRY ABOUT WHAT I SAID LAST TIME... IT JUST SORT-OF SLIPPED OUT.
IT WAS MY FAULT.
SO...
I'M SORRY!
!
OKAY.
I'LL GO PUT IN MY CANCEL-LATION.

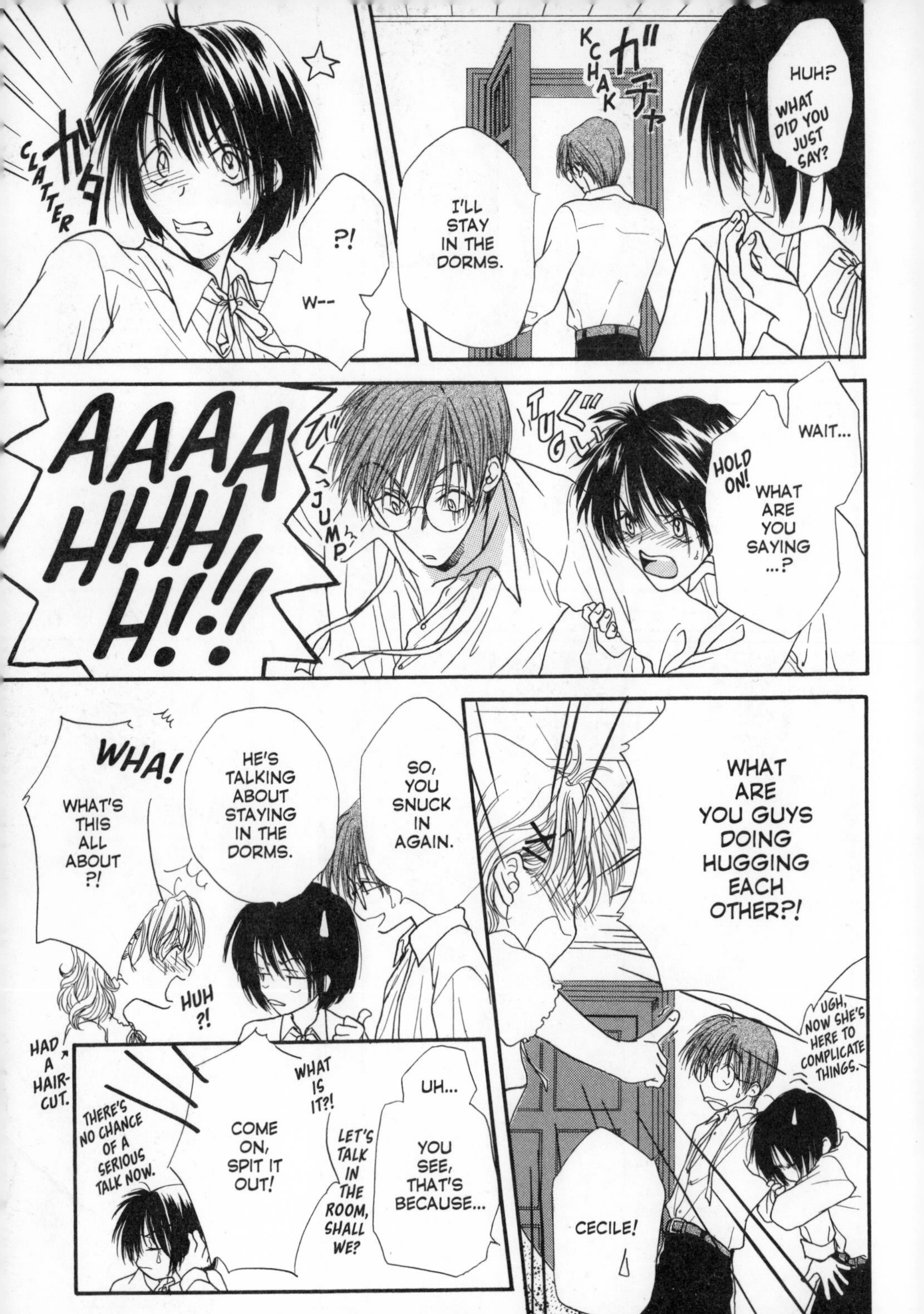
HUH? WHAT DID YOU JUST SAY?
KCHAK
ガチャ
I'LL STAY IN THE DORMS.
?!
W--
CLATTER
ガタ
WAIT...
HOLD ON!
WHAT ARE YOU SAYING ...?
TUG
JUMP
AAAAHHHHH!!!
WHAT ARE YOU GUYS DOING HUGGING EACH OTHER?!
UGH, NOW SHE'S HERE TO COMPLICATE THINGS.
CECILE!
SO, YOU SNUCK IN AGAIN.
HE'S TALKING ABOUT STAYING IN THE DORMS.
WHA!
WHAT'S THIS ALL ABOUT ?!
HUH ?!
HAD A HAIR-CUT.
UH...
YOU SEE, THAT'S BECAUSE...
LET'S TALK IN THE ROOM, SHALL WE?
WHAT IS IT?!
COME ON, SPIT IT OUT!
THERE'S NO CHANCE OF A SERIOUS TALK NOW.

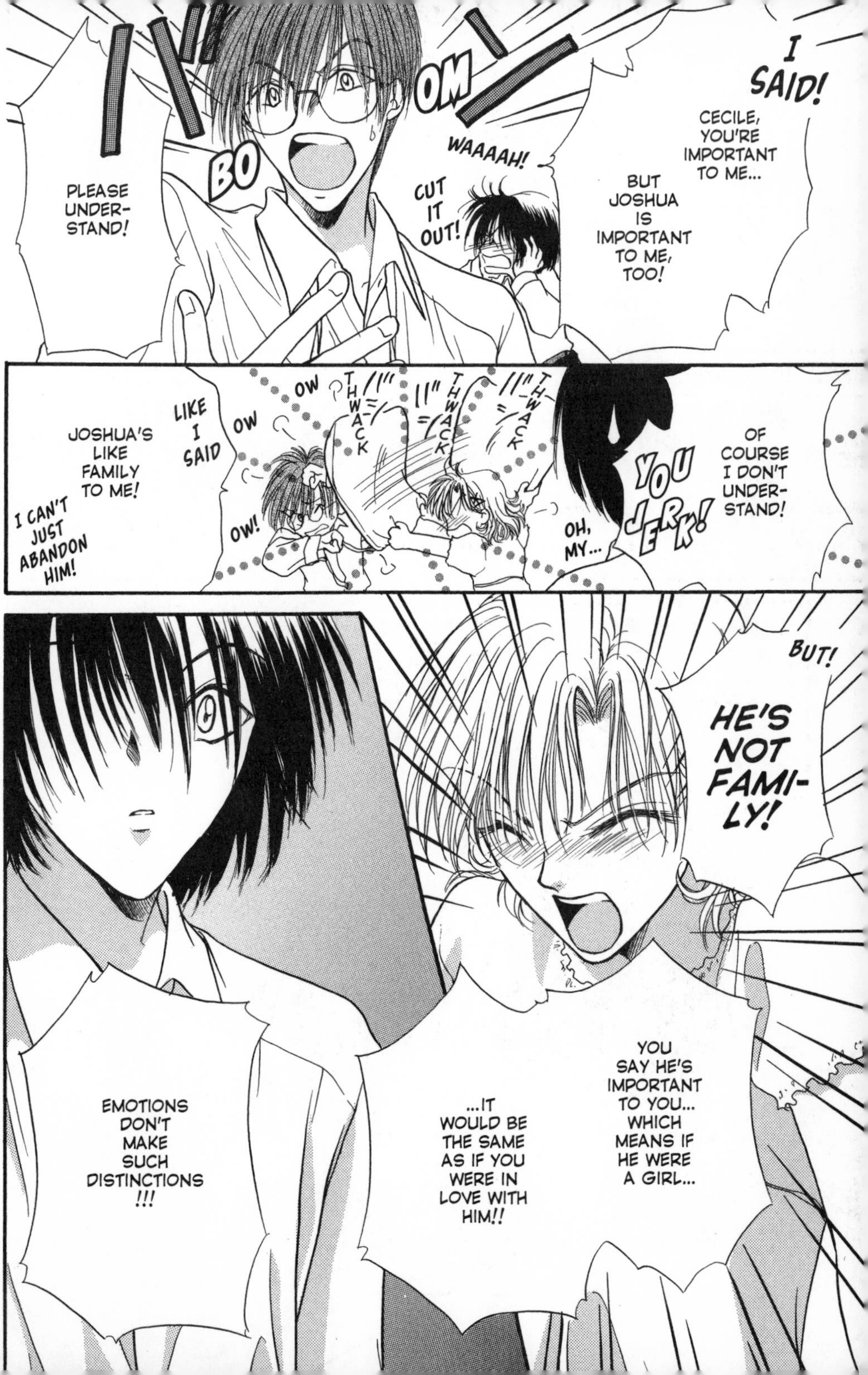
I SAID!
CECILE, YOU'RE IMPORTANT TO ME...
BUT JOSHUA IS IMPORTANT TO ME, TOO!
WAAAAH!
CUT IT OUT!
BOOM
PLEASE UNDER-STAND!
OF COURSE I DON'T UNDER-STAND!
YOU JERK!
OH, MY...
THWACK
THWACK
THWACK
OW
OW
OW!
LIKE I SAID
JOSHUA'S LIKE FAMILY TO ME!
I CAN'T JUST ABANDON HIM!
BUT!
HE'S NOT FAMI-LY!
YOU SAY HE'S IMPORTANT TO YOU... WHICH MEANS IF HE WERE A GIRL...
...IT WOULD BE THE SAME AS IF YOU WERE IN LOVE WITH HIM!!
EMOTIONS DON'T MAKE SUCH DISTINCTIONS !!!

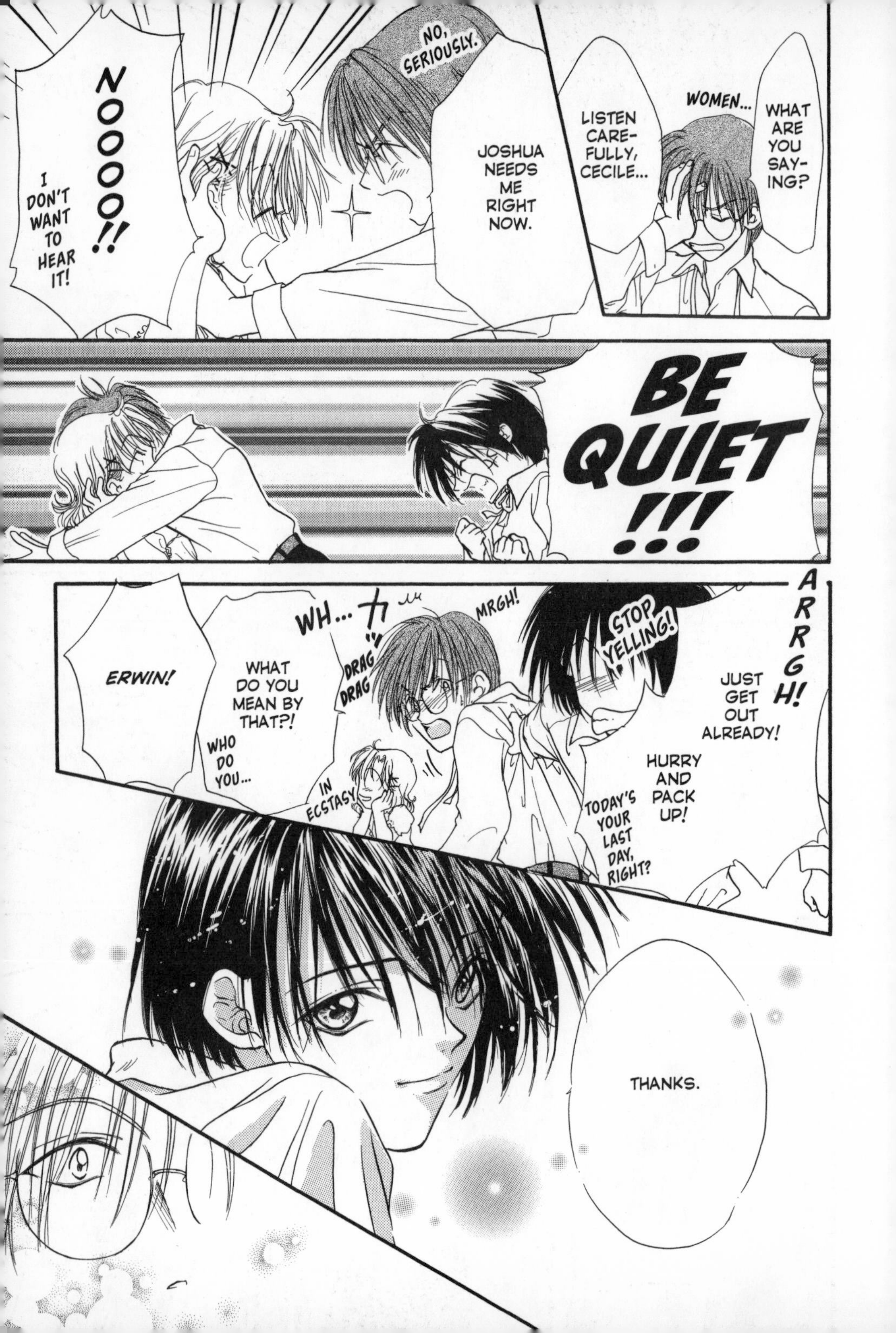
WHAT ARE YOU SAYING?
WOMEN...
LISTEN CAREFULLY, CECILE...
JOSHUA NEEDS ME RIGHT NOW.
NO, SERIOUSLY.
NOOOOO!!
I DON'T WANT TO HEAR IT!
BE QUIET!!!
ARRGH!
STOP YELLING!
JUST GET OUT ALREADY!
HURRY AND PACK UP!
TODAY'S YOUR LAST DAY, RIGHT?
MRGH!
WH...
DRAG DRAG
WHAT DO YOU MEAN BY THAT?!
WHO DO YOU...
IN ECSTASY
ERWIN!
THANKS.

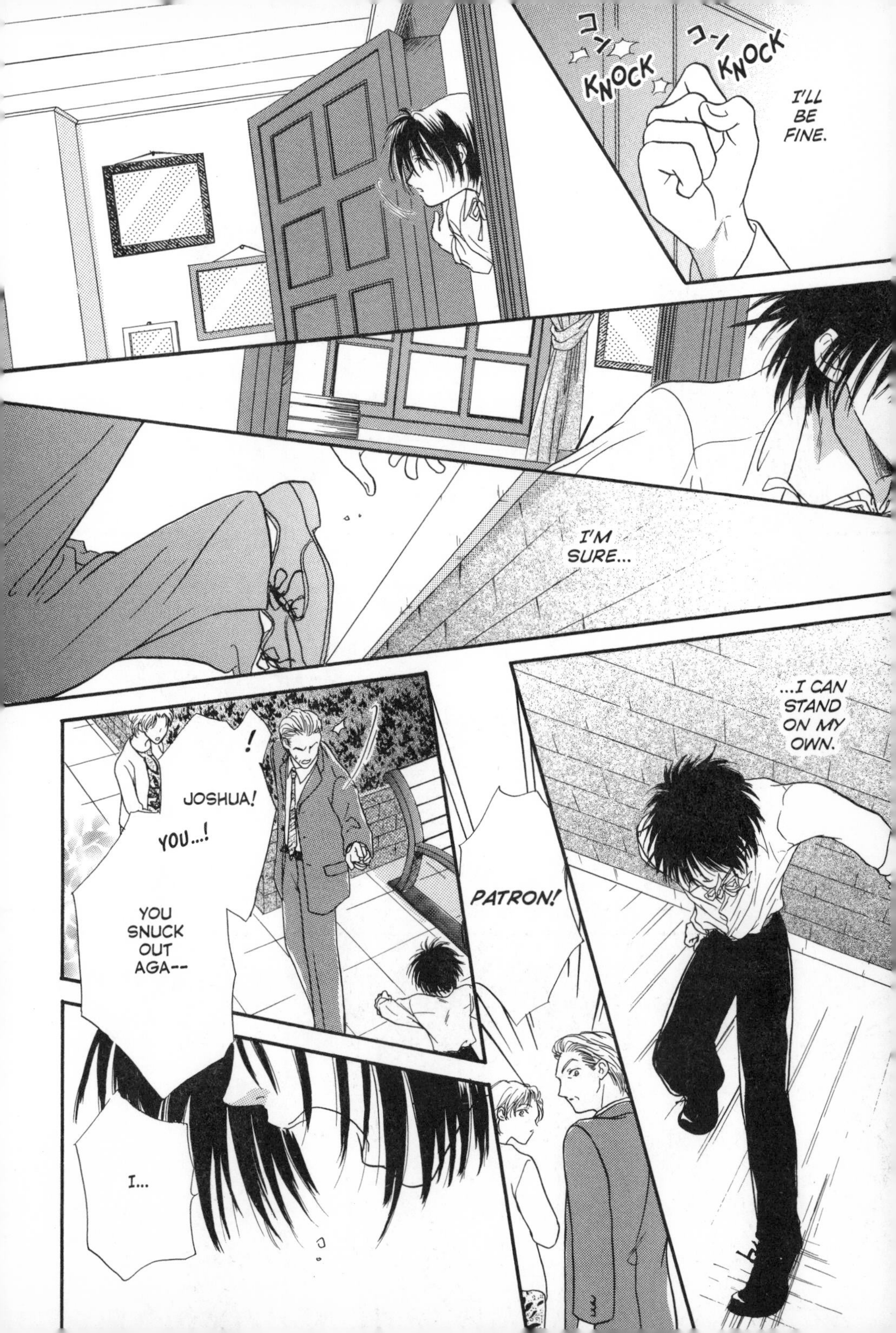

コン
KNOCK
コン
KNOCK
I'LL BE FINE.
I'M SURE...
...I CAN STAND ON MY OWN.
PATRON!
!
JOSHUA!
YOU...!
YOU SNUCK OUT AGA--
I...

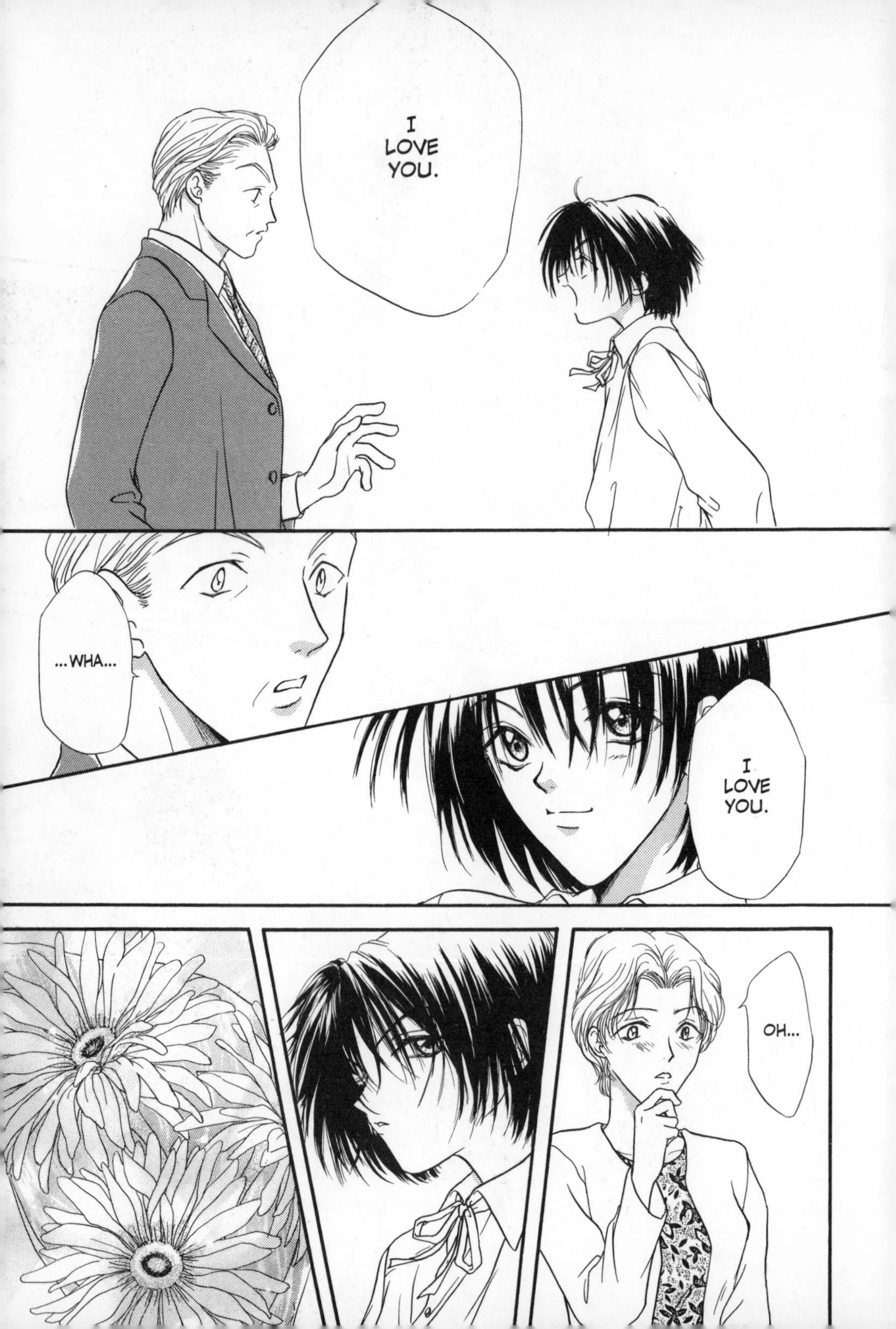
I LOVE YOU.
...WHA...
I LOVE YOU.
OH...

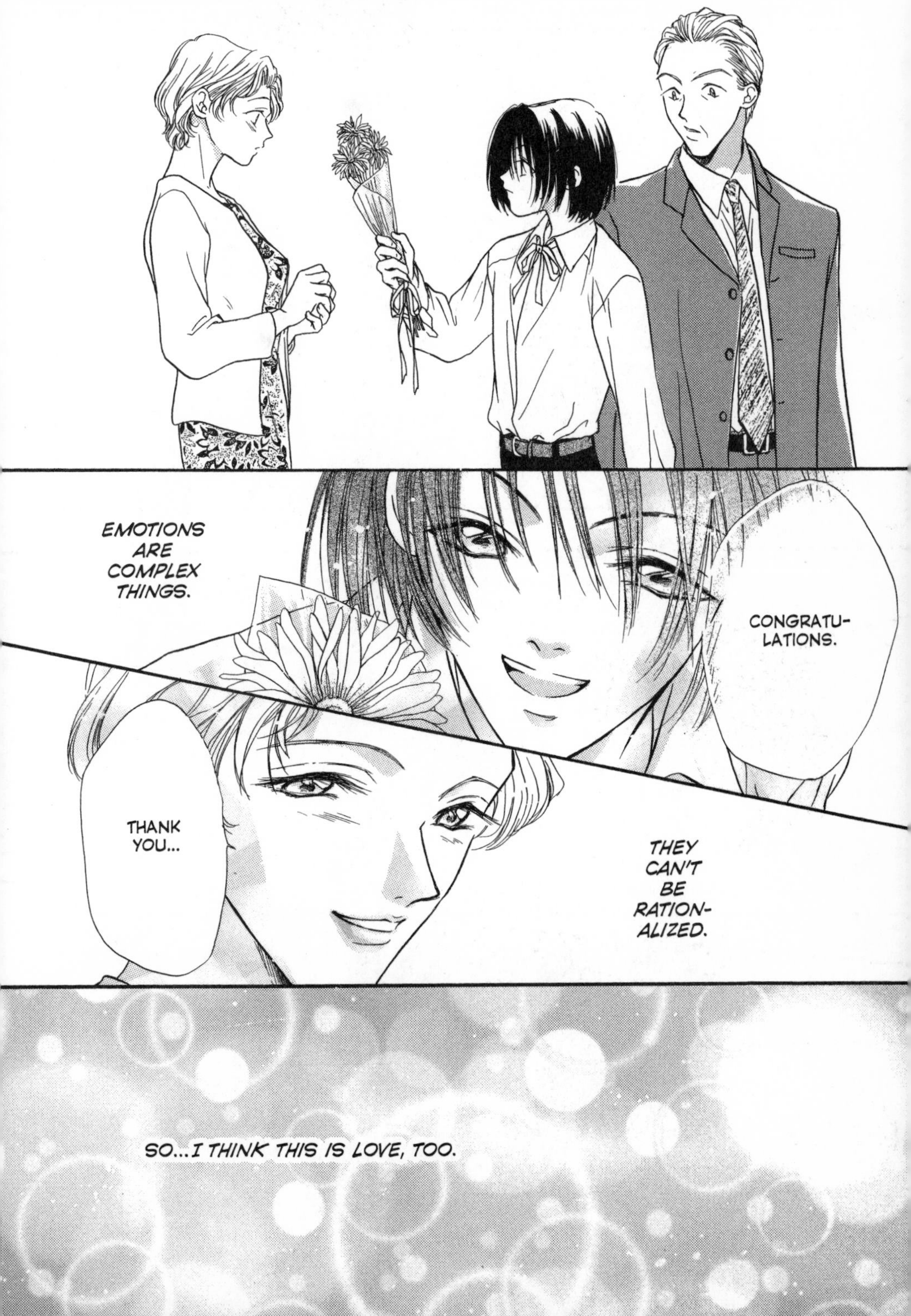

CONGRATULATIONS.
EMOTIONS ARE COMPLEX THINGS.
THEY CAN'T BE RATIONALIZED.
THANK YOU...
SO...I THINK THIS IS LOVE, TOO.

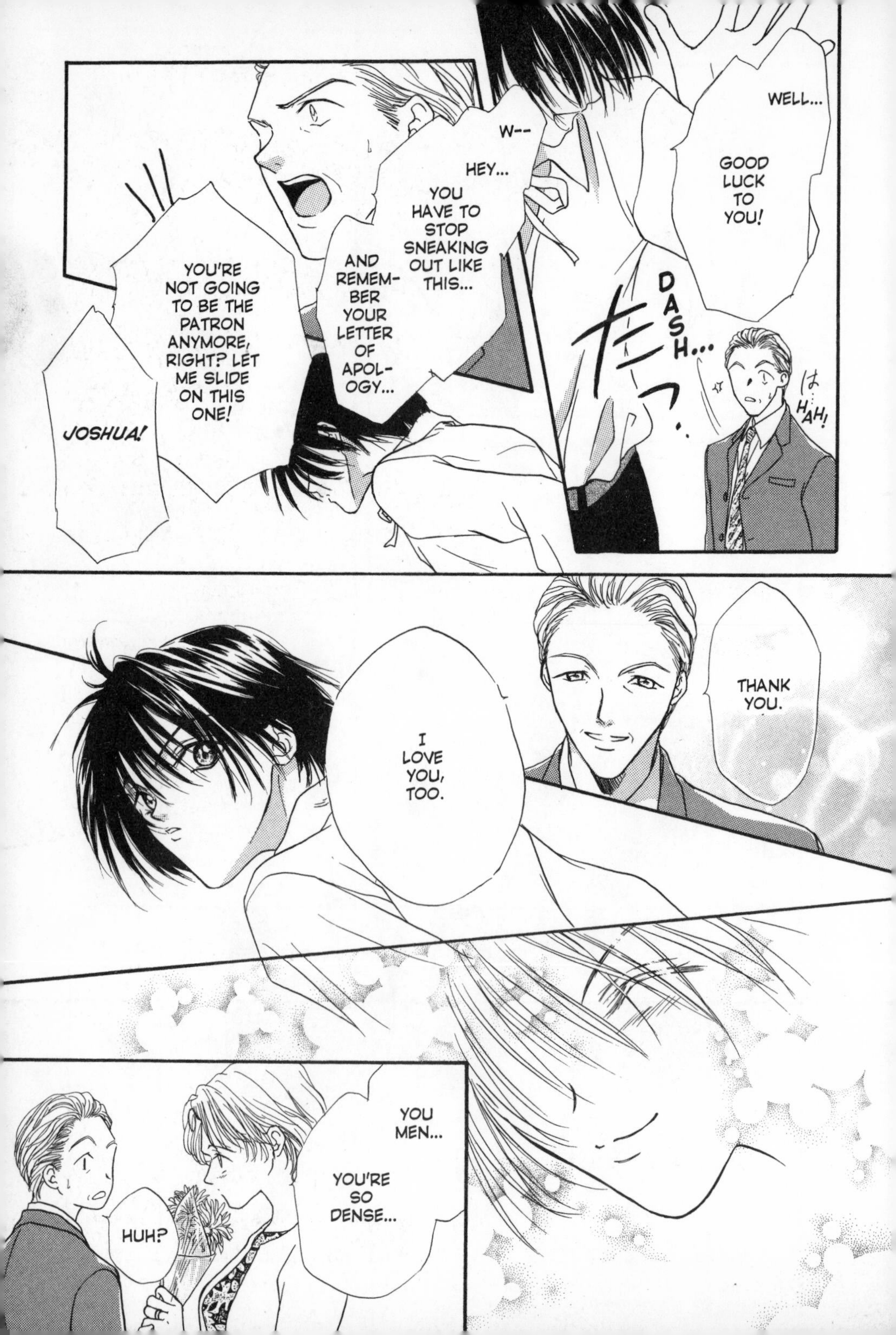
WELL...
GOOD LUCK TO YOU!
DASH...
HAH!
W--
HEY...
YOU HAVE TO STOP SNEAKING OUT LIKE THIS...
AND REMEMBER YOUR LETTER OF APOLOGY...
YOU'RE NOT GOING TO BE THE PATRON ANYMORE, RIGHT? LET ME SLIDE ON THIS ONE!
JOSHUA!
THANK YOU.
I LOVE YOU, TOO.
YOU MEN...
YOU'RE SO DENSE...
HUH?

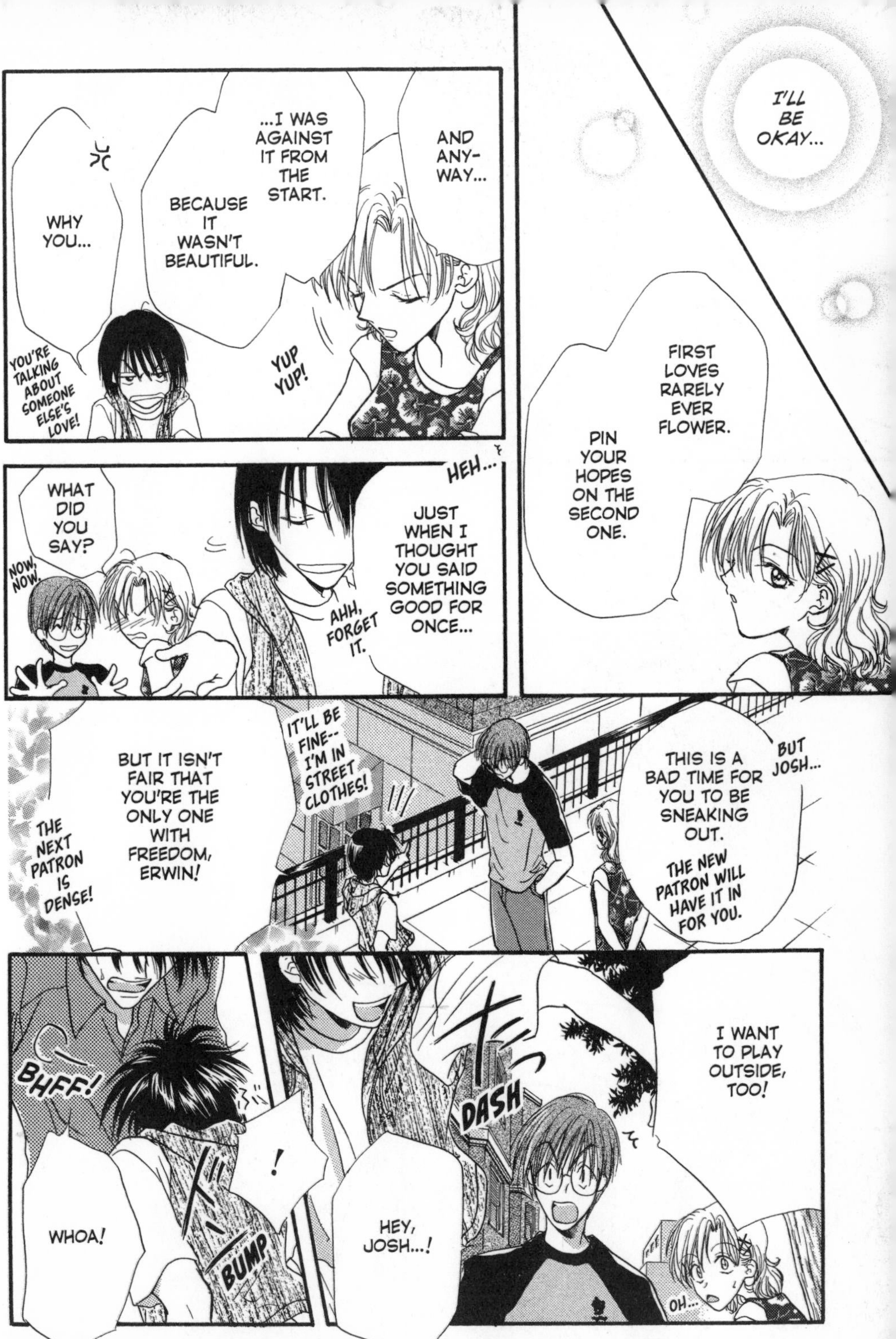
I'LL BE OKAY...
FIRST LOVES RARELY EVER FLOWER.
PIN YOUR HOPES ON THE SECOND ONE.
AND ANY-WAY...
...I WAS AGAINST IT FROM THE START.
BECAUSE IT WASN'T BEAUTIFUL.
YUP YUP!
WHY YOU...
YOU'RE TALKING ABOUT SOMEONE ELSE'S LOVE!
HEH...
JUST WHEN I THOUGHT YOU SAID SOMETHING GOOD FOR ONCE...
AHH, FORGET IT.
WHAT DID YOU SAY?
NOW, NOW.
BUT JOSH...
THIS IS A BAD TIME FOR YOU TO BE SNEAKING OUT.
THE NEW PATRON WILL HAVE IT IN FOR YOU.
IT'LL BE FINE--I'M IN STREET CLOTHES!
BUT IT ISN'T FAIR THAT YOU'RE THE ONLY ONE WITH FREEDOM, ERWIN!
THE NEXT PATRON IS DENSE!
I WANT TO PLAY OUTSIDE, TOO!
DASH
HEY, JOSH...!
OH...
BHFF!
!
BUMP
WHOA!

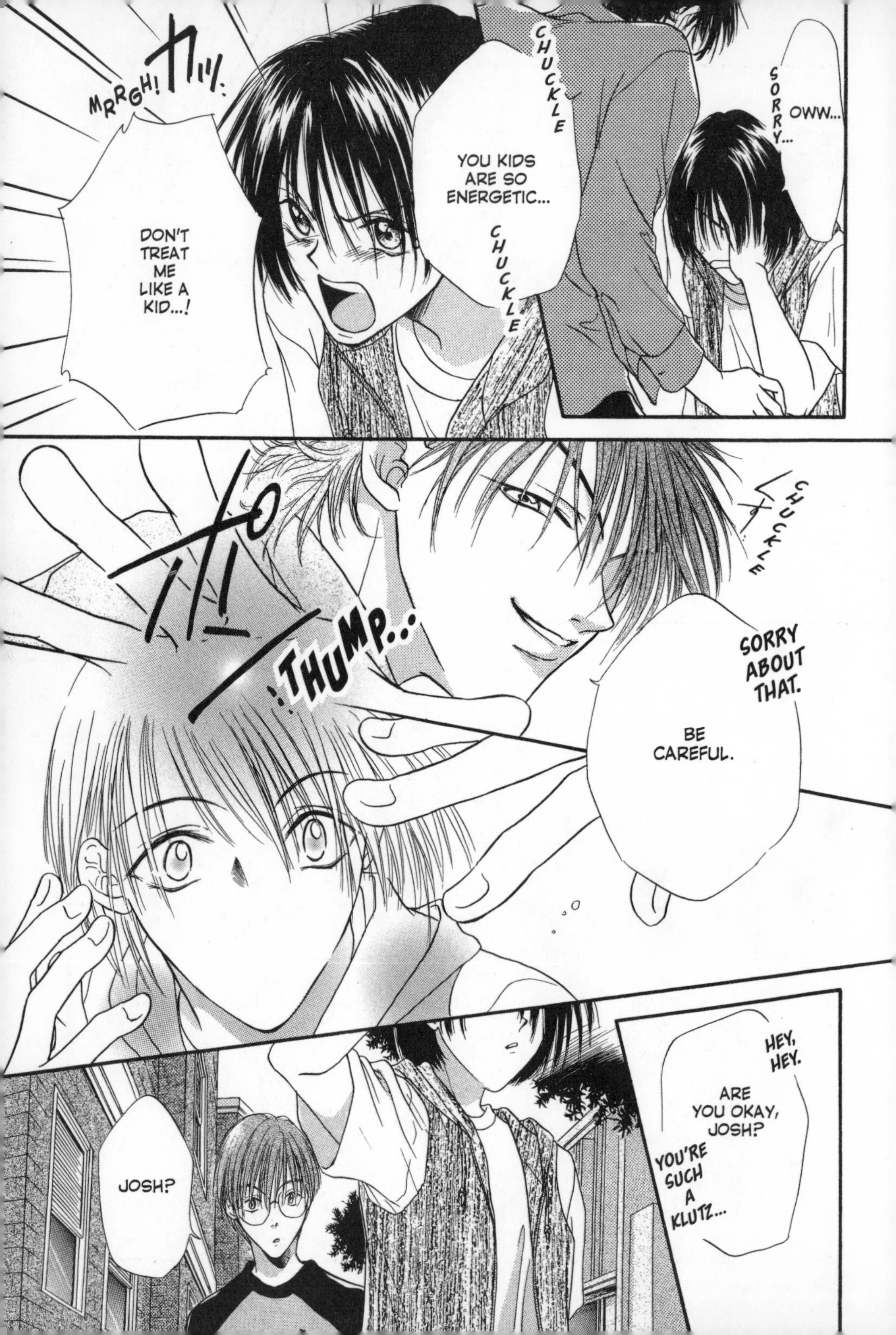

SORRY...
OWW...
CHUCKLE
YOU KIDS ARE SO ENERGETIC...
CHUCKLE
MRRGH!
DON'T TREAT ME LIKE A KID...!
CHUCKLE
SORRY ABOUT THAT.
BE CAREFUL.
THUMP...
HEY, HEY.
ARE YOU OKAY, JOSH?
YOU'RE SUCH A KLUTZ...
JOSH?

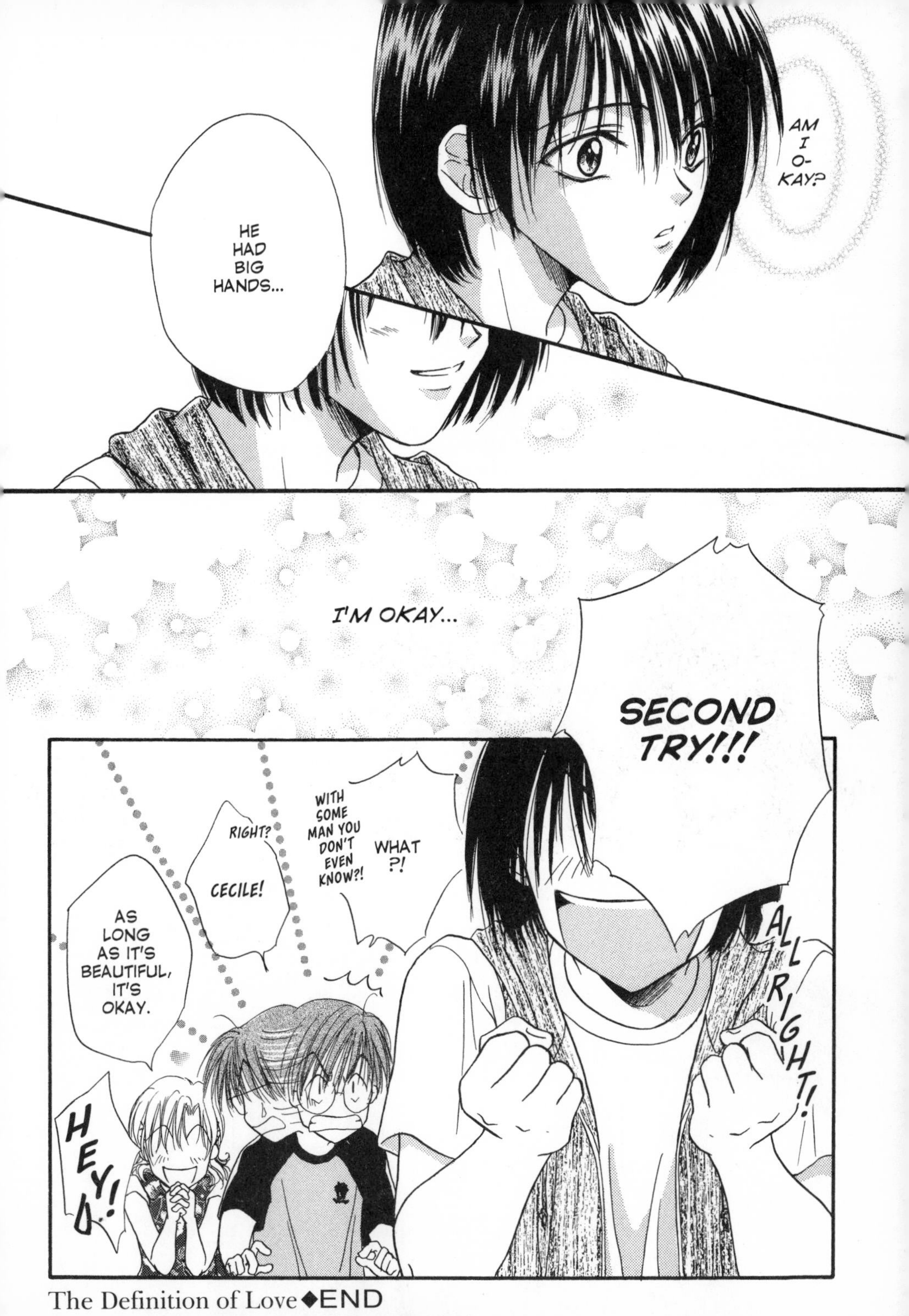
AM I O-KAY?
HE HAD BIG HANDS...
I'M OKAY...
SECOND TRY!!!
ALL RIGHT!!
WHAT?!
WITH SOME MAN YOU DON'T EVEN KNOW?!
RIGHT? CECILE!
AS LONG AS IT'S BEAUTIFUL, IT'S OKAY.
HEY!

The Definition of Love◆END

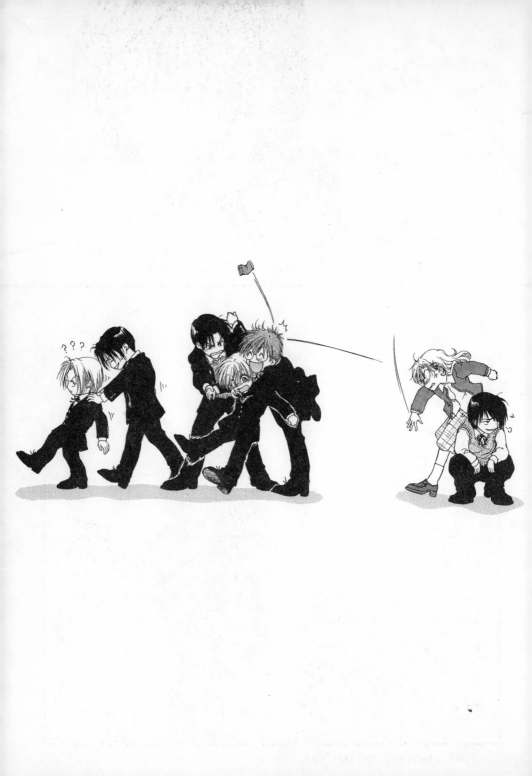

PROMENADE

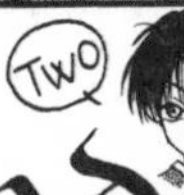
TWO

WELL HELLO! HOW IS EVERYONE? I FAILED ONCE AGAIN THIS YEAR IN MY ATTEMPT AT PLANTING TULIPS--THIS IS CHIGUSA KAWAI. (I'M FOLLOWING THE WRITTEN DIRECTIONS TO THE LETTER...SO WHY...???) HERE IS THE SECOND VOLUME OF "GEORGIE-BOY'S MATURATION DIARY" (←?). IT'S STILL CONTINUING.

WOW. AND IT'S ALL BECAUSE OF YOU SUPPORTIVE READERS. THANK YOU VERY MUCH. I LOVE YOU!♡ NOW, THIS TIME AROUND, TWO EXTRA EPISODES HAVE BEEN CRAMMED IN. WHICH MEANS, NO ORIGINAL STUFF. I'M SORRY. PLEASE MAKE DO WITH THESE PAGES OF MY "EXCUSES". OK?

NOTE: THE CHARACTER DATA IS CURRENT TO THE TIME OF THE "BARRIER" CHAPTER. I'M SORRY IT'S SO CONFUSING...YOU'LL HAVE TO DO YOUR OWN CALCULATIONS.

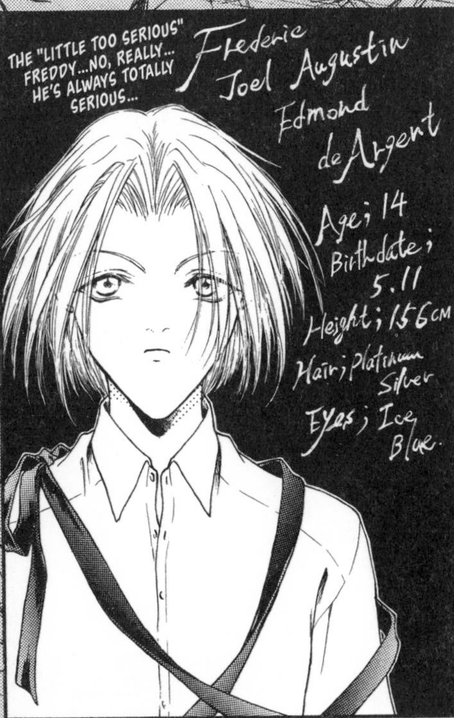
THE "LITTLE TOO SERIOUS" FREDDY...NO, REALLY... HE'S ALWAYS TOTALLY SERIOUS...
Frederic Joel Augustin Edmond de Argent
Age; 14
Birthdate; 5.11
Height; 156cm
Hair; Platinum Silver
Eyes; Ice Blue.

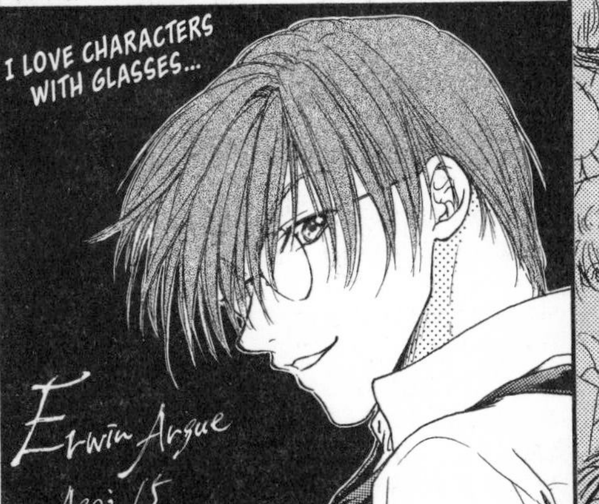
I LOVE CHARACTERS WITH GLASSES...
Erwin Argue
Age; 15
Birthdate; 9.29
Height; 178cm
Hair; Hazel Brown
Eyes; Green

CHAPTER COMMENTARIES.

* CHAPTER 4 -- "BARRIER" (HENRI'S TALE)

I HAD FUN DOING THIS CHAPTER. BECAUSE I DIDN'T HAVE TO THINK TOO HARD (?). IT'S FUN WHEN THERE'S SO MUCH WACKINESS. AND IT'S ALL THANKS TO FREDDY...?

* CHAPTER 5 -- "CALLION" PT.1 AND PT.2 (CHRIS' TALE)

CHRIS, I'M SORRY!! (LAUGH) A "CALLION" IS A BELL AT THE TOP OF THE TOWER IN CHURCHES AND SUCH. THIS TIME, THE STORY TAKES PLACE OUTSIDE OF SCHOOL, SO I USED THE BELL AS THE TITLE WITH THE INTENTION OF TYING TOGETHER THE OUTSIDE (OFF CAMPUS) AND THE INSIDE (ON CAMPUS) LOCATIONS. NO, REALLY...CHRIS...I'M SO SORRY...

* "FOR WHOM THE BELL TOLLS" (TAKES PLACE ONE YEAR BEFORE THE MAIN STORY)

MY DEBUT WORK. YEESH. ABOUT ERWIN...HIS ACTUAL PERSONALITY IS MORE LIKE THE ONE IN THE MAIN STORY.IF ANOTHER SERIOUS ROLE COMES AROUND, MAYBE WE'LL SEE HIM AGAIN...

* "THE DEFINITION OF LOVE" (TAKES PLACE SIX MONTHS BEFORE THE MAIN STORY)

A CONTINUATION OF THE PREVIOUS CHAPTER. UHH... ABOUT THE MAN WHO APPEARS AT THE END... ACTUALLY...OH NO! I RAN OUT OF SPACE.

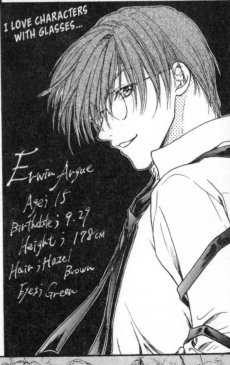

ACTUALLY, AFTER I DID THOSE LAST TWO CHAPTERS, THERE WAS AN OUTRAGEOUS PLAN TO WRITE A BUNCH OF OTHER SIDE STORIES AND PUT OUT AN ENTIRE SEPARATE VOLUME! (I'M PRETTY SURE THE EDITOR'S FORGOTTEN ALL ABOUT IT BY NOW.) IN WHICH CASE, THE MYSTERIOUS MAN AT THE END WAS SUPPOSED TO BE THE NEXT MAIN CHARACTER. THAT GUY, TOO...IF HE GETS A CHANCE...HE MAY APPEAR...IN THE MAIN STORY, I MEAN...

TO EVERYONE WHO WROTE ME LETTERS AFTER THE FIRST VOLUME CAME OUT, THANK YOU SO VERY MUCH. (TO EVERYONE WHO SUPPORTED ME FROM THE BEGINNING, THANK YOU TOO! ♡) I READ THEM ALL. FROM TOP TO BOTTOM. WITHOUT MISSING A SINGLE WORD. (KINDA CREEPY...?) THEY REALLY ARE MY TREASURES--IT'S TRUE. I HAVEN'T BEEN ABLE TO KEEP UP WITH WRITING RESPONSES, BUT YOU'LL BE SURE TO GET ONE SOONER OR LATER...YOU'LL HAVE TO BE PATIENT WITH ME.

FOR SOME REASON, A LOT OF FANS RESIDE IN AICHI.
NOW ATTEMPTING CONQUEST OF ALL TERRITORIES
THANKS, EVERYONE. ♥
GOAL: TO KEEP DRAWING UNTIL I'VE GOTTEN FAN LETTERS FROM PEOPLE IN EVERY PREFECTURE.

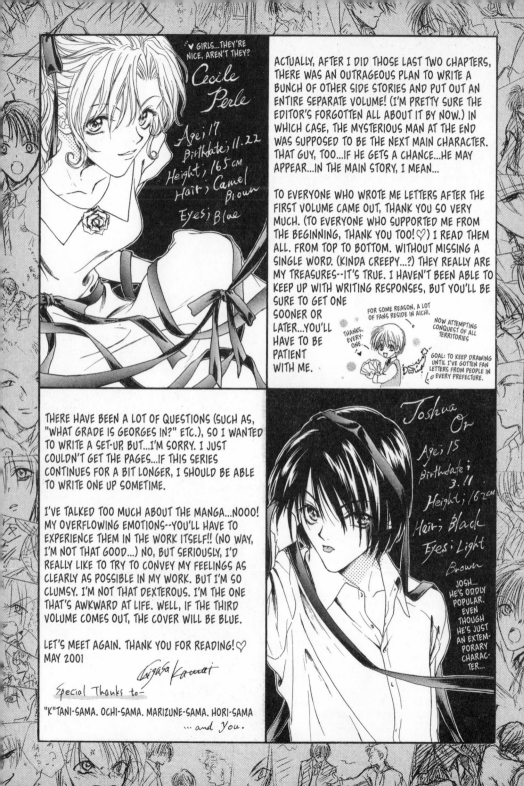

♥ GIRLS...THEY'RE NICE, AREN'T THEY?
Cecile Perle
Age; 17
Birthdate; 11.22
Height; 165 CM
Hair; Camel Brown
Eyes; Blue

Joshua Or
Age; 15
Birthdate; 3.11
Height; 162 CM
Hair; Black
Eyes; Light Brown
JOSH... HE'S ODDLY POPULAR. EVEN THOUGH HE'S JUST AN EXTEMPORARY CHARACTER...

THERE HAVE BEEN A LOT OF QUESTIONS (SUCH AS, "WHAT GRADE IS GEORGES IN?" ETC.), SO I WANTED TO WRITE A SET-UP, BUT...I'M SORRY. I JUST COULDN'T GET THE PAGES...IF THIS SERIES CONTINUES FOR A BIT LONGER, I SHOULD BE ABLE TO WRITE ONE UP SOMETIME.

I'VE TALKED TOO MUCH ABOUT THE MANGA...NOOO! MY OVERFLOWING EMOTIONS--YOU'LL HAVE TO EXPERIENCE THEM IN THE WORK ITSELF!! (NO WAY, I'M NOT THAT GOOD...) NO, BUT SERIOUSLY, I'D REALLY LIKE TO TRY TO CONVEY MY FEELINGS AS CLEARLY AS POSSIBLE IN MY WORK. BUT I'M SO CLUMSY. I'M NOT THAT DEXTEROUS. I'M THE ONE THAT'S AWKWARD AT LIFE. WELL, IF THE THIRD VOLUME COMES OUT, THE COVER WILL BE BLUE.

LET'S MEET AGAIN. THANK YOU FOR READING! ♡
MAY 2001

Kigasa Kawai

Special Thanks to-

"K"TANI-SAMA. OCHI-SAMA. MARIZUNE-SAMA. HORI-SAMA

...and You.

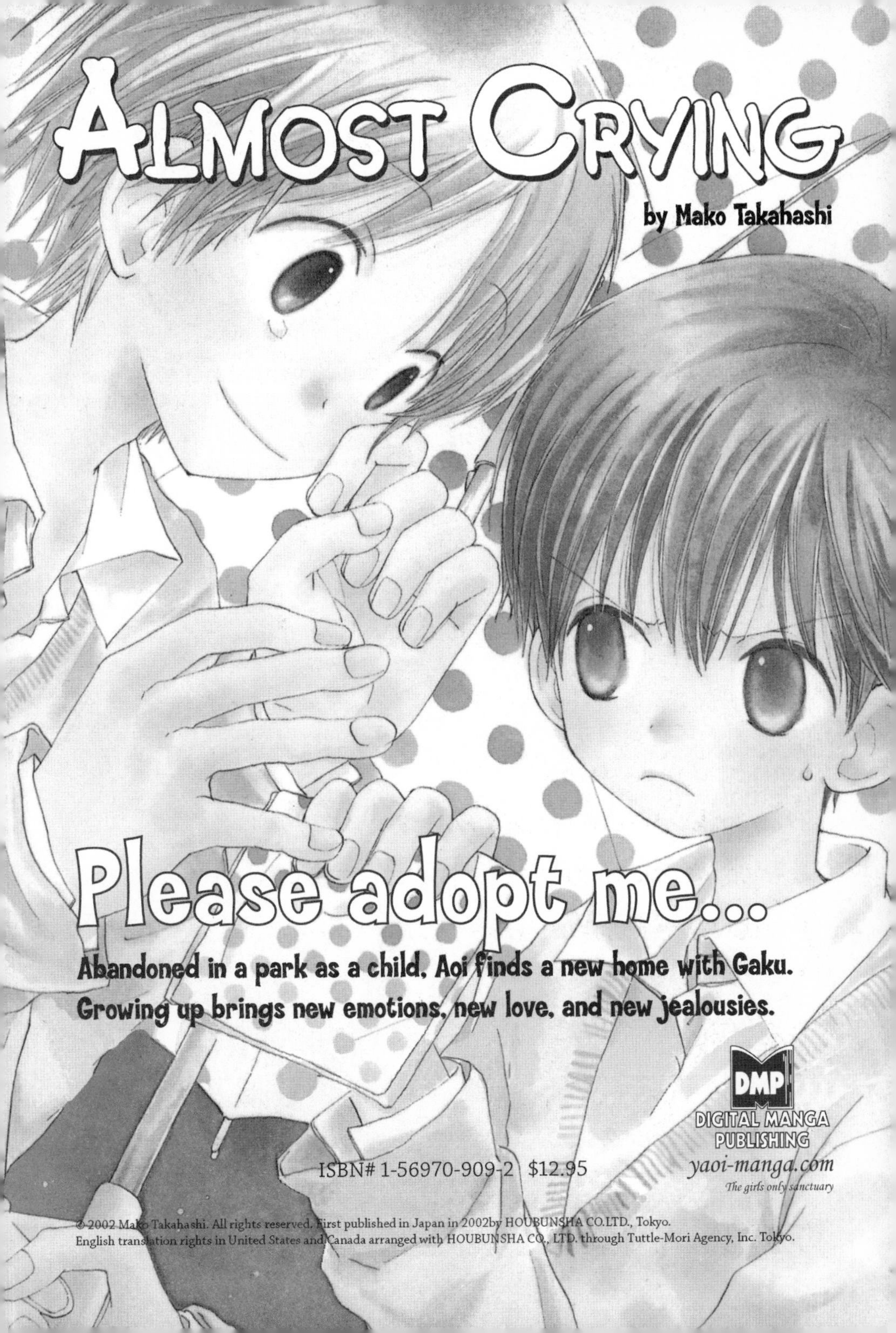
ALMOST CRYING
by Mako Takahashi
Please adopt me...
Abandoned in a park as a child, Aoi finds a new home with Gaku.
Growing up brings new emotions, new love, and new jealousies.
DMP
DIGITAL MANGA PUBLISHING
ISBN# 1-56970-909-2 $12.95
yaoi-manga.com
The girls only sanctuary
© 2002 Mako Takahashi. All rights reserved. First published in Japan in 2002by HOUBUNSHA CO.LTD., Tokyo.
English translation rights in United States and Canada arranged with HOUBUNSHA CO., LTD. through Tuttle-Mori Agency, Inc. Tokyo.

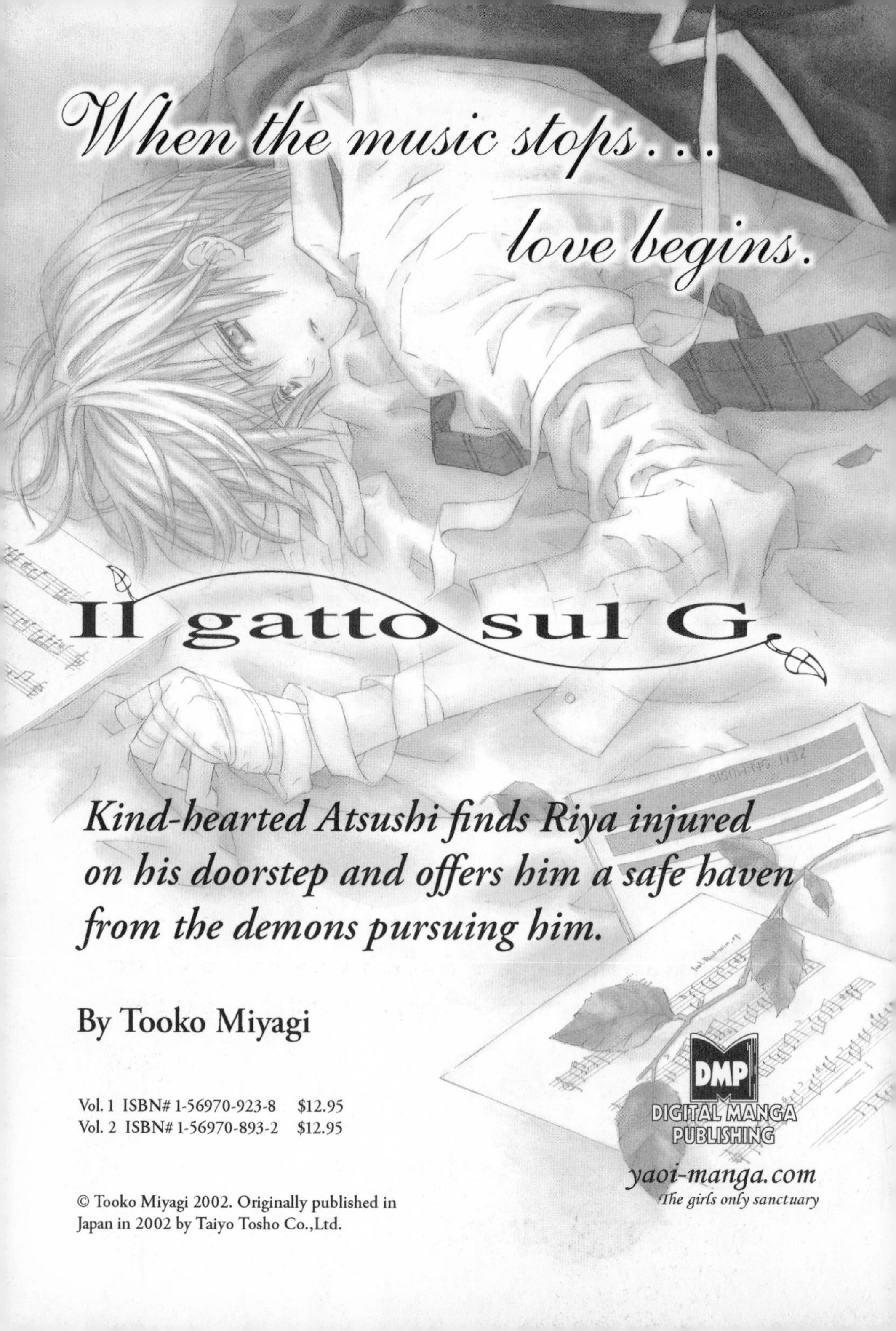
When the music stops . . .
. . . love begins.
Il gatto sul G
Kind-hearted Atsushi finds Riya injured on his doorstep and offers him a safe haven from the demons pursuing him.
By Tooko Miyagi
Vol. 1 ISBN# 1-56970-923-8 $12.95
Vol. 2 ISBN# 1-56970-893-2 $12.95
© Tooko Miyagi 2002. Originally published in Japan in 2002 by Taiyo Tosho Co.,Ltd.
DMP
DIGITAL MANGA PUBLISHING
yaoi-manga.com
The girls only sanctuary

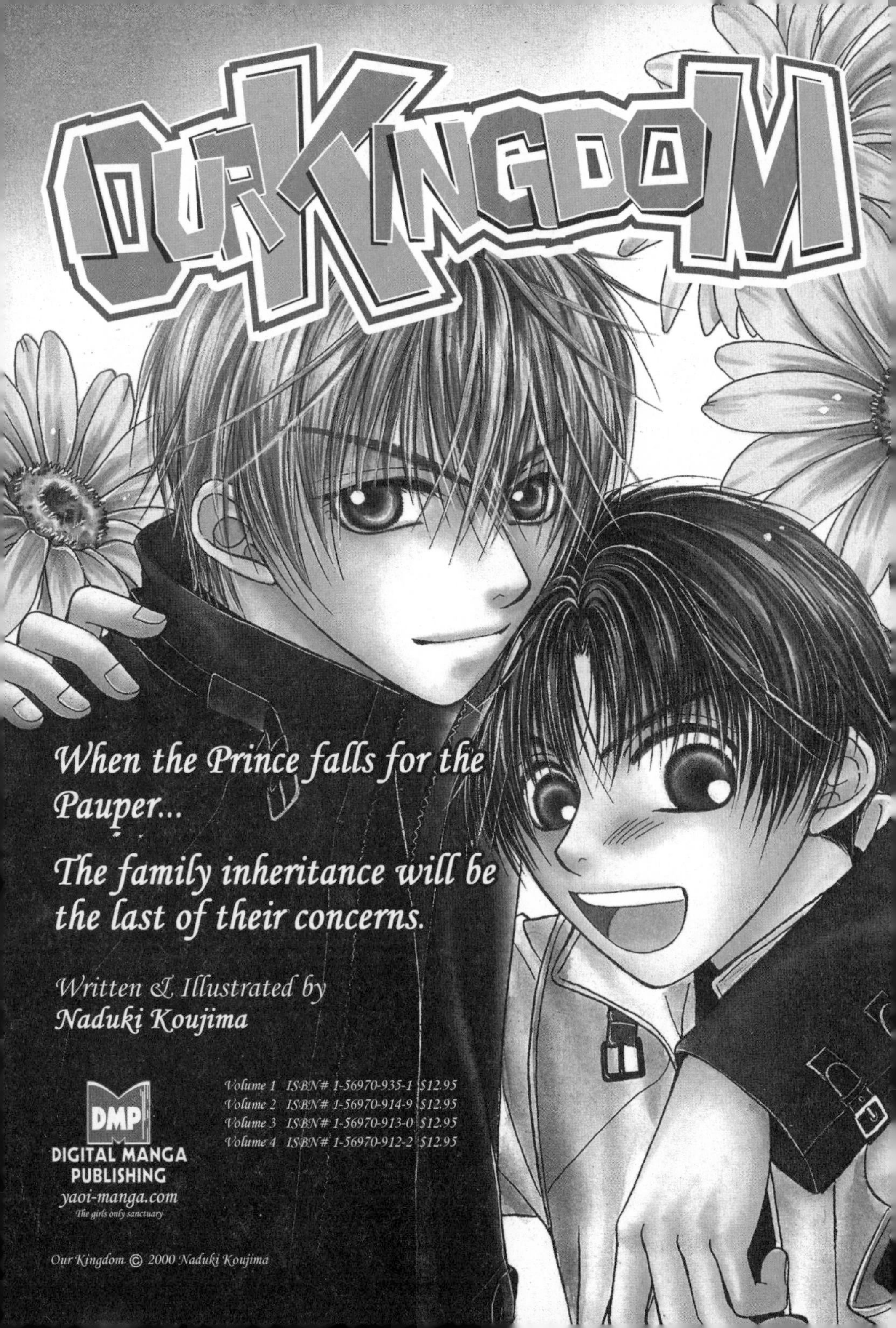
OUR KINGDOM
When the Prince falls for the Pauper...
The family inheritance will be the last of their concerns.
Written & Illustrated by
Naduki Koujima
Volume 1 ISBN# 1-56970-935-1 $12.95
Volume 2 ISBN# 1-56970-914-9 $12.95
Volume 3 ISBN# 1-56970-913-0 $12.95
Volume 4 ISBN# 1-56970-912-2 $12.95
DMP
DIGITAL MANGA PUBLISHING
yaoi-manga.com
The girls only sanctuary
Our Kingdom © 2000 Naduki Koujima

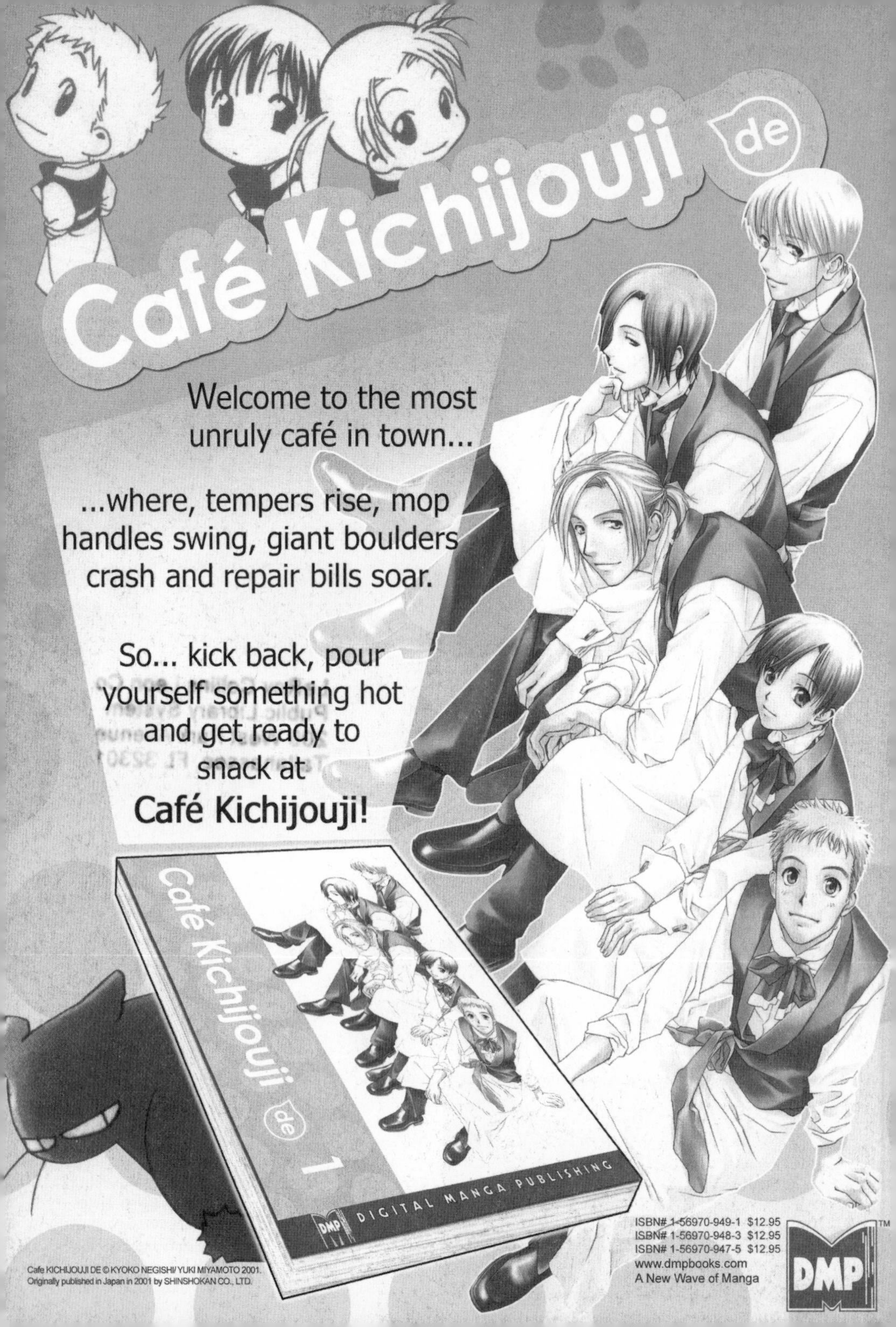
Café Kichijouji de
Welcome to the most unruly café in town...
...where, tempers rise, mop handles swing, giant boulders crash and repair bills soar.
So... kick back, pour yourself something hot and get ready to snack at
Café Kichijouji!
Café Kichijouji de 1
DIGITAL MANGA PUBLISHING
DMP
ISBN# 1-56970-949-1 $12.95
ISBN# 1-56970-948-3 $12.95
ISBN# 1-56970-947-5 $12.95
www.dmpbooks.com
A New Wave of Manga
DMP
Cafe KICHIJOUJI DE © KYOKO NEGISHI/ YUKI MIYAMOTO 2001.
Originally published in Japan in 2001 by SHINSHOKAN CO., LTD.

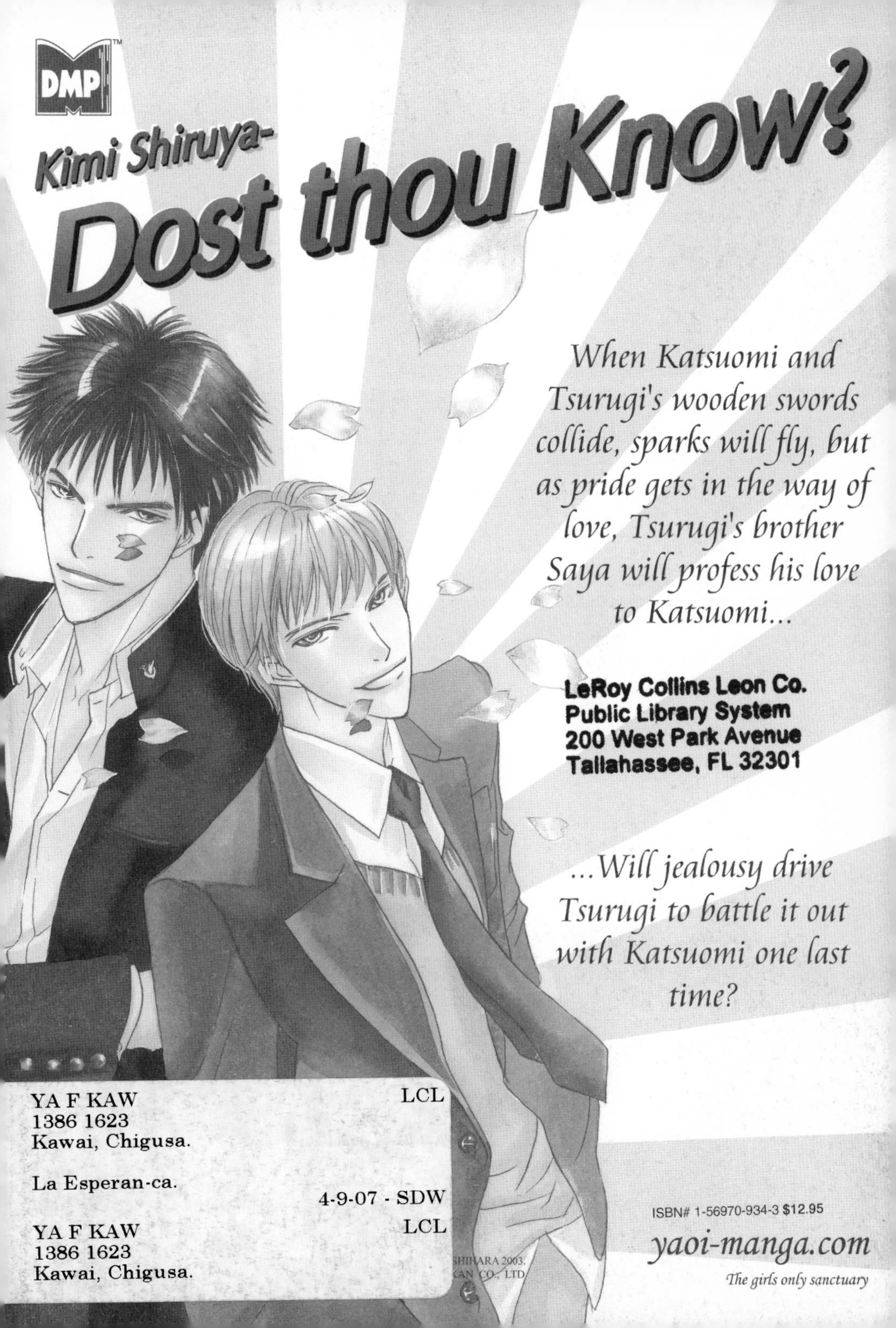
DMP
Kimi Shiruya-
Dost thou Know?
When Katsuomi and Tsurugi's wooden swords collide, sparks will fly, but as pride gets in the way of love, Tsurugi's brother Saya will profess his love to Katsuomi...
...Will jealousy drive Tsurugi to battle it out with Katsuomi one last time?
ISBN# 1-56970-934-3 $12.95
yaoi-manga.com
The girls only sanctuary
SHIHARA 2003.
KAN CO., LTD

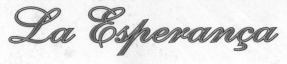

Translation	Sachiko Sato
Lettering	Studio Cutie
Graphic Design	Eric Rosenberger
Editing	Stephanie Donnelly
Editor in Chief	Fred Lui
Publisher	Hikaru Sasahara

English Edition Published by
DIGITAL MANGA PUBLISHING
A division of DIGITAL MANGA, Inc.
1487 W 178th Street, Suite 300
Gardena, CA 90248

www.dmpbooks.com

First Edition: February 2006
ISBN: 1-56970-932-7

1 3 5 7 9 10 8 6 4 2

Printed in China

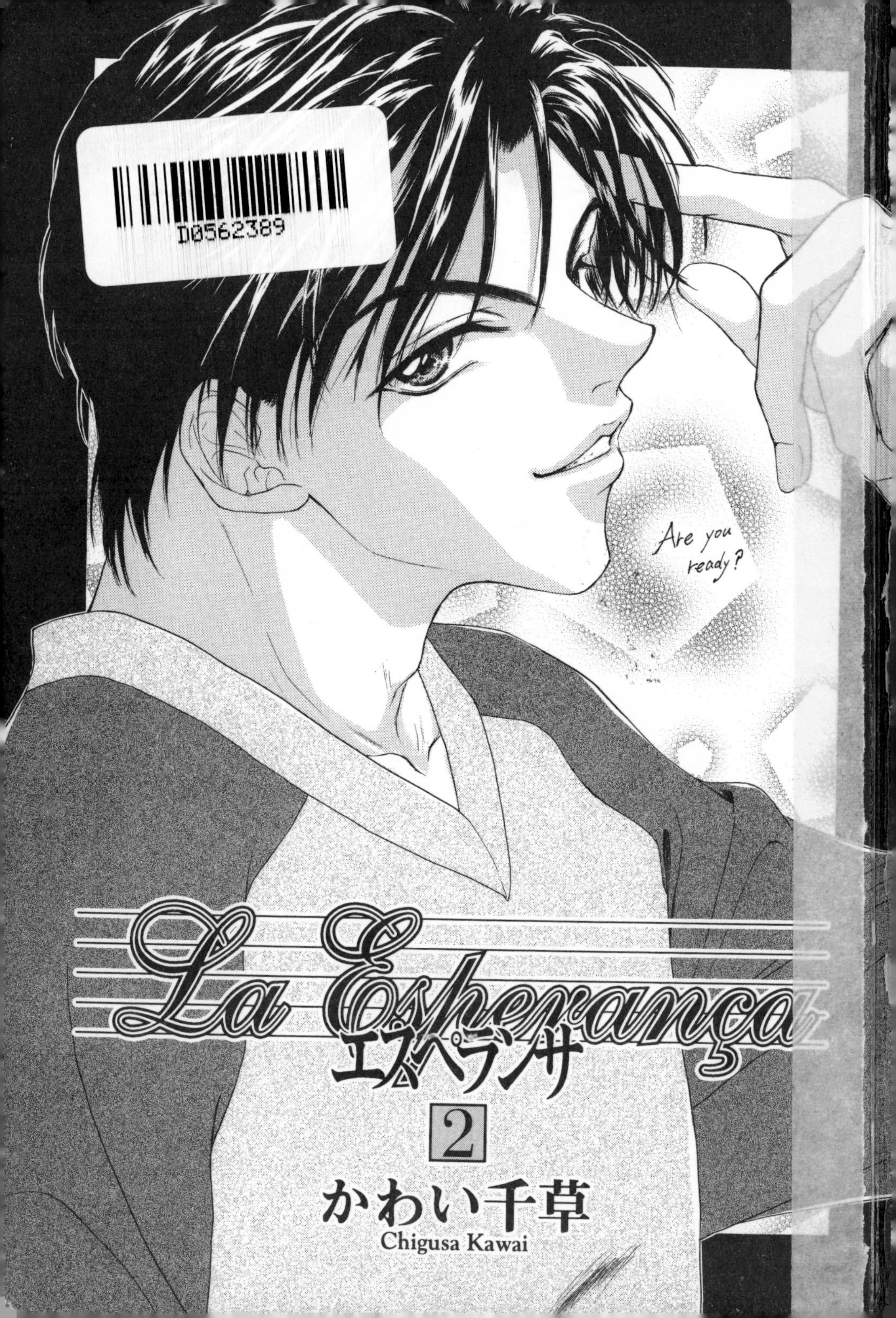
Are you ready?

La Esperança
エスペランサ

2

かわい千草
Chigusa Kawai